And the Bride wore...

And the Bride wore...

The Story of the White Wedding

Ann Monsarrat

Colour plates and initial letters by Elisabeth Trimby

GENTRY BOOKS · LONDON

First published 1973

© Ann Monsarrat 1973

ISBN 0 85614 027 9

Published by Gentry Books Limited,
15, Tooks Court,
London EC4A 1LA
Layout and Design Brian Roll
Made and printed in Great Britain by
William Clowes & Sons, Limited
London, Beccles and Colchester

Acknowledgements

So many people have helped and encouraged me during the writing of this book that a complete list would be almost as long as the work itself. I thank every one of them most heartily, and am particularly grateful to my publishers, who thought of the idea, and to Mrs. Mary Knowler and Mrs. Sadie Gentry who have done invaluable research work. Mr. Claude Prance, of Gozo, unhesitatingly gave me the use of his superb private library and his own detailed knowledge (while Mrs. Patricia Prance constantly kept a sharp eye open for anything to do with weddings, as well as providing the most splendid library teas). Miss Kay Staniland, of the London Museum, has been unfailingly helpful and always encouraging; Mrs. Madeleine Ginsberg, of the Victoria and Albert Museum, pointed me in the right direction at the very beginning. In America, Mrs. Georgia B. Bumgardner of the American Antiquarian Society, Worcester, Massachusetts, and the Smithsonian Institution, Washington, have been of great help, surpassed only by the warm-hearted zeal of Mrs. John C. Pritzlaff, Jr., wife of the former American Ambassador to Malta. Miss Georgia Acton, at the U.S. Embassy in Malta, has also been unstinting in her assistance. To Mr. Paul Cassar and Mr. George Borg, at the Gozo Public Library, Dr. Paul Xuereb and Miss Lillian Sciberras at the Library of the Royal University of Malta, to Miss Magda Camilleri and her helpers at the British Council Library, Malta, and to the British Museum, London, I owe a debt impossible to repay. Mr. John H. Drew, Mrs. Charles Frend, Mrs. K. W. Monsarrat, Sir Rennie Maudslay, K.C.V.O., M.B.E., Keeper of the Privy Purse, and Rear-Admiral J. A. Templeton-Cotill, C.B., have all been particularly generous in spending time and thought in unravelling problems for me. To the writers and publishers of the many books and journals from which I have quoted, I am most grateful of all: without them, this book truly could not have existed. And, finally, my special thanks to my husband, who encouraged me to accept the commission, and never once in the course of the next three years said he wished he had not done so, though there must have been many times . . .

The author wishes to thank

the copyright holders for permission to quote from the following works: *Edwardian Daughter*, copyright © 1958 by Sonia Kepple, Hamish Hamilton, London; *The Wandering Years*, by Cecil Beaton, Weidenfeld & Nicolson Ltd.; *Piaf*, by Simone Berteaut, translated by Ghislaine Boulanger, W. H. Allen & Co. Ltd.; *Queen Mary*, by James Pope-Hennessy, George Allen & Unwin Ltd.; *Life amongst the Troubridges*, ed. Jaqueline Hope-Nicholson, John Murray (Publishers) Ltd.; *My Dear Duchess*, ed. A. L. Kennedy, John Murray (Publishers) Ltd.; *The Recollections of a Northumbrian Lady*, ed. L. E. O. Charlton, David Higham Associates, Ltd.; *Kilvert's Diary*, ed. William Plomer, Jonathan Cape, Ltd.; *Diary of a Black Sheep*, by Richard Meinertzhagen, Oliver & Boyd; *Letters of a Grandmother*, ed. Gladys Scott Thomson, Jonathan Cape Ltd.; *Armstrong's Norfolk Diary*, ed. Herbert B. J. Armstrong, Hodder & Stoughton Ltd.; *George VI*, by John Wheeler-Bennett, Macmillan, London and Basingstoke; *Brides* (a Condé Nast publication), Early Spring, 1970.

Author's Note

In this book I use such phrases as *most brides* and *all weddings*, and in doing so I am, of course, setting myself up as a prime target for those angry armies of statisticians who will delight in pointing out that in the past 2·96 years there were 4·33 recurring more Moslem brides and 6·42 per cent more civil marriages than white weddings in Christian churches. And they may well be right.

But this is the story of the *White Wedding* and, to save a great many qualifications, when I say *most brides* please assume that I mean most brides whose cultural roots are in Europe and the Christian religion, the Jewish faith on which that religion is based, and the pagan rights it absorbed.

It would be wonderful to delve into all the wedding clothes and customs of all the peoples of the world. But that would take more than one book!

Contents

Illustrations

Chapter One

O Hymen! Hymen O!
Hebrew, Greek and Roman Brides
0 – 410 AD

With sweet-odoured marjoram flowers
Wreathe thy beauty-radiant brow;
Seize the veil of flame-bright hue;
Joyous come with saffron shoe
Upon thy foot of snow.
Catullus: *Nuptial Song in Honour*
of Junia and Manlius

HINK of a bride, and what do you see? For millions of Christians, Jews, agnostics, atheists and just plain romantics all round the world the picture is the same: a radiant creature dressed in white—snowy dress and floating veil, trailing bouquet and a touch of orange blossom; something old, something new, something borrowed and something blue. Nostalgic, traditional, and, more often than not, ludicrously extravagant. Whatever else is skimped on this day of days, the bride is going to look right; a vision she and her moist-eyed mother (and, with luck, the bridegroom too) will remember for the rest of their lives. And still, for many, many brides, there is only one way to look 'right'.

In the 1920s it was briefly the thing to get married in beach pyjamas in the South of France. A few years ago a crumpled caftan was considered (by the bride at any rate) to be just the job when a British peer's daughter married the owner of a trendy boutique. See-through tops and bulging hot-pants have found their way to the altar since, but for each one of those unblushing brides, thousands more have chosen white and all the trimmings.

Ask why, and you are likely to receive an odd look and a sharp answer. Brides dress that way because it is traditional; they always have and they always will; old as the hills; honoured through the centuries. . . .

Except, it isn't.

The custom-made, white wedding, with all the frills we know so well, is not so very old. Like many a good thing, it's Victorian. It was not until the middle of last century that all the ingredients we now think of as virtually indispensable to a white wedding

1

came together to make the great tradition. And as tradition goes, a hundred-odd years is historical peanuts.

For centuries after the Romans there was no such thing as an immediately recognizable wedding dress. The rich wore richer versions of their normal clothes; the poor, and even the middle classes, chose the best dress from their closet and made it festive with ribbons, love-knots, and a garland of flowers.

And even for a Roman bride, the dress took second place to the accessories, most of which were loaded on her head. Yellow was the wedding colour then, and an all-enveloping flame-yellow veil a bride's chief insignia. This was pulled over her face during the ceremony 'to shield the downcast looks of virgin modesty' and worn until she arrived at her new home on the night of the wedding, when it was the bridegroom's privilege to do the unveiling.

Under the veil she wore a garland of flowers (picked by herself), and under that, she had an elaborate *coiffure* which involved dividing the hair into six locks with a special spear-shaped comb. Her shoes were important too—they had to be saffron-coloured—and she usually carried in her hand three wheat ears (wheat being one of the many symbols of fertility). The dress in between all this finery lacked significance. It had to be vertically woven and tied with a woollen girdle, but tradition decreed no special colour.

William Vaughan in his *Golden Grove* (published in 1608) says a Roman bride 'was bound to have a chaplet of flowers or hearbes upon her head, and to weare a girdle of sheeps wooll about her middle, fastened with a true-loves knot, the which her husband must loose. Here hence rose the Proverbe: *He hath undone her virgins girdle*; that is, of a mayde he hath made her a woman.'

Not a proverb in every-day use now perhaps, but the custom was still going strong (very strong, in fact) in Scotland at the end of the 18th century—thirteen-hundred years after the fall of the Roman Empire. Sir John Sinclair in his *Statistical Account of Scotland*, 1793, quotes the minister of Logierait in Perthshire on the superstitions of the parish: 'Immediately before the celebration of the marriage ceremony, every knot about the Bride and Bridegroom (garters, shoe-strings, strings of petticoats &c.) is carefully loosened. After leaving the church the whole company walk round it, keeping the church-walls always upon the right side. The bridegroom, however, first retires one way with some young men to tie the knots that were loosened about him; while the young woman, in the same manner, retires somewhere else to adjust the disorder of her dress.'

Ovid (43 B.C.–A.D. 17, and three times married) shows the close association in Roman minds between brides and veils in his story of the love-sick Mars (*Fasti*, Book III).

Woefully in love with Minerva, Mars confides his plight ('I burn and for a long time have nursed this wound') to old Anna Perenna, who had 'but lately been made a goddess'. Naughty old Anna, pretending to mediate, tells him that Minerva has yielded to his entreaties. 'The lover believed her and made ready the bridal chamber. Thither they escorted Anna, like a bride, with a veil upon her face. When he would have kissed her, Mars suddenly perceived Anna; now shame, now anger moved the god befooled. The new goddess laughed at dear Minerva's lover. Never had anything pleased Venus more than that.'

Not a bad joke—played *once*. But the replacement of the real bride with an ugly, old one was common practice for so long that Folk Lore specialists have a name for it: they call it 'The False Bride' (and probably add 'syndrome' afterwards). 'Slavonic, Teutonic, and Romance peoples' were especially fond of it. In Brittany they dragged the joke out even more painfully by introducing first a little girl, then the mistress of the house, and lastly the grandmother. In one district of Bavaria, a bearded man in woman's clothes was the surprise bride; and in Esthonia, the bride's brother had that honour.

A charitable explanation of the custom is that it was an attempt to fool the evil spirits and protect the real bride.

Weddings have always been considered a good excuse for a party. The Greeks looked upon theirs as sacrificial feasts to the household gods; but, whatever the name, the father of the bride was expected to pick up the bill. And, whatever the name, wedding cakes appeared on the menu. These began rather humbly—the Greeks baked up a mixture of pounded grain and honey, and the Romans went one worse with grain and salt. The elaborately iced and marzipanned creations we know today didn't evolve until the 17th century.

It is usually assumed that the Romans introduced the wedding cake to Britain, along with straight roads and central heating, but Sir John Lubbock (in his *Origin of Civilization*, 1870) claimed that 'among the Iroquois, the bride and bridegroom used to partake together of a cake of "sagamite", which the bride offered to her husband. The Fiji Islanders have a very similar custom . . .' and so, he argued, if they could come up with the idea without the help of the Romans, why not the Ancient Britons?

Equally primaeval is the urge to throw things at the bride. The Hebrews combined the two customs and threw cake; and, as late as last century, cake or biscuits were still being scattered or broken over the heads of rural brides in Britain. The Greeks threw grain, fruit and sweetmeats. Roman bridegrooms had a chance to hit back; they traditionally threw nuts to the young men who formed part of the noisy procession which, as with the Greeks, accompanied the bride and groom to their new home. All these missiles were thought of as fertility symbols.

Mercifully, other customs have proved less durable—like the one of the mothers-in-law and the flaming torches. When a Greek bride was taken to her new home on her wedding night, she was accompanied by flute players—and her mother, who must have cut a pretty awesome figure: she bore torches which had been lit at the parental hearth. Judging by some vase-paintings, the entourage was met at the other end of the journey by the bridegroom's mother—also with blazing torches. To add to the conflagration, Vaughan says: 'The Grecians accustomed to burne before the doore of the newe married the axletree of that coach, wherein shee was brought to her husbands house, letting her to understand, that she was ever after to dwell there.' Quite a home-coming!

Roman mothers-of-the-bride had a less flamboyant but equally histrionic part to play: their daughters were symbolically torn from their arms before the procession set out. To her new home, the Roman bride carried three coins (which could be the origin of the silver sixpence in the shoe of more recent times): one for her husband, one for the household gods, and the third for the gods of the nearest crossroads. When she arrived, she rubbed the doorposts with grease or fat (to slip up those evil spirits) and 'decked them with fillets' (decorated them with ribbons). She was then carried over the threshold—a custom said (even by the Romans) to have its origin in the rape of the Sabine women and to 'signifie that she lost her virginity unwillingly'; but it was much more likely to have been done to prevent the ill-omen of a stumble on the new doorstep. (Sir John Lubbock said the 'Redskins of Canada, the Chinese, and the Abyssinians' also carried their brides over the threshold.) In Roman times the actual lifting was a group effort, rather than the one-man job it has now (if possible) become.

All this jollity was accompanied by a chorus of maidens singing the praises of the bride and groom and entreating Hymen, god of marriage, to look upon the union with an especially benign eye. Catullus (87–54 B.C.) gives a delightful and detailed description of it all in the *epithalamium*, or wedding poem, which he wrote for his noble friend and patron Lucius Manlius Torquatus.

Robert Herrick, writing one-thousand-seven-hundred years later, tells of exactly the same goings-on in his *Epithalamy to Sir Thomas Southwell and his Lady*, but he is more likely to have been indulging a taste for the classics than giving a faithful description of what actually took place on that occasion. I would very much doubt that the new Lady Southwell went around rubbing goose fat into the doorposts or draping herself in a saffron veil on her wedding bed in the England of Charles I—though there were a lot of other funny frolics then, and later.

But the conquering Romans did bring their customs with them to Britain, and many of them did take root. Some are still with us. And most of them—like the garland of flowers—were already ancient when the Romans themselves adopted them.

Dr. John Brand, in his *Popular Antiquities* (first published in 1777) says: 'Nuptial garlands are of the most remote antiquity. They appear to have been equally used by the Jews and the heathens. In the eastern church the chaplets used on these occasions appear to have been blessed. The nuptial garlands were sometimes made of myrtle.' (*Myrtle* was considered sacred to Venus and used as an emblem of love.)

He adds dryly: 'I know not Gosson's authority for the following passage: "In som countries the bride is crowned by the matrons with a garland of prickles, and so delivered unto her husband that hee might know he hath tied himself to a thorny plesure." School of Abuse, 1587, or rather the Ephemerides of Phialo, 1579, p. 73.'

Chapter Two

Marriage by Purchase
The Anglo-Saxons   200 – 1000 AD

A king shall buy a queen with goods,
with beakers and bracelets; both shall
first be generous with gifts.
From: *The Exeter Book*

HEN Rome pulled her legions out of Britain in A.D., 410 the Anglo-Saxons took over as the next power bloc. To begin with they were a pretty rough lot—almost as rough as the ancient Britons they ruled—but by the end of the sixth century a slightly more gracious age was dawning. The country was gradually being converted to Christianity and the church was beginning to weave itself into people's lives. One of the first things it took on was weddings.

The Roman upper classes had been married by priests and offered nuptial sacrifices to the gods, but the average Briton went about matrimony in a far more direct and purely secular manner. He believed in marriage by capture. A man saw a girl he fancied, rode off with her and argued later. The argument usually proved long and bloody, involving whole clans in savage feuds; but nothing is so bad that someone can't see a gleam of goodness in it. A marvellously prosy Victorian writer, John Cordy Jeaffreson (in *Brides and Bridals*, 1872) admitted 'it cannot be questioned that marriage by force was miserably fruitful of domestic feuds and private animosities'. But . . . 'Against this inconvenience may be set an advantage which the apologists of marriage by capture may fairly claim for the institution. The duty of wifely submissiveness to marital authority was impressively inculcated in the system that authorized suitors to subdue their mistresses with blows, and required women to accept meekly and without reference to their own secret predilections the rule of their captors. There was small likelihood of a need to kill the cat after marriage, when its nine lives had been so thoroughly taken by the matrimonial process. The system, moreover, spared wives the bitterness of perceiving a diminution of tenderness on the part of their lords after marriage. The bride captured against her will would not cherish unreasonable expectations of happiness in wedlock. Nor would she probably have grounds in the future for complaining that her master was less considerate of her feelings as a husband than he had shown himself as a lover.'

Anglo-Saxon fathers were not so blissfully philosophical. Marriage by capture might be all right for marauding tribes, but to a man busy establishing a more settled community, the loss of a daughter was the loss of a valuable asset. She helped to run

5

the house and farm, spin the flax and wool (hence the word spinster), weave the cloth and make the clothes. If she went, he wanted compensation. And so, in place of marriage by capture, came marriage by purchase.

Like most new ideas it gained ground slowly. Judging by the laws passed at the time, there were many who thought the old ways best, and stuck to them. Ethelbert, King of Kent, decreed at the end of the sixth century, that any man guilty of 'carrying away a maid by force' should 'pay fifty shillings to her owner, and afterwards buy her from him'. If he carried off a married woman, he could keep her, but only if he provided a replacement, at his own cost, for the injured husband.

Young men trying honourably to follow the new customs had to be protected too. To safeguard husbands who had been lured into buying girls who weren't all they'd been said to be, another of Ethelbert's laws ordained that for a marriage to be binding, it must have been made 'without guile' on the seller's part. 'But if there be deceit, let him bring her home again, and let the man give back his money.' (An early version of the Trades Descriptions Act! Just how long the groom could keep his bridal trial offer before returning the goods as unsound, was not made clear.) Ethelbert himself had married a Christian (Bertha, daughter of Charibert, King of Paris), and became the celebrated convert of St. Augustine. But, to his unconverted subjects, all these new regulations must have seemed very radical indeed.*

For those who accepted the new style of marriage this is how it worked. The family elders made the match and, after a great deal of haggling, fixed the bride price. This settled, the money was handed over at the betrothal, or *handfasting*, ceremony, together with as many other presents of jewellery or cattle as the father of the groom-to-be thought suitable to his social and financial position. The bargain was sealed with a drink ('wet bargains' have always been considered more binding than dry ones), and a kiss. The kiss was important. If it didn't take place and the parties later decided not to marry, both of them had to return all the gifts given during the betrothal. If the kiss had been exchanged, the man still had to return all the gifts he had received, but the girl only had to give back half the presents given to her. (According to J. S. Burn's *History of Parish Registers*, this law still held good in 1835 when magistrates in Exeter ordered a man to return the watch he had received from his fiancée, but decided she need only pay back half the value of a brooch she'd had from him.)

The *handfasting* usually took place when the prospective bride and groom were very young, and often many years before the actual marriage. (Which led to more laws having to be passed: unscrupulous fathers had time to sell promising daughters to several suitors before they reached marriageable age, and so, eventually, the money was handed over at the wedding ceremony instead.) But despite the youth of the couple, betrothals were taken very seriously. It was the *handfasting*, not the marriage ceremony, which produced the exchange of vows which are now part of the Anglican wedding service.

And it was the *handfasting* which produced the word 'wed'. This originally meant the pledge, the sum of money handed over to the girl's father. Later it also came to mean the ring which was given at the same time, and which was worn on the bride-to-be's right hand until the marriage. During the wedding ceremony, the groom

---

* Another law of this time forbade widows to remarry until one year after the death of the previous husband. The law is no longer with us, but the sentiment lingers on.

Plate One

transferred the 'wed' to the bride's left hand, holding it in turn over the tips of the thumb and the first two fingers and saying 'in the name of the Father', for the thumb; 'in the name of the Son', for the index finger; 'in the name of the Holy Ghost', for the middle finger; and, finally, 'Amen', as he slipped it into place on the third finger. This nice little ceremony is still continued in the Catholic marriage service. Happily, the Anglo-Saxon bridegroom's next trick is not: having been handed one of the bride's slippers by her father (to signify the transfer of authority), he bopped the bride smartly on the head with it (to signify that he was now her master). The 'weapon' was later carried into the bridal chamber and placed over the bed—on the husband's side, of course, in keeping with its symbolic character. But 'by way of practical joke', says Thomas Wright, in his *Womankind in Western Europe*, 'when the lady was accused of being rather tyrannical in temper, some facetious individual sometimes stole into the room, and slyly transferred the shoe to the other side.'

John Cordy Jeaffreson confidently explained how the shoe got into the act in the first place: 'It is needless to observe that this symbolic use of the shoe was an old Israelitish custom, and still prevails in Oriental lands. My readers will remember how Ruth's kinsman plucked off his shoe, as a sign that he transferred a right. "Now this was the manner in former time in Israel concerning redeeming and concerning changing, for to confirm all things: a man plucked off his shoe and gave it to his neighbour; and this was a testimony in Israel." Nor can they fail to see the aptitude of the symbol, when used to make the transmission of power over a human creature. The covering of the foot was the instrument with which a victor, putting his heel on the neck of a conquered enemy, would demonstrate the subjugation of the fallen foe.'

A charming picture! Especially when applied to marriage. But there is no doubt it could be the origin of the curious custom of tying old boots to the bumpers of honeymoon cars. The Victorians used to throw shoes after the bridal pair as they drove off in their carriage; and long before that German brides tossed a shoe in the way modern brides throw their bouquet—if it was caught by an unmarried girl, she would, so they said, be the next to find a husband.

Today's bride usually aims her bouquet at the bridesmaids—and bridesmaids are another tradition we owe to the Anglo-Saxons. The Romans had surrounded their young girls with chaste matrons (Catullus's 'Matrons! who have faithful been To your faithful husbands'), but an Anglo-Saxon bride had unmarried friends about her, the senior one attending for several days beforehand to help make the decorations for the feast—and the floral garlands.

The bride was crowned with one of these wreaths after the blessing in church—and so was her husband. According to Dr. Brand: 'After the benediction in the church, both the bride and the bridegroom were crowned with crowns of flowers, kept in the church for that purpose.' If she were freeborn, the bride wore hers over long, loose hair. (Daughters of bondsmen were not allowed this privilege: they had to have their hair close-cropped at all times. And married women 'as soon as matrimony had qualified their freedom with something of servile condition' were expected to wear their hair up and covered.)

The veil disappeared with the Romans, but some kind of shield for shy brides was still considered necessary. The Anglo-Saxons decided to include the bridegroom in this, too. Again according to Dr. Brand: 'Among the Anglo-Saxons the nuptial benediction was performed under a veil, or square piece of cloth, held at each corner by a tall man over the bridegroom and bride, to conceal her virgin blushes; but if the bride was a widow, the veil was esteemed useless.' This kind of veil—called a Care Cloth—was probably the Christian version of the canopy used in ancient Hebrew weddings, and still used in Jewish ceremonies today. Leon Modena in the *Rites of the Jews* (1650) says: 'There is a square vestment called Taleth, with pendents about it, put over the head of the bridegroom and bride together.'

To begin with Anglo-Saxons went to church only to have their weddings blessed, but gradually the priests took over the whole operation. They started out as witnesses at the betrothal and marriage ceremonies, moved on to joining the hands and blessing the ring; soon they were making the rules and turning a business agreement into a full religious rite.

They were also keeping an eye on the festivities which followed the wedding. Jeaffreson called these 'gross and riotous banquets at which the earls and thanes of old time caroused riotously and drank to stupifaction in honour of the newly married couples' and the 18th century antiquarian, Joseph Strutt, said that after an Anglo-Saxon nuptial feast 'the remaining part of the day was spent by the youth of both sexes in mirth and dancing, while the graver sort sat down to their drinking bout, in which they highly delighted'.

The poetry of the time leaves a more mellow impression of those gatherings in the great halls; it tells of warriors lounging on the long benches which ranged the shadowy rooms, listening to the minstrels' tales of heroic battles and lands beyond the seas, drinking mead and beer from gleaming metal goblets. Always gold is mentioned —the ceiling of the great hall is 'gold-decked'; the goblets are of 'twisted gold'; the women 'gold-adorned, bedecked with rings'—it is easy to picture the lustre of it winking through the smoke from the open fires; shining on the rich, natural dyes of the clothes. Easy, too, to picture the wife of the giver of the feast circulating amongst the men, like the queen in *Beowulf* ('gold-adorned . . . the free-born queen of the people'), filling their cups from the flagon she carries, bidding them 'be of good cheer at the beer-banquet'. The beginning of the party must have had great simple dignity. But it obviously didn't last. The Church was already hot with indignation, already issuing decrees to stamp out the unseemly levity which followed. Dancing, especially, it viewed with the sternest disapproval.

According to *A Treatise wherein Dicing, Dauncing, Vaine Playes or Enterludes with other idle pastimes, &c. commonly used on the Sabboth day, are reprooved, by the authoritie of the Worde of God and auncient writers. Made Dialoguewise by John Northbrooke, Minister and Preacher of the Worde of God, London, 1579* . . . according to all that: 'In the Counsel (holden in the yeare of Our Lord God, under Pope Liberius) of Laodicia, A.D. 364. it was decreed thus: It is not meete for Christian men to daunce at their marriages. Let them dyne and sup gravely and moderately, giving thanks to God for the benefit of marriages. Let the cleargie arise and goe their waies, when the players on the Instrumentes (which serve for Dauncing) doe byginne to playe, least by their presence they shoulde seeme to allowe that wantonnesse. In this Counsel, which was holden by the time of Theodoricus the King, it was decreed, namely, that no Christian should daunce at any marriage, or at any other time.'

In this department, they were fighting a losing battle.

Chapter Three

The Age of Chivalry
1000 – 1500 AD

*Three ornaments longe pryncypaly to a wyfe: a
ring on hir fynger; a broch on hir brest; and
a garlond on hir hede.*

Dialogue of Dives and Pauper (1493)

OR the rich and for royalty, Mediaeval weddings were
magnificent affairs, splendid with all the trappings of this
Age of Chivalry. Relatives, surrounded by sprawling
trains of retainers, strutting knights and household clergy,
travelled hundreds of miles to take part in the feasting and
the jousting. Great tournaments were held lasting days or
even weeks; enormous banquets were given: at Westminster on St. Clement's day 1243, 'Thirty-thousand
dishes were got ready for those who sat down to dinner'
at the wedding of Queen Eleanor's sister, Cynthia, and the
Earl Richard. The *trousseau* was firmly established and,
now that the girls of noble families were being brought up
to be decorative rather than useful, the dowry had come into being. Fathers were
having to pay to get rid of their daughters.

Even female serfs were allowed to benefit from the new quixotic climate. William
Vaughan (in his *Golden Grove*) records: 'In Scotland the custom was, that the lord of
the soile should lie with the bride before her husband. But because this order was not
decent nor tolerable among Christians, king Malcome, the 3, of that name, in the
yeere of our Lord 1095, abolished that wicked custom, & enacted that every bride
thencefoorth, should pay to the Lord for ransome of her mayden-head, five shillings.'

A descendant of King Malcolm, Alexander III of Scotland, was the bridegroom at
what must have been the most spectacular wedding in Britain during this age of
spectacles. The day after Christmas 1251, Alexander married Margaret, daughter of
Henry III of England, at York. The Benedictine friar, Matthew Paris, keeping the
chronicle of his monastery up to date, told of 'the splendour of this grand nuptial
ceremony' with an eager eye to the brilliance of it all, and a slightly less lively
conscience urging him, now and then, to tut-tut the 'worldly and wanton vanity of the
scene'.

There was such a crush of 'so many people of different kinds, such numerous crowds
of English, French, and Scotch nobles, such hosts of Knights dressed in elegant
clothing, and glorifying in their silk and variegated ornaments'; such 'multitudes of
people rushed and pressed together in an unruly manner', that the 'ceremony was

9

performed early in the morning, secretly and before it was expected'. But that didn't stop the fashion show, which went on for many days (or the feasting, either—sixty pasture cattle were slaughtered for the first course of one dinner alone). 'A thousand Knights and more, clad in silken stuff, commonly called *cointises**** appeared at the nuptials on the part of the King of England and on the morrow, throwing off all these, they again presented themselves to the court in new robes.' The King of Scotland couldn't quite compete: he only had 'sixty Knights and more dressed in a becoming manner, and many of equal ranks of the Knights, dressed in the same style as they'.

The various nationalities were billeted in separate parts of the city, but even so they all fought like mad—one knight was killed outright, and 'others who were wounded never afterwards recovered'—and the poor old Archbishop of York, 'who was as it were the northern prince and host of all', not only had to mediate but also to pay a hefty slice of the bill. The sixty pasture cattle for the feast had been his treat; he also paid for lodgings for the people and fodder for their horses. In all, 'owing to this visit of his lord, in making presents of gold, silver and silken dresses, he sowed on a barren shore four thousand marks, which he never afterwards reaped'.

The bride seems to have been completely forgotten in the *mêlée*—neither she nor her gown get a mention. But then, both the Princess and her bridegroom were absurdly young: Alexander succeeded to the throne at the age of eight and married two years later; his new queen was eleven.

Towards the end of the century, a more suitably mature bridegroom, Philip III of France,✝ had his Court adopt a total, and glittering, colour-scheme for his marriage: the gentlemen were dressed in scarlet and the ladies in cloth of gold embroidered and trimmed with gold and silver lace. Paul Lacroix in his *Manners, Customs and Dress During the Middle Ages*, adds: 'Massive belts of gold were also worn and chaplets sparkling with the same costly metal.'

But this is all rather rare and heady stuff. For the near clandestine marriage of Sir William Plumpton, Constable of Knaresborough Castle, Yorkshire, in 1451, the bridegroom wore 'a garment of green checkery' and the bride one of 'a red colour' with a grey hood (*Plumpton Correspondence*, edited by G. T. Stapleton). Most couples chose something between these two extremes: something rich and festive, but not specifically nuptial. There was only one fashion which marked out the bride from her guests, and that was the custom of wearing her hair long and loose as a sign of maidenhood. It is often shown in old paintings and tapestries: the girl, her head modestly bowed in a gesture of undiluted virginity, has her hair flowing down to her knees in the kind of crimped corrugations which show it spent most of its time in plaits, and on top of it all, is a garland of flowers. She was said to have 'married in her hair'. But even more often, the bride is shown wearing one of the beautifully elaborate winged or conical headdresses which we associate with the Middle Ages, and then trying to discover who is getting married is like playing a game of find the lady. It is usually the grouping rather than the regalia which provides the clue—the couple holding hands or having them joined by the priest is obviously the happy pair. But

---

* *Cointise* or *Quaintise*: 13th and 14th century term denoting the curious or extravagant in fashion (Cunnington's *Dictionary of English Costume*).

✝ Philip III of France, known as 'le Hardi' (the Bold) 'seems to have been an ineffective and colourless man' says *Chambers's Encyclopaedia*. The bold label 'though contemporary, has never been satisfactorily explained'.

the bride's clothes differ very little from those of the other ladies in the picture: the high-waisted, wide-sleeved gown, richly coloured, softly draped, and partially covered by a sleeveless over-dress or -coat; the trimmings of fur and jewels (the look of already advanced pregnancy, even), all conform to the ordinary fashions of the time.

Just how lavishly the bride was dressed depended on the position—both social and financial—of her father; this was the time of rigid sumptuary laws which detailed exactly who could wear what. During the reign of Edward III (1327–77) Knights whose possessions were below the yearly value of 251 marks were not allowed 'cloth of gold, nor clothes, mantle, nor gold furred with miniver, nor of ermine, nor no apparel bordered of stone, nor otherwise' and nor were their families. Knights and their Ladies who possessed 400 marks annually, could wear what they wished, with the one restriction that 'ermine and letuses* and apparel of pearl and stone' were to be worn on the head, only. Esquires had to have 200 marks a year before they could wear 'cloth of silk and silver, ribband, girdle, and other apparel reasonably garnished with silver'. Tradesmen and their wives had to be content with the skins of 'lambs, rabbits, cats, and foxes'. Later, under Henry VII, no one below the rank of knight was permitted to wear silk shirts—'upon peine of forfeityre therof'.

White was not yet thought of as the bridal colour, but it was worn by at least one bride: King Henry IV's daughter, Princess Philippa, married Eric of Denmark in 1406, when she was 12 years old, wearing 'a tunic and mantle with long train of white satin worked with velvet, furred with pured miniver and purfled with ermine; and the sleeves of the tunic also furred with ermine' (*Archaeologia*, Vol. 47, which has a valuable list of the young Princess's *trousseau*, too). White also appears as a symbol in the legends of the time. Sir Thomas Malory, in his round-up of the Arthurian tales, *Le Morte d'Arthur*, described the commotion at the wedding feast of King Arthur and 'Dame Guenever', when 'came a white hart into the hall, with a white brachet [*hunting dog*] next him', followed by 'a lady on a white palfrey'; and in one of the charming Welsh folk tales of the *Mabinogion* (in which King Arthur also features), growing flax to make a white headdress for the bride is one of the trials set the hero. This is the story of *Kilhwch and Olwen*, in which the wicked chief-giant Yspaddaden Penkawr, knowing he will die on the day of his daughter's marriage, sets forty highly improbable tasks for would-be suitors. But so beautiful is the girl ('More yellow was her head than the flower of the broom, and her skin was whiter than the foam of the wave, and fairer were her hands and fingers than the blossoms of the wood anemone amidst the spray of the meadow fountain'), that Kilhwch succeeds in them all, even growing flax in a field which has resolutely refused to grow flax—so that 'it may make a white wimple for my daughter's head, on the day of thy wedding'.

A bride won in a different kind of contest is described by another Mediaeval writer, and this time her finery keeps more closely to the three ornaments which the *Dialogue of Dives and Pauper* stipulated for wives: a ring, a brooch and a garland. This bride is Tibbe, daughter of the Reeve, or magistrate, of Tottenham, and she has obviously been dressed by her creator to epitomise how every girl of this period

---

* *Letuces*—a type of greyish-white fur, probably that of the pole-cat or snow weasel.

should look on her wedding day (in the same way that a satirist now would load on a long white dress, long white veil, bouquet, horseshoes, orange blossom and a final sprinkling of confetti). She appears in *The Turnament of Tottenham: or, the Wooeing, Winning, and Wedding of Tibbe, the Reev's Daughter There*, a marvellous send-up of the Age of Chivalry, by a poet of that Age (the earliest known manuscript dates from the reign of King Henry VI—about 1456). Poor Tibbe (or Tyb as she is more often called) is to be won by combat—her father, the Reeve, offering her as a prize in the Tournament of Tottenham, along with:

> Coppell my brode-henn [*broody hen*] that was broyt out of Kent:
> And my dunnyd kowe [*dun cow*],
>   For no spens [*expense*] wyl I spare,
>   For no cattell [*possessions*] wyl I care,
>   He schal have my gray mare,
>   And my spottyd sowe.

Seated on that other portion of the prize, the grey mare (with a 'sek ful of fedyrs' for a saddle, for 'scho schuld syt soft'), this is how Tibbe makes her entrance:

> A gay gyrdyl Tyb had on, borrowed for the nonys,
> And a garland on her hed ful of rounde bonys [*round bones or beads*],
> And a broche on hur brest ful of sapphyre stonys,
> Wyth the holy-rode tokenyng [*religious token*], [which] was wrotyn
>   [*made*] for the nonys:

According to the *Dialogue of Dives and Pauper*, the brooch 'betokenneth clennesse in herte and chastitye that she oweth to have; the garlande betokeneth the gladnesse and the dignitye of the sacrament of wedlock'. The 'gay gyrdyl Tyb had on' was also important. One 15th century bridegroom, Thomas Betson, a wool merchant, thought his bride-to-be (his 'maystresse Kateryn') should have at least three new girdles for her wedding, and since he lived in London, while she was in the country, he was given the task of getting them made. In a delightful exchange of notes with the girl's mother (included in *The Stonor Letters*, edited by C. L. Kingsford) he shows a marvellous male bewilderment about this transaction and the rest of the *trousseau*: '. . . I must beseech your ladyship to send me how I shall be demeaned in such things as shall belong unto my cousin Katherine, and how I shall provide for them. She must have girdles, three at the least, and how they shall be made I know not, and many other things she must have, yet know well what they be, in faith I know not; by my troth, I would it were done, liever than more than it shal cost. . . .'

Betson had waited many years for Katherine Riche, the daughter of a friend, to grow old enough to marry (which she was judged to have done in 1478, when she was 15), but the final arrangements caused him much harassment. In June 1478, he wrote again to Katherine's mother—this time about the banns: 'Our vicar here, so God help me, shall cry out upon her within this ten weeks and less, and by that time I shall be ready in every point, by God's grace, and so I would she were, forsooth ye may believe me of it.'

Chaucer, that superb 14th century man of many parts (soldier, courtier, diplomat, and civil servant, as well as poet) dressed one of his brides, Grisilde, in much the same way that Tibbe was kitted out, in his *Clerk of Oxenford's Tale*. When the markys (or Marquis) in this story decides to wed the loveliest but also the poorest girl in the village, he not unnaturally asked the ladies of the court to clean her up and dress her in new clothes before taking her off to the castle. And the ladies of the court, not unnaturally, are none too keen on the assignment.

> And for no thyng of hir olde geere
> She sholde brynge into his hous, he bad
> That wommen sholde dispoillen hire right theere;
> Of which thise ladyes were nat right glad
> To handle hir clothes, wherinne she was clad.
> But nathelees, this mayde bright of hewe
> Fro foot to heed they clothed han al newe.
>
> Hir heris han they kembd, that lay untressed
> Ful rudely, and with hir fyngres smale
> A corone on hire heed they han ydressed,
> And sette hire ful of nowches grete and smale.
> Of hire array what sholde I make a tale?
> Unnethe the people hir knew of hire fairness,
> When she translated was in swich richesse.

Which roughly translated means they combed her hair and placed, with delicate fingers, a nuptial garland (*corone*) on her head, and decorated her lavishly with brooches (*nowches*) great and small (earlier we learn that the Marquis had rings and brooches made for this intended bride of gems 'set in gold and in asure'); and altogether made such a splendid job of it the people hardly recognized her when they had finished.

Roger of Wendover, prior of the Benedictine Monastery of St. Albans, gives an excellent contemporary account of a royal mediaeval wedding as his last entry in the monastery's chronicle (translated from the original Latin and now called, charmingly, *Flowers of History*). Written in 1235, one year before the Prior's death, it tells of the marriage of Isabella, the beautiful young sister of King Henry III of England (so beautiful that Henry kept her locked in the Tower of London for safety—he may not have looked after his country too well, but he made very sure of his sister!). The bridegroom was the enlightened, embattled, Holy Roman Emperor, Frederick II, and the fact that it was not his first marriage—or that he was currently engaged in a war against a son by a former wife—was obviously seen as no reason to scale-down this particular wedding. Prior Roger tells it all so well, I'll let him take over:

How the emperor demanded the sister of the king of England in marriage.

In the month of February of this year [1235] two templars, with some knights and other special messengers, came to the king at Westminster, charged with letters, sealed with gold, from the emperor Frederic, demanding the hand of the English king's sister, Isabel, in marriage. They reached the king on the 23rd February, and begged for an answer to the letters and the demand, that they might announce the king's decision to their lord with all haste. The king then held a careful deliberation with the bishops and nobles of his kingdom for three days, when they all, after duly considering the matter, unanimously agreed that the lady should be given to the emperor, and on the 27th of February the king gave his answer agreeing to the demanded alliance. The messengers then asked permission to see the lady, and the king sent some trustworthy messengers to fetch his sister from the tower of London where she was carefully guarded; the messengers conducted her with all honour to the king at Westminster where she appeared before the messengers of the emperor, a lady in her 20th year, beautiful to look upon, adorned with virgin modesty, and distinguished by her royal dress and manners. After they had refreshed their sight for some time with gazing on the lady, they decided that she was most worthy in all respects of the imperial couch, and confirmed the marriage on the soul of the emperor by oath, presenting her with a wedding ring in his name; after they had placed it on her finger they proclaimed her empress of Rome, all exclaiming, 'Long live our empress . . .'

Of the wedding ornaments of the empress and of the noble preparations.

There was such a profusion of ornaments at this marriage that they appeared to surpass kingly wealth; for the empress herself a crown had been most elaborately constructed out of pure gold adorned with jewels, and on it were carved the likenesses of the four martyr and confessor kings of England, to whom the king had especially assigned the care of his sister's soul. She shone forth with such a profusion of rings and gold necklaces, and other splendid jewels, with silk and thread garments, and other like ornaments, which usually attract the gaze and excite the desires of women even to covetousness, that they appeared invaluable. With bridal garments of silk, wool, and thread, she was so well supplied, that it was difficult to say which would be most likely to attract the emperor's affections. Her couch was so rich in its coverlets and pillows of various colours, and the various furniture and sheets made of pure fine linen, that by its softness it would invite those lying in it to a delightful slumber. All the drinking cups and dishes were of the purest gold and silver; and, what seemed superfluous to every one, all the cooking pots, large and small, were of pure silver . . . After he had thus arranged matters the king, on St. John's day, held a solemn festival before the Latin gate at Westminster in company with the archbishop of Cologne and the emperor's other messengers; as soon as all the arrangements had been completed they all took the road towards the borough of Dartford accompanied by the king with a large train of earls and barons . . .

Of the arrival of the empress at Cologne.

After a voyage of three days and nights they entered the mouth of the river Rhine, and after a run of a day and night up that river, they arrived at Antwerp, a city under the imperial jurisdiction. On their landing at this place they were met by an immense host of armed nobles, who had been sent by the emperor to act as guard to the empress, to keep vigilant watch round her person day and night; for it was reported that some of the emperor's enemies, who were in alliance with the French king, were planning to carry off the empress, and prevent the marriage. They were also met by all the priests and clergy of the adjacent districts in solemn procession, ringing bells and singing songs of joy, and with them came all the best masters in every sort of music with their instruments, who accompanied the empress with all kinds of nuptial rejoicings during the journey of five days to Cologne. When her approach became known at that place there went out to meet her, with flowers, palm branches, and in festive dresses, about ten thousand of the citizens, mounted on Spanish horses, who put them to full speed and engaged in jousting with one another. Accompanied by these rejoicing crowds the empress proceeded through the principal streets of the city, which had been decorated in all kinds of ways against her arrival; and, on learning that every one, and especially the noble ladies of the city, who sat in the balconies, were desirous of seeing her face, she took her cap and hood from her head, for all to get a sight of her, for doing which every one praised her, and after they had gazed at her gave her great commendations for her beauty as well as her humility. She then took up her abode outside the walls of the city on account of the noise therein, and there awaited the emperor's instructions.

Of the marriage of the emperor and empress at Worms.

At the time of the empress's arrival at Cologne, the emperor was engaged in a war against his son who had rebelled against him; his father, however, led such a large army against him that he laid siege to ten of his castles at one and the same time . . . ordered him to be enchained and took him away with him to Worms, from which place he sent word to the empress to come to him there, she having then been six weeks at Cologne. The archbishop of Cologne and the bishop of Exeter, with the other nobles of her suite then at once set out on their way to the emperor, and, after a journey of seven days brought the empress to him amidst all kind of nuptial pomp and rejoicing. She was received on her arrival by the emperor with joy and respect, who was beyond measure delighted with her beauty, and the marriage was solemnized at that place on Sunday the 20th of July, and although her beauty pleased the emperor at first sight he was much more pleased after marriage . . .

The following year, King Henry himself married. But he appears to have done so with even more haste and considerably less splendour than he provided for his sister— all those silver saucepans must have made a nasty dent in the royal coffers.

Princess Isabella had received the Emperor Frederick's proposal on 23 February, sailed from England on 11 May, and married on 20 July. Henry asked for the hand of Eleanor of Provence shortly before Christmas; by 19 January, that lady, with a commendable turn of speed, had ridden across the breadth of France, sailed the Channel, married the King at Canterbury and been crowned Queen in London. (Four years later they produced the little Princess Margaret whose marriage to Alexander of Scotland caused such tumult at York.)

Henry and his eager Eleanor were wed on 14 January in the porch of Canterbury Cathedral, which was not as odd as it now sounds. Until the reign of Edward VI (1547–53) in England, and slightly later in Europe, the actual marriage ceremony was always performed at the church door; then, everyone moved inside for the nuptial Mass.

Chaucer said of his Wife of Bath:

> She was a worthy womman al hir lyve,
> Housbondes at the chirche dore she hadde fyve.

And an old manuscript *Concerning the Clergy in the Papal Times* (quoted by Dr.

Brand) shows that this applied to everyone: 'the pride of the clergy and the bigotry of the laity were such, that both rich and poor were married at the church doors'.

Many other reasons, apart from pride and bigotry, have been put forward, from the indecency of granting permission *inside* the church for a man and woman to sleep together, to the amount of business, even last-minute bargaining, which took place just before the ceremony. John Bridges gives a late 13th century example of the commercial side of the transaction in his *History and Antiquities of Northamptonshire*:

> This Robert Fitz Roger, in the sixth year of Edward I entered into an engagement with Robert de Tybetot to marry within a limited time John his son and heir to Hawisia the daughter of the said Robert de Tybetot, to endow her at the church door, on her wedding-day with lands amounting to the value of one hundred pounds per annum out of this Manor of Aynho.

But a little commerce wasn't really going to shake the vaults of a Mediaeval church— most days of the week the aisles looked more like a bustling market than a place of worship, anyway. There is one other explanation, however, which does seem possible: it is the theory that weddings were performed outside the church as a last-ditch stand to keep them out of the clutches of the clergy. It didn't work, but it could have been the one surviving sign of resistance.

The decrees issued by the Catholic Church during the Middle Ages show just how determined it was to gain complete control. Not content with regulating how people should marry, it was now busily deciding who should marry—or, rather, who should not. The Saxons had begun it by forbidding marriage between first cousins; then, in the 11th century, marriages between second cousins were prohibited; a little later even third cousins could not marry without papal dispensation.

If it were discovered—no matter how long after the event—that couples within the forbidden degrees of consanguinity had married, the marriage was automatically null and any children declared illegitimate. To complicate matters further, as matrimony was said to make husband and wife one flesh, so her relatives became his, and *vice versa*; which meant that a widow or widower could not marry the first, second or third cousin of the deceased partner. To compound the complication, god-parents were also looked upon as blood relations. A man and a woman who had stood as god-parents to the same child could not marry each other—though, under these rules, one would have thought they should have done so, and quickly. A god-father certainly could not marry his god-daughter—this was incest just as surely as if the actual father had perpetrated the act. And, if a couple had naughtily slept together out of wedlock (or within a marriage which was later annulled by the church) they could not in future marry cousins of their partners within the prohibited degrees.

Child betrothals were still common practice, and these too could cause hopeless confusion in the children's later lives. The real trouble here was that there were two forms of betrothal ceremony, the difference resting in whether the vows were exchanged in the present or future tense. If the latter were used, the contract could be set aside if the parties decided not to go ahead with the wedding. If, however, the vows were exchanged in the present tense, these were binding for all time—even if they had only been exchanged privately. A couple, however young, who had promised, in the present tense, to marry each other, could marry no one else—ever. If they agreed to keep their vows secret and went ahead with other marriages, it only needed two malicious, unknown witnesses to inform against them to make their unions illegal and immoral. Often the testimony of just one witness was accepted. The young couple did not have to marry each other, but they were allowed to marry no one else until the death of one set the other free.

This labyrinth of chaos was bliss for those of the clergy who enjoyed intrigue and meddling. It was lucrative, too: dispensations, annullments, or a blind eye were all on offer from the church—at a price; a service which some members of the laity were quick to turn to their own advantage. All these rules remained in being until the Reformation, and Margaret Tudor, Henry VIII's sister, was to provide a classic example of how to manipulate them. The widow of James IV of Scotland, she had her second marriage, to the Earl of Angus, annulled on a fictional plea of a previous betrothal. She was then able to get rid of her third husband, Lord Methuen, by proving to a spiritual court that he was a cousin eight degrees removed (i.e., third cousin) to the Earl of Angus, whose union with her had been proved no marriage at all. With a lady like her in the family, it is difficult to understand how Henry VIII ever got into such a mess.

However, for anyone wanting to marry and stay married, the path to the altar was littered with booby-traps. The impossibility of keeping tabs on all those third cousins, real or church invented, gave urgent meaning to the request in the marriage service for anyone knowing of any 'just cause or impediment' why the wedding should not go forward 'to speak now, or for ever hold thy peace'. Nowadays, it lacks drama; then it must have been an absolute show-stopper.

The publishing of banns also became vitally important. This wasn't a new idea— the Carthaginian Tertullian (c. 160–A.D. 230) said that in his time all marriages were considered clandestine that were not announced in church beforehand—but in the Middle Ages it must have provided an essential opportunity for the whole community to start counting on their fingers and unravelling complicated lines of descent.

Walter Reynolds, Archbishop of Canterbury from 1313–27, ordered that every wedding should be preceded by the reading of the banns on three consecutive Lord's days or holidays; and that marriages should be celebrated at church, with reverence, in daylight, and in the face of the congregation. Priests, he said, should use the threat of excommunication to prevent clandestine betrothals and marriages; and any priest breaking any of the church's laws—especially by knowingly performing illegal marriages—would be punished.

Neither flock nor clergy appears to have sprung immediately to heel. The next two Archbishops of Canterbury, after Reynolds, found it necessary to issue even sterner edicts on exactly the same theme.

Rigid laws usually produce their own antidote, and in this case the answer was the *specialis licentia*—the special licence. By the early 14th century, these were already available for people with plenty of money and a position of influence. Then, as now, they allowed a couple to be married anywhere, at any time, and without the formality of announcing it beforehand.

But however they married—whether by special licence in private, or openly before the congregation of the parish church—both bride and groom qualified their vows with the phrase 'if holy church it will ordain', a necessary reservation, even when everything possible had been done before the wedding to ensure its legality. The vows themselves have changed very little over the years, as is shown by this eerie echo of the present-day ceremony, taken from a Missal of Richard II's reign (1377–99):

> Bridegroom: 'Ich M. take the N. to my wedded wyf, to haven and to holden, for fayrere, for fouler, for bettur for wors, for richer for porer, in seknesse and in helthe, for thys tyme forward, til dethe us depart, ʒif holi-chirche will it orden; and ʒerto iche pliʒt the my treuthe;'

and on giving the ring:

> 'with this ring I the wedde, and this gold and selver ich the ʒeve, and with my bodi I the worschepe, and with all my worldly catelle I the honoure.'
>
> The bride: 'Iche N. take the M. to my weddid husbond, to haven and to holden, for fayrer for fouler, for bettur for wors, for richer for porer, in seknesse and in helthe, to be bonlich and buxum in bed and at burde,* tyl deth us departe, fro thys tyme forward, and if holichirche it wol orden; and ʒerto iche pliʒt the my treuthe.'

After the promises and the giving of rings outside the church, and the nuptial mass inside it, came the banquet. The Merchant, in Chaucer's *Canterbury Tales*, provides a delightful description of one such wedding feast in his story of rich old Januarie and lovely young May:

> And at the feeste sitteth he and she
> With othere worthy folk upon the deys [*dais*].
> Al ful of joye and blisse is the paleys [*palace*],
> And ful of instrumentz and of vitaille.

At every course there is 'loud mynstralcye' and eager Januarie, clutching a 'fyrbrond' (or torch) in his hand, dances before his bride and guests.† Then all the men 'daunce and drynken faste, And spices al aboute the hous they caste'. Soon Januarie heartily wishes they would all go away and leave him to a nightcap of 'ypocras, claree and vernage of spices hoote'—and his bride. And at last they do: 'Hoom to hir [*their*] houses lustily they ride'; the bride is brought to the marriage bed, which is 'with the preest yblessed'; and . . .

> And Januarie hath faste in armes take
> His fresshe May, his paradys, his make [*mate*].
> He lulleth hire, he kisseth hire ful ofte;
> With thikke brustles of his berd [*beard*] unsofte.

Considerately he reassures her:

> Ther nys [*is*] no werkman, whatsoevere he be,
> That may both werke wel and hastily;
> This wol be doon at leyser [*leisure*] parfitly.

---

* *Bonlich and buxum in bed and at burde*: meek and obedient in bed and at board—one vow which has gone out of fashion.

† *Torch dances* were particularly popular in Germany, and Royal Prussian weddings were still celebrated with a *Fackeltanz* in the middle of last century (the Ministers of the Crown carried the torches). Queen Victoria did not approve and made Prince William of Prussia promise not to involve her daughter, the Princess Royal, in one when he married her and carried her back to Berlin in 1859.

The Age of Chivalry

And so it is.
  At noon next day, lusty old Januarie leaps out of bed,

                                 but fresshe May
        Heeld [*kept to*] hire chambre unto the fourthe day,
        As usage is of wyves for the beste. . . .

        As custume is unto thise nobles alle.
        A bryde shal nat eten [*eat*] in the halle
        Til dayes foure, or thre dayes atte leeste,
        Ypassed been; thanne lat [*let*] hire go to feeste.

Which only goes to show that some things may change, but others stay the same.

Chapter Four

White for the Pure Young Maid
The Sixteenth Century

Thy smock of silk, both fair and white,
  With gold embroidered gorgeously;
Thy petticoat of sendal right;
  And thus I bought thee gladly.

Thy purse and eke thy gay gilt knives,
  Thy pincase gallant to the eye;
No better wore the burgess wives,
  And yet thou wouldst not love me.
                              Anon: *Greensleeves*

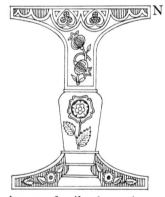

N England, this was the age of the Tudors—the time of Henry VIII and the Virgin Queen. The upstart Henry VII had already been on the throne for fifteen years when the 16th century dawned; his grand-daughter, Queen Elizabeth, was to sweep the country gloriously into the 17th. It was a time of discovery, widening horizons and growing prosperity. The new wealth was reflected throughout social life, and weddings benefitted from it along with everything else. People were able to marry earlier; even the poor could celebrate in some style now that special houses were provided, next to the church, for wedding parties; and the new nobility, though busy build-ing up family dynasties—and vast palaces in which to house them—was charitably minded: in their lifetime, the rich supplied dowries and wedding feasts for their servants, and when they died they left sums 'for poor maydens to marry'. After the Reformation, anxious souls still left money for Masses to be said 'if this be legal'; it wasn't, and these sums, too, were turned into dowries for poor girls.

And it was now that 'white' and 'weddings' began to join forces. It was not yet thought of as the bridal colour, but by the end of the century it was so firmly estab-lished as the symbol of pure young maidenhood that it became the automatic choice for a great many brides. That may seem rather a quibble, but there was still a long way to go before 'dressed all in white' met with the immediate reaction 'Ah, here comes the bride'; to an Elizabethan, 'dressed all in white' meant 'Ah, here we have a pure young maid—a virgin'—marriage had nothing to do with it. But it was the start, the very first sprouting of what was to become the great white wedding tradition. Queen Elizabeth herself, with her red hair and pale skin, wore white to

20

enormous advantage; she also inspired a cult of romantic virginity which affected everything at her court (except the love-life of her courtiers); the combination was seized on by the poets, who immortalised her, her colouring and the colour white in one great poetic package. 'White is my colour', says the Maid firmly in Sir John Davies' *A Contention betwixt a Wife, a Widow, and a Maid*, and white was the colour of many a virgin gown—as well as every brow and every bosom—for nearly fifty years; every female head of hair was red or gold; and every fair young maid was a small reflection of the Queen. Edmund Spenser packed all these fashionable ingredients into his *Epithalamion*. His bride

> comes along with portly pace,
> Lyke Phoebe, from her chamber of the East,
> Arysing forth to run her mighty race,
> Clad all in white, that seemes a virgin best.
> So well it her beseemes, that ye would weene
> Some angell she had beene.
> Her long loose yellow locks lyke golden wyre,
> Sprinckled with perle, and perling flowres atweene,
> Doe lyke a golden mantle her attyre;
> And, being crownèd with a garland greene,
> Seeme lyke some mayden Queene.

'Clad all in white, that seemes [*becomes*] a virgin best'—Spenser's white is specifically the white of maidenhood. It is still the garland on the head and the 'loose yellow locks lyke golden wyre' which show she is a bride, and the same poet makes this very clear in his *Prothalamion*:

> There, in a Meadow, by the Rivers side,
> A Flocke of Nymphes I chauncèd to espy,
> All lovely Daughters of the Flood thereby,
> With goodly greenish locks, all loose untyde;
> As each had bene a Bryde . . .
>
> Two of those Nymphes, meane while, two Garlands bound
> Of freshest Flowres which in that Mead they found,
> The which presenting all in trim Array,
> Their snowie Foreheads therewithall they crownd,
> Whil'st one did sing this Lay,
> Prepar'd against that Day,
> Against their Brydale day, which was not long:
> Sweet Themmes! runne softly, till I end my Song.

Mary Queen of Scots, another regal red-head, wore a gown 'as white as lilies' when she married the young Dauphin of France in 1558—and defied tradition to do so, for white was then the mourning colour for French queens. Even so, she didn't set an immediate fashion for all royal French brides to follow; there was still plenty of competition to the virgin trend, and even if the bride did wear white, it wasn't quite the pure and pristine affair we imagine today. When Mary's youngest sister-in-law, the celebrated Marguerite de Valois, married Henri of Navarre, she was certainly robed in white—white ermine, no less—but this was 'covered by a great blue coat with four ells of train'. Less noble brides also went in for various kinds of colourful

21

decoration. Sometime around 1580, John Heywood (grandfather of John Donne and an early music teacher to the little girl who was to become the original bloody Mary), made a list of all the bits and pieces women managed to drape around themselves—and it sounds like a mad inventory of a 20th century handbag:

> Silken swathbonds, ribands and sleeve-laces,
> Girdles, knives, purses, and pin-cases.

These, together with gloves, garters and scarves, all decorated wedding dresses, too. After the marriage ceremony, the swathbonds (silk 'swaddling bands', worn round the waist), ribbons, sleeve-laces and garters were scrambled for by the guests, who wore whatever they could grab as trophies for the rest of the festivities. Garters were the most prized of all: if the bride were lucky, these went last, as she made her escape to bed; if she were unlucky, she lost them before she left the altar.

Dr. Brand, commenting on this trophy-hunting—a custom which 'strongly marks the grossness of manner that prevailed among our ancestors'—said the young men used 'to strive, immediately after the ceremony, who could first pluck off the bride's garters from her legs. This was done before the very altar. The bride was generally gartered with ribands for the occasion. Whoever were so fortunate as to be victors in this singular species of contest, during which the bride was often obliged to scream out, and was very frequently thrown down, bore them about the church in triumph.' A Yorkshire clergyman told him in the late 18th century that 'to prevent this very indecent assault', it was usual for a bride married at his church 'to give garters out of her bosom'. Brand thought the whole idea was probably 'a fragment of the ancient ceremony of loosening the virgin zone, or girdle, a custom that needs no explanation'.

The bridegroom also wore—and usually lost—ribbon garters, though these were called points as soon as they appeared on masculine legs. Christopher Brooke instructed in his *Epithalamium*:

> Youths, take his poynts, your wonted right;
> And maydens, take your due, her garters

which sounds a slightly more decorous division of the spoils than usual. And Samuel Butler, a few years later, was to show, in *Hudibras*, where these trophies ended up:

> Which all the saints, and some since martyrs,
> Wore in their hats like wedding garters.

Most girls chose two or three colours for all these ribbon fripperies, and as decorations for the feast and bridal bed. The bridemen gallantly wore the bride's colours round their sleeves and carried them aloft during the procession to church. 'Two broad bride-laces of red and yellow buckram begilded' streamed in 'such wind as there was' at a country wedding arranged for Queen Elizabeth's amusement when she visited Kenilworth in 1575.

The knives also mentioned in Heywood's list of trinkets sound less appropriate as wedding finery, but they were certainly worn.

> See at my girdle hang my wedding knives!
> With those dispatch me,

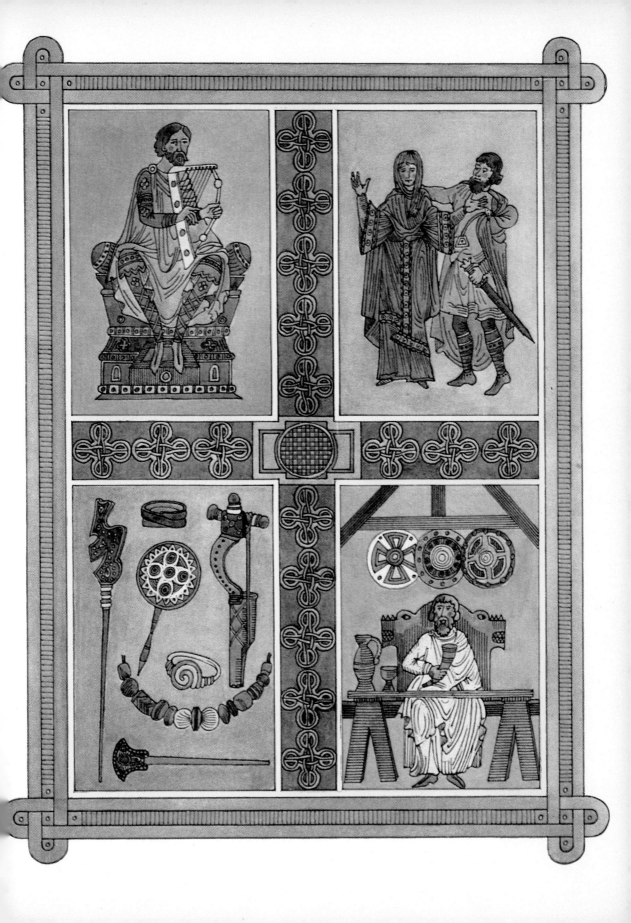

Plate Two

says the bride to her jealous husband in Thomas Dekker's play *Match Me in London*. What kind of knives they were, we don't know, but a book with a charming title— *The French Garden, for English Ladyes and Gentlewomen to walke in* (1621)—offers a wide range from which to choose. In a dialogue describing how a fashionable lady of the day should dress, a mistress commands her waiting-woman: 'Give me my girdle, and see that all the furniture be at it; looke if my cizers, the pincers, the pen-knife, the knife to close letters with, the bodkin, the ear-picker, and the seale be in the case: where is my purse to weare upon my gowne?'

In fact, wedding knives were most probably 'cizers'. These were often called 'a pair of knives' in Tudor times, and were popular as wedding presents, especially if inscribed with a suitable little rhyme. Posy No. 11 in Francis Davison's *A Poetical Rapsodie* (1611) is for 'A Pair of Knives':

> Fortune doth give these paire of knives to you,
> To cut the thred of love if 't be not true.

An even more popular gift was gloves. For many years, these were *the* wedding present and it was a wretched marriage indeed which did not abound in them. 'We see no ensigns of a wedding here, no character of the bridale; where be our skarves and our gloves', says Lady Haughty in Ben Jonson's *The Silent Woman*. And at the very beginning of the 17th century, John Stephens said of his *Plaine Countrey Bride*: 'She hath no rarity worth observance, if her gloves be not miraculous and singular.'

Miraculous they usually were. The gloves of this period were lovely things, made of soft leather, with wide gauntlet cuffs, richly embroidered and often jewelled. The bride's were either a gift from the groom or from a spurned suitor, making one last bid to show her the folly of her choice by sending the most lavish and extravagant pair he could find. Important guests, groomsmen, the boys who escorted the bride to church, and the married men who escorted her back again; the parson . . . all were given gloves. Some clergymen were even prepared to do a little blackmailing to get theirs. At the beginning of the century, Richard Arnold noted in his *Commonplace Book*, among the 'artcles upon whiche is to inqyre in the visitacyons of ordynaryes of churches: Item, whether the curat refuse to do the solemnysacyon of lawfull matrymonye before he have gyft of money, hoses, or gloves'.

They were also given at French weddings. At the mock marriage in Rabelais' *Pantagruel* (1532), as soon as the contract was signed: 'On one side was brought wine and comfits; on the other, white and orange tawny-coloured favours were distributed; on another, gauntlets privately handed.'*

Shakespeare has Hero, in *Much Ado About Nothing*, admire the 'excellent perfume' of the gloves sent by Claudio on their wedding morning. He also chronicled the extraordinarily early hours chosen for marriages, and the fact that many brides did not think it essential to have a new outfit for the wedding. Hero chooses one rabato (a ruff) as she dresses for her marriage and her rather annoying attendant tries to argue her out of it: 'Troth, I think your other rabato were better.' It is obvious that neither was bought specially for the occasion. Her headdress is new and will do

---

* The restrained method of distributing the bride's colours described here—the handing round of white and orange ribbon knots, or favours, instead of fighting for the garters—came to England during the seventeenth century. Odd to have Rabelais, of all people, reflecting such early decorum.

excellently, thinks the aggravating Margaret, though it would have shown to better advantage had Hero's hair been 'a thought browner'. The gown, like the collar, appears to have been chosen from the bride's existing wardrobe, and comes in for the most devastating comment of all: the Duchess of Milan's dress, says Margaret, 'that they praise so' was 'but a night-gown in respect of yours: cloth o' gold, and cuts, and laced with silver, set with pearls, down sleeves, side sleeves, and skirts round, underborne with a bluish tinsel; but for a fine, quaint, graceful, and excellent fashion, yours is worth ten on 't'. *

And all this in the small hours of the morning. ''Tis almost five o'clock, cousin; 'tis time you were ready', says Beatrice when they finally rout her out of bed to help dress the bride. Juliet's wedding was even earlier. Old Capulet, with all the noise and sense of virtue of a man who hasn't been to bed at all, wakes his household at cock's crow—three a.m. Not long after that, County Paris, the eager groom, is on the doorstep with his musicians. Juliet never seems to have considered pleading a 16th century equivalent of 'I haven't got a thing to wear' to delay this dreaded (and bigamous) match. Instead, sleeping potion in hand, she asks, with desperate composure:

> Nurse, will you go with me into my closet
> To help sort such needful ornaments
> As you think fit to furnish me tomorrow?

The house is in an uproar to provide the food and entertainment; Juliet's dress is unimportant.

One of the main reasons why more brides did not have a new gown for their weddings was, of course, the cost. Fine cloth and trimmings were relatively expensive and 16th century fashions took a lot of material. Mary Queen of Scots, always generous with her ladies, paid £125 for the wedding dress of her favourite bed-chamber woman, Margaret Carwood in 1567 (and attended the marriage, even though it did take place the day after Darnley's murder and the massive gunpowder explosion at Kirk o' Field); and when the Lady Jean Gordon married Bothwell (just two years before Mary herself became the wife of that artful man), the Queen presented her with eleven ells (13¾ yds.) of cloth-of-silver for her wedding gown. Lower down the social scale, when Richard Johnson married Margaret Mattyrs of Calais in 1547, the bride's trousseau material comprised: 'In the packet of cloth are 3½ yds. of fine cloth that cost 17s. the yard (et ultra say ye!) for the bride's wedding garment, and an upper body to spare: in a greater piece 6½ yds. for her second gown &c.' The three-and-a-half yards would not have been enough for the whole dress, and was possibly for the two bodices and a kirtle—the kind of 16th century petticoat which showed as a flash of contrasting colour between the open fronts of the over-skirt. (In poorer circles, it could also be a short petticoat, worn over the main skirt, like an all round apron.) To complete Mlle. Mattyrs' wedding gown, material would still have been needed for the over-skirt and for the sleeves; these were often made separately from the dress and then tied to the bodice with ribbons. In this way, one pair of expensively

---

* A *night-gown* was an informal dress, not to be confused with a night-dress for going to bed in; *cuts* were slashed openings in the outer fabric, showing a different material beneath; *down sleeves* were ordinary long sleeves and *side sleeves* were loose outer sleeves, open from the shoulder. *Underborne* meant lined.

embroidered or jewelled sleeves could serve several outfits. Queen Yolande, mother of King René of Sicily and an ardent theatre-goer, was said to have had a costly pair of sleeves (attached in this manner) stolen from her arms while she watched a miracle play.

If every bride could not afford a new dress, however, a garland of leaves or flowers was available to all. In France, a girl with no dowry was said to bring her husband a chaplet of roses, and both in England and on the Continent, floral wreaths were still favoured, especially by country brides. The milkmaid heroine of a popular Elizabethan ballad, *I'm to be married o' Sunday*, prepared to wear one for her marriage:

> Next Saturday night 'twill be my care
> To trim and curl my maiden hair,
> And all the people shall say, Look there!
>   When I come to be married o' Sunday.

> Then to the church I shall be led
> By sister Nan and brother Ned,
> With a garland of flowers upon my head,
>   For I'm to be married o' Sunday.

> And in the church I must kneel down
> Before the parson of our good town;
> But I will not spoil my kirtle and gown,
>   When I'm married o' Sunday.

Petruchio, that most wayward of bridegrooms, carols the refrain from this song in *The Taming of the Shrew*:

> We will have rings and things of fine array;
> And, kiss me, Kate, we will be married a' Sunday.

It was generally agreed that Sunday was a good day for marrying (Mary Queen of Scots chose it for two of her three weddings), but the tricky problem of just what to put into the bridal garland met with no such happy concord. Many people, including Polydore Vergil, an Italian churchman at the court of Henry VIII, thought that gilded wheat ears could not be bettered as a nuptial crown, while Puritan preachers were resolutely against the gilding of anything. In a sermon called *A Marriage Present*, Roger Hacket urged brides to wear 'sweet smelling flowers' with their 'native fragrance' not those 'gilded with the art of man'. Curiously, the Puritans did not object to the use of wheat itself, even with its heathen and fertility connections; and they also managed to overlook the fact that the rose, one of the most fragrant flowers of all, was said to be dedicated to Venus. The rose was also said to be the symbol of discretion and secrecy (hence *sub rosa*), and Laevinus Lemnius neatly wrapped up this dual significance in his *Herbal from the Bible* ('drawn into English' by T. Newton in 1587):

> . . . the myrtle and rose be plants which antiquitie dedicated to Venus; for that, at brideales, the houses and chambers were wont to be strawed with these odoriferous and sweete herbes; to signifie that in wedlocke all pensive sullenness and lowering cheer, all wrangling and strife, jarring variance, and discord, ought to be utterly excluded and abandoned, and that in place thereof al mirth,

25

pleasantness, and cheerfulnesse, mildness, quietness, and love should be maintained, and that in matters passing between the husband and the wife all secrecy
should be used.

City brides used roses and other flowers to decorate the feast, and often wreaths of
flowers or wheat were carried in the bridal procession, but on their heads they
preferred to wear something more durable. Golden circlets or 'goodly caps, garnished
with laces, gilt' were now the fashion for town weddings. Royal brides often had their
hair flowing loose, in a maidenly manner, but they topped it with crown jewels
rather than the kind of flowery crown any country milkmaid could wear. Those who
could afford to, aimed at something like the splendid array Henry VIII's thrice-
married sister wore for her first wedding. In 1503, when she married James IV of
Scotland, Margaret Tudor had 'a varey riche coller of gold, of pyerrery [*precious
stones*] and perles round her neck, and the croune upon hyr hed, her hayre hangynge.
Betwix the saide croune and the hayres was a varey riche coyfe hangyng down behind
the whole length of her bodye'. (The 'coyfe' seems to have been a floor-length veil—
and this part of the outfit was not copied by her contemporaries. 'Coyfe' or 'coif'
usually referred to a tight-fitting cap, like a baby's bonnet, covering the hair and ears
and tying beneath the chin.)
   If the bride could not produce her own golden headdress, the church could sometimes supply one for her. In 1540 St. Margaret's Church, Westminster, 'Paid to
Alice Lewis, a goldsmith's wife of London, for a serclett to marry maydens in, the
26th day of September, £3. 10s.' In 1560, when three young sisters were married on
the same day, they all wore the same kind of 'goodly caps' (what we would now call
Juliet caps—or, I'm afraid, beanies) trimmed with gilded lace. John Stowe's *Survey of
London* contains this account of the wedding:

> In the year 1560, in the parish church of St. Mary Wolneth were married
> three daughters of one Mr. Atkinson, a scrivener, together. They were in their
> hair, and goodly apparel, set out with chains, pearls, and stones. Thus they went
> to church, all three one after another, with three goodly caps, garnished with
> laces, gilt, and fine flowers and rosemary strewed for their coming home; and so
> to the father's house, where was a great dinner prepared for his said three bride-
> daughters, with the bridegrooms and company.

The strewing (or *strawing*, as the word was often written) of flowers and herbs
before the wedding procession was a popular custom—and today's miniscule flower-
girls who hold tight to their baskets of blooms (decorative, rather than decorating),
are, no doubt, directly descended from it. In the 16th century, it was one more
ensign of the wedding which could send the hearts of hopeful young girls fluttering,
as they thought of their own turn yet to come:

> Come, straw apace. Lord, shall I ever live
> To walk to Church on flowers? O 'tis fine
> To see a bride trip to church so lightly
> As she her new choppines would scorn to bruze
> A silly flower.

The choppines which this would-be bride imagined tripping to church on were cork or
iron platforms—something like a skate but with a wider base—which could be strapped

to ordinary shoes. The extra height they gave, lifted hemlines above the dirty streets and protected delicate slippers. Hamlet describes one of the strolling players as being 'nearer to heaven . . . by the altitude of a chopine'. Of all the silly flowers and herbs crushed beneath these contraptions, none was more prized than rosemary: it was worn by the bridemen, carried in the procession, floated in the 'knitting cup' (the wine or ale drunk by bride and groom to celebrate the union), dipped in holy water, blessed by the priest, and cast at the feet of the bride, as it was at the feet of the three Misses Atkinson of St. Mary Wolneth. The poets revelled in explaining why, like the one who produced this little verse for *A Handful of Pleasant Delites* (1584):

> Rosemary is for remembrance
> Between us day and night,
> Showing that I might alwaies have
> You present in my sight.

Shakespeare put it more sparely, and more movingly in *Hamlet*:

> There's rosemary—that's for remembrance;
> Pray you, love, remember;

Being 'for remembrance', it also featured at funerals. Thomas Dekker recorded a sad occasion when the bride died of the plague on her wedding day and the same branch of rosemary was called on to serve both functions within a few hours:

> Here's a strange alteration; for rosemary, that
> Was wash't in sweet water to set out the bridall,
> Is now wet in tears to furnish her burial.

A nice alternative to strewing the path with rosemary and flowers was to scatter it with symbols of the bridegroom's trade: bits of old iron went before a blacksmith, pieces of cloth before a tailor, wood shavings before a carpenter, and so on. And, according to that 'Minister and Preacher of the Worde of God', John Northbrooke, in his *Treatise on Dicing, Dauncing, Vaine Playes, &c* (1579): 'In olde time (we reade) that there was usually caried before the mayde when she shoulde be maried, and came to dwell in hir husbandes house, a distaffe, charged with flax, and a spyndle hanging at it, to the intente that she might be myndefull to lyve by hir labour.'

A typical Tudor wedding procession is described by Thomas Deloney in *The Pleasant History of John Winchcomb, in his younger years called Jacke of Newberrie, the famous and worthy clothier of England*. Deloney was an Elizabethan, but he set this story in the reign of Henry VIII; the wedding, like the rest of the book, shows how the new middle-class—the wealthy burgher families—were learning to live in style.

> So the marriage day being appointed, all things was prepared meete for the wedding and royall cheer ordained, most of the Lords, Knights and Gentlemen hereabout were invited thereunto: the Bride being attyred in a Gowne of Sheepes russet, and a kertle of fine worsted, her head attyred with a fillament of gold, and her hair as yellow as gold hanging downe behind her, which was curiously combed and pleated, according to the manner in those days: She was lead to church between two sweet boys with Bride laces and rosemary tied about their silken sleeves, the one of them was sonne to Sir Thomas Parry, the other to Sir

Francis Hungerford. Then there was a fair bride cup of silver and gilt carried before her wherein was a goodly branch of Rosemarie gilded very faire hung about with silken ribonds of all colours: next was there a noyse of musicians that played all the way before her: after her came all the chiefest maidens of the Countrie, some bearing great bride cakes and some Garlands of wheate finely gilded and to the path unto the Church.

A gross parody of this kind of bridal progress formed part of the Kenilworth wedding which was arranged for Queen Elizabeth. This was an extraordinary event, described in great detail by one Robert Laneham, a clerk to the bedchamber and part of her Majesty's entourage for her nineteen-day visit to Kenilworth Castle. The Queen's host (and favourite), the Earl of Leicester, had assembled a truly prize assortment of yokels to act out this wedding, and Laneham, from the rarified heights of a townsman and a minor court official, sent a devastating account of it to his friend Humphrey Mercer. The day was a Sunday—appropriately for a wedding; the gathering place was the tilt-yard of the Castle; 'And thus were they marshalled. First, all the lusty lads and bold bachelors of the parish, suitably habited every wight, with his blue buckram bride-lace upon a branch of green broom (because rosemary is scant there) tied on his left arm, for on that side lies the heart; and his alder pole for a spear in his right hand, in martial order ranged on afore, two and two in rank: Some with a hat, some in a cap, some a coat, some a jerkin, some for lightness in doublet and hose, clean truss'd with points afore; Some boots and no spurs, this spurs and no boots, and he again neither one nor other: One had a a saddle, another a pad or a pannel fastened with a cord, for girths were geazon: And these, to the number of sixteen wights, riding men and well beseen.' Then came the bridegroom 'in his father's tawny worsted jacket . . . a pair of harvest gloves on his hands, as a sign of good husbandry; a pen and ink-horn at his back, for he would be known to be bookish. . . .' After the bridegroom 'a lively morrice-dance according to the ancient manner: six dancers, maid-marian, and the fool. Then three pretty pucelles, as bright as a breast of bacon, of thirty years old a-piece; that carried three special spice-cakes of a bushel of wheat (they had by measure, out of my Lord's bake-house) before the bride, Cicely, with set countenance and lips so demurely simpering, as it had been a mare cropping of a thistle. After these, a lovely loober-worts, freckle-faced, red-headed, clean trussed in his doublet and hose' whose job was to bear the bride-cup 'formed of a sweet sucket barrel, a fair turn'd foot set to it, all seemly besilvered and parcell gilt adorned with a beautiful branch of broom, gaily begilded for rosemary: from which two broad bride-laces of red and yellow buckram begilded, and gallantly streaming by such wind as there was, for he carried it aloft: this gentle cup-bearer had his freckled physiognomy somewhat unhappily infested, as he went, by the busy flies, that flocked about the bride-cup, for the sweetness of the sucket that it savoured of; but he, like a tall fellow, withstood their malice stoutly—see what manhood may do— beat them away, killed them by scores, stood to his charge, and marched on in good order.

'Then followed the worshipful bride, led, after the country manner, between two ancient parishioners, honest townsmen. But a stale stallion and a well spread (hot as the weather was,) God wot, and ill-smelling was she: thirty years old, of colour brown-bay, not very beautiful indeed, but ugly, foul, and ill-favoured.' After the unsavoury bride came 'by two and two, a dozen damsels for bride-maids, that for favour, attire, for fashion and cleanliness, were as meet for such a bride as a tureen ladle for a porridge-pot.'

A man with a poisoned pen, Master Laneham! But he draws a vivid picture of the scene which is said to have inspired Shakespeare's rustic foolery in *A Midsummer Night's Dream*.

Laneham mentions no musicians in this procession, but it was a rare wedding which had none. From the time a Tudor bride left her house till the end of the boisterous bedding, a constant 'noyse of musicians' was the order of the day—and next morning she was woken with a musical *reveille* beneath her window. The Bishop of Exeter, Miles Coverdale, complained of the 'great noise of harpes, lutes, kyttes, basens,* and drooms, whewyth' matrimonial celebrants troubled the whole church, and hyndred them in matters pertayning to God'. Another churchman, mentioned in John Veron's *The Huntynge of Purgatorye to Death* (1561), artfully made sure of peace at least during the wedding service:

> I knewe a priest (this is a true tale that I tell you, and no lye,) whiche, when any of his parishioners should be maryed, woulde take his backe-pype, and go fetche theym to the churche, playnge sweetelye afore them, and then would he laye his instrument handsomely upon the aultare tyll he had maryed them and sayd masse. Which thyng being done, he would gentillye bringe them home agayne with backe-pype.

Coverdale was an Anglican, and the bag-pipe-playing priest who 'sayd masse' was obviously a Catholic—one from each side of the religious conflict which see-sawed to and fro during almost the entire century. As Catholic and Protestant took turn-and-turn-about, the laws (including those governing matrimony) were changed to suit the beliefs of whoever was in power. On the sidelines were the Puritans, who agreed with the Anglicans almost as little as they approved of the Catholics. And the start of all the chaos was, of course, a marriage: by humbling the priests, Henry VIII hoped to persuade the Pope to annul his union with Catherine of Aragon. Normally, the Pope would have been accommodating; Catherine was the widow of Henry's elder brother, which left the kind of useful loophole needed in these cases. But the lady had powerful support from the Holy Roman Emperor as well as her own royal Spanish family, and eventually the Pope said no; and so, came the Reformation.

Curiously, although Henry's first church reforms had the effect of making marriage easier, they also made divorce more difficult. He did away with the restrictions—no marriages between the first Sunday of Advent and Hilary day, between Septuagesima Sunday and Low Sunday, and between Rogation Sunday and Trinity Sunday—which had previously left only about 32 weeks in which people could marry (without—once again—getting a dispensation); and he also did away with *de praesenti* betrothals—the kind at which the vows were exchanged in the present tense and were therefore binding for ever. These had proved particularly fertile ground for annulments (as we have seen in the previous chapter) and, had he left them alone, they might well have come in useful in his own subsequent matrimonial adventures.

Unlike the close seasons for weddings, which were never reinstated in England (no act of Parliament or canon of the Anglican church has since prohibited marriage

* *Kytte*—an early version of the violin. *Basens*—cymbals.

at any time of the year), *de praesenti* betrothals were brought back soon after Henry's death. According to the preamble to the Act of Edward VI's reign which restored them: 'Sithence the time of which act [Henry VIII's], although the same was godly meant, the unruliness of men hath ungodly abused upon, women and men breaking their own promises and faiths made by the one unto the other, so set upon sensuality and pleasure, that if after the contract of matrimony they might have whom they more favoured and desired, they could be content by lightness of their nature to overturn all they had done before, and not afraid in manner, even from the very church door and marriage feast, the man to take another spouse, and the espouse* to take another husband. . . .'

Obviously with this kind of thing in mind, Heinrich Bullinger, the Swiss religious reformer, urged betrothed couples to keep their engagements short: 'After the hand-fastynge and makynge of the contracte, the church-goyng and weddyng shuld not be differed to long, lest the wickedde sow hys ungracious sede in the meane season.' Bullinger—the son of a priest, the husband of a nun, and the father of eleven children—was much admired by church reformers in Britain. His book, *The Christen State of Matrimonye*, was translated by Miles Coverdale (who translated the Bible for Henry VIII and became Bishop of Exeter) and the lurid picture it gives of lax morals and bad behaviour at weddings was presumably thought to be just as applicable to Britain. 'The devil hath crept in', warned Bullinger, and the English divines agreed.

Richard Whiteforde, in the *Warke for Housholders* (1537) also issued a warning. His was against that other tempter into wickedness—clandestine engagements: 'The ghostly enemy doth deceyve many persons by the pretence and coloure of matrimony in private and secrete contracts. . . . It is a great jeopardy, therefore, to make such contractes, especially amongst themselves secretly, alone, without recordes [*witnesses*], which must be two at the lest.'

The church appears to have been more successful with this kind of tocsin in the towns than in the country. An American professor, turning a Kinseyish eye to old parish registers, recently announced that 33 per cent of the brides in the rural parish of Colyton arrived at the altar pregnant, while only 13 per cent in the city of York were so encumbered. Though the church could not be happy that so many of the flock were allowing 'the wickedde to sow hys ungracious sede in the meane season', they were delighted at the result—for procreation was the patriotic theme of the age. Unlike today, when we are constantly threatened that there won't even be standing room for the world's teeming millions in a few years time, Tudor England was seriously under-populated; a fact which led Cardinal Pole, in the time of Henry VIII, to advocate a tax on bachelors. In a detailed argument, written in the favourite dialogue fashion of the day, he suggested that wilful bachelors should be 'allured to the procreatyon of chyldur' by being prohibited from taking up public office and by taxation: every unmarried man 'schold yerely pay a certayne summe, as hyt were of every pownde xii*d.*, wych yerely cumyth in, other by fe, wagyes, or land; and every man that ys worth in movable godys above iiii *li.* of every pownd iii*d*'. (i.e. out of all his annual income he should pay a shilling in the pound, and on the value of his moveable goods, if he had more than £4-worth of them, he should pay 3d. in the £).

* *Espousal* originally meant betrothal—the engagement, not the marriage. An engaged man was a *spouse*, and his *fiancée* an *espouse*.

'And so, aftur thys mean, I thynke in few yerys the pepul schold increase to a notabul noumber. Thys I juge, among other, to be a syngular remedy for the sklendurness of our polytyke body. How say you, Master Lupton? Ys hyt not so?'

The money gained from such taxation, suggested the good Cardinal, should 'be dystrybutyd partely to them wych have more chyldur then they be wel abul to nurysch, and partely to the dote of pore damosellys and vyrgynys'.

It was an interesting idea but, rather than trying to limit the joys of bachelorhood, Cardinal Pole might have been better occupied making marriage itself more appealling. The religious upheavals made matrimony a worrisome business for many young couples, who were only too eager to fall in with the desire to see them joined in holy wedlock and adding to the 'polytyke body', but who wanted to do it within their own religion. The Catholic church said that the only valid marriage was one performed by a Catholic priest, yet after Henry VIII's break with Rome only Anglican marriages were recognised, and in the England of Elizabeth I, Catholic priests were not supposed to exist at all. The Puritans were miserable because they refused to use the new *Book of Common Prayer*—in which was the now obligatory marriage service. Most Catholics overcame their difficulties by being married in secrecy by Catholic priests who had gone under cover. The Pope gave his blessing out of consideration for the peculiar difficulties of the faithful, but the unions were highly irregular, no banns being called, and no licence bought. The Puritans, likewise, secretly used their own service and did without the wedding ring, which they looked on as a heathen device. Those who could square it with their consciences, submitted to a ceremony in the reformed church, too, to ensure legality and peace with the neighbours.

While Catholic Mary was on the throne, the whole thing was thrown into reverse. Then the church was on the look-out for those who refused to follow the old rites of the Church of Rome—as one of the *Articles of Visitation* in the diocese of London (1554) clearly shows: 'Item, whether there be any that refuseth to kysse the prieste at the solemnization of matrimony, or use any such lyke ceremonies heretofore used and observed in the church.' (The 'kysse' of the priest was the benedictional kiss, the sacerdotal *pax*—an extension of the Anglo-Saxon betrothal kiss. The old form was for the priest to kiss the bridegroom, who passed it on to his new bride. Sometimes one of the assistant priests would then kiss all the guests—a task of mixed attraction.)

But this resurrection of the Catholic religion did not last long, for Mary died young (at 42), after a reign of less than five years. When her Protestant half-sister, Elizabeth succeeded her (at the age of 25), the Pope immediately declared her illegitimate and claimed the right of disposing of the crown himself, England being, he said, a fief of the holy see. A lot of people agreed with his first point (Elizabeth was, after all, the daughter of Anne Boleyn for whom Henry had divorced Catherine of Aragon and rearranged the English religion); but he ruined his case with the second. Zenophobia united the country behind the new Queen—and the new religion. The Anglican church and its *Book of Common Prayer* took such firm root that not all the Stuarts nor Oliver Cromwell could effectively rip it up again. The Church of England marriage service has remained virtually unchanged since this time (though, happily, it is no longer the only recognised service).

The atmosphere in church, however, appears to have changed a great deal. According to Bullinger, 16th century wedding guests behaved rather badly. They came to the Lord's house as if it were a house of merchandise 'to lay forthe their wares and offer to sell themselves into vice and wickedness'; and as they came, so they went forth again 'in shameful pomp and vain wantonness'. In a further roll of thunder from his *Christen State of Matrimonye* he maintained that 'early in the morning the wedding people begynne to exceade in superfluous eating and drinkyng whereof they spytte until the half sermon be done. And when they come to the preaching they are halfe dronke, some altogether, therefore regard they neither the preaching nor prayer but stonde there onely because of the custome. Such folkes also do come unto the church with all manner of pompe and pryde, a gorgiousnesse of rayment and jewels. They come with a great noyse of basens and drommes wherewith they trouble the whole church. . . .'

It was a pity if they really didn't listen to the wedding sermons, because there were some marvellous ones. Under Edward VI a dissertation on the duties of marriage, and a passage from the Scriptures 'calculated to inspire conjugal virtue' and strengthen the happy pair for the 'conflict with the special difficulties of matrimony', became mandatory and, as this nugget from the Rev. Henry Smith's sermon *A Preparative to Marriage* shows, it was the womenfolk who were thought to be most in need of such inspiration: a wife, said 'silver-tongued' Smith, must not examine whether her husband 'be wise or simple, but that she is his wife; and therefore they which are bound must obey, as Abigail loved her husband, though he were a foole; for the wife is as much despised for taking rule over her husband as hee for yielding it unto her'.

At the weddings of poor couples (according to Vaughan) the guests 'at the very instant of marriage doe cast their presents into a bason, dish, or cup, which standeth upon the Table in the Church ready prepared for that purpose. But this custome is onely put in use amongst them, which stand in need'.

Another way for needy brides and grooms to raise money was to give a bride-ale. These were usually held in the church itself, immediately after the wedding ceremony, and worked on the same psychological principle as sherry mornings or charity balls: provide a good cause, a party atmosphere and plenty to drink, and then send round the collection box. Then, as now, it was a popular way of raising funds—there were church-ales, to replenish the parish coffers; clerk-ales, to pay the parish clerk; bid-ales, to bail out a bankrupt or pay for a village project; and bride-ales which paid for themselves and left something over to start the young couple off in their new home. (They also gave us the noun *bridal*.) The church usually benefited from all these events by hiring out the equipment for brewing the beer; sometimes it also provided handsome cups for the chief guests to drink from: Wilsdon parish church, according to an inventory taken in about 1547, had 'two masers that were appointed to remayne in the church for to drynk in at bride-ales'.

Often the guests brought the food as well as paying for their drinks. William Harrison, in his *Description of Britain*, said: 'In feasting, also, the husbandmen do exceed after their manner, especially at bridales, &c., where it is incredible to tell what meat is consumed and spent; ech one brings such a dish, or so manie, with him, as his wife and he doo consult upon, but alwaies with this consideration, that the leefer [*dearer*, or *closer*] friend shall have the better provision.' Wedding cakes would certainly have been among the donated dishes. At the beginning of the century, these were rather uninteresting dry biscuits, baked more for the pleasure of breaking them over the bride's head than for eating; but during Elizabeth's reign eggs, sugar, currants and spices were used, turning them into something of a delicacy. They were still used as missiles, though: if they weren't crumbled over the poor bride's head at the party, they were thrown at her as she crossed the threshold.

Towards the end of the century, many parishes built, or set aside, a house close to the church especially for bride-ales and if the celebrations were held in one of these, or at the home of the bride, a bride-bush or bride-stake was placed outside to attract passers-by and so increase the revenue. The 'bush' (a green bough of a tree or shrub) was the sign used by regular ale-houses to advertise their wares—as it still is today in all the old *Bull and Bush* inn-signs round the country; and a 'stake' was a pole with a leafy branch attached to the top. There was often dancing round the bride-stake, as round a May-pole, and the male guests also wore off their high spirits by running races and taking part in country sports, like tilting at the quintain.

Master Laneham was delighted with the horrible mess the rustics made of tilting at the Kenilworth wedding. The quintain was a post or plank which the combatants aimed at with their lances instead of trying to unseat another rider; if they struck the wrong part of it, they were neatly unseated themselves by a sand-bag which swung out and knocked them off their horses. Most of the Kenilworth 'loober-worts' got 'a good bob with the bag' and one didn't even get close enough for that: while he tried to aim for the post, his amorous mount 'would carry him to a mare among the people'. Another tilter 'would run and miss the quintain with his staff, and hit the board with his head'. Rural buffoonery, indeed, compared with the impeccably organised and executed Court tilts, but a scene which must have enlivened many a country wedding for several hundred years.

A good send-off to married life was obviously considered essential for everyone— and that, happily, included servants. They may not have rated quite the celebrations given for the children of the house, but they didn't do badly. Many of the letters of the 16th century show how the head of the household rallied his family and friends to give his servants a wedding day to remember and a nest-egg to build on. When a gentleman with the resounding name of Bassingbourne Gaudy, Esquire, of Bucken-ham, was High Sheriff of Norfolk, he was asked by a friend to attend the wedding of one of his retainers:

> Sir, Whereas, a servant of myne, which hath bene longe well deserving to-wards my wief and me, is to be married at Lynne, on Sunday, the 14th daie of July next, amongst divers other my good friends; I would earnestly request you to accompany my wief and me ther, or otherwise to extend your favour as shall please you; for which we shall rest beholden unto you, and be ready to requyte you in the like as occasion shall serve. Thus, with my heart commendac'ns, I committe you to God. Lynne, this 24th of June, 1594. Yours to his power, John Peyton.

The meaning of the phrase 'or to extend your favour as shall please you' becomes obvious with another letter to the 'Right Worshippfull Bassingbourne Gawdy'— this time a reply to one written by Mr. Gaudy on the marriage of one of his own servants:

> Gode Sire, in parte of performance of your worshipp's request, made by your letters, I have sent herein enclosed to your servants marryage, a French crowne, which, though yt be small, yet cometh yt freely, and from a willinge mynde, and

therefore praye you that yt may be taken in good parte. If occacyons had not letted, I would have increased your company and the pore'on, and so humbly commendinge myself to your favour, I take my leave this 25th day of Julie. Your worship's sure well-wisher, Th. Baxter.

Servants and the poor of the district also benefited from the weddings of the rich. The festivities in Deloney's *John Winchcomb* went on for ten days 'to the great relief of the poor that dwelt all about'; and when Lady Jane Grey married, 'beef, bread and ale' were provided for three days. This sounds rather frugal, considering the ambitious reasons for making her marriage particularly popular, but it was probably the usual span for most weddings. When Mary Queen of Scots married the 'beardless and lady-faced' Darnley in July 1565, John Knox complained sourly that 'During the space of three or four days, there was nothing but balling, dancing, and banqueting'.

For the rich, there was still the pageantry of grand tilts and tourneys during the day, and now lavish *masques* were added to the evening entertainment. These exotic fantasies, full of allegory and rhyming couplets—like the one Prospero conjured from the air for Ferdinand and Miranda in *The Tempest*—were especially favoured by Queen Elizabeth. Letters to Sir Robert Sidney in June 1600, describing the wedding of the Queen's maid-of-honour, Anne Russell, to Lord Herbert, the Earl of Worcester's son, tell of the splendid *masque* given on that occasion. Her Majesty not only attended the wedding, but naughty Mary Fitton, another maid-of-honour and one of the leading *masqueraders*, persuaded her to dance at it, too:

> This day her Majestie was at Blackfriars to grace the marriage of the Lord Harbert and his Wiffe. The bride mett the Queen at the Waterside, where my Lord Cobham had provided a hectica, made like half a litter wherein she was carried to my Lady Russel's by 6 Knights. Her Majestie dined there, and at Night, went thorough Doctor Puddins Howse (Who gave the Queen a Fanne) to my Lord Cobhams, where she supt. After Supper the Maske came in, as I write in my last; and delicate it was to see 8 Ladies soe pretily and richly attired. Mrs. Fitton went to the Queen, and woed her to downce; her Majestie asked what she was: Affection, she said. Affection! said the Queen, Affection is false. Yet her Majestie rose and downced: so did My lady Marques. . . . The Gifts given that day were valued at 1000L in plate and Jewels at least. The entertainment was great and plentifull and my Lady Russel much commended for it. Her Majestie, upon Tuesday, came back again to the Court, but the Solemnities continued till Wednesday Night, and now the Lord Harbert and his faire Lady are in Court.

No doubt the Queen tried to persuade Mistress Russell against matrimony, the way she tried to disuade yet another maid-of-honour, Frances Howard. 'Many persuasions she used against marriage,' wrote Mistress Howard to the Earl of Hertford in 1585, '. . . how little you would care for me . . . how well I was here and how much she cared for me. But, in the end, she said she would not be against my desire. Trust me, sweet lord, the worst is past, and I warrant she will not speak one angry word to you.' (Frances Howard became Lord Hertford's second wife and the Queen had been right in trying to talk her out of it: they were extremely miserable together for thirteen years.)

Her Majesty—having opted for celebrated virginity herself (a fact she wished proclaimed in her epitaph)—did not approve of other people's urge for matrimony. Married clergy, that strange new phenomenon of the Reformation, she found it difficult to be polite to, and insisted they keep their wives in private lodgings, well away from their official residences. The married clergy themselves, having done the deed, often felt equally embarrassed. Roger Hacket (the man who told brides to wear 'sweet smelling flowers' not those 'gilded with the art of man'), was a forceful character, yet he was so ashamed when he married, he could not bring himself to tell his patron of his 'misbehaviour'.

Most of Elizabeth's subjects, however, felt no such inhibitions. They married with pride, celebrated with zest, and bedded with much publicity. The Puritans were disgusted. 'After the bancket and feast there begenneth a vayne mad and unmanerly fashion for the bryde must be brought to an open dancyng place. Then is there such a renninge, leapinge and flynging amonge them then is there such a lyftinge op and discoveringe of the damesels appareil that man might thinke all these danncers had cast all shame behind them and were become starke madde and out of their whyttes. . . .' The Flemish artist, Peter Brueghel's extremely lewd and lusty painting of a *Peasant Wedding* (1568) gives an astonishingly clear idea of what he was on about.

There was a saying at this time that older, still unmarried sisters of the bride should dance barefoot at the wedding; this would presumably change their luck and get husbands for them, too. Old maids were not highly regarded in this world or the next: in the latter, it was said, they were destined to lead apes in hell. Whether the barefoot dancing was ever actually done, or just talked about—like wearing a willow garland as a sign of lost or rejected love—I don't know. Both ideas are mentioned a lot, but I have never come across a description of anyone ever actually doing either.

Many odd customs also attended the bedding of the bride, and these definitely were acted out, not just spoken of. One of the most curious was that the bride's attendants should take all the pins from her hair and clothes and throw them away—if any were left about the bride her marriage would not be a happy one, and if any of the attendants kept one, they were doomed to spinsterhood, at least until the next Whitsuntide. Usually the bride escaped from the wedding party at night, losing what garters and ribbons she still had about her on the way, and was helped to prepare for bed by her bridesmaids; but when Mary Queen of Scots married Darnley, she cast off the widow's garments she had worn for the early morning ceremony as soon as she returned to her apartments, and her attendants—in this case her male attendants and guests—were each allowed to take a pin from her before she withdrew with her ladies to change. (Although Mary had been a widow for four-and-a-half years, she was still only 22 at the time of this second marriage; Darnley was 19.) Queen Elizabeth's man in Scotland, Sir Thomas Randolph, sent this description of the wedding to the English court:

> She [*Mary Queen of Scots*] had on her back the great mourning gown of black, with the great white mourning hood, &c. The rings, which were three, the middle a rich diamond, were put on her finger. They kneel together, and many prayers were said over them; she tarrieth out the mass, and he taketh a kiss, and leaveth her there, and went to her chamber, whither, within a space, she followeth, and being required (according to the solemnity) to cast off her cares, and leave aside these sorrowful garments, and give herself to a more pleasant life,

after some pretty refusal (more, I believe for manner sake than grief of heart), she suffereth them that stood by, every man that could approach, to take out a pin; and so, being committed to her ladies, changed her garments, but went not to bed; to signifie to the world that it was not lust that moved them to marry, but only the necessity of her country, not, if God will, to leave it without an heir.

A vacillating character, the new King of Scotland was more consistent in his religion than in most things. As a Protestant, he left Mary, a devout but tolerant Catholic, to hear out the Mass alone. But before he left he 'taketh a kiss'—most probably, the benedictional kiss of the Catholic wedding service.

After describing the lavish banquet, the dancing, and then the supper which followed the 5 a.m. ceremony at Holyrood Palace, Randolph ends his report 'and so they go to bed'. He mentions none of the rough high-spirits which often attended this ritual, so perhaps Mary and her husband were allowed to retire with as much dignity as Henry VII tried to preserve at royal weddings in England. Among the *Articles ordained by King Henry VII for the Regulation of his Household* is this one concerning the bedding of newly married princesses: 'All men at her coming in to be voided, except woemen, till she be brought to her bedd: and the man, both: he sitting in his bedd, in his shirte, with a gowne cast about him. Then the bishoppe with the chaplaines to come in and blesse the bedd: then every man to avoide [*leave*] without any drinke, save the twoe estates, if they liste priviely.'

Getting the marriage-bed blessed was often a problem for Henry's less exalted subjects who could not call on a bishop to do the job for them. According to an old document concerning the clergy in papal times: 'The pride of the clergy and the bigotry of the laity were such that new-married couples were made to wait till midnight, after the marriage-day, before they would pronounce a benediction, unless handsomely paid for it, and they durst not undress without it, on pain of excommunication.'

King Henry's subjects would also have had trouble trying to stop their guests drinking in the bridal chamber. Sipping the posset (a drink made of hot wine, milk, eggs, sugar and spices) was the traditional sign-off to the wedding day for the bride and groom, their family and attendants, and as many of the guests as could crowd into the bedroom. (The wine was said to fortify the bridegroom, and the sugar to make him kind.) After that, came the flinging of the stocking—a game to see who would be the next to marry, which varied slightly in different parts of the country: it always involved the young attendants throwing stockings over their shoulders and trying to hit the head, or specifically the nose, of the bride and groom as they lay in bed; but sometimes the bridesmaids, one by one, threw the bride's left hose with the bride's nose as the target; and sometimes, the men aimed at the bride's head or nose with her stocking, while the bridesmaids aimed at the groom with his. Whoever got the correct head or nose with the correct stocking, was next in line for the altar. At the kind of weddings the Puritans kept such an eager eye on, there would still be no peace for the new-married couple, even after the last stocking had been flung, the last drop of posset drunk, the last guest shooed from the room and the chamber door finally closed. Then was the time for 'unmannerly and restless people' to stand outside the door and 'sing vicious and naughty ballads that the devil may have his whole triumph now to the uttermost'.

During the reigns of the Stuarts, many other jolly games and tricks were practised
—like sewing the couple into the sheets and tying a bell beneath the marriage bed;
but the Tudors, even the rumbustious Elizabethans, were slightly more restrained.
Shakespeare, who could turn a bawdy phrase with the best of them, has weddings in
many of his plays, but they are nearly always serious, even sedate, occasions. (The
exception is *The Taming of the Shrew*, and here Petruchio's outrageous behaviour—
wearing terrible old clothes, throwing wine in the priest's face, and swearing in
church—is all part of the taming process, not a reflection of the manners of the time.)
Shakespeare's own attitude seems to have been that of Beatrice in *Much Ado About
Nothing*, when she likens 'wooing, wedding, and repenting' to dance steps: the
wooing is 'hot and hasty, like a Scotch jig, and just as fantastical'; Repentance, 'with
his bad legs, falls into the cinque-pace faster and faster, till he sink into his grave';
but the wedding is 'mannerly-modest, as a measure, full of state and ancientry'.

The furious Puritans searched diligently, and found a very different scene. In the
next century, they were to have even more fuel to stoke their fiery—and extremely
articulate—wrath.

Chapter Five

Years of Social Upheaval
The Seventeenth Century

My wooing's ended; now my wedding's neere;
When gloves are giving, guilded be you there.'
Robert Herrick: *Lines to Rosemary and Baies*

HE Bride was clad in White. . . . & covered also with a white vaile.' John Evelyn saw such a bride in March 1646 and recorded the fact in his diary: 'The 23rd. . . . I was conducted to the *Ghetta* where the *Jewes* dwell (as in a Tribe & Ward) together, where I was present at a Mariage: The Bride was clad in White, sitting in a lofty chaire, & covered also with a white vaile; Then two old *Rabbies* joynd them together, one of them holding a glasse of Wine in his hand, which in the midst of the ceremony, pretending to deliver to the Woman, he let fall, the breaking wherof, was to signifie the frailty of our nature, & that we must expect disasters & crosses amidst all enjoyments: This don, we had a fine banquet, & were brought into the Bride chamber, where the bed was dress'd up with flowers, & the Counterpan, strewed in workes.'

Evelyn was a splendidly enquiring twenty-five-year-old doing the Grand Tour when he was taken to this wedding in Venice. During the rest of his long life, he attended many other marriages, both in England and on the Continent, and he noted them all in his diary, but he never again said what the bride wore. The dress of the Jewish girl had obviously struck him as very unusual; and well it might—the same kind of thing was not to be seen at a Christian ceremony for another 150 years.

In Britain, the Elizabethan wedding formula continued with little change right through to the middle of the 17th century; then came the interregnum, Oliver Cromwell, and complete upheaval. Dedicated Puritans did not believe in celebrating anything, and that included marriages. For three years these were taken out of the churches altogether and matrimony was made a purely civil contract, performed before justices of the peace with the formal sobriety given to any other legal trans-action. With the restoration of Charles II in 1660, the old festivities and frivolities returned; but by the end of the century a curious change had taken place, which had nothing to do with the head of state, religion, or the law. It suddenly became fashion-able to marry secretly: a special licence, a discreet home-visit from the clergyman, a quiet family dinner and possibly a hand at cards, and the deed was done. '. . . the Wedding is clapp'd up so privately, that People are amaz'd to see Women brought to

Plate Three

Bed of legitimate Children, without having ever heard a Word of the Father', wrote a surprised French observer.

It was largely the customs of this century which crossed the Atlantic to America. The settlers were now sailing over by the ship-load to open up the promised land and once there, surrounded by Indians and faced with extraordinary hardships, they kept up a social life as close as possible to the one they had left behind. As often happens with transplants, many of the customs took firmer root abroad than the main plant at home: well into the 20th century, many Americans still preferred to marry in their own front-rooms rather than in church; and in 1971, President Nixon's elder daughter was following strong tradition when she had an altar set up at the White House for her wedding spectacular. (Though she chose an even more romantic spot for it than her predecessors—the rose-garden, in full bloom.)

But, to go back to the beginning and one of the first weddings to take place under Stuart patronage in England: in 1604, less than two years after becoming king, James I celebrated the marriage of the first of his many favourites, the handsome young Sir Philip Herbert. The bride was the Lady Susan Vere, daughter of the Earl of Oxford, and the wedding took place during the Christmas festivities at Whitehall Palace. Little had changed in the short time since Elizabeth's death (no strange new Scottish customs had been added), but now there was a monarch on the throne who threw himself whole-heartedly into such matrimonial enterprises, as can be seen from a letter written by Sir Dudley Carleton, a guest at the Herbert–Vere wedding:

> On St. John's Day we had the Marriage of Sir Philip Herbert and the Lady Susan performed at Whitehall, with all the honour could be done a great favourite. The Court was great and for that day put on the best bravery. The Prince and Duke of Holst led the Bride to Church, the Queen followed him from thence. The King gave her, and she in her tresses, and Trinketts brided and bridled it so handsomely, and indeed became her self so well, that the King said, if he were unmarried, he would not give her, but keep her himself. The marriage dinner was kept in the Great Chamber, where the Prince and the Duke of Holst, and the great Lords and Ladies accompanied the bride. The Ambassador of Venice was the only bidden guest of strangers, and he had place above the Duke of Holst, which the Duke took not well. . . . At night there was a Masque in the Hall, which for conceit and fashion was suitable to the occasion. There was no final loss that night of Chaines and Jewells, and many great ladies were made shorter by the skirts, and were well enough served that they could keep cut no better. The presents of plate, and other things given by the Noblemen, were valued at 2500L, but that which made it a good marriage was a gift of the King's of 500l. land for the Bride's Joynture. They were lodged in the Council Chamber, where the King in his shirt and Nightgown gave them a 'Reveille Matin' before they were up, and spent a good time in or upon the bed, chuse which you will believe. No ceremony was omitted of Bride-cakes, Points, Garters and Gloves, which have been ever since the livery of the court; and at night there was sewing into the sheet, casting off the bride's left hose, with many other pretty sorcerie.

With carryings-on like this, it is hardly surprising that William Bradshaw (a worthy successor to Heinrich Bullinger) should have lashed out at the congregation so bitterly in his sermon *A Marriage Feast* (1620). Most of the spectators at weddings, he said, 'with their hearts, countenances, and words cast dirt and puddle water in the faces of those about to enter the calling of marriage'. The feast too often made a 'brothel house of a bride-house' with 'deep carousing and drinking of healths to bride and bridegroom, and every idle fellow's mistress, till the whole company's wits' were drowned in drink. Dwelling juicily on the Puritans' chief point of complaint, he rounded on the uncontrolled hilarity and its 'beastly and profane' songs, sonnets and jigs 'indicated by some hellish spirit and chanted by those that are the public incendiaries of all filthy lusts; and these are ordinarily made in the scorn and derision of this holy estate to delight and solace the guests withal' as they made marriage a matter of 'obsceneness and filthiness'.

It was not only the Puritans who thought things had gone too far, either. Matthew Griffith, a royalist preacher, also complained of the music, the drinking and the jokes in his *Bethel, or a Forme for Families* (1634). 'Some cannot be merry without a noise of fiddlers, who scrape acquaintance at the first sight; nor sing, unless the divell himselfe come in for a part, and the ditty be made in hell. . . . We joy indeed at weddings; but how? Some please themselves in breaking broad, I had almost said bawdy jests . . . Some drink healths so long till they lose it, and (being more heathenish in this than was Ahasuerus at his feast) they urge their companions to drink by measure, out of measure.'

It all sounds very wicked and Mr. Griffith worked himself into such a fever of excitement over such behaviour, that he burst a blood vessel while preaching in 1665 and died in the pulpit. But sin, like beauty, owes a lot to the eye of the beholder: John Stephens of Gloucester, looked at just the same kind of wedding scene and saw only rough and humorous innocence. Stephens flourished around 1615, but the *Plaine Countrey Bride* he described was certainly about in Elizabethan times and, with very little alteration, could still be found in rural districts way into the 19th century. She was the lady who had no 'rarity worth observance, if her gloves be not miraculous and singular'. On her wedding day she rose 'with a purpose to be extremely sober: this begets silence, which gives her a repletion of aire without ventage: and that takes away her appetite. Shee seemes therfore commendably sober unto all: but she drives the Parson out of Patience with her modestie . . . guilt rases of ginger* Rosemary and Ribbands be her best magnificence. She will therefore bestow a Livery, thoughe receives back wages: behaviour sticks to her like a desease. . . . neither can she take pleasure in the custome: & therefore importunacie with repetition, enforce her to dumbe signes: otherwise you must not expect an answere. She is a curteous creature: nothing proceedes from her without a curtesie. . . . She may to some seeme very raw in carriage: but this becomes noted through the feare of disclosing it. She takes it by tradition from her fellow Gossips, that she must weepe showres upon her marriage day: though by the vertue of mustard and onions, if shee cannot naturally dissemble: but good simplicity hath not taught her the Courte-invention, to squeake loude enough on her marriage night likewise: So She hath little or nothing to confirme her honesty: besides that which plaine innocency affords. Now like a quiet creature she wishes to loose her Garters quickly, that she may loose her maiden-head likewise.'

A plaine Country Bridegroome also came under Stephens' affectionate scrutiny: 'He showes neere affinity betwixt mariage and hanging: and to that purpose, he provides

---

* *Guilt rases of ginger*—gilded roots or sprigs of ginger. If the former, they were dried, gilded, and fastened to the bride's girdle along with her wedding knives and other 'furniture', for the guests to envy and admire, all spices being highly prized delicacies.

a great Nosegay, and shakes hands with every one he meets, as if he were now preparing for a condemned mans voyage.' (Writers were very fond of coupling marriage and hanging. Shakespeare said: 'The ancient saying is no heresy, Hanging and wiving goes by destiny,' and a hundred other poets echoed him in more or less the same words.) As well as his posy, Stephens' bridegroom has a 'faire troublesome cloake' that is half-a-yard too long, and 'Although he points out his bravery with ribbands, yet he hath no vaineglory; for he contemnes fine cloathes with dropping pottage in his bosome. The invitation of guests, provision of meate, getting of children, and his nuptiall garments, have kept his braine long in travaile.... He never was maister of a feast before; that makes him hazard much new complement. ... He hath long forecast with his *Sweet-hart* in some odde corner of the milke-house, how he may goe the sparingest way to worke when he marryes: and he hath only that meanes to make her beleeve he is a frugall good husband.'

In France, at similar weddings, all the neighbours lent a hand to dress the bride. A member of Oxford University, writing in about 1625, after a 'monthes jorney into Fraunce' noted: 'A scholler of the university never disfurnished so many of his friends to provide for his jorney, as they (the French) doe neighbours, to adorne their weddings. At my being at Pontoise, I sawe mistres bryde returne from the church. The day before shee had beene somewhat of the condition of a kitchen wench, but now so tricked up with scarfes, rings, and cross-garters, that you never saw a Whitsun-lady better rigged. I should much have applauded the fellowes fortune, if he could have maryed the cloathes but (God be mercifull to hym!) he is chayned to the wench; much joy may they have together, most peerless couple, Hymen, Hymenaei, Hymen, Hymen O Hymenaee! The match was now knytt up amonst them. I would have a French man marie none but a French woman.'

An English bridegroom who must soon have wished he had married the clothes rather than the girl inside them, was the young third Earl of Essex. His was another court wedding in which King James I took a direct interest, and very grand it sounds: 'On the 5th of January, 1606 Robert Devereux, Earl of Essex was married to Frances Howard, daughter of Thomas, Earl of Suffolk, a bridegroom of fourteen to a bride of thirteen. The men were clad in crimson and the women in white; they had everyone a white plume of the richest hern's feathers, and were so rich in jewels upon their heads, as was most glorious.'

The bridegroom was the eldest son of Queen Elizabeth's Essex; the bride was exceptionally beautiful, and proved to be exceptionally wicked. Before she was 24, Frances Howard had had several lovers; divorced Essex (on the dubious grounds that he could not consummate the marriage with *her*); instigated the death of Sir Thomas Overbury, who opposed her next marriage (she offered £1000 to have him assassinated); married Robert Carr, Earl of Somerset, the greatest and most trouble-some of all James I's favourites; pleaded guilty to Overbury's death; and been, feebly, pardoned by the King. Both her marriages were generously blessed by the most illustrious poets: Ben Jonson wrote the *masque* for the Essex wedding and followed through with a set of verses 'To the most noble and above his titles, Robert, Earle of Somerset, sent to him on his Wedding-day, 1613'; Francis Bacon donated a *masque* (at the cost of £2000 to himself) for this second marriage, and John Donne contributed an *Epithalamium*. (Donne wrote of the bride powdering her otherwise 'radiant hair' and dressing in 'silk and gold'—gold being the correct wear

41

for second marriages, when white was not appropriate. But Frances Howard was having none of that. She married Carr on Christmas day and chose to appear with her hair in virgin disarray, flowing ostentatiously 'almost to her feet'.)

The same year as Frances Howard's scandalous second match, saw the sumptuous wedding of the King's own eldest daughter, the Princess Elizabeth, to Frederick, the 18-year-old German elector palatinate—an occasion of breathtaking extravagance. The poets serenaded this marriage, too: Chapman, Campion, Donne, Wither, all were quick to chronicle the beauty and virtue of the young princess who was later to become Queen of Bohemia and to be called 'the Queen of Hearts'. Thomas Heywood wrote a vast nuptial song, praising the bride whose 'very presence paradic'd the place' and the groom who, 'Having female beauty in a manly looke' was 'for *Venus*, or her sonne mistooke'. He also mentioned 'a bright saffron roab from Hymen borrowed'; but, in fact, the bride's dress was made of 'Florence cloth of silver, richly embroidered' and paid for by a marriage-tax levied on the country as a whole. Getting the people to pay for royal weddings was a traditional right of the crown, just as, for centuries, tenants were legally bound to contribute to the wedding of their lord's eldest daughter and the knighting of his eldest son (a shilling for every £1-worth of land held was the usual sum); but all these customs had fallen out of use. It had been more than a hundred years since the last royal marriage tax, and James's attempt at a revival met with such surly opposition, he wisely decided not to enforce it. Having paid out a hair-raising £53,294 for the festivities and a further £40,000 as the bridal portion, he received only £20,500 from his subjects.

A great deal of the £53,294 went on entertainment: Sir Francis Bacon and Inigo Jones were in charge of this department and, as well as organising lavish court *masques*, they contrived a whole series of magnificent spectacles to set floating on the Thames from 11 February until the 16th (the wedding took place on St. Valentine's day). The highlight of this display was the reconstruction of the Battle of Lepanto, complete with British men o'war, Turkish galleys, and floating castles, forts, rocks and beacons to set the scene. The bride's dress was a minor item compared with all this, but even so, her cloth-of-silver train alone cost £130, and set an expensive fashion for future royal brides to follow. From this time until the beginning of the 19th century (when Queen Victoria chose to be married in white), silver was looked upon as the royal bride's badge of purity.

According to a contemporary account of the wedding (included in John Leland's *Collectanea*) the young Princess Elizabeth wore upon her head 'a crown of refined golde, made Imperiall by the pearles and diamonds thereupon placed, which were so thicke beset that they stood like shining pinnacles upon her amber-coloured haire dependantly hanging, playted down over her shoulders to her waiste, between every plaight a roll or liste of gold-spangles, pearles, rich stones and diamonds'. She was attended by sixteen bridesmaids—one for each year of her age—all robed in white or silver tissue, trimmed with silver lace and with detachable sleeves of 'several colord tyssues'. (The bride's sleeves were embroidered with diamonds of 'inestimable value'.)

Such profligate expense on a court wedding has probably never been repeated in Britain. The Princess's brother, Charles I, did not marry until 1625, a month after coming to the throne, and then the main ceremony took place in Paris, where his bride, the French Princess Henrietta Maria, was married by proxy in the porch of

Notre Dame Cathedral. (She wore for this ceremony, velvet and cloth of gold, and a train so heavy that she had to have a man—'an Officer', and one hopes a gentleman—in there with her, supporting it with his head and hands, as well as the three ladies of the court who carried it in the accepted manner.) Six weeks later, she sailed for England with a retinue of one bishop, twenty-nine priests, and 410 male and female attendants. The King was at Dover to greet her and they were married again at Canterbury. From there, the young Monarch and his bride, both dressed in green, went to London by river, a procession of gaily decked barges following their progress. 'Fifty good ships discharged their ordnance' as they reached the city, 'and the Tower guns opened such a peal as the Queen can never have heard the like.' Bells rang out all over the country until midnight, bonfires blazed and there was great rejoicing, for the new Queen was a 'brave lady' with 'eyes that sparkled like stars'. It was a gay beginning. But the end of Charles's reign—and the end of his life—was darkened by the deadly gloom of Puritanism.

What happened to marriages during the Commonwealth has no real place in a book about 'the white wedding', but it was a fascinating period, and like every other slice of history, it has left its mark on the traditions we observe today. It caused an almighty set-back in the evolution of white, and most probably affected the whole pattern of weddings for the next two hundred years. In short, it's worth a detour.

The Puritans did not approve of white wedding dresses, or anything else which smacked of superstition; they believed that marriages should be performed with the minimum of fuss and ceremony, and for the three years after Cromwell was proclaimed Protector, the only legal marriage was one performed before a justice of the peace.

In August 1653 Dorothy Osborne wrote to William Temple, her servant (as suitors were then gallantly called), saying she had just read in a 'new's book' something 'that may concerne any body that has a minde to marry, 'tis a new forme for it, that sure will fright the Country people Extreamly, for they aprehend nothing like goeing before a Justice; they say noe other Marriage shall stand good in Law; in conscience I beleeve the olde one is the better, and for my part I am resolved to stay till that com's in fashion againe'. A great many people agreed with her. The new 'forme' was that a couple wishing to marry presented all particulars to a parish registrar; they could then choose whether to have the banns called in church on the following three Sundays or in the market place on the following three market days. When the registrar was sure the banns had been cried in one or the other, he issued a certificate to say so. This was then presented to a justice of the peace, who joined the couple's hands, heard them exchange their vows and declared the marriage lawful and complete.

Within the family of the Lord Protector, at least one member preferred the church to the market place when the time came to have her banns called. Frances, Oliver Cromwell's youngest daughter, chose to have her wedding announced in St. Martin's-in-the-Fields and in November 1657 the registrar there recorded in scrupulous detail:

These are to certifie whom it may concerne that, according to the late Act of Parliament, entytuled an Act touching Marriages, and the registering thereof, &c., publication was made in the publique meeting-place, in the parish church of

Martin's-in-the-Fields, in the county of Middlesex, upon three several Lord's Days, at the close of the Morning Exercise, namely, upon the xxv day of October, MDCLVII., as alsoe upon the i and viii day of November following, of a marriage agreed upon between the Honourable Robert Rich of St. Andrew's, Holborne, and the Right Honourable the Lady Frances Cromwell of Martins-in-the-Fields, in the country of Middlesex, all which was performed according to the Act, without exception. In witnesse whereof I have hereunto set my hand the ix day of November, MDCLVII. William Williams, Register of Martins-in-the-Fields.

To conform with Puritan principles, St. Martin's had been stripped of its saintly connections and become plain Martin's-in-the-Fields, a public meeting-place (St. Andrew's appears to have escaped this indignity); and the Sunday service had become the Morning Exercise; but the Cromwells themselves were going up in the world. All the Lord Protector's older children had married within their own social class—the gentry. Now, Frances's husband was the grandson and heir of the Earl of Warwick, and only a few days earlier her sister, Mary, had married Lord Falconbridge. It was all of a piece with Cromwell's own behaviour: for his first inauguration as Lord Protector, he had worn modest black velvet; for his second—after toying with the idea of becoming king—he was robed in purple and ermine. But, if the head of state was taking himself a trifle too seriously, his underlings were still able to rustle up some healthy humour. Richard Flecknoe had a splendid time with the new marriage arrangements in a song *On the Justice of Peace's making Marriages, and the crying them in the Market*:

Now just as 'twas in *Saturns* reign,
The Golden age is returned again;
And *Astrea* again from heaven is come,
When all on earth by Justice is done.

Amongst the rest we have cause to be glad
Now Marriages are in markets made,
Since Justice we hope will take order there,
We may not be cousened no more in our ware.

So husbands shall have this comodity by't
T' have wives by the weight, who are often too light,
And wives (to contentment of every one)
Shall have husbands too (they hope) by the stone.

Nay perhaps in time they may think it fit
That Justice first night by bed-side should sit,
And carefully look (as in market they did)
That Justice too be done in the bed. . . .

Let Parson and Vicar then say what they will,
The custome is good (God continue it still)
For Marriage being a now Trafique and Trade,
Pray where but in Markets shu'd it be made? . . .

44

Meantime God blesse the Parliament,
In making this Act so honestly meant;
Of the new Marriages God blesse the breed,
And God bless us all, for was never more need.

The Puritans found the going tough in their war against the sin of levity. They doubtless had unobtrusive little weddings themselves, and people too close to their scrutiny to do otherwise, followed their example. But, in the country as a whole, things went on pretty much as before. In June 1654, when Cromwell had been Protector for a year, Dorothy Osborne again wrote to William Temple; it looked as though she might be able to marry him at last, after a courtship and correspondence of near seven years, and she wrote to sue for a quiet wedding:

> I have never known a wedding well designed but one, and that was of two person's whoe had time enough I confesse to contrive it; and noebody to please int but themselves. hee came downe to the Country where she was upon a Visitt and one morning marryed her, as soone as they cam out of the Church they took coach and cam for the Towne, dined at an Inne by the way and at night cam into Lodgings that were provided for them, where nobody knew them and where they passed for marryed people of seven years standing; the truth is I could not indure to bee Mrs. Bride in a Publick wedding to bee made ye happiest person on Earth. doe not take it ill, for I would indure it if I could rather than faile, but in Earnest I doe not think it were possible for mee.

Despite the Puritans, quiet weddings were obviously still rare. But Dorothy Osborne, by her eloquence, won one for herself: when she married William Temple later that same year (on Christmas day, another festival the Puritans did not believe in celebrating) it was very quietly indeed. Presumably she overcame her feelings about being married before a justice of the peace, because, by law, no other weddings were valid until 1656; then Parliament confirmed the new matrimonial legislation, with the exception of one clause: 'That no other marriage whatsoever within the Commonwealth of England shall be held or accounted a legal marriage.' After this, most weddings returned to the churches—but not to the Anglican marriage service. The *Book of Common Prayer* was banned and a new *Directory for Publick Worship*, with a much simplified ceremony, replaced it. Wedding rings were officially frowned on —'A Relique of Popery and a Diabollicall Circle for the Devil to daunce in' was how one puritan divine saw them—but most people continued to use them and at least one 'officiating minister' (clergymen went out with royalty) saw that his daughter had one 'lest she should be turned back upon him later'. William Secker, another Commonwealth preacher, bravely published a sermon in 1658 called *A Wedding Ring fit for the Finger; or the Salve of Divinity upon the Sore of Humanity; Laid Open in a Sermon at a Wedding in Edmonton*, and it proved to be extremely popular, in America as well as in England. (It contained a delightful simile: husband and wife, said Mr. Secker, should vie with each other in industry for the good of their off-spring, 'even as the cock and hen both scrape in the dust-heap to pick up something for their chickens'.) The royalist Nathaniel Hardy also refused to be cowed: in *Love and Fear; the Inseparable Twins of a Blest Matrimony; characterized in a Sermon occasioned by the Late Nuptialls of Mr. William Christmas and Mrs. Elizabeth Adams*, Mr. Hardy,

'Mr. of Arts' and preacher to the parish of St. Dionis Backchurch, said in July 1653: 'The ring given in marriage is of a circular figure, and a circle is the image of Constancy, to teach the man how perpetual his love should be.' (He also pointed out that most things come in pairs . . . like heaven and earth . . . and in a man's body 'most of his parts are made in pairs, two eyes, two ears, two nostrils, two lippes, two armes, two thighs, two legs, two feet . . . man being thus made, God said to him, "It is not good that he should be alone;" and therefore as he had made other living creatures male and female, so he provided woman for man.')

One relic of puritanism which is still with us, is the idea that one should not marry on Sundays. The *Directory for Publick Worship* (1644) ordered that no marriage should be solemnised on a day of public humiliation, adding 'And we advise it be not on the Lord's day.' This previously popular wedding day never became fashionable again.

The Pilgrim Fathers who founded Massachusetts in 1620, and all the other Puritans who braved the voyage to America throughout this century, carried their beliefs and laws with them. And they spread them not only throughout their own territories of New England, but even into Virginia—the Old Dominion, founded by Elizabethan adventurers and dashing cavaliers. Around the middle of the century, Virginian magistrates were empowered to perform marriages, and instead of having the banns read in church, couples could pin a notice to the court-house door. Like everything else in Virginia, the price of a wedding licence was costed out in pounds of tobacco: in 1672 the fee for one bearing the Governor's signature was 100 lbs., while banns could be called in church for 40 lbs. To buy one of the 'young, handsome, honestly educated maids, of honest life and carriage', who were shipped out as brides for the early settlers, cost 120 lbs. of tobacco—£12 sterling. (It was politely called a re-imbursement, rather than a payment, to the company which had transported the girls from England.)

New York State (New Netherland before it was captured by the English in 1664) also had civil marriage: as late as 1695 a visiting English clergyman complained that many of the weddings there were performed by justices of the peace.

For most of the century in Virginia and the southern states the law was that marriages should be performed in a church between the hours of eight in the morning and twelve midday—the same ruling that applied in England, except during the Commonwealth. But the gradual development of the new colonies made this impractical: for many people the nearest church was two days' hard, and often dangerous, ride away—there were 'Injuns in them thar hills'—and it was simpler for the parson and the guests to converge on the bride's house. That way the party could start as soon as the ceremony was over. Amongst the lonely early settlers, strung out on large plantations, hundreds of miles from the nearest embryo town, always living with the threat of Indian invasion, weddings were seized on as the perfect excuse for a three-, four-, or even seven-day fiesta. Work and the crops were forgotten: a witness in a court case in York County, Virginia, in 1656 testified that he had found a planter's tobacco untended and had asked: 'Mr. Bushrod, what do you mean by suffering your tobacco to run up so high; and why do you not topp itt?' Mr. Bushrod had replied that 'his overseer, Richard Barkshyre, had gone to a weddinge att Pyanketank without his consent, and he knew not how to helpe it'. In 1666, when Dutch men-o'-war entered the James River (on which the first of all the English settlements was founded) the British guard-ship was caught napping—her captain was ashore, attending a wedding.

Although the far-flung pattern of population was the main cause of home marriages in America, the fact that, in the second half of the century, they were highly fashionable in England certainly had something to do with it, too. There was an insatiable thirst for news of the latest styles and fads from the old country—and not only among the women settlers. When the menfolk wrote to each other within the colonies their letters were full of strange new words—*Sachem* (an Indian chief) and *wampum* or *wampumpeag* (Indian money: strings of shells or beads, calculated by the fathom), and news of Indian up-risings—but when they wrote to England, it was page after page of the minutest detail, explaining the exact shade, the precise fabric, the size of button, and the amount of braid which they wanted for their next suit of clothes, all gleaned from the latest intelligence of London fashions. If they lived in Maryland or Virginia they paid with the next crop of tobacco, and a man ordering a wedding suit was presented with a bill like this one from the year 1643:

To making a suit with buttons to it . . .	80 lb.
1 ell canvas	30 lb.
for dimothy linings	30 lb.
for buttons and silke	50 lb.
for points	50 lb.
for taffeta	58 lb.
for belly pieces	40 lb.
for hooks & eies.	10 lb.
for ribbonin for pockets	20 lb.
for stiffinin for collar	10 lb.
Sum	378 lb.

The American Antiquarian Society in Worcester, Massachusetts, has a delightful cache of letters written by John Hall, a London merchant, to his mother, who (after her fourth marriage) was Madame Rebekah Symonds of Ipswich, Mass., wife of Deputy Governor Symonds (who had two sons and six daughters from two or three previous marriages of his own). 'Good Son' John, in his 'labours of love and pride in London shops', kept Madame, her daughters and her step-daughters right up to the minute in fashions from home—or tried to, for in May 1675 they had obviously been hopelessly out of date in their requests for new supplies:

Honoured Mother. . . . you sent for a fashionable Lawne whiske [*neckerchief*], but soe it is that their is none such now worne either by Gentil or Simple, young or old. Instead wherof I have bought a shape and ruffles which is now the ware of the bravest as wel as the young-ones; such as goe not with naked necks ware a black scarf over it therefore I have not only bought a plaine one that you sent for but also a Lact one such as are most in fashion; secondly, you sent for a Damson coloured Spanish Leather for women's shoes But their is noe Spanish Leather of that Couler and Tuckey Leather is Coulared soe on the graine. Side only both which are out of use for women's shoes Therefore I bought a skin of Leather that

47

is all the mode for Women's shoes all that I fear it is too Thick; But my Cos. Epps told mee that such Thinne ones as here are generally used would by raine and snow in New England be presently rendered of noe service, and therefore persuaded me to send skin which is stronger than ordinary. . . . As to the feathered fan I would also have found in my heart to have Let it alone because none but very grave persons (and of these very few) use it; That now its Growne almost as absolete as Ruffles and more rare to be seen than a Yellow Hood . . .

The fan John Hall forced himself to send was excellent value: 3s. 3d. for 'a feather fan and silver handle', only 3d. more than 'a pare of thred stockings'. In the same bill (squashed into the side of the page with the letter written around it, the way Hall always did his accounting) is a 'plaine Bible' at 4s.; 'two women's Ivory Knives' at 1s. 8d. the pair; '10 yds of silk pudswa' (most probably Paduasoy—a rich silk material) at £4. 5s.; '5 yds sky Callico' at 4s.; one dozen 'sowing Silke' for a shilling; that skin of leather for just three shillings, and the 'Lact Alamode scarfe'* at 5s. 6d. For 24 items—plus customs charges and shipping (6s. 10d.); cord, packing paper, and 'bils' (6d.); and freight paid in London (2s. 6d.)—the total cost came to £11. 5s. 5d.

Just two months before exercising himself over all this finery, John Hall was commiserating with his mother on the troubles in New England: 'Dear Mother your sorrows in N.E. are Much upon mee; And I have Lively Ideas in my minde of the frights and distractions that those Salvages put you too.' The 'salvage' Indians had just fired a nearby town in the Nashua valley and ridden off with some of the women; all of them, no doubt, dressed in the very latest fashions.

When there was plague in London, Madame Symonds was afraid it would be carried over to America with her new clothes, but her 'most dutiful and obedient son' assured her that he bought everything himself from safe shops and reliable dealers and kept it all for a month in his own home, where none had been infected. And so the traffic continued. When John Hall's sister was about to marry, he sent out a pair of white leather gloves which were sure to have been of the most stylish design. On both sides of the Atlantic, gloves were still much given at weddings and if nothing else about the ceremony was white, the gloves were almost bound to be. Thomas Dekker wrote of 'five or six pair of white innocent wedding gloves' in his *Satiromastix* and the bride in John Fletcher's *The Night Walker*, understandably a little crazed by the unfortunate happenings of her wedding-night (she is thought to have died, placed in a coffin, which is stolen in mistake for a casket of treasure, and dumped in a graveyard), babbles about being offered 'five pairs of white gloves' to dance at the wedding of the only man she has ever loved.

In England, the poet Henry Oxinden wrote to his cousin, Elizabeth Dallison, for fashionable supplies for his 'privat' second wedding of 1642 (*The Oxinden and Peyton Letters*). His bride-to-be, he said, 'hath a desire to have a paire of speciall good gloves for my mother, and a paire for my sister and 3 paire for her sisters, of 6d. 8d. the peice at least. . . . I conceive I shall want a paire of plaine perfumed gloves for myselfe. . . .' (He also thought he would want 'what is most in fashion to hap my

* This almost certainly meant a 'laced' scarf, in the sense that it was trimmed with lace. *Alamode*—all run together like that—was a type of black silk.

48

sword in . . . a plain band [*collar*] and cuffes and boot hose tops of the newest and best fashion that is'.) In America, the Rev. Andrew Eliot, pastor of North Church in Boston, calculated he had had '29 hundred' pairs of gloves given to him in thirty-two years—though many of these would have been for funerals, when gloves were also given. (He sold most of them, but didn't tell how much he made.)

Many ministers in New England put all the misfortunes of the new colonies down to the vanity and extravagance of the women (even the Indian outbreaks were charged to this score) and they certainly dressed oddly for a new-frontier life. A quick comparison of Governor Symonds' estate and his wife's wardrobe gives some idea of their topsy-turvy values: the Governor was worth £3000 when he died, and one of his homes—Argilla Farm, on Heart-Break Hill, by Labour-in-Vain Creek—was valued at £150. Just one of his wife's cloaks, an 'embroidered satin Manto', sent from London by good son John, cost £30. Even in Puritan territory, sumptuary laws had to be invoked. In Salem, Massachusetts, in 1652, a man appeared in court charged with 'excess in boots, ribbonds, gould and silver lace', and in Newbury, the following year, two women were had up for wearing silk hoods and scarfs, but were discharged on proof that their husbands were worth £200 each. Another Massachusetts town, Northampton, had a thorough purge on 'wicked apparell' in 1676: thirty-eight women of the Connecticut valley were brought before the judge at the same time; a 16-year-old girl, called Hannah Lyman, was accused of 'wearing silk in a fflaunting manner, in an offensive way and garb not only before but when she stood presented'; and thirty young men were charged with wearing silk, long hair, and other extravagances. With all this attention given to everyday fashion, it is not surprising that weddings called forth truly astonishing effort. From the time a request for supplies went out from the colonies to the final delivery of goods, there was a delay of about a year; most brides were content to wait that long to be married in style. Judge Samuel Sewell, who presided over the notorious witchcraft trials in Salem in 1692, sent vast lists from Boston to England when his daughters married, demanding everything from dining tables to dress material. (None of the material was white; most of it was patterned and brightly-coloured, which one might have thought was for practical reasons, except most of these ladies don't appear to have been practical.) Having waited so long for their finery, new Americans made the most of it. Families living within reasonable distance of the church made a brave nuptial show not only on the day of the wedding, but on the following Sunday, and sometimes on the following four Sundays, as they paraded *en masse* to the meeting house in the most glorious array they could muster. It was a custom called 'Coming Out Bride'. In England, wedding parades of this kind also took place, but with less of a flourish, and they don't appear to have been given a name. On Sunday, 3 August 1662, Samuel Pepys recorded in his diary: 'A full church, and some pretty women in it; among others, Beck Allen, who was a bride-maid to a new married couple that came to church to-day, and, which was pretty strange, sat in a pew hung with mourning for a mother of the bride's, which methinks should have been taken down.'

Pepys was writing two years after Charles II's restoration to the throne, when wedding feasts and festivities were no longer frowned upon, but they still had not quite overcome the dampening effects of the Commonwealth, and they never quite did. The full-blooded, three- or four-day wedding celebrations, the tournaments and *masques*, the breath-taking extravagance, never fully returned. It was all a little more piece-meal now: often the bridal pair married at one place, had the party at another, and went to a third for the bedding. Sir Samuel Tuke almost habitually took his brides to his friend John Evelyn's at Deptford for his wedding nights. On 9 June 1664, Evelyn recorded in his diary: '*Sir Samuell Tuke* being this morning married to a Lady kinswoman to my Lord *Arundel* of *Wardoer*, by the Queenes Lord *Almoner* L. *Aubignie* in St. James's Chapell, solemniz'd his Wedding night at my house with much companie.' And again on 2 July 1668: 'Sir *Sam: Tuke* Baronet & the Lady he had married but this day came & bedded her at night at my house, many friends accompanying the Bride.'

When Evelyn's daughter, Susanna, married in April 1693, he wrote: 'Much of this Weeke spent in Ceremonie, receiving Visites and Entertainments of Relations.' But it was all on a reasonably intimate scale. The custom was no longer for relatives to converge from all parts of the country for the wedding. Instead, it was the bridal pair who did the travelling: a week or so after the ceremony they took off on a grand tour, living with each relation for several weeks and usually staying away for many months. In November 1693, seven months after Susanna's marriage to William Draper, Evelyn noted: 'My Son Draper & Daughter, now with Child, came to see us; after their some monthes absence in Visiting their Relations in divers places of the Country &c.'

Evelyn and Pepys, the two great diarists of the century, knew and admired each other, although socially they were worlds apart. Pepys, the son of a tailor, rose to heights of which even he had not dared to dream, but he could never achieve Evelyn's easy acceptance of, and into, the noblest society. The weddings Evelyn attended sound decorous and impeccably organised, even if they were not all as grand as that of his niece in June 1670: 'To Lond: in order to my *Niepce* Evelyns Marriage, daughter to my Late Brother of Woodcot, with the Eldest son of Mr. *Attourney Montague*, which was celebrated at *Southampton* house Chappell, after which a magnificent Entertainement, Feast & dauncing, diner & supper in the greate roome there; but the bride &c was bedded at my Sisters Lodging in Drurie-Lane &c.' He would never have been caught in a situation like this: '23rd [*January 1662*] . . . by coach by invitãcon to my uncle Fenner's, where I found his new wife, a pitiful, old, ugly, ill-bred woman in a hatt, a midwife. Here were many of his, and as many of her relations, sorry, mean people; and after choosing our gloves, we all went over to the Three Crane Tavern, and though the best room in the house, in such a narrow dogg-hole we were crammed, and I believe we were near forty, that it made me loathe my company and victuals; and a sorry poor dinner it was too.' Or this: ' . . . . we found Mrs. Carrick very fine, and one Mr. Lucy, who called one another husband and wife, and after dinner a great deal of mad stir. There was pulling of Mrs. bride's and Mr. bridegroom's ribbons, with a great deal of fooling among them that I and my wife did not like. Mr. Lucy and several other gentlemen coming in after dinner, swearing and singing as if they were mad, only he singing very handsomely.' (Pepys the music-lover being scrupulously fair!) But even Evelyn on occasion found himself in rackety company. In 1671 when King Charles II went to Newmarket for the racing, Evelyn stayed at nearby Euston, Lord Arlington's palace: 'where we found Monsieur *Colbert* (the *French Ambassador*) & the famous new *french* maid of honor, *Mademoisell Quierovil* now comeing to be in greate favour with the K——: Came his Majestie almost every second day with the Duke [*of York, his brother*], who commonly returned againe to New-market; but the King lay often here. . . . It was universaly reported that the faire Lady —— was bedded one of these nights, and the stocking flung, after the manner of a married Bride: I acknowledge she was for the most part in her undresse* all day, and that there was fondnesse, & toying, with that young wanton; nay 'twas said, I was at the former ceremonie, but tis utterly false, I neither saw, nor heard of any such thing whilst I was there, though I had ben in her Chamber & all over that apartment late enough; & was my selfe observing all passages with curiosity enough: however twas with confidence believed that she was first made a *Misse* as they cald these unhappy creatures, with solemnity, at this time &c:'

The King's official wedding, to his Portuguese princess, was more restrained. There had been a proxy marriage in Portugal before the 24-year-old Catherine of Braganza set sail for England, and there was another quiet ceremony at Portsmouth when she landed. At this the new queen wore a richly-coloured dress, with wide, lace-trimmed panels of a lighter fabric at either side of the skirt, a matching stomacher, a low-cut lace collar, and large, puffed sleeves, handsomely slashed to show the lighter material beneath. She also wore a farthingale, which was thought to be absurdly old-fashioned by the British. Pepys, the tailor's son who once signed himself 'Dapper Dick', was particularly scathing, and even the gentler Evelyn commented on the 'Portuguese ladies in their monstrous fardingales' and the curious way the princess had of arranging her hair: 'her foretop long and turned aside very strangely'. King Charles was thought to be most elegantly dressed for the occasion in the very latest fashion of petticoat breeches, which were tight to the knee and then flounced out in a frill of lace at least a foot deep.

One of the main reasons for the subdued wedding celebrations in England was the King's choice of a Catholic for his bride; and the country's displeasure was even more marked a decade later when Charles's brother, James, Duke of York, also married a Catholic—and had the King of France and the Pope to help with the match-making. At the age of 26 the Duke (later James II) had secretly married an English girl (Anne Hyde, daughter of the Earl of Clarendon) but when she died twelve years later, he looked abroad for a second wife. Charles II and Queen Catherine still had no children after eleven years of marriage, and the Duke of York had only two daughters; it was important that he should, if possible, produce a male heir to the throne. A careful survey was made of likely princesses, and a short list of eleven drawn up. Of these, the Archduchess Claudia of Innsbruck looked the most promising and the Earl of Peterborough, as proxy for the Duke of York, was dispatched to Austria to marry her, carrying with him £20,000-worth of jewels as a wedding present. But before he reached Innsbruck, the Earl received word that another recent widower, the Holy Roman Emperor, Leopold I, had also decided to marry the Duchess; the Duke of York was now offered her sister. After an indignant retreat, Lord Peterborough was sent off to look at number two on the list, the Duchess of Guise, but she proved to be 'low of stature and ill-shaped'. By a lucky chance, the Duke's envoy now saw a painting of the young sister of the Duke of Modena, who was also on the list, and was so completely captivated by it himself, he set off with eagerness to secure her for his royal master. 'It bore the appearance of a Young Creature about Fourteen years of

---

* The *undresse* of Mademoisell Quierovil (or, to give her her full and proper name, Mademoiselle Louise-Renée de Penancoët de Kéroualle, later Duchess of Portsmouth) would not have been quite so informal as it now sounds. Undress, in the age of corsets, was a loose gown, as opposed to the heavily boned and laced-in variety.

Age,' he wrote, 'and carried such a light of Beauty, such Characters of Ingenuity and Goodness as surprised the eyes.' But, unfortunately, this creature of delight had decided to become a nun. Sadly, the good Lord Peterborough pressed on to look at the next candidate, the Princess Eleanor of Neuburg, who had 'a neck as white as snow', which was good, but 'was inclined to be fat', which was not. (How these poor girls were surveyed and publicly summed up!) In Wurttemberg, the by now much travelled envoy found the Princess Mary Anne 'possible' but his heart obviously wasn't in it, and when instructions arrived to return to Modena and pursue the young princess there, the Earl leapt into speedy action.

Mary of Modena had been 'so innocently bred' she had heard neither of the Duke of York, nor of England, until the marriage was proposed to her, and her immediate reaction was 'Why *me?*' She received the Earl bewildered but determined not to yield: although 'she was much obliged to the King of England and the Duke of York for their good opinion', she 'could not but wonder why, when there were so many other princesses of more merit, who would esteem the honour, and be willing to embrace it, they should require her, when she had vowed herself, as much as she was able, to another life.' And her sentiments do seem very reasonable. But not to the King of France, the glorious Louis XIV, who wanted to see this alliance with Britain concluded; he now stepped into the bargaining with an offer to guarantee a dowry of 400,000 crowns on the part of the bride; Charles II, on his side, undertook to provide £15,000 a year for his brother; but in the end it was Pope Clement X who won round the truly pious princess, by suggesting she should 'place before her eyes the great profit that might accrue to the Catholic faith' through such a marriage, which would 'open a wider field than the virginal cloister' and be more 'conducive to the service of God and the public good'. With great haste the proxy marriage was arranged so that it could take place on the same day (30 September 1673) that the marriage settlement was signed.

After public rejoicings in Modena, Lord Peterborough set out for England with the new Duchess (in constant tears and writing long letters back to her convent at every halt). Charles II wanted them home before the next session of Parliament, hoping to forestall the anger of the country with a *fait accompli* and a winning (albeit Catholic) bride. But the harassed Earl could not get his caravan to move more than 20 miles a day, and was not sure how his royal masters would feel about an additional passenger, the mother of the young Princess, who 'could not be diverted from coming by any means'. At Dover, the 40-year-old bridegroom was waiting to greet his 15-year-old bride; and she cried again. A second marriage ceremony was quickly performed, 'after a fashion', by the Bishop of Oxford, acting on the sole authority of the King. At Gravesend, Charles II and his courtiers were waiting with the royal barge to conduct the wretched (still crying) bride up the Thames to Whitehall Palace in what should have been a gay litttle flotilla. Parliament, which had long-since been in session, called on His Majesty to declare the proxy Catholic wedding void; and, as a result, Parliament was adjourned. (And after all this trouble, though the Duke of York and Mary of Modena did have a son—Bonnie Prince Charlie—he never succeeded to the British throne, whilst the two daughters of Anne Hyde, Mary and Anne, both in turn became queen.)

These dockside weddings of Charles II and his brother do not seem to have been very impressive occasions. Lady Fanshawe, who was present at the King's Portsmouth marriage in 1662, dismissed it in one sentence in her *Memoirs*: 'The Bishop of London declared them married in the name of the Father, the Son, and the Holy Ghost; and then they caused the ribbons her Majesty wore to be cut in little pieces; and as far as they would go, everyone had some.' Very soon this on-the-spot mutilation of the bride's outfit was to disappear and in place of it came the presentation of knots of ribbons, which had been made up in the bride's chosen colours prior to the ceremony. These knots were called 'favours' and, although they did not appear at his own wedding, it was most probably Charles II and his French followers who brought the custom to England. Both Pepys and Evelyn record being given favours, but neither of them was made particularly happy by the experience.

Evelyn wrote in 1672: '*August* 1. I was at the Marriage of my L: Arlingtons onely Daughter, (a Sweet Child, if every there was any) to the *Duke* of *Grafton*, natural sonn, of the King, by the *Dutchesse* of *Cleaveland*, the *Archbishop* of Cant: officiating, the King & all the grandees present: I had a favour given me by my Lady, but tooke no great joy at the thing for many reasons:' (Evelyn did not approve of court morality and, possibly, was not happy that the bride was only five years old and the bride-groom nine.) Seven years later, he continued the story: 'Dind at the Co: of *Suther-lands*, & was this evening at the re-marriage of the *Dutchesse* of *Grafton* to the Duke (his Majesties natural son) she being now 12 yeares old: the Ceremonie was per-form'd in my *Lord Chamberlaines* (her fathers Lodgings) at *Whitehall* below, by the Bish: of *Rochester*, his Majestie Present: a suddaine, & unexpected thing (when every body believed that first marriage, would have come to nothing;) But the thing being Determined, I was privately invited by my *Lady* her mother, to be present; but I confesse I could give her little joy, & so I plainely told her; but she told me, the *King* would have it so, & there was no going back: & this sweetest, hopefullest, most beautiful child, & most vertuous too, was Sacrific'd to a boy, that had ben rudely bred, without any thing to encourage them, but his Majesties pleasure.' Evelyn 'staied Supper where his Majestie sate between the *Dutchesse* of *Cleaveland* (the incontinent mother of the Duke of Grafton) & the sweete *Dutchesse* the Bride, with severall greate Persons & Ladies, without Pomp;'

It was commonplace for girls to be married at 12; Evelyn himself, when nearly 27, had married a 12-year-old and then gone off travelling for four years, 'my Wife being yet very Young, and therefore dispensing with a temporarie & kind separation, whilst under the care of an excellent Lady, & prudent Mother'. But not everyone approved. When Sir Stephen Fox, friend to both Evelyn and Pepys and, like the latter, a man who had risen through the ranks, was offered Lord Spenser, son of the Countess of Sunderland, as a husband for his daughter, he said: 'that his Daughter was very Young, as well as my Lord, & he was fully resolv'd never to marry her, without the parties mutual liking, which she could not judge of 'til more advanc'd in age . . .' His daughter was then about 12 and he thought 16 or 17 the proper time.

Pepys' experience with favours left an equally sour taste; he had watched his neighbour and Admiralty colleague, Sir William Penn, distributing the things 'up and down the town long since' while he had to wait until a week after the wedding to get his. He was not in a mood to approve of anything Sir William did at this time, but the way he went about the marriage of his 15-year-old daughter had Pepys chuntering into his diary for weeks. It began on 15 February 1667: 'home and to dinner, where I hear Pegg Pen is married this day privately; no friends, but two or three relations on his side and hers. Borrowed many things of my kitchen for dressing their dinner.' Later, a friend, Mrs. Turner, 'did give me account of this wedding to-day, its being private being imputed to its being just before Lent, and so in vain to make new clothes till Easter, that they might see the fashions as they are like to be this summer; which is reason and good enough. Mrs. Turner tells me she hears (Sir W. Pen) gives £4,500 or £4,000 with her. They are gone to bed, so I wish them much sport.'

But the next morning, Sir William shocks his inquisitive neighbour again: 'One wonder I observed to-day, that there was no musique in the morning to call up our new-married people, which is very mean, methinks, and is as if they had married like dog and bitch.'

On the 20th Pepys was muttering once more: 'Up, with Sir W. Batten and Sir W. Pen by coach to White Hall, by the way observing Sir W. Pen's carrying a favour to Sir W. Coventry, for his daughter's wedding, and saying that there was others for us, when we will fetch them, which vexed me, and I am resolved not to wear it when he orders me one. His wedding hath been so poorly kept, that I am ashamed of it; for a fellow that makes such a flutter as he do.'

But, on the 22nd: ". . . myself, to Sir W. Pen's house, where some other company. It is instead of a wedding dinner for his daughter, whom I saw in palterly clothes, nothing new but a bracelet that her servant* had given her, and ugly she is, as heart can wish. A sorry dinner, not anything handsome or clean, but some silver plates they borrowed of me. . . . We had favours given us all, and we put them in our hats, I against my will, but that my Lord and the rest did . . . home to supper and to bed, talking with my wife of the poorness and meanness of all that Sir W. Pen and the people about us do, compared with what we do.'

The following Sunday, Pepys, Sir William Penn and the other Navy Commissioners went to Whitehall Palace for an early morning conference with the Duke of York, and then on to church together. There, Lady Penn spooned a final dollop of salt into all Pepys' open wounds: 'My lady Pen there saluted me with great content to tell me that her daughter and husband are still in bed, as if the silly woman thought it a great matter of honour, and did, going out of the church, ask me whether we did not make a great show at Court to-day, with all our favours in our hats.'

To a Frenchman, all this fuss about ribbons seemed extremely old-fashioned. Francis Maximilian Misson, a French Protestant who found refuge in England towards the end of the century, pointed out that 'Formerly in *France*, they gave *Livrées de Nôces*, which was a Knot of Ribbands, to be worn by the Guests upon their Arms; but that is practis'd now only among Peasants. In *England* it is done still among the greatest Noblemen: These Ribbands they call Favours, and give them not only to those that are at the Wedding, but to five hundred People besides; they send them about, and distribute them at their own Houses. 'Tother Day, when the eldest Son of *M. de Overkerque* marry'd the Duke of *Ormond's* Sister, they dispers'd a whole Inundation of those little Favours; nothing else was here to be met with, from the Hat of the King, down to that of the meanest Servant. Among the Citizens, and plain Gentlemen, (which is what they call the *Gentry*) they sometimes give these Favours; but it is very common to avoid all Manner of Expence as much as possible.'

---

* *Servant*—most probably meaning Peg Penn's new husband.

Plate Four

(Poor Monsieur Misson: as he was tutor to the Duke of Ormonde's grandson, he most probably had to grit his gallic teeth and wear one of the disgracefully dated things himself.)

Gold, silver, carnation and white ribbons were used for the Ormonde favours, a combination which would not have met with the whole-hearted approval of the bridesmaids in a book called *The Fifteen Comforts of Marriage* (quoted in Brand's *Popular Antiquities*). For them, every shade had deep significance, which made choosing them a tricky business. First of all they tried to decide how to decorate the bridal bed—

> not, say they, with yellow ribbands, these are emblems of jealousy—not with *feuille mort*, that signifies fading love—but with true-blue, that signifies religion; this was objected to as being too grave: and at last they concluded to mingle a gold tissue with grass-green, which latter signifies youthful jollity. For the bride's favours, top-knots, and garters, the bride proposed blew, gold-colour, popingay-green, and limon-colour,—objected to, gold-colour signifying avarice —popingay green wantonness. The younger bridemaid proposed mixtures,— flame-colour—flesh-colour—willow—and milk-white. The second and third were objected to, as flesh-colour signifies lasciviousness, and willow forsaken. It was settled that red signifies justice, and sea-green inconstancy. The milliner, at last, fixed the colours as follows: for the favours, blue, red, peach-colour, and orange-tawny: for the young ladies' top-knots, flame-colour, straw-colour (signifying plenty), peach-colour, grass-green, and milk-white; and for the garters, a perfect yellow, signifying honour and joy.

Often the ribbons were still called true-love knots (a very ancient term) rather than favours. There is a nice theory that both the knots and the name were an early import from Denmark where *Trulofa, fidem do* meant 'I plight my troth', or 'faith'. The little bows were seen as pledges, and when they reached England, the transfer from '*trulofa*' to 'true-love' was simple and suitable. (But not, I think, true.) A mid-17th century writer, again quoted by Brand, cynically, and sadly, preferred the knots to the marriage: 'In *Paradoxical Assertions and Philosophical Problems*, by R.H. 1664, we read: "I shall appeal to any enamoreta but newly married, whether he took not more pleasure in weaving innocent true-love knots than in untying the virgin zone, or knitting that more than Gordian knot which none but that invincible Alexander, Death, can untye?"'

Another thing which changed during this century was the wedding cake, and once again it is the French influence brought to Britain by Charles II which is held responsible for the transformation. Even before Charles's Restoration, however, the mixture had become yet richer. In *A Sing-song on Clarinda's Wedding* (R. Fletcher's *Poems & Fancies*, 1656), the bridegroom and the 'Plum-cake' arrived on the bride's doorstep together:

> The *Bridegroom* and the *Parson* knock,
> With all the *Hymeneall* flock,
> The *Plum-cake* and the *Fidle*.

John Evelyn described how he remembered the old bride-cakes when he was a little boy 'before the Civil Wars' and had seen, 'according to the custom then, the bride and bridegroom kiss over the bride-cakes at the table. It was at the latter end of dinner;

and the cakes were laid upon one another, like the picture of the shew-bread in the old Bibles. The bridegroom waited at dinner.' Country and provincial bridegrooms continued to wait on their guests into the next century, and, no doubt, many still kissed their brides over the plates of bride-cakes. But Evelyn (who was born in 1620) obviously regarded both the waiting and the arrangement of the cakes as old fashioned. At the court and society marriages he attended as an adult, the wedding cakes were more substantial efforts, decorated with marzipan and elaborate icing in much the way we know today. To begin with the icing was put over the mounds of small cakes, so that although they looked like one large, handsomely decorated confection, they could still be broken satisfactorily over the heads of bride and groom: one crack in the outer casing, and out fell a traditional cascade of individual bride-cakes.

Towards the end of the 17th century, marriages themselves underwent a remarkable change. High society, and the people who followed its example, decided to cut out most of the trimmings and to marry as unobtrusively as possible. Our French friend, Monsieur Misson, who kept a sharp eye on the social habits of the British (and published his findings in a neatly organised dictionary of English life), followed the new trends avidly, though he did not at all approve the results. Under *Weddings*, in his *Memoirs and Observations in his Travels over England*, he first explains that he is speaking of customs 'ordinarily practis'd only among those of the Church of *England*, and among People of a middle Condition: To which we may add, that live in or near London'. With this in mind, he continues: 'Persons of Quality, and many others who imitate them, have lately taken up the Custom of being marry'd very late at Night in their Chamber, and very often at some Country House. They increase their common Bill of Fare for some Days, they dance, they play, they give themselves up for some small Time to Pleasure; but all this they generally do without Noise, and among very near Relations. When those of a middle Condition have a mind to be so extravagant, as to marry in Publick, (which very rarely happens) they invite a Number of Friends and Relations; every one puts on new Cloaths, and dresses finer than ordinary; the Men lead the Women, they get into Coaches, and so go in Procession, and are marry'd in full Day at Church: After Feasting and Dancing, and having made merry that Day and the next, they take a Trip into the Country, and there divert themselves very pleasantly. These are extraordinary Weddings.'

At the more usual 'incognito' marriages, the bride and bridegroom 'conducted by their Father and Mother, or by those that serve them in their room, and accompany'd among others by two Bridemen, and two Bride-maids, go early in the Morning, with a Licence in their Pocket, and call up Mr. Curate and his Clerk, tell him their Business; are marry'd with a low Voice, and the Doors shut; tip the Minister a Guinea, and the Clerk a Crown; steal softly out, one one Way, and t'other another, either on Foot, or in Coaches; go different Ways to some Tavern at a Distance from their own Lodgings, or to the House of some trusty Friend, there have a good Dinner, and return Home at Night as quietly as Lambs.'

The bedding ceremony apparently still took place, even at these quiet weddings, for Misson goes on to describe the taking of the bride's garters ('which she had before unty'd, that they might hang down, and so prevent a curious Hand coming too near her Knee'), the flinging of the stocking, and the drinking of the posset.

At one royal marriage earlier in the century, wedding and bedding were given equal importance, and both were equally jolly. It was another union aimed at producing a male Stuart heir (even though the bride's step-mother, the reluctant Mary of Modena, was also currently busy about the same task). Charles II, uncle of both the unwilling bride, Princess Mary (daughter of the Duke of York and his first wife, Anne Hyde), and the weakly bridegroom, Prince William of Orange, gave hearty encouragement both at the altar and at the bedside. According to the diary of the bride's physician: 'At nine o'clock at night the marriage was solemnized in her highness's bed-chamber. The King, who gave her away, was very pleasant all the while; for he desir'd that the Bishop of London would make haste, lest his sister [*the Duchess of York*] bee delivered of a son, and so the marriage be disappointed; and when the prince endowed her with all his worldly goods, hee willed to put all up in her pockett for 'twas clear gains. At eleven o'clock they went to bed, and his majesty came and drew the curtains and said to the prince 'Now, nephew, to your worke! Hey! St. George for England!'

At the new style quiet weddings it was the following day that everyone dressed up and made really merry. The bride, having been married in nothing more festive than an every-day mob-cap, now 'more gay and more contented than ever she was in her Life, puts on her finest Cloathes (for she was marry'd only in a *Mob*) the dear Husband does the same, and so do the young Guests; they laugh, they dance, they make merry; and these Pleasures continue a longer or shorter Time, according to the several Circumstances of Things'. There was a growing sensitivity, a turning away from the bawdy presentation of Mistress Bride to all the world. And there was also a healthy regard for money. It may have cost a little more to buy a special licence and tip the parson and his clerk, but the savings on a quiet wedding were considerable. Making money during the 17th century was no easy matter: England was being bled dry by successive wars with the Dutch and the French, and industrial growth had not yet started. Family fortunes, of any size, had to be conserved. The wrangling that went on over marriage settlements was all part of this, and though it seems mercenary and heartless to us now, it was so often essential then. With no welfare state, the practical certainty of many children, and the limited ways of increasing income, a man was a romantic fool—and a liability to his relations—if he did not ensure that he had enough money to support a family before rushing into matrimony. The touching seven-year wait of Dorothy Osborne and William Temple seems pointless judged against present-day circumstances; but Temple, who was to become such a brilliant diplomat, could not get a job; his father could not afford to support him and a family, and the Osbornes (who did not approve of his politics) did not see why they should dilute their wealth when Dorothy had many suitors who would have brought money into the family rather than have taken it out. For very often it was not just the bridal couple who benefited from marriage settlements. In 1690 Mary Woodforde, wife of the Prebendary of Winchester, wrote in her diary of the negotiations over a bride for her stepson: 'Mrs. Lamport and her daughter were here, and my Husband and they treated about the intended match between the Young Woman and Son Heighes. And they came to an agreement which God grant may be for their good, and enable us to bring up the rest of our Children in his fear, and to pay what we owe to everybody that we may serve God without distraction.' Pepys, thirty years earlier, had 'dined with my Lady [*Sandwich*] and my Lady Pickering, where her son John dined with us, who do continue a fool as he ever was since I knew him. His mother would fain marry him to get a portion for his sister Betty, but he will not hear of it.' (Sister Betty had to wait another eight years before the portion was found.)

This family belief that the marriage of any one member should, if possible, benefit the whole, or at least allow the marrying pair to live up to their social station, was one of the main reasons for a less innocent kind of quiet wedding. Under *Marriage* (as opposed to *Weddings*), Monsieur Misson described a 'greater Abuse'; the existence of some chapels where it was possible to marry secretly *without* a licence. 'Take the two first People you meet, two Beggars if you think fit, carry them along with you to the privileg'd Church as early in the Morning as you please, Mr. Curate will marry them so fast, that neither King nor Parliament can unmarry them; and for two Crowns your Business is dispatched. Hence come the Matches between Footmen and young Ladies of Quality, who you may be sure live no very easy Life together afterwards: Hence too happen polygamies, easily conceal'd, and too much practis'd.'

Running off with an heiress, or any other girl for that matter, was called trepanning. Pepys' rather worthless brother-in-law, Barty, took Mrs. Pepys along to see 'a young lady which he is a servant [*suitor*] to, and have hope to trepan and get for his wife.' And Daniel Defoe, looking back on the situation some years later, described it in technicolour prose in an article he printed under three eye-catching titles: *Conjugal Lewdness, A Treatise Concerning the Use and Abuse of the Marriage Bed*, and *Marital Whoredom*:

> The arts and tricks made use of to Trepan, and, as it were, Kidnap young Women away into the Hands of Brutes and Sharpers, were very scandalous, and it became almost dangerous for anyone to leave a Fortune to the disposal of the Person that was to enjoy it; and where it was so left, the young Lady went always in Danger of her Life; she was watch'd, laid wait for, and, as it were, beseiged by a continual Gang of Rogues, Cheats, Gamesters, and such like starving Crew, so that she was obliged to confine herself like a Prisoner to her Chamber, be lock'd, and barr'd, and bolted in, and have her Eyes every moment upon the Door, as if she was afraid of Bailiffs and Officers to arrest her; or else she was snatch'd up, seized upon, hurry'd up into a Coach-and-six, a Fellow dressed up in a clergyman's Habit to perform the Ceremony, and a Pistol clapt to her Breast to make her consent to be marry'd, And thus the work was done.

By the time Defoe wrote this in 1724 'stealing ladies' had become a capital offence, and rightly so, he thought: 'It seemed a little hard that a Gentleman might have the satisfaction of hanging a thief that stole an old horse from him, but could have no justice against a rogue for stealing his daughter.'

The 'privileg'd Churches' referred to by Misson were St. James's, in Duke's Place, and St. Trinity in the Minories. Both claimed that they did not come under the jurisdiction of the Bishop of London and could therefore make their own rules. Surprisingly, they got away with this for a good many years, and did brisk matrimonial business from the reign of Charles II until the end of the century. One of the marriage registers of St. James's, Duke's Place, showed that in the twenty-seven years from November 1664, nearly 40,000 weddings took place there—an average of almost 1500 a year. As the incumbent could fix his own fee for a quick no-questions-asked ceremony, it was highly lucrative. Pre-dated certificates were also available, which proved helpful in the case of embarrassingly premature heirs.

Poor people could find the same type of facilities in the less salubrious neighbour-hood of the Fleet prison, and towards the end of the 17th century Fleet marriages were becoming notorious. Prisoners with enough money to bribe the warden were allowed to live 'Within the Rules' of the prison but outside its walls. Many a criminal clergyman set himself up in comfortable lodgings in the streets and yards round about and made a handsome living out of weddings at five shillings a time. Shady men of God still at large teamed up with tavern keepers, who provided a wedding parlour—and brandy on the house—in gratitude for the wedding-breakfast business which came their way. None of the marriages was legal (no banns were called, no licence bought) and the only certificate issued, if one were issued at all, was a grubby piece of paper with an illegible signature. Most of the rogue clergymen kept marriage registers to some degree of accuracy, which were frequently produced in court as evidence in bigamy cases. During the last few years of the century, in the reign of William and Mary, a duty was put on marriage licences and certificates, after which both, to be legal, had to carry a five-shilling government stamp. (Under the same Act, bachelors and widowers were taxed, just as advocated by Henry VIII's Cardinal Pole; though the money went not to 'pore damosellys and vyrgynys' but to 'carrying on the War against France with vigour'.) The new stamp duty, and the introduction of a £100 fine on clergymen caught performing illegal marriages, caused a brief lull in the irregular marriage trade; but it soon got going again, brisker than ever. A couple who had had their hands joined by a clergyman, however disreputable, said their vows and handed over five shillings—or even half a crown and a glass of cheap brandy—*felt* married. Most of them were content with any scrap of paper for their marriage lines and they certainly were not going to pay another five shillings to the government for something that was none of its business.

With all this going on, it is not surprising that we hear little of white weddings. A bride embarking on marriage in such an under-cover way (either legally or illegally) was not going to advertise the fact by sporting virgin white and a wreath of flowers. And a lady of fashion, marrying late at night in her chamber, preferred powdered hair, jewels and a low-cut gown to the charms of sweet simplicity; like Fletcher's bride, Clarinda, who was

> Deck'd in her robes and garments gay
> More sumptuous than the live-long-day
> Or Stars enshrin'd in Amber.

A more intimate view of mid-century fashions was given by Richard Braithwaite. He urged: 'Eye those rising mounts, your displayed breasts, with what shameless art they wooe the shamefast passenger.' The trappings of virginity were not in vogue.

However, there was one kind of white wedding which gained a limited following during this century: it was thought that if a girl wore only a single long white garment on her wedding day, her husband could not, in the future, be held accountable for her debts. It was never true, but lingered way into the 18th century, and seems to have been founded on the idea that a husband was only deemed responsible because on marriage he acquired absolute interest in his wife's estate. If, it was argued, the husband gained nothing with his wife, then surely he could not be held to account. Several parish registers of the 16th, 17th and early 18th centuries record weddings where the bride was dressed 'only in her shift and bareheaded'. (In 1774 there was a particularly sad case at Saddleworth where a bride of 70, who was already 'a little in Debt' was 'obliged' by her 30-year-old bridegroom to be 'married in her shift'; but 'the weather being very severe, threw her into such a violent fit of shaking as induced the compassionate Minister to cover her with his coat'.) A companion piece to this fallacy was the belief that a man could lawfully sell his wife, provided he handed her over with a halter round her neck. This wretched custom lasted even longer: in the early 19th century, men quite frequently led their wives into the cattle-market and offered them for sale; and as late as 1858 a man auctioned his wife in a beer shop in Little Horton, near Bradford. By then, however, a certain delicacy of feeling was becoming apparent even in the north: this last bride had round her neck not a rope, but a ribbon. Such lots usually fetched from 6d. to 10 or 11 shillings, though one lady in Birmingham brought in a gratifying £15.

In the 17th century the bride-ale became the penny-bridal and moved out of the churches and church houses and into the taverns and ale-houses. The young couple struck a bargain with the landlord for a room and food in exchange for the wine, ale, and spirit trade the wedding would bring his way. The guests, once more, paid for their own drinks and made a collection for the bride and groom. During the Civil War, the General Assembly passed an Act for the restraint of 'pennie brydals' but, as with the attempt to close the theatres, it didn't really work. The Minister of the parish of Monquhitter, Scotland, said that these events 'involved every amusement and every joy of an idle and illiterate age' and told how they were organised: 'When a pair were contracted, they, for a stipulated consideration, bespoke their wedding at a certain tavern, and then ranged the country in every direction to solicit guests. One, two, and even three hundred would have convened on these occasions to make merry at their own expense for two or more days. This scene of feasting, drinking, dancing, wooing, fighting, &c. was always enjoyed with the highest relish, and until obliterated by a similar scene, furnished ample materials for rural mirth and rural scandal.' In Essex, church houses were still used; writing in the middle of the 18th century, Philip Morant (in his *History of Essex*) said of the village of Great Yeldham: 'A house near the church was anciently used and appropriated for dressing a dinner for poor folks when married, and had all utensils and furniture convenient for that purpose. It has since been converted into a school.' And in the *History of Sir Billy of Billericay, and his Squire Ricardo* (a not at all bad parody of *Don Quixote*), there is a description of the kind of celebration which took place in them:

> In most parts of Essex it is a common custom, when poor people marry, to make a kind of dog-hanging, or money-gathering, which they call a wedding-dinner, to which they invite tag and rag, all that will come; where, after dinner, upon summons of the fiddler, who setteth forth his voice like a town-crier, a table being set forth, and the bride set simpering at the upper end of it, the bridegroom standing by with a white sheet athwart his shoulders, whilst the people march up to the bride, present their money and wheel about. After this offering is over, then is a pair of gloves laid upon the table, most monstrously bedaubed about with ribbon, which by way of auction is set to sale at who gives most, and he whose hap it is to have them, shall withall have a kiss of the bride.

In most parts of the country a reward was also given to the first guest home after the wedding ceremony, and although the prize was not much in itself, it provided an excellent excuse for wild behaviour. In some areas of Scotland there was 'running for the broose', or 'brose', which was a cup of porridge, and in other northern regions 'riding for the Kail', a cabbage or vegetable soup. As the church could be ten miles or more from the bride's home, the honour of winning one of these was often fought out in a hard—and dirty—cross-country steeplechase. Further south there was 'riding for the bridecake' and sometimes this was turned into a complicated and attractive ceremony which took place when the bride was taken to her new home for the first time. The Reverend Aulay Macaulay, writing in the late 18th century, told how the custom used to be carried out in the village of Claybrook, Leicestershire:

> A custom formerly prevailed in this parish and neighbourhood, of riding for the bridecake, which took place when the bride was brought home to her new habitation. A pole was erected in front of the house, three or four yards high, with the cake stuck upon the top of it. On the instant that the bride set out from her old habitation, a company of young men started off on horseback; and he who was fortunate enough to reach the pole first, and knock the cake down with a stick, had the honour of receiving it from the hands of a damsel on the point of a wooden sword, and with this trophy he returned in triumph to meet the bride and her attendants, who, upon their arrival in the village, were met by a party, whose office it was to adorn their horses' heads with garlands, and to present the bride with a posy. The last ceremony of this sort that took place in the parish of Claybrooke was between sixty and seventy years ago [*around 1720–30*], and witnessed by a person now living in the parish. Sometimes the bridecake was tried for by persons on foot, and then it was called throwing the quintal, which was performed with heavy bars of iron; thus affording a trial of strength.

In Westmeath, Ireland, Sir Henry Piers discovered a less friendly greeting for the bride on her journey to her new home, which still had sinister undertones of marriage by capture. The bridegroom and his friends appeared on horseback when the bride had reached the half-way mark (the spot where the young couple's parents had originally met to arrange the match) and they then 'cast short darts at the company that attended the bride but at such a distance that seldom any hurt ensued, yet it is not out of the memory of man that the lord of Hoath on such an occasion lost an eye'. By the end of the century, the darts were no longer thrown; but the marriage itself was still being arranged in ancient fashion:

> The parents and friends on each side meet on the side of an hill, or, if the weather be cold, in some place of shelter, about midway between both dwellings; if agreement ensue they drink the agreement bottle as they call it, which is a bottle of good usquebaugh: for payment of the portion which generally is a determinate number of cows, little care is taken. Only the father or next of kin to the bride sends to his neighbours and friends and everyone gives his cow or heiffer which is all one in the case, and thus the portion is quickly paid. Nevertheless caution is taken from the bridegroom on the day of delivery for restitution of the cattle in case the bride die childless within a certain day limited by agreement, and in this case every man's own beast is restored. Thus care is taken that no man shall grow rich by often marriage.

61

And the Bride Wore . . .

In the towns of Britain the more prosperous of the lower classes, who could afford to pay for their own wedding feast, usually held the celebration in a tavern, often ordering a private room for the occasion, like Samuel Pepys' Uncle Fenner and his awful new bride in the 'hatt'. The cavalier poet, Sir John Suckling, in his *Ballad upon a Wedding*, gives a delightful picture of a marriage feast at an inn near Charing Cross, with the bridegroom dressed so 'Pest'lent fine' and the plump little bride attracting a wealth of amorous glances:

> If wishing should be any sin,
> The parson himself had guilty bin,
>   She look'd that day so purely;
> And did the youth so oft the feat
> At night, as some did in conceit,
>   It would have spoil'd him surely. . . .
>
> Just in the nick the cook knock'd thrice,
> And all the waiters in a trice
>   His summons did obey;
> Each serving-man, with dish in hand,
> March'd boldly up, like our train'd band,
>   Presented, and away.
>
> When all the meat was on the table,
> What man of knife or teeth was able
>   To stay to be entreated?
> And this the very reason was
> Before the parson could say grace
>   The company was seated.
>
> Now hats fly off, and youths carouse;
> Healths first go round, and then the house,
>   The bride's came thick and thick;
> And when 'twas nam'd another's health,
> Perhaps he made it hers by stealth:
>   (And who could help it, Dick?)
>
> O' the' sudden up they rise and dance;
> Then sit again, and sigh, and glance;
>   Then dance again and kiss:
> Thus several ways the time did pass,
> Whilst ev'ry woman wish'd her place,
>   And ev'ry man wish'd his.

Many 17th century taverns were most respectable places. Pepys frequently took his wife to them, and in his early days as Clerk to the Acts at the Admiralty, when he was flattered by the attentions of his superiors, the two Sir Williams (Sir William Penn and Sir William Batten, both of whom he came to despise so thoroughly), he often dined or supped with them at London inns, together with their wives and sometimes even their young daughters. But no one of any status would have used them for important entertaining.

All in all, this was a messy century for weddings, which is not surprising considering the series of national and religious crises which acted as a backdrop to the social scene: four years of Civil War and the assassination of Charles I were followed by the iron rule of Cromwell; Charles II's reasonably stable, and in many ways glorious, reign was punctuated by two Dutch wars and constant skirmishing, the plague and the great fire of London; James II unleashed fresh chaos by re-establishing the Catholic religion and answering Monmouth's abortive rebellion with the Bloody Assizes; after three turbulent years on the throne, he escaped to France as his son-in-law and nephew, William of Orange, marched on London to scoop up the British crown for himself and his wife, Mary. With all this going on, it is little wonder that the consolidating social patterns of Elizabeth's reign shattered. Only one generalisation can be made—marriages themselves were very popular indeed. In the new world and the old, most people married early and married often. While the plague was raging in London, families moved a little further out into the country week by week, carrying on protracted wedding negotiations as they went. In America, where marriageable women were out-numbered by about three to one, it was a very peculiar girl who was not promised within a few months of setting foot in the new colonies; and widows were wooed afresh almost before they had ordered their mourning clothes. In Britain one widow was not only wooed but wed before her weeds arrived: John Rons recorded in his diary, in January 1638, that 'a gentleman carried his wife to London last week and died about eight o'clock at night, leaving her five hundred pounds a year in land. The next day before twelve she was married to the journeyman woolen-draper that came to sell mourning to her'. A Scots gentleman, embarking on his fifth marriage, was said to be 'unco' wastfu' o' wives', but he had a long way to go before he was as wasteful as a woman in Haarlem, Holland, was of husbands. John Evelyn was shown her cottage in 1641 and told she had been married twenty-five times, 'and being now a Widdow, was prohibited to marry for the future; yet it could not be proved, that she had ever made any of her husbands away, though the suspicion had brought her divers times to trouble'.

Pepys heard a sermon in 1660 in which the preacher spoke 'largely in commendation of widowhood, and not as we do to marry two or three wives or husbands, one after another'. One family which not only married often but chose the same family to marry into, ended up in a very nasty tangle. William Hone, in his *Table Book*, sorted out the two familes—the Hawoods and the Cashicks—and discovered that the eldest Hawood daughter had married one John Cashick, while her younger sister had married his father, also named John Cashick. Mr. Hawood, the girls' father, had married old Cashick's daughter by his first wife, and by her had had a son. With the exception of the first Mrs. Cashick Senior, all protagonists were living in Faversham in February 1650, and old Cashick's second wife (née Hawood) was able to say:

> My father is my son,
>   And I am mother's mother;
> My sister is my daughter,
>   I am grandmother to my brother.

Chapter Six

Marriage by Stealth
The Eighteenth Century

Weddings are going forward, some wise *some* other wise.
Mrs. Delany

LANDESTINE marriages which had gained favour during the last few years of the 17th century, became an absurd society cult during the 18th; and now another, and a most incongruous, ingredient was added: the bride wore white. To go with her special licence and top-secret ceremony, a bride with any pretension to fashion was dressed from low-cut bosom to pointed toe in white and silver. She also had to be—or, at least appear to be—overcome by the 'awfulness' of the occasion and distressed beyond words at the mere thought of having the banns called publicly in church. If it could be so arranged that the wedding took place in the midst of a whirling house-party, with only the parson and a couple of witnesses in the know, this was very stylish indeed. If the marriage could then be kept secret for several days, or even months, the very pinnacle of *bon ton* was achieved. It is difficult to find the cause for such curious behaviour, unless the pseudo-discreet marriage was a balance to the noisy commercialism of the match-making. As we have seen in previous chapters, money and marriage had long gone hand in hand, but during this century, they got a wrestler's lock on each other. Heiresses were bartered so openly that their weddings soon came to be called 'Smithfield matches' or 'Smithfield bargains', after the London meat market.

Girls were brought up to know very exactly what they might expect to inherit or have settled on them, and to understand in which precise social and economic strata to look for a husband. 'He has married a fortune' was the phrase of the day, and a girl who was not 'a fortune' stood little chance of making a good match. Dr. Johnson's friend, Mrs. Thrale, wrote a hectic account of her young life, during which her expectations went up and down like a thermometer, according to the humours of a rich uncle. When she was the intended heiress, all eyes turned to the eldest Radcliffe boy of Hitchin Priory, Herts.; when a parson cousin stirred up trouble (or her father behaved foolishly to the man with the money), sights were lowered and a younger brother was considered; in the end, out of favour completely, she was thought lucky to get the handsome Henry Thrale, a man of no family (a brewer, indeed!) but with lots of money of his own and the beautiful Streatham Park in Kent.

Newspaper editors knew it was much more important to give a bride's fortune than her name, and the wedding columns of the *Gentleman's Magazine* were typical of the time, with items such as these:

> 25th March 1735, 'John Parry, Esq., of Carmarthenshire, to a daughter of Walter Lloyd, Esq., member for that county, a fortune of 8,000l.'

> 'Sir George C. to the widow Jones, with 10,000l. a-year, besides ready money.'

> 'The Lord Bishop of St. Asaph to Miss Orell, with 30,000l.'

Sometimes the information was even more precise. In 1731, the same magazine announced: 'Married, the Rev. Mr. Roger Waina, of York, about twenty-six years of age, to a Lincolnshire lady, upwards of eighty, with whom he is to have 8,000l. in money, 300l. per annum, and a coach-and-four during life only.'

Private news reports had the same financial bias. Writing to her cousin, Mrs. Delany, in 1748, Lady Dysart detailed the main features of the wedding of her sister, Lady Frances Carteret, to the 4th Marquis of Tweeddale:

> I think my sister Fanny to all appearance happily established: the Marquis is a sensible reasonable man, and quite her lover. He has £4000 a-year in Scotland and two houses—one of them, I am told, is a very fine place; my sister has £1200 a-year jointure rent-charge. He has given her a very fine pair of brilliant earrings, one drop, a girdle buckle, and five stars for her stays; her clothes (she was married in) were white satin flounced, with a magnificent silver trimming all over the gown and petticoat.

Thirty years later, Mrs. Delany took the same line when she informed her god-daughter that 'The match at present *most* talked of is Lord Shelburn to Miss Moles-worth; a fortune of £40,000, and a right to twice as much.' The young heiresses' resistance to this mercenary mating was splendidly parodied by Richard Brinsley Sheridan in *The Rivals* (1775): his heroine, Miss Lydia Languish, longs to elope with the penniless Ensign Beverley, blissfully forfeiting most of her £30,000 fortune in the process: '— how charming will poverty be with him!' she murmurs (*Aside.*) But, the romantically unsuitable Ensign Beverley is really the eminently eligible Captain Jack Absolute, son of Sir Anthony Absolute, and the choice of her guardian, Mrs. Malaprop; a blow scarcely to be born.

'Why, is it not provoking?' she cries to her friend Julia, 'when I thought we were coming to the prettiest distress imaginable, to find myself made a mere Smithfield bargain of at last! There, had I projected one of the most sentimental elopements!— so becoming a disguise!—so amiable a ladder of ropes!—Conscious moon—four horses—Scotch parson—with such surprise to Mrs. Malaprop—and such paragraphs in the newspapers!—Oh, I shall die with disappointment! . . . Now—sad reverse! what have I to expect, but, after a deal of flimsy preparation, with a bishop's license, and my aunt's blessing, to go simpering up to the altar; or perhaps be cried three times in a country church, and have an unmannerly fat clerk ask the consent of every butcher in the parish to join John Absolute and Lydia Languish, spinster! Oh that I should live to hear myself called spinster!'

Miss Languish recalls her forbidden romance with dramatic rapture: 'How mortifying, to remember the dear delicious shifts I used to be put to, to gain half a minute's conversation with this fellow! How often have I stole forth in the coldest night in January, and found him in the garden, stuck like a dripping statue! There would he kneel to me in the snow, and sneeze and cough so pathetically! he shivered with cold and I with apprehension! and while the freezing blast numbed our joints, how warmly would he press me to pity his flame, and glow with mutual ardour!— Ah, Julia, that was something like being in love.'

A real-life Lydia Languish had slightly better luck in December 1734 when she ran off with her uncle's *valet-de-chambre*; she, at least, got as far as a Fleet marriage and paragraphs in the newspapers before her luck ran out. According to one London paper, the young couple were traced to the Fleet district where they had been married by 'a Roman Catholic priest' and were later 'caught up with in a house in Queen Street, near Guildhall'. The bride was taken home by her friends and the bridegroom thrown into prison. 'So it seems,' moralised the paper, that the bridegroom 'is to suffer for endeavouring to get himself a rich wife, which is a practice followed by all the young gentlemen of quality in England; but the difference is that this young fellow had married or endeavoured to marry an heiress without the consent of her friends, whereas the others generally marry or endeavour to marry heiresses without their own consent.'

The funniest elopement of the century must certainly have been that of Lady Mary Pierrepoint, daughter of the Marquis of Kingston. She wanted to marry Edward Wortley Montagu, nephew of Lord Sandwich, and a most suitable match in every way but one: he refused to entail his estate to the first son born of the marriage, explaining in great detail to Lady Mary's father that he did not believe in a system which could put all the family's wealth in the hands of an unsuitable child, just because he was the eldest, and leave a more promising son without any inheritance at all. In reply to this reasoned argument, Lord Kingston thundered that he wasn't going to have his grandson a beggar, and called the whole deal off. Wortley promptly sent all his entail notes and calculations to his good friend Richard Steele who used them in two blistering articles in *The Tatler* (18 July and 12 September 1710). But the romance was not crushed so easily: rather against his will, Wortley found he still had Lady Mary on his mind, and they soon took up their clandestine correspondence again, beginning a fresh series of love-hate letters which was to last the next two years. Wortley wanted to find out if the Marquis would take a larger sum as a settlement in lieu of the entail agreement; Lady Mary said, contrary to what happened in most families, she and her sister were told nothing '. . . since I am so unfortunate to have nothing in my own disposal, do not think I have any hand in making Settlements. People in my way are sold like slaves, and I cannot tell what price my Master will put on me.' Wortley was in a dilemma; he didn't want to offer more than he had to.

While they went on bickering at each other, Lord Kingston was spending his time more productively: he married off his 19-year-old only son to an illegitimate girl, whose father had agreed to by-pass his legitimate family and settle his entire estate not on the daughter or her husband or even on their first-born son, but on Lord Kingston himself—an operation which required an Act of Parliament to bring about. By sacrificing his son to a 'silly, childish girl', the Marquis managed to raise dowries for his own daughters and was then able to make his own choice of a husband for Lady Mary. He settled on the delightfully named Honourable Clotworthy Skeffington, son and heir of the 3rd Viscount Massereene, a match to which Lady Mary took strong exception. She wrote a letter to her father: 'to let him know my Aversion to the Man propos'd was too great to be overcome, that I should be miserable beyond all things could be imagin'd, but I was in his hands, and he might dispose of me as he thought fit.—He was perfectly satisfy'd with this Answer, and proceeded as if I had given a willing consent'. £400 was laid out on 'wedding Cloaths' for the bride; while Wortley hivered and hovered; finally, they decided to elope (and to quarrel about who would be sacrificing most by taking such a step). On 8 August 1712, Wortley began to make the arrangements:

> You may appoint the time and place, and I will provide a Coach, a Licence, Parson, etc. A Coach and six looks much better than a pair for such a service, but will it not be more likely to have company about it while it stands near your house?
> If we should once be in a coach let us not say one word till we come before the parson, least we should engage in fresh disputes; but why should we meet at all, if we are so likely to have 'em? It is plain we shou'd not.

Despite the rather awesome last paragraph, Lady Mary appointed the time and place, and waited on the balcony from six until seven one morning, but no lover came. Her father, hearing something was a-foot, ordered her to leave for the country immediately, under the care of her brother. She managed to get a note to Wortley who was belatedly galvanised into action; with a special licence in his pocket, he rushed after her. Then came the absurd high peak of the melodrama: on the first night of the flight from London, both Lady Mary and her rescuer stayed at the same inn, without knowing it. 'We have more ill Luck than any other people,' wailed Lady Mary in a note next day. Had she known, she said, 'I could have ris up by my selfe at 4 o'clock and come to your chamber, perhaps undiscover'd.' Wortley and his servant acted so furtively at the inn, they were taken for highwaymen, and had there been a robbery in the district they would surely have been accused. The following day the lovers' luck must have changed for somehow, somewhere, they were married and returned to London in time for Wortley to have lunch with Richard Steele the next day. It wasn't a happy marriage, but he had been right not to entail his estate: his only son was the biggest scoundrel imaginable (amongst the least of his sins were two unsuitable marriages—both secret and one of them bigamous).

Both in Britain and America a special licence was thought to be virtually indispensable to any fashionable marriage, not just an elopement. It did away with the need to have the banns called and meant couples could marry in their own homes at whatever time of the day or night they liked, or even in church outside canonical hours. When wedding announcements were not dwelling on the fortunes of the bride and groom, they often stressed this fashionable aspect of the affair: 'Last Saturday evening at Batch, by special licence, the Right Hon. Arthur, Earl of Donegall, to Mrs. Moore' (The Times, 29 October 1788). In America most weddings were still celebrated at the home of the bride. Gertrude Lefferts Vanderbilt, writing of Flatbush, New York, in the later 1870s said it was 'only 20 years ago that a bridal party assembled in the church for a marriage service. It is now quite common'. In New England it was socially acceptable to have the banns called or to 'post' them in a public place, but in the state of New York this was thought to be extremely ungenteel. There, pretty well all fashionable marriages were performed by Governor's licence, and a notice in a New York newspaper dated 13 December 1765 shows how extraordinary any other form of wedding had become:

> We are creditly informed that there was married last Sunday evening, by the Rev. Mr. Auchnuty, a very respectable couple that had published three different times in Trinity Church. A laudable example and worthy to be followed. If this decent and for many reasons proper method of publication was once generally to take place, we should have no more of clandistine marriages; and save the expense of licenses, no inconsiderable sum these hard and depressing times.

But this 'laudable example' was brought about by necessity rather than choice, for *Holt's New York Gazette and Postboy* had announced only seven days earlier:

> As no Licenses for Marriage could be obtained since the first of November for Want of Stamped Paper, we can assure the Publick several Genteel Couple were publish'd in the different Churches of this City last Week; and we hear that the young Ladies of this Place are determined to Join Hands with none but such as will to the utmost endeavour to abolish the Custom of marrying with License which amounts to many Hundred per annum which might be saved.

As soon as government stamped paper (stamped in England, which was where the money went) became available again, the young ladies, curiously, soon lost their reforming zeal.

In December 1752, Mrs. Delany had written to her sister from Ireland: 'My young friend Miss Forde . . . will be very soon married: wedding clothes are bought; —they are to be asked in the church—Lord Limerick's daughter was—and so it will now be *the fashion*, and *I think a very good one.*' But once again, the fashion was short-lived, and those who could afford to were soon buying their special licences again, or taking that even swifter route to matrimony—a trip to the Fleet quarter or to one of the many wedding 'chapels' which had sprung up in more salubrious areas of London to deal with the rush-wedding trade. Throughout the reigns of Queen Anne and George I, fines were increased and laws tightened in an effort to end these illegal marriages, but on 29 June 1723 the *Weekly Journal* was still able to report:

> From an inspection into the several registers for marriages kept at the several alehouses, brandyshops, &c., within the Rules of the Fleet Prison, we find no less than thirty-two couples joined together from Monday to Thursday last without licenses, contrary to an express act of parliament against clandestine marriages, that lays a severe fine of £200 on the minister so offending, and £100 each on the persons so married in contradiction to the said statute. Several of the above-named brandy-men and victuallers keep clergymen in their houses at 20s. per week, hit or miss; but it is reported that one there will stoop to no such low conditions, but makes, at least, £500 per annum, of divinity-jobs after that manner.

Robert Chambers quotes several entries from the records and registers of such establishments in his *Book of Days*:

Marriage by Stealth

'5 November 1742, was married Benjamin Richards, of the parish of St. Martin's-in-the-Fields, Br. and Judith Lance, Do. sp. at the Bull and Garter, and gave (a guinea) for an antedate to March ye 11th in the same year, which Lilley comply'd with, and put' em in his book accordingly, there being a vacancy in the book suitable to the time.'

June 10, 1729.—John Nelson, of ye parish of St. George, Hanover, batchelor and gardener, and Mary Barnes of ye same, sp. married. Cer. dated 5 November 1727, to please their parents.

Mr. Comyngs gave me half-a-guinea to find a bridegroom, and defray all expenses. Parson 2s. 6d. Husband do., and 5.6 myself.

One man was married at least four times under different names, and received five shillings on each occasion 'for his trouble'. Sometimes the details were so sketchy they hardly seem worth recording at all; on other occasions explanatory material was added: 'To be kept secret, the lady having a jointure during the time she continued a widow.' Even the small fees charged by Fleet parsons were too much for some of their clients: 'Had a noise for four hours about the money,' noted one harassed clerk. 'Married at a barber's shop one Kerrils, for half-a-guinea, after which it was extorted out of my pocket, and for fear of my life, delivered,' wrote a windy parson.

Thomas Pennant (in *Some Account of London*) described the Fleet Street of the 1740s like this: 'In walking along the street, in my youth, on the one side next the prison, I have often been tempted by the question: *"Sir, will you be pleased to walk in and be married?"* Along this most lawless space was hung up the frequent sign of a male and female hand enjoined, with *Marriages performed within*, written beneath. A dirty fellow invited you in. The parson was seen walking before his shop; a squalid profligate figure, clad in a tattered plaid nightgown, with a fiery face, and ready to couple you for a dram of gin, or a roll of tobacco.' He makes the wedding touts sound most genteel with their 'will you be pleased to walk in and be married?', but the letter columns of the day were less polite about these 'plyers for weddings', who came in both sexes and all degrees of morality, from straightforward hustlers to virtual kidnappers. Any pedestrian or carriage travelling down Ludgate Hill or Fleet Street was soon surrounded and threatened by this competition for clients. However, on the day of *The Bunter's Wedding** (a ballad of George II's reign) it all sounds very jolly. The bride is 'dainty plump Kent Street fair Kitty, A vermin-wool-cutter by trade'; and the bridegroom 'Ben of the Borough, so pretty, Who carries a basket, 'tis said'. The wedding takes place at the *Hand and Pen*—probably the original *Hand and Pen*, a pub near Fleet Bridge which proved so popular for illegal weddings that three more establishments were set up close by, all with the same name: one was in a barber's shop and another was run by a redoubtable Mrs. Balls. In the song, Ben and his fair Kitty set out for the marriage quarter in a hackney-carriage:

> But when at Fleet Bridge they arrived,
> The bridegroom was handing his bride,

* *Bunter*: most dictionaries (including Dr. Johnson's which was written in the middle of the 18th century) give the meaning of this word as 'a woman who picks up rags about the street'. Either Ben was a rare male rag gatherer, or, as 'he carries a basket, 'tis said', perhaps in some parts of London it also meant a street hawker.

And the Bride Wore . . .

The sailors they all to him drived,
  'Do you want a parson?' they cry'd.
But as they down Fleet Ditch did prance,
  'What house shall we go to?' says Ben,
When Kitty in raptures made answer,
  'Let's go to the Hand and the Pen.'

Then into the house they did bundle,
  The landlady show'd them a room,
The landlord he roared out like thunder,
  'The parson shall wait on you soon;'
Then so eager he came for to fasten,
  He staid not to fasten his hose,
A fat-bodied, ruddy-fac'd parson,
  That brandy had painted his nose.

But before he the couple did fasten,
  He looked all around on the men,
'My fare's half-a-crown,' says the parson.
  'I freely will give it,' says Ben;
Then Hymen he presently followed,
  And the happy knot being ty'd,
The guests they whooped and hollowed,
  All joys to the bridegroom and bride.

And as they was homewards advancing,
  A-dancing and singing of songs,
The rough music met them all prancing,
  With frying-pans, shovels, and tongs,
Tin canisters, salt-boxes plenty,
  With trotter-bones beat by the boys,
And they being hollow and empty,
  They made a most racketing noise.

The street, or 'rough' musicians were on the look-out for weddings this century, as in the previous one, and they now had competition from an unlikely quarter—bands of butchers, marrow-bones and cleavers at the ready, were also eager to supply a nuptial serenade. If there were enough of them, with eight marrow-bones to represent a full octave, they were said to produce some surprisingly harmonious results. Robert Chambers, writing in the middle of the 19th century said that the 'Marrow-bone-and-Cleaver epithalamium' was 'rapidly passing among the things that were'; a sad loss, as it 'seldom failed to diffuse a good humour throughout the neighbourhood':

It was wonderful with what quickness and certainty, under the enticing presentiment of beer, the serenaders got wind of a coming marriage, and with what tenacity of purpose they would go on with their performance until the expected crown or half-crown was forthcoming. The men of Clare Market were reputed to be the best performers, and their *guerdon* was always on the highest scale accordingly. A merry rough affair it was; troublesome somewhat to the police, and not always relished by the party for whose honour it was designed; and sometimes, when a musical band came upon the ground at the same time, or

70

Plate Five

a set of boys would please to interfere with pebbles rattling in tin canisters, thus throwing a sort of burlesque on the performance, a few blows would be interchanged. . . . When this serenade happened in the evening, the men would be dressed neatly in clean blue aprons, each with a portentous wedding favour of white paper in his breast or hat.

A surprisingly large number of aristocratic bridegrooms patronised the Fleet district, and even more favoured the unconsecrated chapels which had set up shop in smarter areas of London. Out at Hampstead, the Sion Chapel offered package deals of wedding-ceremony and wedding-dinner at an all-in price, and discreetly mentioned its fashionable clientele. Marriage licences were said to be necessary, but they were never studied too carefully, if at all. In 1716, it launched an advertising campaign in London newspapers:

> Sion Chapel, at Hampstead, being a private and pleasure place, many persons of the best fashion have lately been married there. Now, as a minister is obliged constantly to attend, this is to give notice that all persons bringing a license, and who shall have their wedding-dinner in the garden, may be married in the said Chapel without giving any fee or reward whatsoever, and such as do not keep their wedding dinner at the gardens, only five shillings will be demanded of them for all fees.

By far the most famous of these higher-class establishments was the Mayfair Chapel, run by the Reverend Alexander Keith. This debonair young man started out in 1730 as the incumbent of the Mayfair Proprietory Chapel, a perfectly ordinary Church of England concern where, for several years, he behaved as a model Church of England parson. His handsome looks and witty sermons won him a fashionable congregation and a steady flow of society weddings—mostly at the expense of St. George's, Hanover Square, traditional spiritual home of high society. The Rector of St. George's was understandably saddened by the shift in allegiance, and when Keith began celebrating irregular marriages on the side (being the darling of his fashionable flock was an expensive business), the Rector moved in. In October 1742, Keith was excommunicated, and in the following April was committed to the Fleet Prison for contempt of court, or, as a writer in the *Daily Post* put it, 'for contempt of the Holy and Mother Church'.

Between excommunication and committal, the enterprising Mr. Keith opened up a marriage shop in the shadow of his old living and cheekily called it the Mayfair New Chapel. When other commitments no longer allowed him to preside there himself, he installed a substitute clergyman, and when he was apprehended, yet another. Weddings at a guinea a time enabled them all to live most comfortably (Horace Walpole called it 'a very bishopric for revenue') and for the next ten years, Mr. Keith kept elegant lodgings within the Rules but without the walls of the Fleet. There, he occupied himself in giving amusing little dinner parties and writing advertisements for his chapel:

> The way to Mayfair Chapel is through Piccadilly, by the end of St. James Street, and down Clergy [*Clarges*] Street, and turn to the left-hand. The marriages (together with a license on a five-shilling stamp and certificate) are carried on for a guinea, as usual, any time till four in the afternoon, by another

clergyman, at the little chapel in Mayfair, near Hyde Park Corner, opposite the great chapel, and within ten yards of it. There is a porch at the door like a country church porch.

He always stressed that 'porch at the door like a country church porch'. It was pleasantly innocent-sounding and a distinctive landmark, typical of Keith's commercial flair. His most famous client was the Duke of Hamilton, who married the 18-year-old Elizabeth Gunning (youngest of the two glorious Gunning girls), at the Mayfair Chapel on St. Valentine's Day 1752. Horace Walpole gave a characteristically whimsical account of the public courtship and the private wedding:

> About six weeks ago Duke Hamilton, the very reverse of the Earl, hot debauched, extravagant, and equally damaged in his fortune and person, fell in love with the youngest of the masquerade and determined to marry her in the spring. About a fortnight since, at an immense assembly at my Lord Chesterfield's, made to show the house, which is really most magnificent, Duke Hamilton made violent love at one end of the room, while he was playing at pharaoh at the other end; that is, he saw neither the bank nor his own cards, which were of three hundred pounds each: he soon lost a thousand. . . . However, two nights afterwards, being left alone with her while her mother and sister were at Bedford House, he found himself so impatient, that he sent for a parson. The doctor refused to perform the ceremony without licence or ring: the Duke swore he would send for the Archbishop—at last they were married with a ring of the bed-curtain, at half an hour after twelve at night, at Mayfair Chapel, on the 14th of February.

But the days of the Mayfair Chapel were numbered. In 1753, George II's Chancellor, Lord Hardwicke, presented a sweeping new bill before Parliament which, when it came into effect the following year, finally succeeded where nearly a century of piecemeal measures had failed: over ninety marriage chapels in and around London (including the Sion at Hampstead and Mr. Keith's in Mayfair) were forced to close their doors, and deportation instead of fines gradually cleared the Fleet area of brandy-nosed parsons. Lord Hardwicke did not win through without a struggle, however—or without figuring in many a vicious lampoon. The poor saw the bill as depriving them of cheap marriages just to protect a few heiresses, and many of the rich saw nothing wrong with the *status quo*. Leading the objectors in the House of Commons was Henry Fox,* who, appropriately, had himself run off with an heiress nine years earlier. His unlikely ally was Horace Walpole, also an M.P. At the time of Fox's marriage, Walpole had written acidly to Sir Horace Mann: 'The town has been in a great bustle about a private match . . . Mr. Fox fell in love with Lady Caroline Lenox (eldest daughter of the Duke of Richmond), asked her, was refused, and stole her. His father was a footman, her great-grandfather a king—*hinc illae lachrymae*! All the blood-royal have been up in arms.'

Fox became a mob hero: crowds followed him wherever he went, cheering and shouting 'Take care, your honour, of our wives and children!' Time and again the people took the horses from his carriage, and pulled him through the streets to

* The future Lord Holland, son of Sir Stephen Fox and father of the great Whig statesman Charles James Fox.

Westminster themselves. Walpole, on the whole, reserved his antipathy to the bill for private comment. On 22 May 1753, he wrote to Mr. Conway:

> It is well you are married! How would my Lady Ailesbury have liked to be asked in a parish church for three Sundays running? I really believe she would have worn her weeds for ever rather than have passed through so impudent a ceremony! What do *you* think? But you will want to know the interpretation of this preamble. Why, there is a new bill, which, under the notion of preventing clandestine marriages, has made such a general rummage and reform in the office of matrimony, that every Strephon and Chloe will have as many impediments and formalities to undergo as a treaty of peace. Lord Bath invented the bill, but had drawn it so ill, that the chancellor [*Lord Hardwicke*] was forced to draw a new one, and then grew so fond of his own creature, that he has crammed it down the throats of both Houses, though they gave many a gulp before they could swallow it.

Both Houses of Parliament did a fair amount of nibbling at Lord Hardwicke's proposals before they attempted to swallow at all and, as a result, Scotland escaped the new laws completely (which led to the popularity of Gretna Green), but over the rest of the country everyone except the royal family, 'the people called Quakers' and 'the persons professing the Jewish religion' had to marry with a special licence or in churches or chapels where 'banns of matrimony had been usually published' and anyone solemnising matrimony without banns or licence in any other kind of establishment, was liable to transportation 'to some of His Majesty's plantations in America for the space of fourteen years'. Destroying, forging or falsifying, with evil intent, an entry in a marriage-register, became a capital offence, and, as a final dividend, binding pre-contracts (the kind of betrothals which were virtually as serious as marriage) were done away with for ever.

There was a considerable pause between the Marriage Act being passed by Parliament and its coming into effect on Lady Day (25 March) 1754, and this, inevitably, was turned into a great irregular-marriage spree. As early as July 1753 Horace Walpole was informing George Montagu that: 'Lady Anne Paulett's daughter is eloped with a country clergyman. The Duchess of Argyle harangues against the Marriage-bill not taking place immediately, and is persuaded that all the girls will go off before next Lady-day.'

Alexander Keith had done a great publicity job against the bill, which he grandly saw as directed exclusively against himself: On the day before the bill became law, sixty-one couples were married at the Mayfair Chapel, but this was the last fling. The rest of Keith's life was spent fast within the walls of the Fleet where, deserted by smart society, all his money gone, he died four years later in a filthy communal cell in the most wretched part of the prison. As part of his campaign against the Act, he wrote an account of the lower class's attitude to marriage (*Observations on the Act for preventing Clandestine Marriages*); it was loaded to suit his argument, of course, but still most interesting:

> As I have married many thousands, and, consequently have on those occasions seen the humour of the lower class of people, I have often asked the married pair how long they had been acquainted; they would reply, some more, some

less, but the generality did not exceed the acquaintance of a week, some only of a day, half a day. . . . Another inconveniency which will arise from this Act will be, that the expense of being married will be so great that few of the lower class of people can afford it; for I have often heard a Fleet parson say that many have come to be married when they have had but half-a-crown in their pockets, and sixpence to buy a pot of beer, and for which they have pawned some of their clothes. . . . I remember once upon a time I was at a public-house at Radcliff, which then was full of sailors and their girls; there was fiddling, piping, jigging, and eating. At length one of the tars starts up and says, '— me, Jack, I'll be married just now; I will have my partner!' The joke took, and in less than two hours ten couple set out for the Fleet. I staid their return. They returned in coaches, five women in each coach; the tars, some running before, others riding on the coach-box, and others behind. The cavalcade being over, the couples went up into an upper room, where they concluded the evening with great jollity. The next time I went that way I called on my landlord, and asked him concerning this marriage adventure. He at first stared at me, but recollecting, he said those things were so frequent that he hardly took any notice of them; 'for,' added he, 'it is a common thing when a fleet comes in to have two or three hundred marriages in a week's time among the sailors.'

That the poor should have wanted cheap weddings, and young heiresses romantic ones, is understandable. But that great families with great fortunes should have happily contrived secret or, at best, unobtrusive alliances for their offspring remains mysterious. These were the people who believed in the solid marriage settlement and the glory of the great match (as opposed to the love match); it is provokingly inconsistent of them not to have wanted to cap their dynastic efforts with a suitably grand celebration. In aristocratic circles, it certainly wasn't stinginess which caused the swing away from gala nuptials, because some of the quietest weddings were given by the most brilliant hostesses, and one of the most furtive ceremonies of all took place while 500 guests were celebrating the bridegroom's 21st birthday in another part of the house, unaware that there was any additional cause for con-gratulations. One factor which may have had a bearing on the new vogue, was the growth of sentimentality. What we now think of as a Victorian simper did in fact make its appearance a good fifty years before Victoria was born. In the second half of the 18th century it was thought correct for a bride to be overcome by 'virgin sen-sibility' and over-awed by the 'awful solemnity' of the occasion. Most plays and novels were full of 'genteel sentiments' and the works of the popular Samuel Richard-son were drenched in them: *Sir Charles Grandison's* bride is much too overwhelmed by virgin confusion to attend the tenants' party celebrating her marriage; and Lady G. comments to her sister on this occasion: 'After all, Lady L——, we women, dressed out in ribands, and in gaudy trappings, and in virgin-white, on our wedding days, seem but like milk-white heifers led to sacrifice.' A public wedding in a crowded church was more than modesty could bear, and as for a public bedding. . . .

This was not the climate in which garter-grabbing and stocking-flinging could survive and except in boisterous country areas all these customs now died out. In their place the honeymoon began to emerge and, for the first time, a degree of seclusion was allowed to newly-weds. To begin with they took off the morning after the wedding to spend a few days quietly at the home of close friends; later, some young couples drove away immediately the ceremony was over, leaving relatives and guests to celebrate without them; a few even went to one of their own houses entirely alone: a most startling idea. It was a trend which began with the nobility and filtered down the social scale very slowly, and it was called 'going away'. The word *honeymoon* had been in use as early as the 16th century and before that *honey-month* described the blissful first weeks of marriage, but these were rather low-class words. *Going away* was very genteel.

This early seclusion was usually very brief. Social duty soon called society couples back to town to receive and return the calls of well-wishers, and any girl who had the *entrée* at court, was expected to be presented anew, as a married woman, within a few days of the wedding. Most brides wore white and silver again for their curtsey to the king and queen, though usually not the same white and silver they were married in. In January 1778, Mrs. Delany described Lady Caroline Dawson, who had been presented that morning, 'in her bridal apparel, glittering like the moon in a lympid stream, white and silver, or rather all silver—the prettiest silk I ever saw—and richly trimm'd with silver, festooned and betassel'd, and her lace as fine as if my *enemy* had woven it' (Mrs. Delany was much admired for her needlework). In 1774 she reported: 'The fashion for brides being presented in white *is out*, and so, tho' she [*the new Lady Clanbrassil*] has a very pretty white and silver, she is to be presented in *pink* trimmed with Brussels lace—the trimming cost 70 pound.' It was only a passing fad, and white and silver were soon firmly back in favour once more.

Mrs. Delany was a splendid correspondent who, through her letters, first to her sister and then to a favourite god-daughter, has left us one of the best social portraits of England during the 18th century. She was born Mary Granville, a niece of Lord Lansdowne; and as a beauty but not 'a fortune', was married off at 18 to Alexander Pendarves, a man more than three times her age and very unattractive indeed; then, later in life, she married an Irish friend of the Irish Dean Swift, the Reverend Patrick Delany. (As she is usually known by her last married name, this is the one I have kept to throughout; it is not strictly accurate for the first half of her life, of course, but it is a lot less confusing.) Even Mrs. Delany fails to throw any light on why weddings had become so secretive, though she gives many a delightful description of the new *mariages à la mode*. Although she never made a great match herself, she lived for most of her life in very high society and had a wealth of glittering, relentlessly fashionable friends and relations; of them all, none shone more brightly than her cousin, Georgiana Caroline Carteret, daughter of John Lord Carteret (afterwards Earl Granville), a god-daughter of George II and Queen Caroline, and very much a beauty. In 1734, at the age of 18, cousin Georgiana made a suitably brilliant match, marrying the favourite grandson of the great Sarah, Duchess of Marlborough (by then, the dowager duchess). Mrs. Delany filled in the details for her sister, Ann:

> Now you expect some account of our cousin Spencer. They were married on Thursday between eight and nine o' the clock at night. After they were married they played a pool at commerce, supped at ten, went to bed between twelve and one, and went to Windsor Lodge the next day at noon, and are to return on Monday. . . . Her clothes were white satin embroidered with silver, very fine lace; and the jewels the Duchess of Marlborough gave. . . . The rest of her clothes are a pink and silver, a flowered silk, white ground, a blue damask night-gown, and a white damask the robing and facings embroidered with gold and

colours; a pink plain poudesoy, a flowered silk, green ground, her laces and linen very fine. Everybody at the wedding was magnificent. Lady Dysart, white and purple and silver, Lady Weymouth, blue and silver. Their clothes are now laid by for the royal wedding, which will be about three weeks hence, 'tis thought.

Lady Dysart and Lady Weymouth were sisters of the bride; and the royal wedding for which they were reserving their finery was that of George II's eldest daughter, the Princess Royal, which did in fact take place a month later, on 14 March. Mrs. Delany also described marriages in the next two generations of the Spencer family: those of her cousin's son (John, once more, like his father), and of his daughter (another Georgiana). By the time these events took place, John Spencer senior had died, and his beautiful widow had married Lord Cowper; but she was still way out in the van-guard of fashion, as she remained all her life, and the wedding she organised for her son was the very epitome of *chic*. The triumphant return to London, and the pre-sentation at court, which followed, were remembered and talked of for half a century and more.

Young Spencer had been wooing Miss Margaret Georgiana Poyntz (or Pointz as it was usually spelt at that time) for more than a year and hoped to marry her as soon as he came of age. This happened during the Christmas holidays of 1755 when both families were gathered at the Spencer country home, Althorp, in Northamptonshire. The house party had begun on 12 December and on the 19th, John Spencer's 21st birthday, he asked Mrs. Poyntz's permission to marry her daughter the following day. Mrs. Delany caught up with the story in mid-January and speedily relayed it to her sister:

> There were magnificent doings at Althorpe, and nobody could have acquitted themselves with more dignity and given more universal content than Mr. Spencer did. When his birthday came he told Mrs. Pointz it was his firm resolution to make Miss Pointz his wife as soon as he was master of himself; that now he was, he entreated her leave that he might be married the next day. You may believe that request was granted, and it was so managed that nobody in the house, though near 500 people, knew anything of the matter but Lord and Lady Cowper, Mrs. Pointz and her eldest son; and it was not declared till the Saturday after. On the 20th of December, after tea, the parties necessary for the wedding stole by degrees from the company into Lady Cowper's dressing-room, where the ceremony was performed, and they returned different ways to the company again, who had begun dancing, and they joined with them. After supper every-body retired as usual to their different apartments, and the marriage was not known till the Saturday following.

Mrs. Poyntz and her daughter were obviously not caught unprepared; in the same letter, Mrs. Delany lists the bride's *trousseau*: 'She had four negligees, four night-gowns, four mantuas and petticoats.* She was married in a white and silver with embroidered facings and robings in silver done by Mrs. Glegg. Her first suit she went to Court in was white and silver, as fine as brocade and trimming could make it;

---

* *Negligees* and *mantuas* were dresses for day wear. *Nightgowns* were what we now call 'evening dresses'. *Petticoats* sometimes formed the complete skirt of an ensemble (with a separate bodice to make 'a suit of clothes'), sometimes they were partly covered by the divided or decoratively tucked-up skirt of the negligée, mantua or nightgown.

the second, blue and silver; the third, white and gold and colours, six pounds a yard; the fourth, plain pink-coloured satin. The diamonds worth twelve thousand pounds: her earrings three drops all diamonds, *no paltry scrolls of silver*. Her necklace more perfect brilliants, the middle stone worth a thousand pounds, set at the edge with small brilliants. . . . Lady Cowper says he [*the bridegroom*] may spend near thirty thousand pound a-year without hurting himself.'

Lady Hervey, another of the spirited beauties in which the 18th century abounded, described the wedding party's dramatic return to London in a disapproving letter to the Reverend Edmund Morris: 'One has heard of nothing for some time past but the magnificence, or rather the silly, vain procession on account of Mr. Spencer's wedding; and, what is most extraordinary is, that it was quite disagreeable to both young people, and entirely the effect of the vanity and folly of a daughter of Lord Granville's; I mean Lady Cowper, Mr. Spencer's mother. They came to town from Althorp, where they were married, with three coaches and six horses, and two hundred horsemen. The villages through which they passed were put into the greatest consternation: some of the poor people shut themselves up in their houses and cottages, barricading themselves up as well as they could. Those who were more resolute or more desperate, arming themselves with pitchforks, stakes and spades; all crying out it was the *invasion* which was come; and to be sure, three coaches and six horses, both the Pretender and King of France were come too. In short, great was the alarm, and happy they were when the formidable cavalcade passed through without setting fire to the habitations.' (The Hanoverians had been kings of England for more than 40 years by this time, but the 1745 Stuart uprising was still reasonably sharp in people's minds.)

In mid-February, seven weeks after the wedding, Mrs. Delany told her sister: 'Mrs. Spencer is pulled to pieces about visiting, which is unreasonable; she has had 600 persons to visit her, has been in London but five weeks, and twice confined with a cold; but it is the *only* fault laid to her charge, so she is well off.'

At the beginning of the century, London brides were at home to friends the day after the wedding. Later, when 'going away' became popular, the visiting became more spread out, and, as with the new Mrs. Spencer, paying return visits could take many weeks. In America, according to a letter quoted by Mrs. A. M. Earle (who wrote on American costume at the turn of this present century), the bride and groom, the bride's parents, and the bridegroom's parents all kept open house the day after the wedding. Describing the social whirl caused by this custom in New York, the writer said:

> The Gentleman's Parents keep Open house just in the same manner as the Bride's Parents. The Gentlemen go from the Bridegroom's house to drink Punch with and give Joy to his Father. The Bride's visitors go in the same manner from the Bride's to her mother's to pay their compliments to her. There is so much driving about at these times that in our narrow streets there is some danger. The Wedding-house resembles a bee-hive. Company perpetually flying in and out.

In Boston, by the end of the century, the pace was gentler, as young Anna Green Winslow shows with an entry in her diary for 1771; 'On the 6 Mr. Sam Jarvis

77

married Miss Suky Pierce; on the 11 I made her a visit in company with Mamma and many others. The bride was dress'd in a white Satin night-gownd.'

On both sides of the Atlantic, visiting was often prolonged by tours to see relatives in different parts of the country, as had been done the previous century. And in America, the young people also went off on one-day jaunts to neighbouring plantations or townships, riding on horseback in their best wedding finery: the gentlemen in embroidered velvet coats and waistcoats, satin knee-breeches and silk stockings, their curled and powdered hair topped by tricorn hats; and behind them, riding pillion, the girls in brightly-coloured petticoats, high-heeled shoes, hats tipped over their foreheads, and waving feathers to crown the lot.

When the former Miss Poyntz had long since returned all her 600 visits, she produced a daughter, and called her Georgiana: and 17 years later, in June 1774, it became the turn of the Lady Georgiana to marry. (Her father had been created Earl Spencer in the meantime, which was how the bride became a Lady.) Her bridegroom was 'the first match in England', the 5th Duke of Devonshire, 26 years old and immensely rich. The wedding itself was slightly less dashing than that of her parents, but once again it took place in the midst of birthday celebrations and was wreathed in mystery. The main anniversary this time was that of the King, George III, who was 36 on 4th June. The royal birthday was marked by a grand court ball, and Lady Georgiana danced at this with her husband-to-be, on the eve of her wedding—though apparently the secrecy was so thick on this occasion that even she did not know she was to be married next day. The wedding had been expected to take place two days later, on the 7th, as Mrs. Delany explained to her god-daughter, Mrs. Port:

> The *great* wedding is over, and at last a surprise, for this was the expected day; but they managed very cleverly as they were all at the birthday, and the Duke and Duchess danced at the ball. It was a great secret to Lady Gᵃ Spencer as to the world. *Sunday morning* she was told her doom; she went out of town (to Wimbleton) early on Sunday, and they were married at Wimbleton church, between church and church, as quietly and uncrowded as if John and Joan had tied the Gordian knot. Don't think because I have made use of the word '*doom*,' that it was a melancholy sentence (though a *surprise*) to the young lady; for she is so peculiarly happy, as to think his Grace *very agreable*, and had not the least regret—a bliss which I most sincerely hope will prove a lasting one. The Duke's intimate friends say he has sense and does not want merit—to be sure the jewel has *not* been well *polished*. . . . Nobody was at the wedding but the Duchess of Portland and Lady Cowper, as fine and as gay as a bride herself.

Mrs. Delany doesn't quite seem to have approved of her cousin who was still 'fine and as gay as a bride' at the age of 58; but as Mrs. Port was the loving god-daughter of Lady Cowper as well as of Mrs. Delany, the disapproval was never expressed. The Devonshire match had been generally expected for a considerable time before it came off (Horace Walpole was announcing it to friends the previous March); only the date was kept darkly secret. We don't know what the new Duchess wore for that early morning trip to Wimbledon church, but it was almost certainly white and silver like her mother and grandmother before her. Throughout the century, in town and country, it was an unusual bride who could afford white and yet did not wear it. 'But what are your wedding clothes, sister?' asks Fanny, in Colman and Garrick's play,

The Clandestine Marriage; 'Oh, white and silver, to be sure you know', answers Miss Sterling, daughter of a wealthy city merchant. And in the Reverend Henry Rowe's *Happy Village*, the gay colours worn by the guests give 'pleasing contrast' to the country bride's 'modest white'.

In America the virgin trend gained ground more slowly. There, judging by the many wedding dresses still in existence (in small museums or kept as private family treasures), yellow was the favourite colour, and heavy brocade the most popular fabric. An excellent example is the dress worn by Miss Mary Leverett when she married Lieutenant-Colonel John Denison of Salem, Massachusetts, in 1719: it has a low-cut neck, very tight, pointed bodice, a full skirt bouncing from a tiny waist, and elbow-length sleeves ending in two flattering frills—all in the same rich yellow brocade. According to Mrs. Earle, this gown was also worn by 'a bride of later years who threw it out of her window, jumped after it, and was married in it to the man of her choice'. Second favourite colour in the eastern states was blue, and Mrs. Vanderbilt (in her *Social History of Flatbush*), tells of a most striking 'his' and 'hers' wedding duet, when the bride wore a gown of fawn-coloured silk over a light-blue damask petticoat and the bridegroom wore a waistcoat of the same blue damask. By the middle of the century, bridal white was beginning to emerge. The Library of the American Antiquarian Society (Worcester, Mass.) has a delightful piece of tapestry, embroidered in 1756, which shows a wedding procession to the Old South Church, Boston, with the bride in a white lace cap and white gown with panier-hoops (a hoop on each hip, extending the skirt as much as 18 inches either side). It is a dress which would not have looked out of place at a reception at St. James's Palace, but outside the very bare, very new little Boston church and next to a gentleman on horseback, it looks a little too defiant of its surroundings.

A flesh-and-blood bride who wore white was Elizabeth Pepperell, daughter of Sir William Pepperell, the first native-born American to be made a baronet. When she married Colonel Nathaniel Sparhawk, her father wrote to England for the *trousseau* in the best established manner, ordering 'white watered *Tabby*,* with *Gold Lace* for trimming of it' for her wedding dress, plus a fan mounted in leather (for 20 shillings); two pairs of silk shoes with clogs (chopines, for wearing in the street) a size larger; 'twelve yards of Green Padusoy; thirteen yards of lace for a woman's Head Dress 2 inches wide as can be bought for 13 shillings a yard . . . silk to make a woman a full suit of Clothes; the Ground to be white Padusoy and flowered with all sorts of Coulers suitable for a young woman'.

This last material sounds remarkably similar to one chosen by a slightly earlier Sparhawk bride, but this time for her wedding gown: when Miss Jane Porter married the Reverend John Sparhawk, minister of the First Church of Salem, in 1736, she wore 'white silk, brocaded—to use Dante's words "in flowers of noble colours"'. The design was of great baskets of red, blue and raisin-coloured blooms, with trailing green ferns and branches to link them. It was made up into a gown with a loose sack-back (ideal for showing off the bold pattern), elbow-length sleeves, and a deeply-scooped neckline; not the kind of outfit we associate with church today, but the minister's wife is said to have worn it not only for her quiet wedding, but also for her first appearance 'coming out bride'.

---

* *Tabby*—a silk material, sometimes plain but more often watered.

America had given up the battle with sumptuary laws, though there were still inducements to dress plainly: in Connecticut, anyone who wore gold or silver lace, gold or silver buttons, silk ribbons, silk scarfs, or bone lace worth more than three shillings a yard, was automatically taxed as being worth £150 a year. In Virginia, unmarried men were taxed according to what they wore; and married men according to what their families wore. The Abbé Robin, who visited America just after the Revolution, shows what a cruelly realistic piece of legislation this last tax must have been: 'Piety', he said, 'is not the only motive which induces American women to be constant in their attendance at church. Having no places of public amusement, no fashionable promenades, they go to church to display their fine dress. They often appear in silks, and covered with superbe ornaments.'

Surprisingly, this also appears to have been true of the Quakers. Mrs. Amelia Gummere gives a wonderful description of a Quaker bride and groom (in her book *The Quaker, A Study in Costume*) and it is the exact opposite of the gloomy picture which comes most easily to mind:

> In the month of May, 1771, Isaac Collins, of Burlington, N.J., married Rachel Budd, of Philadelphia, at the 'Bank Meeting', in that city. His wedding dress was a coat of peach blossom cloth, the great skirts of which had outside pockets; it was lined throughout with quilted white silk. The large waistcoat was of the same material. He wore small clothes, knee buckles, silk stockings and pumps— a cocked hat surmounted the whole. The bride, who is described as 'lovely in mind and person', wore a light blue brocade, shoes of the same material, with very high heels—not larger at the sole than a gold dollar—and sharply pointed at the toes. Her dress was in the fashion of the day, consisting of a robe, long in the back, with a large hoop. A short blue bodice with a white satin stomacher embroidered in colours, had a blue cord laced from side to side. On her head she wore a black mode hood lined with white silk, the large cape extending over the shoulders. Upon her return from meeting after the ceremony, she put on a thin white apron of ample dimensions tied in front with a large blue bow.

The apron would have been purely decorative, in the style of the day, and the black hood (a German fashion) was thought to be as essential to an 18th century Pennsylvanian bride as a white veil today. Men, everywhere, were just as fashion conscious as their wives, though in summer in the Southern States it was often difficult to persuade them to wear wigs, even for such important occasions as weddings. In 1735, William Byrd (the tobacco planter who founded the town of Richmond, Virginia) said that at home the planters went around in 'negligee costumes, banians and night caps'. The banians, or banyans, were loose robes of light-weight cloth, rather like a dressing gown, and these were generally confined to the home, but a surprised English traveller, writing to the *London Magazine* ten years later, shows that the night-caps had escaped and were freely worn all over the place: '''Tis an odd sight, that except some of the very Elevated sort few Persons wear Perukes, so that you would imagine they were all sick or going to bed; common People wear Woolen and Yarn Caps, but the better ones wear white Holland or Cotton. Thus they travel fifty miles from Home. It may be cooler for ought I know, but methinks 'tis very ridiculous.' It would certainly not have done for London where (according to Lady

Mary Pierrepoint) the gentlemen wore 'Fring'd Gloves, embroider'd Coats, and powder'd wigs in irresistable Curl'.

Not every British bride wore white, of course, and for those who chose a coloured wedding dress the two most favoured alternatives were the same two shades chosen by most American girls: yellow and blue. (Lilac was a close runner-up in both countries.) Blue has long been associated with constancy (most probably because it is the traditional colour of the Virgin's robe) and in the 16th century it was a favourite choice for bride-laces. Yellow was the classic colour of Hymen, god of marriage. But whether any of this actually influenced 18th century brides on either side of the Atlantic, is dubious. About the importance of white and silver, however, there is not a shadow of doubt, as Oliver Goldsmith makes clear in *The Good-Natur'd Man* (1768); while his heroine prepares to elope to Gretna Green, her maid laments: 'I wish you could take the white and silver to be married in. It's the worst luck in the world, in anything but white.' (Inevitably, she knew of a disaster when a bride had worn another colour: 'I knew one Bet Stubbs, of our town, that was married in red; and, as sure as eggs is eggs, the bridegroom and she had a miff before morning.')

In 1769, Lady Mary Coke described a girl 'who by her dress was a bride . . . in white and silver', but it was still a discerning eye which could make such an assessment; for, white and silver a wedding dress might be, but in all other respects it closely followed the fashion of the day and was expected to do duty on other occasions, too. To add to the difficulty, while nowadays we usually leave white for the bride alone, in the 18th century the bridesmaids and even the guests were often dressed in white, too; and, if the guest were a recent bride herself, the white she wore might well be her own wedding gown. Mrs. Georgiana Spencer was dressed in 'white satin embroidered with silver', the exact description of the dress she was married in, when she attended the wedding of the Princess Royal a month after her own marriage. Her sister, Lady Weymouth, who had been married a good deal longer, was also in white, 'white brocaded lutestring* with silver'. When a daughter of the future Viscount Curzon married in 1778, her *stepmother* was dressed all in white. And in 1791, at the fashionably quiet wedding of the Lady Charlotte Bertie and Lord Cholmondeley nearly all the ladies were in white, as Horace Walpole told Miss Mary Berry: 'Well, our wedding is over, very properly, though with little ceremony, for the men were in frocks [*frock-coats*] and white waistcoats, most of the women in white, and no diamonds but on the Duke's wife; and nothing of ancient fashion, but two bride-maids: the endowing purse I believe has been left off, ever since broad pieces were called in and melted down.† We were but eighteen persons in all, chiefly near relations of each side, and of each side a friend of two . . . the poor Duchess-mother [*the Dowager-Duchess of Ancaster, mother of the bride*] wept excessively . . . she goes directly to Spa, where the new-married are to meet her. We all separated in an hour and half.'

---

* *Lutestring*—a fine, shiny taffeta, sometimes called *Lustring*, a more descriptive version of the name.

† *The endowing purse, or dow purse*—this refers to the custom of the bridegroom presenting a purse of money to the bride as he promised 'with all my worldly goods I thee endow'. A relic of marriage by purchase, it was still practised in parts of rural England during the next century, but not at society weddings.

And the Bride Wore . . .

The wedding took place at the Dowager-Duchess's house in Berkeley Square. Lord Cholmondeley and his bride drove off immediately afterwards, to spend a few days alone at his seat at Beckenham, Kent, before joining the Dowager-Duchess at Spa (most probably the Belgium health resort of that name, which was popular with English society throughout the century). It was all most stylish, which must have been a great relief to Walpole, for, even at the age of 73, he was trendy as ever. When the date was first set for this marriage (at fashionably short notice) he had told Miss Berry: 'The wedding is to be this day sevennight—save me, my old stars! from wedding-dinners! but I trust they are not of this age. I should sooner expect Hymen to jump out of a curricle and walk into the Duchess's dressing-room in boots and a dirty shirt.'

It was an odd situation: this surreptitious attitude to marriage, and yet everyone dressing up in white. The idea of wedding favours seems even more incongruous, yet they were still given, even at the quietest affairs. By the end of the century, these too were white, coloured ribbons being used only by what an 18th century commentator would have unflinchingly called 'the vulgar'. Fanny Burney mentioned white favours in an account of a most informal wedding which took place in 1790, while she was living at Court as Assistant Keeper of the Robes to Queen Charlotte. In her diary, Miss Burney had code names for the main characters in this episode: the real life Miss Gunning became, wittily, 'Miss Fuzilier', and Colonel Digby, an equerry to George III, 'Mr. Fairly'. Miss Burney had had her own sights on the Colonel and had persuaded herself that her chances were good. Even when everyone else could see the way things were shaping, she was still protesting to her sister that Miss Fuzilier, though 'pretty, learned, and accomplished' had not 'heart enough to satisfy Mr. Fairly'; and in June 1788 she was sure that there was 'no manner of truth in the report relative to Mr. Fairly and Miss Fuzilier'. Eighteen months later, in January 1790, she had to record the bitter truth:

> Mr. Fairly was married the 6th. . . . One evening, about this time, Mr. Fisher, now Doctor, drank tea with us at Windsor, and gave me an account of Mr. Fairly's marriage that much amazed me. He had been called upon to perform the ceremony. It was by special licence, and at the house of Sir R—— F—— [*the bride's father*].
>
> So religious, so strict in all ceremonies, even, of religion, as he always appeared, his marrying out of a church was to me very unexpected. Dr. Fisher was himself suprised, when called upon, and said he supposed it must be to please the lady.
>
> Nothing, he owned, could be less formal or solemn than the whole. Lady C., Mrs. and Miss S., and her father and brother and sister, were present. They all dined together at the usual hour, and then the ladies, as usual, retired. Some time after, the clerk was sent for, and then, with the gentlemen, joined the ladies, who were in the drawing-room, seated on sofas, just as at any other time. Dr. Fisher says he is not sure they were working, but the air of common employment was such, that he rather thinks it, and everything of that sort was spread about, as on any common day—work-boxes, netting-cases, etc. etc.!
>
> Mr Fairly then asked Dr Fisher what they were to do? He answered, he could not tell; for he had never married anybody in a room before.
>
> Upon this, they agreed to move a table to the upper end of the room, the ladies still sitting quietly, and then put on it candles and a prayer-book. Dr

Marriage by Stealth

Fisher says he hopes it was not a card-table, and rather believes it was only a Pembroke work-table.

The lady and Sir R. then came forward, and Dr Fisher read the service.

So this, methinks, seems the way to make all things easy!

Yet—with so little solemnity—without even a room prepared and empty—to go through a business of such portentous seriousness! 'Tis truly amazing from a man who seemed to delight so much in religious regulations and observances. Dr Fisher himself was dissatisfied, and wondered at his compliance, though he attributed the plan to the lady.

The bride behaved extremely well, he said, and was all smile and complacency. He had never seen her to such advantage, or in such soft looks before; and perfectly serene, though her sister was so much moved as to go into hysterics.

Afterwards, at seven o'clock, the bride and bridegroom set off for a friend's house in Hertfordshire by themselves, attended by servants with white favours. The rest of the party, father, sister, and priest included, went to the play, which happened to be Benedict.

The veil, most tell-tale of all bridal gear today, was not worn at all during the 18th century; and the garland of flowers was replaced, at both private and public weddings, by caps, bonnets or hats, all usually trimmed with lace (the variety known as *blonde* was the most favoured). At several times hair-styles rose to such absurd heights that any ardent follower of fashion could place nothing on top of them but trimmings—though there was plenty of room for these. During Queen Anne's reign, in the winter of 1711, Lady Mary Pierrepoint sent news of London *modes* to a friend in Yorkshire: 'As to Dresse, tis divided into Partys; all the High Church Ladies affect to wear Heads in the Imitation of Steeples, and on their Muffs roses . . . the other Side, the low Party (of which I declare my selfe) wear little low Heads and long ribbands to their Muffs.' Again in the 1770s, the cartoonists had tremendous fun with milliners climbing ladders to add the final touches to their creations and clients wedged tight into doorways, trapped by the outrageously decorated mountains balanced on their heads. Beaulard, a French milliner, became a national hero by inventing *bonnets à la bonne mamman*, which could be lowered to present a reasonable 'head' to a disapproving mother, or instantly raised to a fashionable three-feet when out of her sight. These were also a boon in carriages and sedan chairs where most women had to kneel or sit with their faces in their laps to accommodate the mounds of false-hair, horse-hair, wool, glue, feathers, ribbon and gauze.

The daughter of Assheton Curzon (later Viscount Curzon) obviously kept her head to a reasonable height, because she was able to top it with a 'beautifull white hat trimm'd with blond' when she married Sir George Smith of Nottinghamshire in January 1778.

Horace Walpole's niece Maria (illegitimate daughter of his brother Sir Edward Walpole) had also worn a hat when she married the Earl of Waldegrave some nineteen years earlier. Uncle Horace was charmed by everything to do with this wedding, as he told his old friend George Montagu on 16 May 1759: 'Well! Maria was married yesterday. Don't we manage well? the original day was not once put off: lawyers and milliners were all ready canonically. It was as sensible a wedding as ever was. There was neither form nor indecency, both which generally meet on such occasions. They were married at my brother's in Pall-Mall, just before dinner, by

Mr. Keppel; the company, my brother, his son, Mrs. Keppel, and Charlotte, Lady Elizabeth Keppel, Lady Betty Waldegrave, and I. We dined there; the Earl and new Countess got into their post-chaise at eight o'clock, and went to Havestock [*in Essex*] alone, where they stay till Saturday night: on Sunday she is to be presented. . . . Maria was in a white silver gown, with a hat very much pulled over her face; what one could see of it was handsomer than ever; a cold maiden blush gave her the sweetest delicacy in the world.'

Walpole was even more delighted by his niece's second wedding. In 1766, she married George III's brother, the 24-year-old Duke of Gloucester, in the secret wedding to beat all secret weddings: at the evening ceremony in the same Pall Mall drawing-room, there were no witnesses at all, except the bride's own domestic chaplain who married them and then, with considerable tact, died shortly afterwards. As Lord Hardwicke's Act had not covered royal unions, the marriage was eventually allowed to be legal (just in time to make the first child born of it legitimate). Another royal brother, the Duke of Cumberland, announced, at about the same time, that he too was secretly married, and his union was also reluctantly recognised by the King. When the *furore* died down, the Royal Marriage Act was drawn up, making it illegal for any member of the royal family to marry in the future without the prior consent of the sovereign. (Only the approval of both houses of parliament could over-rule a royal negative, and then only if the petitioner were over 25.)

Apart from clandestine efforts such as these, Hanoverian weddings were kept with commendable style, though, after the first one, which was celebrated with extra-ordinary pomp, even these more orthodox occasions were family rather than public events. None of Queen Anne's seventeen children lived to marriageable age, and when she, the last of the Stuarts, died without an heir in 1714, it was her third cousin, the 54-year-old Elector of Hanover, who became king (George I) of England, inheriting through his grandmother, the little Princess Elizabeth (daughter of James I) whose wedding in 1613 had been carried out with such fairy-tale extravagance. The new king had been married in Hanover in 1682, divorced his wife for infidelity twelve years later, and brought only mistresses with him to England. His dapper little son, the future George II, also married in Germany; so it was not until his children reached marrying age that Britain had her first taste of royal wedding excitement for over fifty years. And then, it was unusually worth waiting for. George II's eldest daughter, Anne, the Princess Royal, was the first to make it to a British altar and she did so amidst celebrations which were patterned on none other than the extravaganza which had launched James I's daughter on married life 120 years before. This time, however, neither bride nor groom were quite the stuff of which story-book romance is made. The Princess was short, fat, 25 and badly marked by the smallpox; and her husband-to-be, the Prince of Orange, was uncharitably called 'a monster' by British courtiers. (The Princess had been told she could refuse the Prince if she wished, but said she would marry him if he were a baboon. 'Well then,' answered the King, 'there is baboon enough for you.') The marriage date was set for 12 November 1733 and in preparation for the ceremony, a large wooden gallery was built to link St. James's Palace with the small French Chapel a few hundred yards away in the grounds. The old Duchess of Marlborough (favourite of Queen Anne and no great friend of the Hanoverians), whose Marlborough House stood next to the chapel, had not been pleased with anything she had heard about the wedding, and now she was furious. The wretched wooden building could be seen from her windows and darkened many of them; she was afraid 'the mob', trying to see what was going on inside, would pull down her garden wall and 'do a mischief to the house, or rob it'. Leaving soldiers on guard in London, she moved herself well out of the way, and, from the comfortable distance of Windsor, fired off a series of acid letters to her grand-daughter, the Duchess of Bedford, about 'our pompous wedding'.

She had heard that the Prince of Orange was not going to be allowed to see the Princess 'till they go in procession to be married, which seems to me very odd'; and, remembering the simple, inexpensive weddings of Queen Mary and Queen Anne in the previous century, deplored the high cost of this one, especially at a moment when the economy was unstable. No marriage tax was levied this time, but like any other citizen, the Duchess had a shrewd suspicion that she would still end up paying the bill: 'This great fall in stocks which affects so many, must make this ridiculous expense in the state of this wedding, I should think very provoking, for by some contrivance or other, to be sure, the nation must pay for all. . . .' She also bristled at the news that peers and peeresses were 'to be summoned to walk at this great ceremony. I am glad to know that two very considerable peers of my acquaintance will not be there, and they say that the peeresses are to walk in gowns as they did at the coronation. This must put them to a great expense, which is no matter since I think none but simple people and sad wretches will do it. The writing sent to the ladies that carry up the train is that the King requires them to attend the Princess Royal for that purpose and to come in a proper dress. It seems the precedent for this great pomp is that of King James the first when his daughter was married, who was a weak and poor creature as ever you have seen and nonsense has followed that precedent, as these great ladies carry up the Princess Royal's train when she goes to church. I want to know if they will carry it when she comes back, and is the wife to the Prince of Orange, who all his countrymen sit down with.'

Her sentiments were not so much republican as anti-Hanoverian, for when she heard that the Lord Mayor of London had been allotted 300 tickets for the spectacle, she uttered a fine snort of disapproval about the 'sturdy beggars' they would go to. For two weeks she built up a marvellous head of vituperation, and then came the anti-climax: the day before the wedding, the bridegroom was taken ill during Sunday morning service at the Dutch Church in London, and the whole thing was postponed indefinitely. 'I wonder when my neighbour George will remove his orange chest', said the Duchess, regarding the monstrous wooden gallery with a slight return to good humour.

The Prince of Orange, recovered, embarked on a convalescent tour of Britain, and it was not until four months later that wedding excitement struck again. On 2 March, Mrs. Delany wrote to her sister: 'The day for the royal nuptials is not yet named; the Prince is to be in town on Monday next.' On the 14th the marriage was on. It took place that evening 'in the greatest order'. The inside of the despised wooden gallery was transformed with gold, silver and velvet draperies and hundreds of candles, and through this brightly lit passage-way, flanked by rows of spectators (it was said to be large enough to hold 4000) passed the royal family in great state, surrounded by their suites and led by drums, trumpets and kettle-drums, the Serjeant Trumpeter bearing the mace, the Master of Ceremonies, the Lord Chamberlain and the Vice-Chamberlain.

First came the bridegroom, between two bachelor Knights of the Garter, his

85

numerous Household walking fore and aft. Then the Court officials and musicians (not playing) returned to the Palace for the bride, who, dressed in 'Virgin robes of silver tissue', a coronet on her head and 'several bars of diamonds' on her sleeves, walked between her two brothers, the Prince of Wales and the Duke of Cumberland, with eight unmarried peers' daughters to carry her train ('six yards long laced around with massy lace adorned with fringe and tassells'). The suites of the Princess and her brothers preceded them, walking 'one by one in a line'. Then came more unmarried daughters of peers, followed, despite the Duchess of Marlborough's gloomy prophesies, by the peeresses, walking in pairs according to precedence.

The ceremony over, everyone was led back to the royal apartments through the gallery in the same manner, but this time the Prince of Orange was supported by two married dukes (according to the ancient custom); and his bride, though still with her brothers and the same bridesmaids, was immediately followed by the married peeresses, while their unmarried daughters now brought up the rear. (The Duchess of Marlborough thought bride and groom should have been allowed to walk back to the Palace together, instead of in separate processions.)

At 11 o'clock that night, the Royal family supped in public, in the great state ballroom, and at 'about one the Bride and Bridegroom retired, and were afterwards seen by the nobility, &c. sitting up in their bedchamber in rich undresses'.

The wedding was an opportunity for the whole country to show their allegiance to the House of Hanover—and to cast a side-long glance at any neighbour thought still to be harbouring hopes of a Stuart revival. On 20 March, Ann Granville wrote from Gloucester: 'There are many places more polite than our city, but I assure you *none more loyal*. There was such *general rejoicing* that it really *gave one spirits*, and great illuminations at night. My mother made all her windows very bright, as was the whole square, only one house, and they *suffered for it*.'

For royal brides there was still no 'going away'. On the evening following this wedding the Prince of Orange and his Princess were on show at a court 'drawing-room', accepting the good wishes of all who had the *entrée*. The bride's dress on this occasion was, according to Mrs. Delany 'the prettiest thing that ever was seen—a *corps de robe*, that is, in *plain English*, a stiff-bodied gown . . . white damask, with the finest embroidery of rich embossed gold and festoons of flowers intermixed in their natural colours. On one side of her head she had a green diamond of vast size, the shape of a pear, and two pearls prodigiously large that were fastened to wires and hung loose upon her hair: on the other side small diamonds prettily disposed; her earrings, necklace, and bars to her stays all extravagantly fine, presents of the Prince of Orange to her.' The bridesmaids, 'the eight peers' daughters' that held up her train, 'were in the same new style of gown: all white and silver, with great quantities of jewels in their hair, and long locks: some of them were very pretty and well shaped —it is a most becoming dress'. The bridegroom was in 'gold stuff embroidered with silver' which 'looked very rich but not showy'.

Three years later, when the Princess's brother, Frederick, Prince of Wales, married Princess Augusta of Saxe-Gotha, Mrs. Delany told Dean Swift: 'Monstrous preparations are making for the royal wedding. Pearl, gold and silver, embroidered on gold and silver tissues.' But never again in this century were the preparations to be quite as 'monstrous' as those for the Princess Royal. Future Hanoverian brides and

Plate Six

bridegrooms married in the Chapel Royal, within St. James's Palace (no more wooden orange boxes); court society was present both for the evening ceremony and for the drawing-room next day, but the great state fanfare was not repeated. The public could watch the arrival of the foreign bride or bridegroom into the city, after that they had to rely on the newspapers; the main ceremony took place behind high palace walls, witnessed only by the privileged 'family' of the court. (Royal marriages reflected one more social trend: brides and bridegrooms were getting older. Many royal brides were over 25 and most of their husbands were over 30; slightly lower down the social scale, 18 was considered to be a good marrying age for girls and the middle-to-late-twenties for the men. Twelve-year-old brides had gone out of fashion.)

One of the most written about royal weddings of the 18th century was that of George III and the young Princess Charlotte of Mecklenburg-Strelitz—and Horace Walpole did most of the writing. George III was only 22 when he came to the throne (his father, Frederick, Prince of Wales, had died ten years earlier, and so he succeeded his grandfather, George II). After two stolid, Hanover-loving monarchs, the young King appeared to be most promising: 'This Sovereign don't stand in one spot, with his eyes fixed royally on the ground, and dropping bits of German news; he walks about and speaks to everybody', wrote Walpole approvingly after attending one of the new King's first *levées*. He was thought to have 'extreme good-nature' and 'great grace to temper much dignity'. He also had a hopeful eye on Lady Sarah Lennox, daughter of the Duke of Richmond; but, less than a year after his accession, his strong-minded mother saw him firmly tied to a German princess. The lovely Lady Sarah became a bridesmaid.

The date of this wedding depended on the bride's arrival from Germany, and as the September weather grew more and more stormy, this became more and more uncertain. The Court had been on tenterhooks for a fortnight when she finally sailed into Harwich on 7 September 1761, after an uncomfortable nine-day crossing. The 17-year-old Princess and her party spent a quiet first night ashore at the Essex home of Lord Abercorn; then, most of the next day was taken up with travelling to London. She arrived at St. James's Palace in mid-afternoon, and that same night, between ten and eleven o'clock, was married. Not surprisingly, she was thought to look a little pale. Horace Walpole described it all, from the agony of waiting to the drawing-room next day, in a letter to the Honourable H. S. Conway:

> . . . the Queen is come; I have seen her, have been presented to her—and may go back to Strawberry [*Strawberry Hill, his house at Twickenham*]. For this fortnight I have lived upon the road between Twickenham and London: I came, grew impatient, returned; came again, still to no purpose. The yachts made the coast of Suffolk last Saturday, on Sunday entered the road of Harwich, and on Monday morning the King's chief eunuch, as the Tripoline ambassador calls Lord Anson, landed the Princess. She lay that night at Lord Abercorn's at Witham, the palace of silence; and yesterday at a quarter after three arrived at St. James's. In half an hour one heard of nothing but proclamations of her beauty: everybody was content, everybody pleased. At seven one sent to court. The night was sultry. About ten the procession began to move towards the chapel, and at eleven they all came up into the drawing-room. She looks very sensible, cheerful, and is remarkably genteel. Her tiara of diamonds was very pretty, her stomacher

sumptuous; her violet-velvet mantle and ermine so heavy, that the spectators knew as much of her upper half as the King himself. You will have no doubts of her sense by what I shall tell you. On the road they wanted her to curl her toupet: she said she thought it looked as well as that of any of the ladies sent to fetch her; if the King bid her, she would wear a periwig, otherwise she would remain as she was. When she caught the first glimpse of the Palace, she grew frightened and turned pale; the Duchess of Hamilton smiled—the Princess said, 'My dear Duchess, you may laugh, you have been married twice, but it is no joke to me.' . . . They did not get to bed till two. To-day was a drawing-room: everybody was presented to her; but she spoke to nobody, as she could not know a soul. The crowd was much less than at a birth-day, the magnificence very little more. The King looked very handsome, and talked to her continually with great good-humour. It does not promise as if they would be the two most unhappy persons in England, from this event. The bridemaids, especially Lady Caroline Russel, Lady Sarah Lenox, and Lady Elizabeth Keppel, were beautiful figures. With neither features nor air, Lady Sarah was by far the chief angel. . . .

Wedding fever had attacked everyone. 'Mr. Pitt himself would be mobbed if he talked of anything but clothes, and diamonds, and bridemaids', said Walpole. And Sir James Lowther, who had himself been married the night before the King, was reported to have laid a wager of 1,000 guineas with the young monarch, on the date of the first pregnancy.

The Duchess of Northumberland, casting a woman's eye over the young princess's outfit, came up with more details: beneath that dragging velvet mantle was a 'silver Tissue stiffen body'd Gown, embroidered and trimmed with Silver, on her head a little cap of purple Velvet quite covered with Diamonds, a Diamond Aigrette in Form of a Crown, 3 dropt Diamond Ear Rings, Diamond Necklace, Diamond Sprigs of Flowers on her Sleeves and to clasp back her Robe a Diamond Stomacher'. The mantle itself (which Walpole called 'violet' and the Duchess 'purple') was 'laced with Gold and lined with Ermine'. The King 'was dressed in a Stuff of new manufacture, the Ground Silver flower with embossed plate and frosted silver'. Walpole, in another letter, described the diamond stomacher as 'worth three score thousand pounds' and said Her Majesty was to wear it at the coronation, too.

Although this was not a royal love-match, it worked out very well indeed. After a century of predatory monarchs and royal mistresses, cosy domesticity now became the scene. Even the censorious Fanny Burney could find nothing to complain of during her five years' attendance on the Queen—except the dullness of court life (and the fact that she was expected to do some work). George III and Queen Charlotte applied themselves most successfully to the task of filling the royal nurseries with princesses and princes (fifteen of them in all) and to ensuring them a happy family up-bringing. But, when the time came for this next generation to start thinking about marriage, few of them were inclined to follow their parents' excellent example. Their eldest son, the glorious 'Prinny', Prince of Wales, who was later to become Prince Regent and King George IV, began his rackety career at 18 by having an affair with an actress. At 20 he secretly married the widowed Mrs. Fitzherbert. As she was a Roman Catholic, this should have forfeited him the throne (the king, as Defender of the Faith, has to marry a member of that faith), but the Royal Marriage Act, instigated by George III when his brothers kept marrying unsuitably, made the union illegal.

Marriage by Stealth

The permission of the Sovereign had neither been asked for nor given. (In the eyes of the Catholic church, however, the marriage held good, and when the Prince decided to resume the liaison, after his disastrous state marriage to Caroline of Brunswick, he did so 'with the pope's consent'.) Most of the Prince's brothers also preferred mistresses to royal brides, and even his sisters showed no great urge to rush to the altar. In December 1797, when the eldest daughter of George III, the Princess Royal, was finally married (to Prince Frederick of Wurttemberg) she was a rather mature bride of 31. Nevertheless, her loving mother set about sewing the wedding dress with her own hands, and made much of the *trousseau*, too. Fanny Burney, who long after resigning her post as Assistant Mistress of the Robes, was allowed one visit to court a year, to pay her duty to the queen, made her 1797 excursion in good time to hear all about the recent nuptials. First of all she spoke to the bride's sister, the Princess Augusta: '. . . when I told her I had heard that her Royal Highness the bride had never looked so lovely, she confirmed the praise warmly, but laughingly added: "'Twas the Queen dressed her! You know what a figure she used to make of herself, with her odd manner of dressing herself; but mamma said: 'Now really, Princess Royal, this one time is the last, and I cannot suffer you to make such a quiz of yourself; so I will really have you dressed properly.' And indeed the Queen was quite in the right, for everybody said she had never looked so well in her life."'

'The word *quiz*, you may depend, was never the Queen's', noted Miss Burney in her diary. More homely wedding gossip came when she was ushered in to see Her Majesty. There were more serious matters on the Queen's mind (a mutiny in the fleet at The Nore was then causing general alarm) and: 'She looked ill, pale, and harassed', but she was still delighted to talk about her daughter's marriage. 'She permitted me to speak a good deal of the Princess of Wurtemberg, whom they still all call Princess Royal. She told me she had worked her wedding garment, and entirely, and the real labour it had proved, from her steadiness to have no help, well knowing that three stitches done by any other would make it immediately said it was none of it by herself. "As the bride of a widower," she continued, "I know she ought to be in white and gold; but as the King's eldest daughter she had a right to white and silver, which she preferred."'

There was in fact some doubt as to whether the bridegroom was a widower at all. He had previously married a Brunswick princess who, while they were in Russia, had run off and had an illegitimate baby. For this undutiful behaviour, she was said to have been cast into prison and to have died there. But, people asked, had she really died? To complicate matters, the runaway wife was the sister of Princess Caroline of Brunswick, who was married to the Princess Royal's brother, the exotic 'Prinny'. Princess Caroline was reported to have said she was sure her sister was still living—in Russia, with her Russian lover and child—and that she knew people who had seen her; but her own marriage was so wretched she would probably have enjoyed saying anything which was likely to embarrass her husband's family.

The omens for this last disastrous marriage had been wondrously foreboding. Princess Caroline was another German bride who had a delayed and storm-tossed crossing to England: at the end of December 1794 the British fleet sent to escort her through the enemy lines of Dutch and French ships (Britain was again at war) had to put back to port because of bad weather, and the Princess had a three-month wait at

Hanover before they set out again. The reluctant bridegroom used the delay to announce that he would only go ahead with the wedding if the country paid his debts. There were prophesies of doom on all sides. Mrs. Thrale wrote on 17 March 1795: 'Well! here is a furious Frost again—Like Decr and a heavy Snow covering all the Mountains . . . and *such* Tempests last Week!—*such* storms! if this princess Caroline of Brunswick does not get safe over, People will think about the nasty Prophet very seriously.' (Parsley rose to 'two Shillings an Ounce' because of the weather; 'Beef 9^d o' Pound Wheat at an exorbitant Price—Sorrow in all Faces, and Sedition in many Hearts.') Mrs. Thrale covered the financial aspect of the royal drama, too: 'A new Affliction frights our People *now*: the Prince of Wales refuses to marry his Cousin when she does come: unless we pay his Debts—cruel Alternative! they amount to eight hundred Thousand Pounds Stirling it seems, the King will not—the Nation cannot pay them—Nay the King cannot, without greatly distressing himself and his Family—some of these Debts too are of a Nature so disgraceful, that he dares not show the *Articles*, the *Items* I am told: Some think them of a Political Kind, others say he has paid 10 or 20 Thousand for quiet Possession of Lady Jersey—a woman who has no less than Six Grand Children—What Times! What Manners are these? besides the immense Expense of buying Mrs. Fitzherbert's Consent to his Marriage —another Old Grimalkin of fifty Years standing at least.'

Mrs. Fitzherbert was, in truth, 39 at the time of the Prince's marriage (Lady Jersey, the current mistress, was 42; the Prince 32; and the bride 29); his debts were rather less than Mrs. Thrale thought—£630,000—but he was also demanding an increase in his income from £60,000 to £125,000 a year, £17,000 for various expenses incurred by the marriage, and a jointure of £50,000 a year for his wife. Parliament offered £650,000 and the marriage was on again. The Princess landed at Greenwich on 5th April and was married on the 8th. Mrs. Thrale heard only good reports of the bride: 'The Princess pleases People however, if *any* thing will do, *She* will do: 'twas a good measure to bring her over; She is pretty, & that will delight the many, She is chearful & entertaining it seems, and that will charm the King; She is pious too I am told, & very attentive to the Exteriors of Religion—*That* likewise is a good Thing—Tho' one is not oneself quite Young enough to think well of any Woman's Principles who could solemnly accept our Heir Apparent's Hand at the Altar if he ever did—as is still asserted—marry Mrs Fitzherbert according to the Rites of the Romish Church: whoever weds a Man plighted thus seriously to another Woman, most certainly in the Sight of God is committing Adultery; & had I been Archbishop—I would not have joined their Hands for all this World could give. Will the Almighty bless such polluted Nuptials with Children? and will he bless those Children? *I think not.*'

Dr. Johnson's friend was in good visionary form: there was only one child of the marriage, the Princess Charlotte Augusta, born exactly nine months after the wedding day, and she died twenty-one years later, giving birth to a still-born son. Princess Caroline claimed that the Prince of Wales fell down drunk with his head in the hearth on their wedding night—the only night they spent together; the Prince said he would rather see toads and vipers crawling over his victuals than sit at the same table with her; and other people noticed that even in an age not over-given to washing, the Princess was particularly uninterested in keeping clean. Ironically, this unloved 29-year-old bride was married with her hair loose about her shoulders in the ancient romantic style, and she and the distraught bridegroom (he had to be revived with brandy after their first meeting and supported to the altar between two stout friends three days later) went away on one of the first royal honeymoons. But, after that, until the Princess's death in 1821, they lived in mutual hatred several miles apart.

Royal betrothals don't appear to have existed in Britain during this century: in most cases, a match was decided upon, a settlement worked out, and a proxy marriage arranged, all within months; then the main wedding ceremony took place within hours of the bride's arrival in her new country. Child betrothals had gone right out of fashion and the policy of using royal marriages to cement political ties was waning: only good Protestant German, Dutch or Danish spouses were thought suitable for Hanoverian brides and bridegrooms. Even with less exalted unions, the pause between making the match and celebrating the marriage was now very brief. Once the papers had been signed, there was rarely more than a month before the wedding. Young Mary Curzon told Miss Heber how these matters were arranged when her sister married in 1778:

> . . . there is a wedding. . . . We have had a house full of Company for this fortnight; have a deal to dinner today, but my head is full.
>
> My Sister is going to be married. There is a Gentleman has offer'd; she has accepted of him, Sir George Smith of Nottinghamshire. He is a fine handsome fellow, a large estate, an excellent Character & a Charming Young Man; he is attached to my sister. He is tall, Well made, a beautifull pair of eyes, & I shall like him beyond all things for my Brother-in-Law. They will, I fancy, be married next month. . . . I hope they will be vastly happy—she has a good prospect from so good a Young Man.
>
> We are going next week to tour through Nottinghamshire to look at his houses—he has three in that County. He has been with us a good while, left us yesterday. We have been so busy writing for Wedding Clothes, a deal to do with the Lawyers, settlements drawing. I have had the hooping cough to a Violent degree, which, as soon as declar'd, I was order'd to ride as much as possible. . . . My sister, attended by Sir George, has hunted several times a hare hunting & rode very hard.

If the bride were half as charmed by Sir George as her sister, she stood a 'good prospect' of being happy indeed, though in most cases this was pure luck. When Lady Mary Pierrepoint had decided she would rather marry no one than the Hon. Clotworthy Skeffington, she was advised to consult her relations: 'I objected I did not love him. They made answer they found no Necessity of Loveing; if I liv'd well with him, that was all was requir'd of me, and that if I consider'd this Town I should find very few women in love with their Husbands and yet a manny happy. It was in vain to dispute with such prudent people; they look'd upon me as a little Romantic, and I found it impossible to perswade them that liveing in London at Liberty was not the height of happinesse.'

Most people found no necessity either for bride and groom to become too well acquainted before marriage: 'Pray tell Dr. Greville that it is not the fashion in London to make long courtships, and he will be very unpolite if he dangles any longer', Mrs.

91

Delany wrote to her sister in November 1728. Twelve years later, in March 1740, she described a typically rushed matching, meeting and marrying: friends had acted as brokers for Grace Granville, daughter of Lord Lansdowne, and Thomas Foley of Stoke Edith, Herefordshire, leaving them only to say yea or nay on their first meeting. Both decided they were content with their friends' choice; Mr. Foley proposed on 24 February; and on 29 March, Mrs. Delany was writing: 'This moment we are returned from Audley Chapel, where we have been witness of the union of two people that seem made for the happiness of each other. It has at last been concluded in so great a hurry that I hardly think I am awake, but fear I shall start and rub my eyes, as out of a dream, before I can finish my letter. The writings were signed this morning, and at twelve all the company assembled in the vestry. . . .' Neither bride nor groom was in the first flush of youth and one wonders what the rush was all about.

One of the most charming and detailed descriptions of a marriage amongst the substantial county 'gentry' is included in *The Houblon Family*, by Lady Alice Houblon. The Reverend Stotherd Abdy, the fat and jolly parson who performed the ceremony, kept a blow-by-blow account of it all in his pocket-book from the day he joined the wedding party until he reluctantly took his leave nearly a month later. The bride was the young, high-spirited Miss Susanna Archer, eldest daughter and heiress of Mr. Archer of Coopersale. The bridegroom was Jacob Houblon, of Hallingbury Place, thirty-five, and saddened by an early love-affair. The match had been arranged by old Squire Houblon shortly before his death and was purely one of convenience. Hallingbury and Coopersale were neighbouring estates in Essex: the marriage would bind them profitably together. Mr. Archer also had property in Berkshire and it was here, at Welford, that the wedding took place. The ceremony was planned for 13 September 1770, and when our merry parson and his wife arrived from Essex three days beforehand, the bridegroom was already there with the bride, her sister Charlotte, her father and mother (Lady Mary Archer), and Mr. John Shirley, brother of the local vicar.

Large meals, lots of chatter, fishing, partridge shooting, hare coursing, billiards, cards (usually Brag), and a great deal of horse-play filled every day. The breakfast bell rang at half past nine each morning (breakfast was always 'elegant'); outdoor activities then occupied the party until just after 2 p.m. when it was time to change for 3 o'clock dinner ('Soup, Fish and Venison and several other elegant dishes, and a dessert of Fruit' was the menu for the 11th); after dinner the ladies retired to the drawing-room while the gentlemen continued with their wine in 'the eating parlour', sometimes lingering there until 'summon'd to Tea & Coffee' (and 'many eatables of the cake and bread and butter kind') around 7 p.m. At ten o'clock they all sat down to supper ('Partridge & Rabbits & collared Eels and pickled Pidgeons & Jelly, & many more good things' led them 'into Temptation' on the 16th); at 12 o'clock they usually 'took their leaves of each other for the night'. During the week of the wedding a superior French cook was hired and they all went into gales of mirth over his menus which, on the wedding day, had as many as fifteen 'hard-named dishes' in each course. The good-hearted Parson Abdy, who preferred people to laugh at him rather than not laugh at all, was always ready to put his wig on the wrong way, read just one line from each column of a newspaper to make a silly story ('twenty-four Sloops of War found temporary Relief from bathing in the Sea'), or do a series of tricks with a straw, to stop the party flagging. Two days before the proposed wedding day, the bridegroom's younger brother and sister arrived—with bad news. For 'some unavoidable cause' (most probably a lawyer's delay with the settlement papers) the wedding had to be deferred until the 18th. 'The remainder of the evening was not exceedingly joyous.' But, after everyone had got used to the idea, the next six days were spent merrily enough: one morning was taken up with 'drawing the great Pond' for carp, another, with a two-hour walk round the kitchen garden, hot walls and menagerie, and on wet days everyone adjourned to Lady Mary's dressing room where they 'rummaged all the book cases, examined the Knick Knacks upon the Toilet, and set a parcel of shells a dancing in vinegar. Lady Mary and the Miss Archers worked; Mr. Houblon gazed with admiration upon his Bride; Mrs. Abdy and Mr. Archer were engaged in stamping Crests upon doilys with the new invented composition,' and the jolly parson himself 'read to the Company a most excellent Chapter out of the *Art of Inventing, adressed to the Patronesses of Humble Companions*'. On Sunday, the house party went *en masse* to church. On Monday, Mr. Abdy obliged the local vicar by burying a corpse for him.

Then it was Tuesday, 18 September, and the wedding was on. The day appeared 'uncommonly clear and cheerful'; the good parson dressed himself in a new habit and 'everybody except the intended Bride herself seated at Breakfast in the Parlour, in new and elegant undresses by ten o'clock. Soon after eleven o'clock, Mr Archer handed his eldest Daughter down from Lady Mary's dressing Room. Her apparell was a nightgown [*evening dress*] of silver Muslin, with a silver Blond Hat and Cap admirably adapted to the gown. Mr. Houblon [*the bridegroom's brother*], the Bride-Maid Miss Charlotte Archer; who looked enchantingly in an undress of white Lustring ornamented with a Silver Blond, with the serpentine Line of Beauty hanging pendent from her neck in the appearance of a Silver Snake. Mrs. Abdy, Miss Houblon, and Mr. John Shirley closed the Procession.

'We past through a Lane of Tenants, and a groupe of servants in new rich Liveries, to the Church; and there with the greatest propriety of behaviour in everybody, and the most solemn Decency, Mr Houblon and Miss Archer were legally united in the bands of Wedlock. The Bridegroom then led his Bride out of the Church; the Bride-Maid followed, Mr Archer handed Lady Mary back, the Bells were set a ringing, & we all adjourned to the Drawing Room in order to insert the marriage in the Register. We then (as the morning was exceedingly fine & it was too early for dressing for the great appearance) walked round the garden, & thro' the Wilderness, after which we came again into the Drawing Room, where a profusion of Bride Cake was placed ready for refreshment; & salvers of rich wine, & a gold Cup containing an excellent mixture, were handed round. The Bride and Bridegrooms healths were drank, & pieces of cake were drawn properly thro' the Wedding Ring for the *dreaming* Emolument of many spinsters & Batchelors.'

The purpose of this last trick was to thread a piece of wedding cake through the bride's ring a certain number of times (nine was thought to be the most magic figure) and sleep with it beneath the pillow: dreams of future marriage partners were then pretty well guaranteed. The superstition that removing a wedding ring brings bad luck (which is said to be very ancient) obviously wasn't taken too seriously at this time, for, with the ring still on the finger, the operation is extremely messy, if not impossible. It was almost certainly this cake-threading custom which led to the millions of little white boxes of wedding cake which go out each year to the millions of friends and relations who couldn't be there on The Day. A verse in the *Progress of Matrimony*, 1733, indicates how it started:

> But, madam, as a present take
> This little paper of bride-cake;
> Fast any Friday in the year,
> When Venus mounts the starry sphere,
> Thrust this at night in pillowbeer;
> In morning slumber you will seem
> T' enjoy your lover in a dream.

Now we just eat it: not half as much fun!

At many weddings the cake was still broken over the bride's head and occasionally the very old-fashioned biscuit (which began to disappear in Elizabethan times) is still mentioned. Giving evidence in a bigamy trial at the Old Bailey in 1731, one Samuel Pickering, testified that the accused had certainly been married at his tavern by a Fleet parson because he had seen the ring put on her finger and the biscuit broken over her head.

Parson Abdy's account of the Houblon–Archer procession to church, passing through a lane of tenants and servants who behaved with 'the greatest propriety of behaviour' is very similar to Samuel Richardson's description of the wedding of Sir Charles Grandison. Richardson's fictional ladies were all in raptures at the 'decent behaviour' of the 'crowds of spectators of all ranks, and both sexes. Miss Needham declared, and all the young ladies joined with her, that if she could be secure of the like good behaviour and encouragement, she would never think of a private wedding for herself'. Sir Charles and his bride had their path strewn with flowers, which does not seem to have been done for Miss Archer: 'Four girls, tenants' daughters, the eldest not above thirteen, appeared with neat wicker-baskets in their hands, filled with flowers of the season. Cheerful way was made for them. As soon as the bride and father, and Sir Charles, and Mrs. Shirley, alighted, these pretty little Floras, all dressed in white, chaplets of flowers for head-dresses, large nosegays in their bosoms, white ribands adorning their stays and their baskets; some streaming down, others tied round the handles in true lovers' knots; attended the company; two going before; the two others here and there, and every where; all strewing flowers: A pretty thought of the tenants among themselves.'

Back in Berkshire, after eating their bride cake, the Houblons and the Archers retired to change for dinner and emerged in fresh magnificence. After dazzling their eyes 'with the uncommon splendour of their new toilettes' yet another brilliant scene awaited them: 'In the great eating Parlour, about sixteen servants stood in rich Liveries; the Table was spred in a most elegant & superb manner; the Sideboards loaded with massy Plate; the Bride & Bridegroom sat at the top, the Father & Mother at the bottom; with the worthy Steward John Heath, in a handsome suit of Cloaths, & the Body Coachman behind their Chairs. There were fifteen hard-named dishes in each course, besides Removes. The desert consisted of Temples, gravel walks, Ponds, etc.; and twenty dishes of Fruit, & Champagn, Burgundy, Malmsey, Madeira and Frontiniac, were handed about incessantly. Bumpers it may be imagined were drank to the joy, health, & happiness of M^r & Mrs Houblon; the Bells were

94

ringing the whole dinner time, & in short everything had the appearance of the true hospitality of a fine old Family, joined to the elegance of modern taste.'

Coffee and a little mild gambling at cards led them on to ten o'clock supper. Even the food-loving Parson Abdy found it 'impossible to recollect the different situation, of the Lambkins, the Pegodas & the Colonades, & the Comportes & the Hobgoblin's Heads' which were served for this meal, or 'to recapitulate the cheerful *Bon mots* or the laughable observations that were introduced, or to describe upon paper the heart-felt joy which appeared upon every countenance'. The servants had a party, too: in the 'Laundrey in the Yard; a Tabor & Pipe were *dub dubbing* there the whole evening, & to that & a Fiddler's harmonious sound, they were footing it for several hours. Nothing, however, the least indecent, riotous, or drunken could be heard.'

Mr. Houblon and his bride took off next day in their brand new coach, their postillions resplendent in their brand new green and silver jackets, but there was to be no seclusion for this young couple. Right there in the coach with them were the bridegroom's sister and the jolly, fat parson; and hard on their heels were the rest of the party in Mr. Archer's coach and six. The excursion took them just as far as Lord Craven's neighbouring estate, where they looked over the park and plantations and returned in time for dinner.

On the Friday they turned out in a cavalcade of coaches, gentlemen on horseback, and liveried out-riders, for a trip to Newbury, seven miles away: 'This was a glorious treat for all the inhabitants of the Town; for as the Welford Family are naturally well known and honoured there, and as Mr Houblon was in a white and silver frock & his Lady in the wedding muslin, it was soon whispered from House to House that the Bride & Bridegroom were walking thro' the Town. The Bells were immediately set a ringing, & the doors and windows in every street were crowded with spectators.'

The Sunday after the wedding all dressed for church in 'their best Bridal Ornaments' and 'the glistering appearance of the Procession thro' the Isle of the Church from the great House, seemed to set all the Congregation in astonishment'. Mr. Abdy, who was conducting the service, was afraid that most of them were 'but little edified by the solemnity of the Prayers as their eyes seemed to be fixed entirely upon the silver image which Mr Houblon had set up, and their attention to be wholly paid to the Lustre of Lady Mary's Jewels'. The waggish parson vowed that he 'preached by the hour to them, and talked earnestly and much of vanity and vexation of Spirit; but they seemed totally wrapped up in the former, and were not at all inclined to be vexed at anything'. After the service, 'the Bells were set a ringing, and the whole company returned through a crowd of gazing Spectators'.

During the whole bridal month, the party made only two real social visits: once to take breakfast and once to take tea and play cards. And very few people called on them. The whole celebration was an extremely close, family affair and goodness knows how it was sustained with such good humour. But it was, and it was still going remarkably strong when the parson and his wife had to leave on Thursday, 3 October, in order to celebrate the marriage of a sister in Essex. 'Nothing but this should have moved us from the happy spot we were placed in, till we had paid our personal Compts to Mr Archer on his Birthday the Tuesday following, and had attended the Bridal Cavalcade to Newbury Assembly', said the good man. It was obviously all set to go on for a great deal longer.

Mr. Abdy's journal reflects his own robust nature to such a degree it is difficult to imagine a single maidenly blush or furtive motherly tear during the entire Welford celebration; but a chirpy young lady called Miss Emelia Clayton gives a delightful picture of the more sentimental side of 18th century nuptials in a letter to her good friend Georgiana Port. In November 1786, her sister, Marianne, married Colonel Henry Fox (son of the Henry Fox who had run off with the Duke of Richmond's daughter and battled against the Marriage Act), at the magnificent Tudor mansion, Audley End, home of Lord George Howard. As soon as she could set quill to paper, young Miss Clayton told young Miss Port all about it:

> As you insisted upon it, I am set down to give you a full and long account of my dear Marianne's marriage, which was performed this morning at half past eight.
> We all were in the Galery at that time, except herself, who Miss Yates and I was to go for, and lead her in. Her dress was a silver muslin night-gown trimmed with white sattin, a very fine sprigged muslin apron, and handkerchief [*necker-chief*] trimmed with beautiful lace, and white and silver shoes; a blue ennamelled beautiful watch, a present of Lady Howard, a pair of bracelets I gave her, and a diamond ring Ld Howard gave her. Colonel Fox was in a dark green coat, with a very pretty waistcoat, (she *net him*). . . . Miss Yates and I were exactly alike, in white muslins and handkerchiefs trimmed with lace, and blue sattin ribbans. Lord Howard was in dark blue, my b^r in brown, Mr. Neville in dark blue, and the Bishop, Mr. Hayes, and Mr. Gretton in black.
> It is impossible to express what I felt holding her dear trembling hand when I lead her up the gallery. Her heart seemed quite to sink at first, till we reminded her, how *bad a compliment* it would be to him, then she commanded herself vastly well, and was, as *she always is*, just what *she ought to be*. . . .
> What a variety of sensations I felt during the ceremony! surely nothing can be so awfull? sweet angel, God Almighty grant it may be for her eternal happiness! She trembled, and had her eyes quite full, but she did not cry, and I assure you we all behaved vastly well; for there was no crying to be *heard*, tho' I am afraid it might be *seen*. It was serious, but not distressingly so.
> *He* had his eyes quite full also, and looked agitated. which was just what I wished. . . . After having signed our names as witnesses, we went to breakfast, which was vastly pretty. She quite recovered her flurry, and was quietly chearful, as were the rest of the party. Mama and I then went with her whilst she undressed and put on a great coat for travelling. At half past ten I parted from the dearest friend and best sister anybody ever was blessed with.

When a quite private wedding could arouse such tremulous emotions, what an ordeal it must have been for a bride to make a festive entry into church the following Sunday or parade around the nearest country town in her wedding gown, with everywhere the church bells pealing out to greet her—and to alert a hundred prying eyes. How much easier it is to face a dining-room full of strangers in a honeymoon hotel, and pretend you don't look like a honeymooner, than to run the gauntlet of friends and neighbours who already know so much about you and are now avid to surmise the rest. For, as every bride knows, when people eye a newly-married couple, one thing springs most easily to mind—and it always has, as Lady Mary Pierrepoint shows in this amusingly scurrilous letter written from Arlington Street, London, in 1710:

Marriage by Stealth

Next to the great ball, what makes the most noise is the marriage of an old Maid that lives in this street, without a portion to a Man of £7,000 per Annum, and they say £40,000 in ready money. . . . They was marry'd friday and came to church en Parade Sunday. I happen'd to sit in the pue with them and had the honour of seeing Mrs. Bride fall fast asleep in the middle of the Sermon and snore very comfortably, which made several women in the Church think the bridegroom not quite so ugly as they did before. Envious people say 'twas all counterfeited to oblige him, but I believe that's scandal, for she's so devout, I dare swear nothing but downright necessity could make her miss one Word of the Sermon.

In America the scrutiny was still more prolonged, with up to four Sundays of 'Coming out Bride'. But some girls obviously revelled in it, for Mrs. Earle quotes the diary of a young Melford girl, whose sister was determined not to marry in April in case April showers spoiled her bridal progress; she finally timed the wedding so as to have the last Sunday in May for the parade, and as these things happen, there was such a violent thunderstorm that day, she couldn't go to church at all. The sister of another young diarist, Betsey Heath, of Brookline, had better luck in 1783: she was married on the Thursday in 'a Lilock colour'd Lutestring gownd and coat' and the following Sunday 'came out bride drest in strip'd Lutestring Negligie, three white waving plooms in her hat'. On at least one occasion, it was the bridegroom who turned all eyes with his magnificence: in 1810 when a Long Islander called Gabriel Furman jotted down his memories of a wedding of his youth, he didn't give the bride's clothes so much as a passing mention, but the bridegroom, he recalled, wore white broadcloth the first Sunday after the wedding; brilliant blue and gold, on the second; and peach-bloom with pearl buttons, on the third.

Back in Britain, Thomas Pennant described how the custom was kept in North Wales: 'on the Sunday after marriage, the company who were at it come to church, i.e. the friends and relations of the party make the most splendid appearance, disturb the church, and strive who shall place the bride and groom in the most honourable seat. After service is over, the men, with fiddlers before them, go into all the ale-houses in the town.'

Touring Scotland in 1769, Pennant found odd wedding customs there, too. 'The courtship of the Highlander has these remarkable circumstances attending it: after privately obtaining the consent of the Fair he formally demands her of her father. The lover and his friends assemble on a hill allotted for that purpose in every parish and one of them is dispatched to obtain permission to wait on the daughter: if he is successful he is again sent to invite the father and his friends to ascend the hill and partake of a whisky cask, which is never forgot: the lover advances, takes his future Father-in-law by the hand, and then plights his troth, and the fair one is then surrendered up to him.' During the wedding ceremony, great care was taken that dogs should not pass between the bride and groom and particular attention was paid to leaving the bridegroom's left shoe without 'a buckle or latchet to prevent witches "from depriving him, on the nuptial night, of the power of loosening the virgin zone"'. In the Western Highlands, he discovered a custom which was just beginning to die out: 'the morning after the wedding: a basket was fastened with a cord round the neck of the bridegroom by the female part of the company, who immediately filled it with stones, till the poor man was in great danger of being strangled, if his bride did not take compassion on him, and cut the cord with a knife given to her to use at discretion. But such was the tenderness of the Caledonian Spouses, that never was an instance of their neglecting an immediate relief of their good man.'

In Scotland, Wales, Cumberland and some other country districts penny-weddings were still held, though these were now becoming rare in the south of England. In Wales they were called bidden-weddings or bridal-biddings and the guests (according to the *Cambrian Register*, 1796) were 'bidden' to the festivities either by a 'herald, with a crook or wand adorned with ribbons' who 'makes the circuit of the neighbour-hood, and makes his "bidding", or invitation, in a prescribed form'; or by a written notification, like this one which was reprinted in a 1789 *Gentleman's Magazine*:

> *Bidding.*—As we intend entering the nuptial state, we propose haveing a bidding on the occasion on Thursday the 20th day of September instant, at our own house on the Parade, where the favour of your good company will be highly esteemed; and whatever benevolence you please to confer on us shall be gratefully acknow-ledged, and retaliated on a similar occasion, by your most obedient servants,
>
> WILLIAM JONES,⎱Caermarthen,
> ANN DAVIES, ⎰Sept. 4, 1787.
>
> N.B. The young man's father (Stephen Jones), and the young woman's aunt (Ann Williams), will be thankfull for all favours conferred on them that day.

According to a Welsh contributor to the same journal in May, 1784, such biddings were frequently held when 'servants, trades-folks, and little farmers' married. He described the gifts ('from a cow or a calf down to half-a-crown or a shilling') as being given at an 'entertainment' provided some time before the wedding, and said he had frequently known of £50 being collected, and had heard 'of a bidding which produced even a hundred, to a couple who were much beloved by their neighbours; and thereby enabled to begin the world with comfort'. Careful note was kept of all gifts received (sometimes they were even entered in the parish register) so that the bridal pair could 'retaliate' in an appropriate manner when they were bidden in their turn to the festivities of their benefactors.

In William Hone's *Table Book* 'a Lady' tells in more detail how these events were carried out in 'Myrther Tidvel', Glamorganshire (a 'rural and lovely situation' inhabited by simple and 'humble villagers'). There, any girl with 'a fortune of from one hundred to two hundred pounds' married very quietly and privately, returning to her father's house for a few weeks after the wedding: 'where friends and neighbours go to see her, but none go empty-handed'. But the wedding of a girl unlucky enough to have no fortune, was 'forwarded' much more publicly. As most biddings in this area were similar, Mr. Hone's 'Lady' describes one she attended in her youth, as 'bride's-maid to a much valued servant'. Some weeks beforehand the bidder, 'a person well-known in the parish', went round the district inviting everyone 'without limitation or distinction'. The night before the wedding 'a considerable company assembled at the bride's father's, and in a short time the sound of music proclaimed the approach of the bridegroom. The bride and her company were then shut up in a room, and the house-doors locked; great and loud was the cry for admittance from without, till I was directed, as bride's-maid, by an elderly matron, to open the window, and assist the bridegroom to enter'. All the doors were then flung open and the bridegroom's party trooped in. 'A room was set apart for the young people to dance in, which continued for about an hour, and having partaken of a common kind of cake and warm ale, spiced and sweetened with sugar, the company dispersed.'

At eight o'clock next morning the bridesmaid called at the bridegroom's house to lead him and all his supporters to the bride's home, a harper going before them, playing *Come, haste to the wedding*. There, all the bride's supporters were gathered ready to join the procession, the bride, escorted by her brother, taking her place behind the bridegroom and the bridesmaid. 'After the ceremony the great door of the church was opened, and the bride and her maid having changed partners were met at it by the harper, who struck up "Joy to the bridegroom" and led the way to a part of the church-yard never used as a burial ground; there placing himself under a large yew-tree the dancers immediately formed, the bride and bridegroom leading off the first dances,—"The beginning of the world," and "My wife shall have her way".' By this time it was twelve o'clock and 'the bride and bridegroom, followed by a certain number, went into the house, where a long table was tastefully set out with bread of two kinds, one plain, and the other with currants and seeds in it; plates of ornamental butter; cold and toasted cheese; with ale, some warmed and sweetened. The bride and her maid were placed at the head of the table and the bridegroom and her brother at the bottom. After the company had taken what they liked, a plate was set down, which went round, each person giving what they chose, from two to five shillings; this being done, the money was given to the bride, and the company resigned their places to others. . . . Dancing was kept up to seven, and then all dispersed. At this wedding upwards of thirty pounds was collected.'

In the Isle of Man, the food donated for such events was a great deal richer. George Waldron, His Majesty's excise officer on the island at the beginning of the century, said that only sickness ever prevented relatives or friends attending a Manx wedding or contributing handsomely to the feast. He had seen 'a dozen of capons in one platter, and six or eight fat geese in another; sheep and hogs roasted whole, and oxen divided but into quarters'. The only wedding music ever played on the Isle of Man, he said, was *The Black and the Grey*, which sounds rather gloomy. Musicians always led the bridal procession to church with this tune and then marched it three times round the outside of the building before entering for the service. In Scotland, the minister of the rural parish of Monquhitter said (*Statistical Account of Scotland*) that penny weddings were dying out: 'now the penny bridal is reprobated as an index of want of money and want of taste'. But Sir John Eden, in *The State of the Poor* (1797) was happy to find they were still going strong in most areas and could not 'figure' to himself 'a more pleasing or more rational way of rendering sociableness and mirth subservient to prudence and virtue'.

In Cumberland, Bride-wain was the name given to these celebrations, and often here the summons came in the sophisticated form of an advertisement in the newspapers, like this one from the *Cumberland Pacquet*:

George Hayto, who married Anne, the daughter of Joseph and Dinah Colin, of Crosby Mill, purposes having a bride-wain at his house at Crosby, near Maryport, on Thursday, the 7th day of May next, (1789), where he will be happy to see his friends and well-wishers; for whose amusement there will be a variety of races, wrestling-matches, &c. &c. The prizes will be a, — saddle, two bridles, a pair of *gands d'amour*, gloves, which whoever wins is sure to be married within the twelve months, a girdle (*ceinture de Venus*), possessing qualities not to be described, and many other articles, sports, and pastimes too numerous to mention, but which can never prove tedious in the exhibition.

At *The Colliers Wedding* in Northumberland there were only two sports and pastimes—drinking and dancing—but these were tackled with such enthusiasm half the county must have heard the noise. In this Newcastle poem (written by one Edward Chicken in 1764) we get the whole story, in rumbustious, bawdy detail, of the courtship of a Geordie lad ('who gets his Living under Ground'), from first wooing to lights out on the wedding night. In this case, the bridegroom provides the feast (as did Stephen's *Plaine Country Bridegroome* 150 years earlier) while the bride is given choice of venue (and chooses her own home). The superstition that bride and groom should not see each other on their wedding day before meeting at the altar didn't scare anyone in the 18th century, and Tommy, the collier bridegroom, escorts his bride to church in person, riding dramatically across country, at the head of a posse of fellow miners, to collect her:

> The Day appears, the Bride is drest;
> The Music makes the Village ring,
> The Children shout, the old Wives sing.
> *Tom* comes in Triumph o'er the Plain,
> With Collier Lads, a jolly Train;
> They smoke along the dusty Way,
> Whips crack for Joy, the Horses play.
> The Bridegroom rides in State before,
> 'Midst Clouds of Dust the bagpipes roar. . . .
> Like Streamers in the painted Sky,
> At ev'ry Breast the Favours fly.

On foot, come all the young girls of the district:

> The blithsome, bucksome, Country Maids,
> With Knots of Ribbons at their Heads,
> And Pinners flutt'ring in the Wind,
> That fan before, and toss behind,
> Came there from each adjacent Place,
> Strength in their Limbs, Health in their Face,
> To do the Honours to the Bride,
> And eat and drink, and dance beside.

The girls, with fans and posies in their hands, welcome the bridegroom and his band; old Bessy, the bride's mother, broaches the barrels of ale and hands around great plates of cakes:

> They all rise up, and think it Time
> To haste for Church, the Clock's struck Nine.
> Two lusty Lads, well dress'd and strong,
> Stept out to lead the Bride along;

Marriage by Stealth

And two young Maids of equal Size,
As soon the Bridegroom's Hands surprize:
The Pipers wind, and take their Post,
And go before to clear the Coast:
Then all the vast promiscuous Crowd
With thund'ring Tongues, and Feet as loud,
Toss up their Hats, clap Hands, and hollow,
And mad with Joy, like *Bedlam* follow:
Some shout the Bride, and some the Groom,
Till just as Mad, to Church they come;
Knock, swear, and rattle at the Gate,
And vow to break the Beadle's Pate. . . .
The gates fly open, all rush in,
The Church is full with Folks and Din;
And all the Crew, both great and small,
Behave as in a common Hall:
For some perhaps that were Threescore,
Was never twice in Church before,
They scamper, climb, and break the Pews,
To see the Couple make their Vows.
With solemn Face the Priest draws near,
Poor *Tom* and *Jenny* quake for Fear;
Are singl'd out from all the Band
That round about them gaping stand. . . .
Whole Troops of COLLIERS swarm around,
And seize poor *Jenny* on the Ground;
Put up their Hands to loose her Garters,
And work for Pluck about her Quarters;
Till Ribbons from her Legs are torn,
And round the Church in Triumph borne. . . .
The Wedding now is fairly o'er,
The Fees are paid, but nothing more. . . .
Four rustic Fellows wait the While,
To kiss the Bride at the Church Style;
Then vig'rous mount their felter'd Steeds,
With heavy Heels, and clumsy Heads;
So scourge them going Head and Tail,
To win what Country call the Kail.

Everyone home, the party now begins:

The greasy Cook at once appears,
And thunders Mischief in their Ears: . . .
Come take your Seats, and stand away,
My Laddle has not Room to play:
The Hens and Cocks are just laid down;
I never thought you'd come so soon:
And thus with such-like Noise and Din,
The Wedding Banquet does begin. . . .
The Bridegroom waits with active Force,
And brings them Drink 'twixt ev'ry Course,
With Napkin round his Body girt,

101

And the Bride Wore . . .

> To keep his Cloaths from Grease and Dirt. . . .
> Now all are full, the Meat away,
> The Table drawn, the Music play;
> The Bridegroom first assumes the Floor,
> And dances all the Maidens o'er;
> Then rubs his Face, and makes a Bow,
> So marches off, what can he do:
> He must not tire himself outright,
> The Bride expects a Dance at Night.

The whole party dance all day and drink the barrels dry. At nightfall, Jenny is taken to her chamber by the women; the posset is made and left to 'stand'; currant cakes are set floating in ale; and all agree that anyone who steals a sip or takes a bite before the bride and groom will be 'accurst'. Jenny weeps and old Nanny Forster comes up with some comforting advice:

> Come, wipe your Face, for Shame don't cry,
> We all were made with Men to lie,
> And *Tommy*, if I guess but right,
> Will make you have a merry Night;
> Be courteous, kind, lie in his Arms,
> And let him rifle all your Charms. . . .
> Some loose her Head, and some her Stays,
> And so undress her sundry Ways;
> Then Quickly lay the Bride in Bed,
> And bind a Ribbon round her Head:
> Her Neck and Breasts are both display'd,
> And ev'ry Charm in Order laid.
> Now all being ready for *Tom's* Coming,
> The Doors are open'd by the Women;
> Impatient *Tommy* rushes in,
> And thinks that they have longsome been:
> The Maids unwilling to withdraw;
> They must go out, for that's the Law.
> Now *Tommy* next must be undrest,
> But which of them can do it best?
> It is no Matter, all assist;
> Some at his Feet, some at his Breast:
> Soon they undress the Jolly Blade,
> And into Bed he's fairly laid.
> Between the Sheets now view this Pair,
> And think what merry Work was there:
> The Stocking thrown, the Company gone,
> And *Tom* and *Jenny* both alone. . . .
> Now he is Master of his wishes,
> And treats her with a thousand Kisses:
> Young *Tommy* cock'd, and *Jenny* spread,
> So here I leave them both in Bed.

Servants and tenants had their own festivities to mark the marriages of their masters, as at the Houblon-Archer wedding. New liveries were provided, and the poor

Plate Seven

benefitted, too. In Richardson's *Sir Charles Grandison*, the day after the wedding the house-guests 'entertained one another' with reports of what had passed the day before: 'what people said; how the tenants' feast was managed; how the populace behaved at the houses [*inns*] which were kept open. The church-wardens' list was produced of the poor recommended by them: it amounted to upwards of one hundred and forty, divided into two classes; one of the acknowledged poor, the other of poor housekeepers and labouring people who were ashamed to apply; but to whom the church-wardens knew bounty would be acceptable. There were above thirty of these, to whom Sir Charles gave very handsomely.' (To the 'acknowledged poor', who were to have received five shillings apiece, Sir Charles gave ten 'on condition that they shall not be troublesome on the day'—paternalism could often be quite stern.) Several local ale-houses were kept open on the wedding day, from *after* the ceremony until ten at night, for 'the sake of all who choose to go thither'; the squire paid the bill.

What happened when it was the servant who married is shown in two letters written by those two cousins, Mrs. Delany and Lady Cowper (and the events they describe are as different from each other as the ladies themselves). When Mrs. Delany's cook in Ireland suddenly decided to wed, she asked her husband, the Reverend Patrick Delany, the Dean of Down, to perform the ceremony, and saw that there was a gala wedding dinner in the housekeeper's room afterwards: 'Condole with me,' she had written to her sister on 14 December 1751. 'Sally is just on the brink of matrimony, and has sent to speak with me: you shall know the particulars of our conversation.—Why, it was very short; she is to be married this evening, had bespoke supper in the neighbourhood; but that I can't allow. The Dean will marry her himself, they are to have their wedding-supper and lodging here, and I shall soon lose my pretty cook. Her lover is a mason, settles above two hundred pounds on her, lives at Clogher, an old widower, and she has known him fifteen years!'

A day or two later, she was able to tell the end of the tale: 'Last Sunday Sarah Hipwell was married at Glassinivin church, by the Dean of Down, to Robert Rames, mason; I gave all the maidens and men new white ribbon favours, and we all marched and made a gallant show through the garden, D.D. [*the Dean*], Mrs. Don. [*Mrs. Donnellan, a friend of Mrs. Delany's*], and I at the head of the company, to the church, as soon as the bell began to ring, and the ceremony was over just before the congregation came, and I gave them for dinner as much beef, mutton, and pudding as they could devour. Fourteen people dined in Smith's room (besides the servants of the family,) and now the bride is packing up to go away today; I am really sorry to part with her.'

It was all a great deal more genteel when Lady Cowper's waiting woman married in 1768: 'This morning Godwin was married at nine o'clock at Richmond Church. Her relation, Coll. Godwin, paid her the compliment to come with the bridegroom to give her away. She had a new white satin nightgown and petticoat, a white spotted satin cloak, and bonnet trimmed with blond, new lace handkerchief and ruffles upon gauze, a clear apron, and I gave her a very handsome pair of stone shoe-buckles. After they were married they came here, and I ordered that breakfast should be ready for them in the steward's room—Chocolate, tea and coffee, and as soon as they had breakfasted, I received them in the great room with a fire at each end. The bridegroom is not unlike the bride in the face—not vulgar, for such a sort of man; he seems to be about thirty. One of her sisters came here on Monday from Stafford, and is to stay with her a month. The bride and bridegroom went from hence at eleven o'clock in one of their own post-chaises, and another Richmond one for her sister and Coll. Godwin. The bells here rang, and music at the door, quite in a high style! I wish it had proved a fine day for them, but 'tis rather triste.'

It sounds far less fun than the party Mrs. Delany laid on, but much more in keeping with the bride's fashionable *toilette*. In the etiquette of the servants' hall, a waiting woman was as far above a cook as a Countess was above a waiting woman, and Godwin obviously had this kind of distinction very much at heart. Usually, even superior servants, when choosing their wedding dresses, bore in mind the same kind of sentiments as Goldsmith's *Vicar of Wakefield* and his lady: for, 'I chose my wife', said the Vicar, 'as she did her wedding-gown, not for a fine glossy surface, but such qualities as would wear well.'

Another gentleman who most certainly would have appreciated the good vicar's dour economics was Joseph Nollekens, one of the most successful sculptors of the 18th century, but an extremely mean little man (and dirty, too, even by contemporary standards: 'How dirty you go!' Boswell exclaimed one day when they met at the theatre). At his death in 1823, Nollekens left an impressive miser's hoard of £200,000 —and an even more valuable record in marble of all the great men of his time, from George III and the Duke of Wellington, to David Garrick and Oliver Goldsmith himself. In 1772, this odd little character married the statuesque Mary Welch, a lady who 'had no small sprinkling of pride in consequence of a compliment paid her by Dr. Johnson'. (She was also said to have been the inspiration of Sophia Western in Fielding's *Tom Jones*.) Nollekens' pupil and assistant, John Thomas Smith, surveyed this oddly assorted couple on their wedding day with an artist's eye for detail, and later, when he wrote a biography of his master, he set it all down on paper. While most 18th century bridegrooms felt as obliged as their brides to buy new finery for their weddings (often spending as much as £400 on half a dozen new coats and a supply of lace-trimmed linen), Joseph Nollekens saved money on his nuptials as he did on every other occasion: he wore the clothes he had bought in Italy two years earlier and smuggled into England inside one of his sculptor's casts (appropriately one for a bust of the novelist Laurence Sterne, who wrote *A Sentimental Journey through France and Italy*, as well as his more famous *Tristram Shandy*). As a result: 'The bridegroom's dress was a suit of "*Pourpre du Pape*", silk stockings with broad blue and white stripes, and lace ruffles and frill, the whole of which articles he had brought from Rome. His hair was dressed in curls on either side, with an immense toupée, and finished with a small bag tied as closely as possible to his neck.'

The Juno-esque Miss Welch, who was later to rival her husband in penny-pinching, was on this occasion arrayed all a-new, in very splendid style, at the expense of her father. According to Smith:

> This lady's interesting figure on her wedding day, was attired in a saque and petticoat of the most expensive brocaded silk, resembling net-work, enriched with small flowers; which displayed, in the variation of the folds, a most delicate shade of pink, the uncommon beauty of which was greatly admired. The deep and pointed stomacher was exquisitely gimped and pinked, and at the lower part was a large pin, consisting of several diamonds, confining an elegant point-lace apron; certainly, at that period, rather unfashionable, but, on this happy event,

affectionately worn by the lady in memory of her dear mother, who had presented it to her: indeed, Mrs. Nollekens was frequently heard to declare, that she was above 'the fleeting whimsies of depraved elegance'. The sleeves of this dress closely fitted the arm to a little below the elbow, from which hung three point-lace ruffles of great depth: a handkerchief of the same costly texture partly concealed the beauty of her bosom; wherein, confined by a large bow, was a bouquet of rose-buds, the delicate tints of which were imperceptibly blended with the transparency of her complexion, and not a little increased the beauty of a triple row of pearls, tied behind with a narrow white satin ribbon. Her beautiful auburn hair, which she never disguised by the use of powder, according to the fashion of the day, was, upon this occasion, arranged over a cushion made to fit the head to a considerable height, with large round curls on either side; the whole being surmounted by a small cap of point-lace, with plaited flaps, to correspond with the apron and ruffles. Her shoes were composed of the same material as her dress, ornamented with silver spangles and square Bristol buckles, with heels three inches and a half in height, as if she meant to exult in out-topping her little husband, whose head, even when he had his hat on, reached no higher than her shoulder.

Mrs. Nollekens's father was at the expense of her marriage wardrobe, which cost about two hundred pounds: among her dresses, was one of a fashionable Carmelite, a rich purple brown, and enriched with bouquets of carnations, auriculas, and jessamines the size of nature.

A complete *trousseau* list for this period is included by the poet, Robert Southey, in his *Commonplace Book*. It was given to him, early in the 19th century, by Sir Edward Littleton who said it was in his mother's handwriting, 'probably a List of her Wedding Garments—not worth sending you, it is too modern'. But Southey (who was born in 1774) thought otherwise, noting that he didn't 'know the names of half the things' himself:

A black paddysway gown and coat,
A pink unwatered pabby sute of cloaths,
A gold stuff sute of cloaths,
A white worked with sneal, sute of cloths,
A pink lutstring quilted petticoate,
A velvet scarff and hood,
A velvet manteel primed,
A love hood, and a sneal hood,
A pallereen, and a Turkey hancerchief,
An imbroidered short apron,
A pink short apron,
Two paire of silk stocking,
Two paire of shoes,
A sute of knots,
Four Fanns,   The watch and equepage.

   Linen.

A Brusells laced head ruffles, handkerchieff and tucker,
A sute of Brussels drest night cloaths and rufles,
A Macklen-face lace drest night cloaths, and hancerchieef,

And the Bride Wore . . .

A Paries cap, double hankerchieff, and ruffles,
A dormoizeen mobb and tucker edged,
A pinner and quoiff of face lace, Macklen double ruffles, hankerchieff, and a hood
   of muslen edged,
A plain cambrick head ruffles and tipett, and tucker,
A laced cambrick apron, a spoted cambrick apron,
A plain cambrick apron, a lawn apron.

And now, finally, a trip to Gretna Green: the most romantic and lasting legacy of the 18th century. Lovers no longer gain any worth-while benefit by heading for this small border village, but they still run there, from all over the world, when parents say 'No'. It all began with Lord Hardwicke's Marriage Act and the uproar in parliament which allowed Scotland to escape the stringent marriage laws which came into effect in England and Wales. To start with, eloping lovers fled to the Channel Islands and the Isle of Man, but the price (five guineas per couple) and the misery of what could sometimes be two or three days on a stormy crossing from Southampton to St. Peter Port, Guernsey, soon ruled out the former. The Isle of Man tackled the problem itself by bringing in new laws which included the threat that anyone caught solemnising a lawless marriage would be pilloried, lose his ears and be imprisoned until the governor saw fit to release him, on payment of a fine not exceeding fifty pounds.

And so Scotland came into favour. Edinburgh's Canongate area was first to gain a reputation for quick marriages and was soon swarming with a very disreputable mob of phoney parsons (unlike the Fleet clergy, these were not even de-frocked or badly-behaved priests, but usually lawyers' clerks or out-of-work servants). Soon logic stepped in: Edinburgh was eighty miles and more over the Scottish border, and for runaway lovers with a pack of irate relatives on their heels, every mile was a threat to future happiness; marrying in a town on the border itself made more sense; and so came the popularity of little Gretna Green, right on the dividing line, and just nine miles from the last English posting-stage, and fresh horses, of Carlisle. The popular idea that the Gretna Green 'coupler' was a blacksmith seems to have been pure myth, which an official report in the *Statistical Account of Scotland* tried to explode as early as the 1790s:

> The persons who follow this illicit practice are mere imposters—priests of their own creation, who have no right whatever either to marry or exercise any part of the clerical function. There are at present more than one of this description in this place, but the greatest part of the trade is monopolized by a man who was originally a tobacconist, and not a blacksmith, as is generally believed. He is a fellow without education, without principle, without morals, and without manners. His life is a continued scene of drunkenness; his irregular conduct has rendered him an object of detestation to all the sober and virtuous part of the neighbourhood. Such is the man (and the description is not exaggerated) who has the honour to join in the sacred bonds of wedlock many people of great rank and fortune from all parts of England. It is forty years and upwards since marriages of this kind began to be celebrated here. At the lowest computation, about sixty are supposed to be solemnized annually in this place.

The man so charmingly pictured was Joe Paisley, alias the 'Old Blacksmith', a smuggler, then a tobacconist, who first turned his hand to the coupling trade in about

1789. He used to wear a strictly clerical rig of gown, cassock, bands, and three-cornered hat; and, after taking legal advice, stopped giving mis-spelt, scarcely legible marriage certificates, signed with a false name, and supplied official-looking documents (testifying that he had witnessed the couple exchange the binding promises of marriage) which he signed properly. In this way he satisfied his customers, was not breaking the law himself, and the marriages were recognised as legal in England. An enormous drinker (he was said to down a Scotch pint—two English quarts—of brandy a day), he ended up weighing 25 stone. Before Paisley there had been a man named Scott, 'a shrewd, crafty fellow', who was probably the first of all the Gretna Green 'parsons'; and George Gordon, an old soldier, whose professional attire was an ancient full military costume of red coat, cocked hat, jack boots and 'ponderous' sword. Whenever his authority for performing marriages was challenged, Gordon claimed (according to Hone): 'I have a special licence from government, for which I pay fifty pounds per annum.' He must have said it with remarkable conviction, because for a long time he was believed.

None of these gentlemen, and none of their successors, had ever been or was to be a blacksmith, but the desire to turn them all into men of the forge was unassailable. The myth is thought to have begun with some high-flown literary reference to a Scottish Vulcan riveting the hymeneal chains of matrimony, but whatever the origin, it met with most enthusiastic support, as a wealth of delightful Victorian prints still show.

Chapter Seven

Marriage by Fascination
The Nineteenth Century

In a glimmer of gems and a sheen of white,
With the orange wreath on her snowy brow.
The Bride Flown

THE great white wedding: a church crowded with friends and relatives; the bridegroom waiting at the altar; the blushing bride in veil and orange blossom: Wagner and Mendelssohn; bridesmaids and best man; wedding cake, and wedding breakfast; showers of rice and old shoes; all the superstitions in the repertory; and a proper honeymoon, just for two. This was when it all happened, when all the jig-saw pieces which make the young girl's golden dream (and her mother's fixed determination) came together to form the great white wedding tradition. Many of the ingredients had been around for centuries, as we have seen, but it was now that they took the precise shape we know today and were called by the names we call them. During the 19th century, *bride-cake* gradually became *wedding cake*; *Bride-maids*, bridesmaids; *Bride-men*, turned first into *groomsmen* and then, finally, the *best man* of all appeared. *Going away* became the *bridal tour* (and stopped there for the very aristocratic), then, almost universally, was accepted as the honeymoon, with *honeymoon hotels* to cater for the trade. Wedding music meant Wagner's *Bridal Chorus*, from *Lohengrin* ('Here comes the Bride!') and Mendelssohn's *Wedding March* from *A Midsummer Night's Dream*. Wedding hymns were sung (services became 'fully choral'), churches were banked with flowers, parsons directed sentimental words to sentimental congregations, and healths were drunk in champagne at 'a dinner called a breakfast'. Marrying for love was now a hope, if not always an expectation.

In short, weddings became a romantic blend of religious pomp and secular splendour which gladdened Victorian hearts. Or *some* Victorian hearts, for religion was still a red-hot issue and the Protestant-Catholic contest continued to smoulder dangerously. Parliament ended legal discrimination against Catholics at the beginning of the century, with the Catholic Emancipation Act of 1829, which made them first-class citizens once more with, in theory at any rate, all the rights and opportunities of Protestants; and the new Marriage Act of 1836, which introduced civil registrars, no longer required that Catholics should be married at an Anglican ceremony; but there were still squeals of 'Papal aggression' from the country when the Pope set up territorial bishops in England in 1850, and many Protestants looked upon the idea of dressing up their own churches and filling them with music and singing, as one more slippery step towards incense and Rome. Disraeli, in his cliff-hanger of a religious thriller, *Lothair* (who will get the hero? The cardinals or the beautiful—and Anglican —Lady Corisande?) shows the temper of the times in his description of the marriage of Lothair's two cousins, the Ladies Flora and Grizell (two stunning Scottish 'giantesses' whose 'dimples . . . white shoulders and small feet and hands were much admired'). Lord Carisbrooke and the Duke of Brecon were the bridegrooms at this double wedding (and double weddings were another Victorian fancy):

> It was August, and town was thinning fast. Parliament still lingered, but only for technical purposes. . . . One social event was yet to be consummated: the marriages of Lothair's cousins. They were to be married on the same day, at the same time, and in the same place. Westminster Abbey was to be the scene, and as it was understood that the service was to be choral, great expectations of ecclesiastical splendour and effect were much anticipated by the fair sex. They were however doomed to disappointment, for although the day was fine, the attendance numerous and brilliant beyond precedent, Lord Culloden [*father of the brides*] would have 'no popery'. Lord Carisbrooke, who was a ritualist murmured, and was encouraged in his resistance by Lady Clanmorne and a party, but as the Duke of Brecon was high and dry, there was a want of united action, and Lord Culloden had his way.
>
> After the ceremony, the world repaired to the mansion of Lord Culloden in Belgrave Square, to inspect the presents, and to partake of a dinner called a breakfast.

Lord Culloden, a man of few words, iron jaw, and dour faith in the Free Kirk of Scotland, almost certainly met with the approval of his real-life compatriot, Jane Welsh Carlyle. Like a good middle-class Scot, Jane Baillie Welsh was married to that pillar of Victorian letters, Thomas Carlyle, at a no-nonsense ceremony in a private family home (in this case, her grandfather's). That was in 1826, and it was not until thirty-six years later, when she was 61 and rather frail, that she inspected, for the first time, one of the new-style English weddings. Writing from London in February 1862, she told of her curiosity—and her reaction:

> . . . the wedding was an immense affair! It was my doctor's little daughter, who was being married, after a three years' engagement, and as soon as she was engaged, she had made me promise to attend her wedding. I had rather wished to see a marriage performed in a church with all the forms, the eight bridesmaids &c. &c. but I had renounced all idea of going to the church for fear of being laid up with a fresh cold, and meant to attend only the breakfast party after, in which I took less interest. But imagine how good the people here are to me. Our rector, in whose church (St. Lukes) the marriage was to take place, being told by his wife I wished to go, but durstn't for fear of the coldness of the church, ordered the fires to be kept up from Sunday over into Tuesday morning! Besides a rousing fire in the vestry, where I sat at my ease until the moment the ceremony began! I was much pressed afterwards to acknowledge how superior the English way of marrying was to the Scotch, and asked how I had liked it. I said my feelings were very mixed. 'Mixed?' the rector asked, 'Mixed of what?' 'Well,' I said, 'it looked to me something betwixt a religious ceremony and a—pantomime!' So it is. There were forty-four people at the breakfast.

Pantomine or not, almost from the beginning of the century, this was how most people now wished to marry. The introduction of registry office weddings emphasised that the state regarded marriage as a purely civil contract, but it also, as John Cordy Jeaffreson pointed out (in *Brides and Bridals*), 'concurs with popular feeling in encouraging our brides to think that marriage should be beautiful and hallowed with religious observances. Prevailing opinion may be said to hold that, though matrimony may be *lawful*, it can scarcely be called *holy* unless it has received the sanction of spiritual authority.'

And 'spiritual authority' now meant a great deal more than a cursory joining of hands over a Pembroke work table with a couple of candles on it. Sales of marriage licences, special or otherwise, plummeted. Banns were back in vogue, as a fitting prelude to the pomp of the wedding day (and suddenly no one seems to have minded hearing themselves called spinster any more). In many rural churches the cry of 'God speed them well' was added to each reading, and the congregation replied with a fervent 'Amen'.

The nation was turning away from the cynicism of the 18th century, and glowing all over with romanticism instead. Jane Austen, that mistress of restrained emotion, heralded the new right to marry for love in a letter to her sister, Cassandra, in December 1808 (a letter which still has all the brittle overtones of the previous century):

> Lady Sondes' match surprises but does not offend me; had her first marriage been of affection, or had there been a grown-up single daughter, I should not have forgiven her; but I consider everybody as having a right to marry *once* in their lives for love, if they can, and provided she will now leave off having bad headaches and being pathetic, I can allow her, I can *wish* her, to be happy.

(The widowed Lady Sondes, mother of four sons and two daughters, had just married Sir Henry Montresor.) Queen Victoria's Foreign Secretary, Lord Clarendon, was an active advocate in the cause of true love, though by August 1860 he seems to have thought the day already as good as won. In a letter to the Duchess of Manchester, he explained how he had helped Lord Derby's only daughter, Emma, to the man of her choice (the Hon. Chetwynd Talbot, brother to Lord Shrewsbury):

> . . . having heard of Lady E's unhappiness I encouraged Miss Eden to speak to Lady Derby about it & told her that want of great fortune or rank was all nonsense & that we had long ago made up our minds that our daughters shd: marry any one we thought wd: really make them happy provided the poverty was not extreme.
> I know Miss E: did speak to Lady D: & she may have quoted me but I can't think such a banal opinion can have weighed much with D. . . .

Between these two letters, in 1833, Benjamin Disraeli struck an extravagantly discordant note when he wrote to his sister:

> By the bye, would you like Lady Z—— for a sister-in-law, very clever, 25,000l., and domestic? As for 'love,' all my friends who married for love and

beauty either beat their wives or live apart from them. This is literally the case. I may commit many follies in life, but I never intend to marry for 'love,' which I am sure is a guarantee of infelicity. . . .

With a politician's flair for having his cake and eating it, Disraeli, six years later, married a rich widow (20 years his senior) and fell in love with her too.

In France 'marriage by fascination', as one Victorian writer termed the new love matches, was still not in vogue. Towards the end of the century, Matilda Betham Edwards, an Englishwoman who had spent much of her life on the other side of the Channel, described French attitudes to mating and marrying in her book *Home Life in France*, and in doing so, obliquely threw a good deal of light on British customs. Many of the French traditions and beliefs which struck Miss Betham Edwards as odd, or at any rate 'foreign', were the customs and beliefs of England during the previous century; but, from her reaction to them, it is obvious that they had not only vanished, but been completely forgotten, in perfidious Albion.

In France the marriage settlement was still of primary importance. Wedlock, there, she said, was 'no mere individual, but a family matter, a kind of joint-stock affair. An Englishman marries a wife. A Frenchman takes not only his bride for better, for worse, for richer, for poorer, but her entire kith and kin. . . . For centuries, alike in the humblest as well as the highest ranks, matrimonial settlements have kept family possessions together in France—and enriched village notaries! . . . outside Bohemia, slumland, or the world of the *déclassé*, portionless brides in France are an anomaly. No matter what her rank or condition, a girl brings her husband something.'

Until the middle of the 19th century, this was true in Britain, too. Charlotte Bronte's Jane Eyre, newly engaged to the falcon-eyed Mr. Rochester, was delighted to hear that an uncle was thinking of making her his modest heiress: 'It would, indeed be a relief,' she thought, 'if I had ever so small an independency . . . if I had but a prospect of one day bringing Mr. Rochester an accession of fortune, I could better endure to be kept by him now.' It sounds curiously Women's Lib. (though it is hardly the kind of cause modern women's libbers fight over). Brainwashed as we are into thinking that no one had given a thought to women's rights (other than the right to vote) until the present army of noisy militants came on the scene, it is easy to forget that women were changing the pattern of their lives just as dramatically a hundred years ago. And, as usually happens, there were those who delighted in abusing rather than using any new release from restraint. This showed itself especially in the attitude to betrothals, which were no longer blessed by the church nor legally binding, and were called engagements. By 1872, John Cordy Jeaffreson could write: 'Every street in modern London is inhabited by a husband who, without cherishing any unfriendliness to his wife's early admirers, is aware that, before becoming his conjugal partner, she was engaged successively to two or three men of his acquaintance, each of whom she in turn threw over without his consent.' The Victorian miss, he said, 'enjoys greater liberty than the maiden of former time. She may retract any number of lightly given matrimonial promises; and after promising herself with interchangement of rings and holy close of lips to half-a-dozen different suitors, she may become the wife of a seventh admirer, and ask her six jilted lovers to be spectators of her wedding.' There was, however, one drawback to the new rules of the game, for: 'if she has greater freedom she has less security. The law that allows her to trifle with a bevy of lovers, also permits men to jilt her. And it sometimes happens that the frivolous beauty, after playing falsely and cruelly with a true man's passion, receives appropriate, though terrible, punishment from a masculine trifler, who wins her love only to show his disdain of it.'

Such hideous revenge was, happily, not the lot of most young girls, who flirted only a little and not too unkindly before settling down to a long engagement with the man they eventually married. In the 18th century, men had entered into marriage negotiations when they could afford to, and not before. The Victorians were more inclined to promise themselves romantically and wait for better times. Charles Dickens, at the age of 24, was all set for a long engagement to Catherine Hogarth when the success of his first book, *Sketches by Boz*, changed the situation. In March, 1836, he wrote to his uncle:

> The great success of my book and the name it has established for me among the Publishers, enables me to settle at an earlier period than I at first supposed possible; I have therefore fixed Saturday next, for my marriage with Miss Hogarth.

The wedding was unfashionably discreet—'altogether a very quiet piece of business', according to Dickens' friend Thomas Beard. The author's brother-in-law, Henry Burnett, described Miss Hogarth as 'a bright, pleasant bride, dressed in the simplest and neatest manner,' looking 'better perhaps than if she had been enabled to aim at something more'. (Dickens had sold the copyright of *Sketches by Boz* outright for £150, which makes the quietness of the wedding less surprising than the fact that he now felt able to 'settle' at all.)

Lengthy engagements meant that brides were rather more mature. The legal ages for marriage were still 12 for girls and 14 for boys, but, said Jeaffreson: 'very early marriages have fallen altogether out of practice, and brides of thirty years are thought to marry none too late . . . any parents in our prosperous ranks, who should now-a-days couple in wedlock a bride and groom of those tender years, would outrage society, and run some risk of being declared by a lunacy-commission incapable of managing their own affairs.'

The urbane Lord Clarendon was almost as shocked when Queen Victoria suggested that his youngest daughter, Emily, might marry in her late teens. In 1861 he told the Duchess of Manchester that the Queen had appointed Emily a bridesmaid for the wedding of her own daughter, Princess Alice, 'if she *herself shd: not be married in the mean time*—of wh: I hope there will be no chance as she is not $17\frac{1}{2}$ yet'.

Preparing the *trousseau*, was now something which could be spread over months or years, rather than weeks, and as a consequence these grew to alarming proportions. A dozen of everything was the rule of the day. *The Tatler* (30 June 1877) published an amusing lament on the subject—the extravagance of women, claimed the writer, was putting men off matrimony:

> Propound to her the question of marriage and you will speedily arrive at the truth of the fact. You will find she has not a single article of attire from a night cap to a shoe lace but must first be replaced and then reduplicated; and the trousseau with all its horrors, rises before you as the first female bar to matrimony.

True, you will (probably) not have to pay for it yourself but it will be the first shadow of a fearful burden you must bear all the rest of your life and its monstrous proportions indicate a Giant Horror from which you will shrink back appalled. Why a girl cannot be married 'all standing' has ever been a mystery to us but as a matter of fact she WILL not go to church with out an entirely new rigout and as she is on her wedding day so you will be expected to keep her hence forth and for ever.

For the bride herself—and her mother—it was a delightful experience. Whenever a marriage is mentioned in Victorian correspondence or diaries, the very next thing we hear of is a constant flow of visitors—all the friends of the bride and all the friends of her mother—calling round 'to discuss the *trousseau*'. And it wasn't only the ladies who got excited over such matters. Lord Clarendon, again, described the scene at his house when his eldest daughter, Alice, was about to marry Lord Skelmersdale in 1860:

> Little Dunmore overflows with love for his angel & is an unceasing amusement to us—he runs in and out of the house all day like a great Newfoundland puppy. . . . Yesterday he brought a pocket full of patterns as he wished Alice to select the color of the trowsers in wh: he shd: attend her wedding & he said *every thing* he had on wd: be new & worn for the first time on that day—he is awfully cracky. . . .

For the wedding dress white remained the established rule (and the exceptions to it were few); but the 19th century bride was a far more demure 'vision in white' than her 18th century predecessor. A great deal of jewellery was still worn, though silver trimmings soon disappeared and white satin and lace replaced the glittering brocades and silver muslins of the 1700s. The bridal veil made a come-back, not as a conscious revival of Roman wedding veils, but as part of the general trend towards classical fashions. Soon after the French Revolution, the Duchesse d'Abrantès wrote that every dress possessed something 'Turkish, Greek, Mediaeval, or Roman, in short a little of everything except good French taste'. Out of this international rag-bag, the Greek and Roman influence was by far the strongest and the most durable. Throughout the Directoire period in France and the Regency in England, women dressed in clinging, high-waisted gowns (more often white than not) which were quite obviously descended from the classical draperies of ancient Greece and Italy (and very often they damped them down to make them cling the more). As they bound their hair with Roman fillets and wound it into Grecian buns, the best-dressed women of the turn of the century added a trailing scarf of lace or gauze, pinning it centrally to the back of the head, and winding the long ends loosely round otherwise bare arms. Many years after the return to whale-bone and laces, nipped-in waists and massive skirts, Grecian hair-styles and floating veils remained. (And often, as late as the 1830s, fashion magazines still referred to bridal veils as 'scarves', since this is what they had started life as.) Throughout the rest of the century, small veils were virtually obligatory for older women appearing at court functions, and many, married and unmarried, young and old, wore them for all full-dress occasions. At Queen Victoria's wedding, her mother, the Duchess of Kent, and her aunt, the Dowager Queen Adelaide, both wore veils as well as the bride, and when the Lady Caroline Leveson-Gower married the Marquis of Kildare in 1847 the bride's mother and all her bridesmaids wore them.

To begin with, for weddings as for other occasions, veils were for decoration only: they were pinned to the top, or more often to the back of the head, and trailed down behind the bride, sometimes to within an inch or so of the hem of her gown, sometimes not so far. The fashion for wearing them over the face—thus providing once again a modest shield for maidenly blushes, did not evolve until the 1860s and '70s; and the custom of arriving at the church, veil demurely down, and leaving triumphantly bare-faced, was an even later refinement. At first, once the veil was in place, it tended to stay there until the bride got around to eating something at the breakfast, and there is still many an early wedding photograph in existence which shows everyone beaming clear-eyed and gleaming-toothed at the photographer as they leave the church, except the bride, who can only dimly be seen through a haze of lace or tulle.

Royal brides have never been allowed the privilege of hiding behind their wedding veils—and they are still denied it today. There is a tradition that this royal ban was introduced as a precaution against the surprise appearance of substitute brides, but it is more likely to have originated with the first royal wedding veil—Queen Victoria's, which was a small affair even for the 1840s—and with the insatiable desire of the British subject to be allowed free scrutiny of all royal faces on all royal occasions. (A desire which also put an embargo on wide-brimmed hats for the royal family, until Princess Anne over-rode it so thoroughly, and so stylishly, a few years ago.)

At the beginning of the century there is an occasional description of a bride with a veil 'hanging all over her', but this does not necessarily mean over the face. Lady Augusta Bruce, describing the Empress Eugénie on her wedding day said 'a sort of cloud or mist of transparent lace enveloped her', but paintings of this elegant Spanish countess show her with a veil of reasonably modest proportions, hanging only round her shoulders and down her back. At least one early print, *The Courtship & Marriage of Jerry & Kitty*, London, 1814, does show a bride with a veil literally hanging all over her—over her head and face and down to the hem of her skirt all round—but this was rare.

During the 1830s and '40s the fashion was definitely for something much smaller, and bridal plates in journals such as *The Ladies Cabinet* and the *World of Fashion* all show complicated hair-styles with ringlets at the side and buns on top, sprinkled about with sprigs of flowers and leaves, the veils attached either centrally behind the bun, or at either side behind the ears. Most veils were made of lace, and usually of the most expensive lace the bride's family could afford (Brussels and Honiton produced the most costly and most coveted: Valenciennes and Alençon came next; English point lace and Mechlin from Belgium were popular; and our old friend blonde was resorted to by the not so well off). The prickly Jane Eyre prepared a 'square of unembroidered blond' to wear on her 'low-born head' on her wedding day, while Mr. Rochester, with 'princely extravagance' sent to London for lace at least as valuable as the jewels she would not allow him to buy her. This gift was to meet with a nasty end at the hands of the first Mrs. Rochester, the mad-woman with rolling red eyes, who draped it over her own purple and swollen countenance, then tore it in two and trampled on it. But most of these hand-made treasures, which cost several hundred pounds, were treated with due reverence: they either became family heirlooms, worn by several generations of brides, or were worn again by the original bride on special occasions in later life. Queen Victoria's wedding lace was often to appear in sadder years over her widow's black: she wore both her veil and the lace from her wedding dress at the marriages of two of her own children, and at that of her grandson, the future King George V; and in 1897—fifty-seven years after her wedding day—she again donned both for her official Diamond Jubilee photographs.

Humble brides who married humble bridegrooms usually wore a bonnet rather than a veil (Bethnal Green Museum, London, has a charming example from 1845—a very chaste affair of white tulle, with a band of orange blossom). The poked brims gave excellent cover from prying eyes but even so, they were often reinforced with a 'fall' of lace or net, which hung over the brim and over the face. This was a general fashion of the time (like hats with veils which have been in and out of favour many times this century). More specifically bridal was a combination of 'bonnet and veil'; in this case, lace or tulle was either draped over the entire bonnet, or attached to the crown and allowed to hang down behind like a large and exotic streamer. The first bride in a country district to announce that she was going to swop her bonnet for a veil proper was sure to cause such a splendid ripple of anticipation that even a *blasé* young parson could be made aware of her enterprise. The Reverend Benjamin Armstrong, 36-year-old vicar of East Dereham, Norfolk, vowed that all weddings were the same and he preferred a funeral any day, yet on 7 February 1854, he wrote in his diary (*Armstrong's Norfolk Diary*): 'A day of excitement in the parish in consequence of Miss Dingle's wedding and her wearing a *veil*, supposed to be the first ever seen in Dereham. The church was crowded. All weddings are alike. The mind reverts to new wellfitting gloves and bouquets imported from Covent Garden—postboys with huge favours and smirking servant girls—a handsome breakfast with lots of champagne—wretched speeches on the part of the men and tears on the part of the women. Then come the corded boxes; the bridegroom has another glass, an old shoe is thrown into the carriage for luck and off they go. For my part I dislike weddings and would sooner attend a funeral.'

Mrs. Earle recorded a very early, and rare, appearance of a wedding veil in America (in her book *Two Centuries of Costume in America*):

> The earliest wedding-veil and all-white bridal gown made distinctly for a wedding dress, which I have known was worn by Mrs. James H. Heyward, of Charleston, South Carolina. She was Decima Cecilia Shubrich, a lovely creature, married at nineteen. Her portrait was painted by Malbone, who was in Charleston in the year 1800. She wears a tulle wedding-veil placed on the head as would be a similar bridal veil today [*1903*]. Also a splendid tiara of pearls, and ear-rings of pear-shaped pearls. These rich jewels were sent her from England by her godmother Mrs. Rutledge, as a wedding gift.

America also appears to have given an early welcome to bridal orange blossom. Miss Mary Hellen, a badly-behaved young lady, who trifled with the affections of all three sons of President John Quincy Adams before settling for the middle one, wore it for her White House wedding in Washington in the winter of 1828, when, according to her cousin and bridesmaid, Abigail Adams, she 'looked very handsome in white satin, orange blossoms and pearls'. This symbol of fertility (there are few trees, it is said, so prolific as the orange) hit Britain around the same time. Fashion magazines of the early 1820s make no mention of it, but in the June 1827 edition of *La Belle Assemblée* a passage from a moving tale entitled *The Bridal Morn* indicates that it was, by then, an accepted piece of British wedding regalia: 'In silence were adjusted the white garments—the wreath of orange flowers—the bridal veil, scarcely whiter than the cheek it shaded.' The following June, the fashion pages of the same magazine carried a description of the latest

> Bridal Costume. Dress of spotted tulle over white satin; corsage *a là Marie Stuart*. Hair arranged *à la Greque* and placed over the summit of the head was a short plume of white feathers. On the left side was a bouquet of orange flowers with a small part of the green foliage; on the right a full blown white rose.

By the early 1830s, the whole of Britain was singing:

> A wreath of orange blossoms
> When next we met she wore

as the second verse of one of the top pop songs of the day: T. Haynes Bayly's *She Wore a Wreath of Roses*, a ballad rendered with great feeling at drawing-room pianos throughout the land.

Floral headdresses had made a general fashion come-back several years before the appearance of orange blossom. These natural blooms and garlands suited the simple styles and floating muslins of the day, and sat well on the curls, ringlets and Grecian buns as they would not have done on the Pompadours and monstrous *coiffeurs* of the previous century. To begin with the rose, that old favourite, the flower of Venus, was most in demand, and myrtle (another symbol of love) was also brought back into harness. Princess Charlotte of Wales (only child of the disastrous union between the Prince Regent and Caroline of Brunswick) wore a wreath of roses on her upswept red-gold hair when she married Prince Leopold of Saxe-Coburg in May 1816, while two of her old-fashioned aunts (both daughters of George III), who became some- what aged brides around the same time, chose the more lasting adornments of diamonds and feathers: the 40-year-old Princess Mary married the Duke of Gloucester in July 1816 in a wreath of diamonds; while her sister, the Princess Elizabeth, who, two years later, finally clasped a German prince to her bosom at the age of 46, did so in a diamond bandeau surmounted by ostrich plumes.

By the time Queen Victoria married her 'fascinating' Albert in February 1840, orange blossom had, however, triumphed over all rivals, and the young Queen acknowledged the fact by wearing it in a substantial wreath, undiluted by jewels, feathers, or any other bloom. The Spanish Countess Eugénie de Montijo, whose elegance Queen Victoria much admired, was not so abstemious when she married Napoleon III, thirteen years later. Her wedding was an artistic triumph on several fronts, for, according to Philip Guedalla (in *The Second Empire*), the novelist Prosper Mérimée, 'drafted a wonderful marriage contract with an interminable recital of his young friend's dignities and quarterings, and Félix wrestled with the problems of *coiffeur* presented by a veil, a wreath of orange blossoms and an Imperial crown'.

The vogue for orange flowers is said to have originated in France, but I have not found any indication that the British ever considered it a 'foreign fashion'. Wherever it came from, it was swiftly adopted and all alien origins speedily forgotten; though this doesn't mean that it immediately ousted all competition. To begin with the blossom was combined with other flowers and foliage, especially the rose, and was often overshadowed by them. *La Belle Assemblée* of May 1835 described a typical

116

bridal hairstyle as: 'Hair in large plain bands with *touffes* of orange blossom surrounding a pink rose'; and exactly one year later, the *World of Fashion* added a veil to a similar arrangement and called it the 'Newest London Fashion'. Fairly early on, the blossoms were also used to trim the dress. In September 1835, for instance, *La Belle Assemblée*, again, produced some Frenchified prose to describe a wedding gown of the season: 'Bridal Dress of rich blond lace finished at the bottom in *feston* bows of ribbon *en tablier* with small sprigs of orange blossom: the corsage is *drapé* with jockeys of three frills of blond lace; head-dress of hair and blond scarf attached to the back of the head and flowing over the shoulders.'

Usually the orange flowers were made of wax, but in the reports of some weddings 'real orange blossoms' are specified, and journalists at grand nuptials occasionally vowed that the air was heavy with the scent of these flowers, but that might have been over-enthusiasm, or over-writing.

By the early 1870s, Jeaffreson was pleading for relief from all-white headdresses, composed solely of 'yellow-white orange-flowers and other white buds and blossoms', a style which 'not one lovely girl in a thousand' could wear 'without disadvantage'. He also found the connection between orange blossom and fertility extremely distasteful: 'Custom and romance have raised the chaplet of orange-blossoms to unmerited respect. The white of the orange-flower is an impure white, and the symbolism of the plant is a reason why some other flower should be adopted by the English bride.' He had no fault to find with the all-white wedding dress, however, pointing out that 'in our polite and richer classes, the girl who arranges to be married in any colour but white, takes a sure means of making her bridal doing talked about as savouring of eccentricity'.

White had now truly caught on in America, too. In 1840, Mary Stanley Bunce Dana wrote (in *Passing under the Rod*):

> I saw the young bride in her beauty and pride,
> Bedecked in her snowy array

and the same could have been said by guests at virtually all high society and middle class weddings on both sides of the Atlantic from 1820 on. Even the horses which pulled the bride to church were now white. In June 1844 when the American President John Tyler, a widower of 54, married a lovely young bride of 24, the nation first learned of the affair when he was seen leaving the Church of the Ascension, on New York's Fifth Avenue, in an open barouche, drawn by four white horses, with his bride at his side in white chiffon, white gauze veil and a circlet of white flowers. And that was a very quiet wedding.

Another bride with Presidential connections who wore white was the pretty little Quaker girl from Philadelphia, Sarah Yorke. She married the adopted son of the great Andrew Jackson in 1831, and again, as in the previous century, her bridal finery was far from the prim (if not grim) Quaker image. Her wedding gown (which she also wore for the White House dinner given by President Jackson, a few days after the marriage, to introduce her to Washington society) now forms part of the Smithsonian Institution's 'First Ladies' collection, and it is a charming combination of white satin and muslin. The bodice, of satin, is deeply pointed at the waist, back and front, and off-the-shoulder at the top; it has no sleeves, but a deep Bertha collar of fine lace covers the arms almost to the elbow. The skirt, of fine muslin, is exquisitely embroidered with panels of flowers worked in white silk thread.

There were some notable exceptions to the all white rule, however, and the beautiful Maud Burke of San Francisco was one of them. This strong-minded young lady, who was later to re-christen herself Emerald ('the jewels I wear are Emeralds and since I am nicknamed The Emerald Queen I have adopted it as my Christian name') and to lead royal and fashionable London a fine old dance, married Sir Bache Cunard (of the Cunard shipping line) in New York in April 1895, wearing a 'tailor-made gown of grey cloth and a bonnet to match'.

Lower down the social scale it was still 'coming out bride' which produced the most exotic creations and these, at the beginning of the century, were mostly coloured. According to Mrs. Earle, this ceremony was now even more alarming, for: 'At a certain point in the service, usually after the singing of the second hymn, the happy couple, in agonies of shyness and pride, rose to their feet, and turned slowly twice or thrice around before the eyes of the whole delighted assembly, thus displaying to the full every detail of their attire.' The stimulus of a performance like this often produced outfits verging on the fancy dress. In 1810, a young Salem couple appeared —both of them—in pink: the bride in a pink silk and plush coat, with elaborately puffed short sleeves over tight, wrist-length ones; a high waist and gently gathered skirt; and, on her head, a shirred plush bonnet, in matching pink (all decidedly boudoir); while her new husband sported a wide-brimmed, pink plush hat with a large satin bow (also pink), and a waistcoat of the same figured-silk as the bride's coat. A year or so earlier, a couple in more subdued fawn watered silk had caused just as great a sensation, since the bridegroom's share of the silk had been made up into trousers—the very latest male invention. Usually the congregation in American churches was segregated, the men sitting in one section, and the ladies in another; but wedding groups, which arrived a little late for maximum effect, all sat together like a pride of peacocks.

On both sides of the Atlantic there were stern rules for widows who chose to re-marry and these forbad all thought of white. John Cordy Jeaffreson put the English point of view like this: 'A widow at her re-marriage, provokes no criticism by wearing a silk of sober or fuscous tint. It is indeed held by some critics that any colour, with the single exception of black, is more appropriate than white for a gentlewoman's robe of state at her second marriage, and that she has no more right to the dress of virginal brides than to the decoration of wreath and veil, or the services of bridesmaids.' Mrs. Earle illustrated the same maxim with a story of one of her own 'kinswomen' who was married first at 17, widowed within a few weeks, and then married again ten years later. 'She wore "coming out bride" a silver gray satin gown, and a gray pelisse of uncut velvet with a silken stripe; this was lined with cherry-coloured satin and trimmed with marabout plumes. Her bonnet was of shirred gray velvet with natural gray feathers and cherry-coloured face trimmings of very full ruches of ribbon loops . . . a charming costume, but she was exceedingly unhappy because, having been a widow, she could not in etiquette appear in a white bonnet and feathers and veil. And she felt that coming a stranger to her new home it was so unfortunate to appear in a gray bonnet; that it made her seem like an old woman, and was "so conspicuous".'

There was also a certain delicacy on the part of brides who were *known* to have

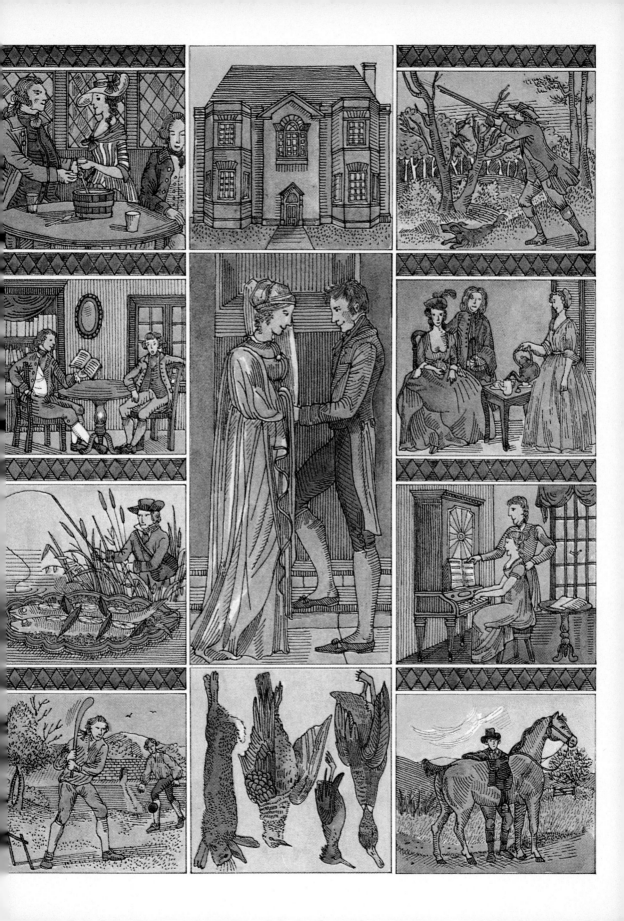

Plate Eight

forfeited their right to virgin white even though they had not precisely been married before. The Reverend Francis Kilvert, in his lively diary, told a sad little tale of a Welsh 'concubine' who wore lilac when her philandering lover finally made an honest woman of her:

> Wednesday, 5 July [1871]: This morning Edward Morgan of Cwmpelved Green brought his concubine to Church and married her. She was a girl of 19 rather nice looking and seemed quiet and modest. She had a pretty bridesmaid and they were both nicely prettily dressed in lilac and white. After the ceremony I saw the stout dwarf Anne Beavan pinning on bright nosegays.

A couple of weeks later Curate Kilvert paid a call on the new bride at her spotless cottage with its little garden 'flaming with nasturtiums':

> A vase of bright fresh flowers stood upon each table and I could have eaten my dinner off every stone of the floor. . . . The oven door was screened from view by a little curtain and everything was made the most and best of. I don't wonder Edward Morgan married the girl. It was not her fault that they were not married before. She begged and prayed her lover to marry her before he seduced her and afterwards. She was very stanch and faithful to him when she was his mistress and I believe she will make him a good wife. . . . The girl said no one ever came near the house to see it, and she kept it as clean and neat and pretty as she could for her own satisfaction.

Ah, Victorian morality! A year earlier, the fine bridegroom had been before the magistrates on a paternity charge: 'An unsuccessful attempt by Samuel Evans' daughter and wife of the Bird's Nest to father the daughter's base child upon Edward Morgan of Cwmpelved Green. It came out that Mrs. Evans had been shameless enough to let the young man sit up at night with Emily after she and her husband had gone to bed. Mrs. V. most properly reprimanded her publicly and turned her out of the Club. Such conduct ought to be strongly marked and disapproved.' (Mrs. V. was the vicar's wife, and the 'Club', no doubt, was the Mother's Union. Such retribution!) No one seems to have done so much as cluck their tongue at the busy Mr. Morgan.

Earlier, Thackeray described the wedding of another unreliable bridegroom, Captain George Osborne, in *Vanity Fair*. The attendant menservants wrote off this occasion as a 'reg'lar shabby turn hout . . . with scarce so much as a breakfast or a wedding faviour', but it did have one 19th century essential—a glass coach. These covered carriages with large glass windows all round were the equivalent of today's big black limousines with white ribbons flying, and the sight of one immediately signified a wedding. Although Captain Osborne's bride, newly impoverished and disgraced by her father's bankruptcy, was dressed only in a 'brown silk pelisse . . . a straw bonnet with a pink ribbon' and a veil of white Chantilly lace, the gentlemen were very elegant indeed. The bridegroom wore a 'blue coat and brass buttons, and a neat buff waistcoat . . . his friend Captain Dobbin, in blue and brass, too', while Mr. Jos Sedley, the bride's brother, was magnificent: 'His shirt collars were higher; his face was redder; his shirt-frill flaunted gorgeously out of his variegated waistcoat. Varnished boots were not invented as yet; but the Hessians on his beautiful legs shone so, that they must have been the identical pair in which the gentleman in the old picture used to shave himself; and on his light green coat there bloomed a fine wedding favour, like a great white spreading magnolia.'

119

And the Bride Wore . . .

At the beginning of the century men's clothes were still as important as those of the ladies and just as open to criticism; but gradually the peacock plumes disappeared and the gentlemen became (and rightly so) a handsome, dark foil for the fashionable absurdities of their partners. Charles Lamb, in his essay *The Wedding*, a whimsical account of the marriage of Sarah Burney (daughter of Rear-Admiral James Burney and niece of the diary-writing Fanny), told how he had met with great disapproval by wearing a sombre black coat while coloured ones were still the vogue. After the ceremony, at which he had stood in for his old friend, the gouty Admiral, and given away the bride, a fellow guest:

> . . . was pleased to say that she had never seen a gentleman before me give away a bride, in black. Now black has been my ordinary apparel so long— indeed, I take it to be the proper costume of an author—the stage sanctions it— that to have appeared in some lighter colour—a pea-green coat, for instance, like the bridegroom's—would have raised more mirth at my expense than the anomaly had created censure. But I could perceive that the bride's mother, and some elderly ladies present (God bless them!) would have been well content, if I had come in any other colour than that.*

That was in 1821; by 1880, Lamb would have met with equal displeasure had he appeared in anything but black. Miss Burney's bridesmaids, 'the three charming Miss Forresters', were also in the vanguard of fashion, wearing coloured dresses rather than white; but they, unfairly, met only with smiles of approval for being so *avant garde*. Lamb himself thought nothing could have been 'more judicious or graceful' than their choice of *toilettes*: 'To give the bride an opportunity of shining singly, they had come habited all in green . . . while *she* [*the bride*] stood at the altar in vestments white and candid as her thoughts, a sacrificial whiteness, *they* assisted in robes such as might become Diana's nymphs . . . as such who had not yet come to the resolution of putting off cold virginity.' The bridal party had arrived at the church 'a little before the clock struck eight', the ceremony having been fixed for 'an early hour, to give time for a little *déjeûne* afterwards, to which a select party of friends had been invited'. This *déjeûne* was held at the Admiral's house, where 'all was merriment, and shaking of hands, and congratulations, and kissing away the bride's tears, and kissing from her in return, till a young lady, who assumed some experience in these matters, having worn the nuptial bands some four or five weeks longer than her friend, rescued her, archly observing, with half an eye upon the bridegroom, that at this rate she would have "none left"'. (An abundance of kissing appears to have been standard practice at weddings in all ages. Stephens said of his *Plaine Countrey Bride* in 1615: 'Her best commendation is to be kist often: this onely proceeds from her without interruption.') At the Burney wedding, 'after a protracted breakfast of three hours—if stores of cold fowles, tongues, hams, botargoes,† dried fruits, wines, cordials, etc., can deserve so meagre an appellation—the coach was announced, which was come to carry off the bride and bridegroom for a season, as custom has sensibly ordained, into the country'.

Then came the moment we all know so well: 'No one knew whether to take their leave or stay. We seemed assembled upon a silly occasion.' Unhappily, not all residue

---

* *The Wedding* was first published in *The London Magazine* (from which the above quotation is taken), in June 1825, and later reprinted, with slight alterations, in *The Last Essays of Elia*.
† *Botargoes*—relishes of mullet or tunny roe.

wedding parties are blessed with a guest like Lamb, a man with a 'foolish talent' for 'thinking and giving vent to all manner of strange nonsense'. After he had 'rattled off' some of his 'most excellent absurdities', this gathering gained new life and continued (with additional aid from whist) until midnight.

Forty years later, in 1861, the high priests of *Minister's Gazette of Fashion* felt obliged to issue a public rebuke to gentlemen who, like Lamb, persisted in wearing black. 'Unfortunately,' they sighed, 'invisible green and even black frock coats are occasionally seen at weddings but both are inconsistent with the occasion except in the case of the marriage of a clergyman.' Instead, they advised blue, claret or mulberry frock coats, pale drab or lavender doeskin trousers, and waistcoats of white quilting. In 1869, the *West End Gazette of Fashion* suggested, for the bridegroom, a short blue frock coat with a velvet collar and edging of silk cord; dove grey trousers; lavender gloves; and a light blue tie. 'The groomsman wears a frock coat with trousers and tie not quite so light and gay as the bridegroom's.' Despite such knowledgeable edicts, tail coats were still frequently worn instead of the newer 'frock' (Prince Louis of Hesse wore one when he married Queen Victoria's daughter, Princess Alice, at Osborne in July 1862), and some people with particularly nice judgment in such matters thought that a frock coat was 'not quite correct' for the bridegroom if the bride wore a veil. In the 1870s and '80s the battle was between frock coats and the even newer morning coat. The *Tailor and Cutter*, downing scissors and pins in 1886, had to admit to fashion anarchy on this point: 'There is no set style nowadays', they confessed. By 1899, however, all was firmly under control once more and they were able to make an absolute ruling for both bridegroom and best man: 'Black frock coat faced with silk. Double-breasted waistcoat of light colour and a dark tie, or a dark waistcoat with a light tie. Grey striped trousers. Patent-leather button boots. Pale tan kid gloves or grey suede. Silk hat.' Throughout the century, the hat gave least trouble of all: a black silk topper went with all manner of coats—tail, frock or morning—whatever the colour.

One bridegroom who was instructed to wear a tail-coat, and a black one at that, was the 'immortal Mr. Adolphus Minn', who learned to become a gentleman by reading the *Manual for Ladies* (and whose tussle with the etiquette of matrimony was unfolded in *The Tatler* of 15 December 1877). According to this 'immortal' gentleman's social bible: 'A black dress coat and trousers, white waistcoat, either silk or other good material—not satin—with white necktie and white gloves, are in much better taste than coloured clothes.' Mrs. Mary Sherwood, a New Yorker who wrote an American etiquette book, *Manners and Social Usages*, in 1884, brought sound common sense to bear on the problem: 'No man ever puts on a dress coat before his seven o'clock dinner, therefore every bridegroom is dressed in a frock coat and light trousers of any pattern he pleases, in other words, he wears a formal morning dress, drives to the Church with the best man, and awaits the arrival of the bride in the vestry room. He may wear gloves or not as he chooses. The best man . . . follows him to the altar, stands at his right hand a little behind him and holds his hat during the marriage service.'

The best man, or groomsman as he was called until late in the century, needed only two qualifications for the job: he was expected to be a friend or relation of the groom, and he had to be a bachelor. There was no male equivalent of the matron-of-honour,

And the Bride Wore . . .

as Charles Dickens discovered when he asked his married publisher, John Macrone, to stand by him on his wedding day and then had to withdraw the honour:

> My dear Macrone.
> The unanimous voice of the ladies, confirms the authority of Mrs. Macrone. They say, with her, that I *must* be attended to the place of execution, by a single man: I have therefore engaged a substitute, and inclose you an Invite to the subsequent ceremonials, which of course you accept. . . .

In feudal times the bridegroom's closest friend had assisted in the capture of the bride and, according to Jeaffreson, he was still 'expected to bleed freely in his friend's cause', though now in a more commercial manner: by buying a costly present. He was usually expected, too, to answer the toast to the bridesmaids, though this does not always seem to have been the case.

The bridesmaids themselves blossomed, multiplied, and flowered in greater and more exotic profusion as the century wore on. Or, as Jeaffreson put it: 'It is no uncommon thing for a bride of Victorian London to ask ten, or even twelve, maidens to gratify her love of display, and encourage her in the execution of a work of sublime self-sacrifice, by appearing in her bridal train with sympathising looks and harmonious dresses.' The lesser ranks of these platoons had little to do except look appealing, but their commander-in-chief, the senior bridesmaid, had an assortment of tasks and occasional perks. According to Mr. Minn's *Manual for Ladies* it was her job to remove the bride's gloves when the priest asked 'Who giveth this woman . . .' and to hold them during the rest of the ceremony. Afterwards she could claim them 'as her guerdon or badge of office'. (In America, according to Mrs. Sherwood, brides had learned a little trickery on this point: 'Formerly brides removed the whole glove, now they adroitly cut the finger of the left hand glove so that they can remove that without pulling off the whole glove for the ring.') Before the wedding, again according to Jeaffreson, the chief bridesmaid was expected to spend 'a few hours in attending the bride on shopping excursions, and gossiping with her about her *trousseau*. Like the inferior maidens [*the other bridesmaids*], she must grudge no needful time or expense for the execution of her official toilet. The night before the wedding she is sometimes required to pass in comparative unrest and imperfectly successful endeavours to reassure the bride that she will never repent the next day. On the wedding-day she enjoys herself more than any other woman concerned in the solemnity. Standing close to the bride in church, she holds the dear girl's fan and scent-bottle, and signs the register as witness after the performance of the marriage ceremony. Breakfast follows, and when the slipper has been thrown after the retiring carriage of the happy couple, her work is at an end, unless it is a wedding "with cards", and she is engaged to help in directing envelopes, and making out the invariably incomplete list of persons to whom cards ought to be sent.'

Cards were a printed notification that the wedding had taken place. They varied in style a great deal during the century, and were often on the verge of disappearing completely; but brides who failed to send them obviously felt they might well have been expected to do so, for the warning 'No cards' can sometimes be seen at the end of Victorian wedding announcements, in the same way that the plea 'No flowers' appears at the end of funeral notices today. Jeaffreson, writing in 1872, gave a potted history of the custom: 'In the days of our grandmothers, a bride's nuptial card was always an

122

invitation to a banquet of sweetmeats, as well as an announcement of her marriage and future residence.' It gave her change of name and change of address, told the date of her return from the honeymoon and the 'particular days on which she would sit in state, to receive callers and regale them with wine and wedding-cake'. But from 1830 onwards 'fashion has been notably capricious and changeful with respect to wedding-cards and bridal receptions. She abolished successively the feast of sweetmeats and the ceremonious call on one of several stated days. Then, for a while, she declared that a bride's cards should merely state her abode and the time "after" which she would be "at home" to callers fortunate enough to find her there. She next ordained that the bridal placard should say nothing about the sender's "home", should not even give its address. It should be a single undated card, sent in a plain envelope; it should be a contrivance of two cards joined together with silver thread; it should consist of two ordinary calling-cards—one the sender's, the other her groom's. Having invented half-a-hundred varieties of the bridal note, and discarded each of them after taking into brief favour, Fashion grew weary of nuptial cards, and proclaimed them antiquated things that should no longer be tolerated in polite society. At the present moment it is an open question amongst the guardians of our social proprieties, whether a bride should "send cards" or be married "without cards". But I am assured by many judicious ladies, who are greatly authoritative in feminine affairs, and hold fashion in no high esteem, that nuptial cards, announcing the bride's maiden name, wifely name, and London address, are never likely to go altogether out of use, as the neglect to distribute them is fruitful of divers inconveniences in the vast Babylon.'

Despite the prophesies of these authoritative ladies, this convenient custom has virtually died out in Britain. In North America, however, it flourishes still, though in its least communicative form. In both the United States and Canada, cards are regularly sent out to friends and relatives who could not attend the wedding (and sometimes, rather superfluously, even to those who did), but these handsome folded quarto sheets of light card or embossed paper (usually printed in black) almost invariably state only that Miss ——, married Mr. ——, at ——, on such-and-such a date, and it is left to the recipient to play detective and find out where to write to congratulate them.

In Victorian times, there also appears to have been some confusion amongst the arbiters of etiquette as to who should pay for the dresses of the bridesmaids. Jeaffreson inferred that the cost was borne by the girls themselves; while Mr. Adolphus Minn's *Manual for Ladies* ruled that: 'the bridegroom, if able and of a generous disposition will give a wedding dress to the bridesmaid, should there be only one. Should he not do it, she must provide her own. So likewise where there are several, the bridesmaids provide their own attire. The bride sends to each, the day before the wedding, the gloves to be worn on the occasion, wrapped up in white paper and tied with white ribbon'. Thackeray, however, in *Snobs and Marriage*, which he wrote for *Punch* in the 1840s, indicated that the grand gesture was for the bridegroom to pay for the lot. When the dashing young snob, Lieutenant Pump Temple, married his cousin Fanny Figtree:

> You should have seen the wedding! Six bridesmaids in pink, to hold the fan, bouquet, gloves, scent-bottle, and pocket-handkerchief of the bride; basketfuls of white favours in the vestry, to be pinned on to the footmen and horses; a genteel congregation of curious acquaintance in the pews, a shabby one of poor

on the steps; all the carriages of all our acquaintance, whom Aunt Figtree had levied for the occasion; and of course four horses for Mr. Pump's bridal vehicle.

Then comes the breakfast, or *déjeûner*, if you please, with a brass band in the street, and policeman to keep order. The happy bridegroom spends about a year's income in dresses for the bridesmaids and pretty presents; and the bride must have a *trousseau* of laces, satins, jewel-boxes and tomfoolery, to make her fit to be a lieutenant's wife. There was no hesitation about Pump. He flung about his money as if it had been dross.

There was no hesitation about Mary Lamb (sister to Charles), either. When she acted as bridesmaid at the marriage of Sarah Stoddart and the writer William Hazlitt in May 1808, she knew exactly who should pay for her dress—herself. But what colour it should be, that was more difficult. And then, the bride being such a fine needlewoman, there was the question of whether the gown should bear witness to this fact. An additional complication was the arrival of some fine silk from a mutual friend, Thomas Manning, the intrepid Tibetan traveller, now in China. . . . Miss Lamb (a mature bridesmaid of 44) thrashed over all these points in a letter to the bride-to-be on 16 March 1808:

> I never heard in the annals of weddings (since the days of Nausicaa,* and she only washed her old gowns for that purpose) that the brides ever furnished the apparel of their maids. Besides, I can be completely clad in your work without it, for the spotted muslin will serve both for cap and hat (Nota bene, my hat is the same as yours) and the gown you sprigged for me has never been made up, therefore I can wear that—Or, if you like better, I will make up a new silk which Manning has sent me from China. Manning would like to hear I wore it for the first time at your wedding. It is a very pretty light colour, but there is an objection (besides not being your work and that is a very serious objection) and that is, Mrs. Hazlitt tells me that all Winterslow would be in an uproar if the bridemaid was to be dressed in anything but white, and although it is a very light colour I confess we cannot call it white, being a sort of a dead-whiteish-bloom colour; then silk, perhaps, in a morning is not so proper, though the occasion, so joyful, might justify full dress. Determine for me in this perplexity between the sprig and the China-Manning silk. . . .

As the century advanced white became the exception rather than the rule for bridesmaids. To give the bride 'an opportunity of shining singly' the attendants were dressed in colourful contrast. Pale blue and pink (often some of each) were the favourite colours, with lilac and pale green close behind. Rich shades were often used for trimmings, and sometimes for the dresses themselves. In November 1859, Lord Clarendon wrote to the Duchess of Manchester:

> My niece's wedding *came off* yesty: & *went off* very well. She had 12 bridesmaids very prettily dressed in red (groseilles soummises) of a crapy sort of stuff wh: made the church look gay. She has the most entire confidence in her husband for whom I entertain the most profound distrust, but he is worshipped by his own family wh: is something & he is as clever as he is unpopular wh: is saying a good

* The tale of Nausicaa, had just been rewritten by Lamb in his *Adventures of Ulysses*, and thus was fresh in his sister's mind.

deal, & I can only hope it may be well as she is the best of girls & recd: nearly 150 presents.

Every conceivable type of headdress was worn by bridesmaids, from garlands of flowers and veils like the bride, through bonnets and little hats, rosebuds and jewels, to the large picture hats which came into vogue in the 1890s. Usually they carried posies (or at the end of the century, 'shower bouquets'), supplied by the bridegroom, and wore a keepsake of the occasion—most often a bracelet, locket or brooch—also 'a gift of the bridegroom'.

Their dresses, like that of the bride, usually followed the fashion of the day but, towards the end of the century, period costume also came into favour. The *Illustrated London News*, of 1 January 1885, reported that the bridesmaids of the Hon. Dulcibella Eden, daughter of Lord Auckland, wore outfits 'designed after Sir Joshua Reynolds' (who had flourished a hundred years earlier). They 'consisted of white satin petticoats, and overskirts of soft white silk, with pointed bodices and fichus of the same, large caps, and yellow shoes and stockings'; and each bridesmaid carried 'a bunch of yellow chrysanthemums'. The pages 'were in Gainsborough costumes of cream ribbed serge, cloaks lined with yellow silk, and three-cornered white hats'. Eight years later, the *Lady's Pictorial* (15 July 1893) described a very pretty Norwich wedding, at which the bridesmaids wore 'Empire costume'. The bride and her family all strolled to church together on this occasion—as wedding parties had done in the 18th century—but everything else was strictly contemporary.

Even at weddings where the bridesmaids were dressed in coloured gowns, the guests still did not always respect the bride's right to shine alone. At many grand marriages the bride's and often the bridegroom's mother wore white, and when Lady Audrey Townshend married the Hon. Greville Howard, son of the Earl of Suffolk, in September 1873, two young guests arrived in white trimmed with pale blue, while the bridesmaids wore pale blue trimmed with dark red. The white and blue ensembles were described in great detail in her diary* by Laura Troubridge, the 15-year-old god-daughter of the bride (who wore one of them—her 18-year-old sister, Amy, wore the other); and she did an excellent job on reporting what everyone else was dressed in too:

> Amy and I had white nansook gowns, two large flounces on the underskirt, a very pretty polonaise† of the same, trimmed with insertion with sky blue ribbon run through the lace on both sides. The bodies were made crossing over, we had capes to match, also trimmed, sky blue sashes, snoods and neck ribbons, white straw hats, very high crowns and with large round brims, trimmed with black grosgrain and white feathers, (Amy's had also a little blue one, and mine had a lovely pale blue rose).

Primrose kid gloves, 'silver ornaments, white tulle ties, black silk stockings and high kid boots' completed the outfits, and the young lady thought they were both

---

* Edited by her daughter, Jaqueline Hope-Nicholson, and published in 1966 as *Life Amongst the Troubridges*. Laura Troubridge was later to put her talent for precise observation to good use as a successful artist, commissioned by Queen Victoria and other members of the royal family.

† *Polonaise*—what, in the 18th century, had been called a *Mantua*: a bodice with a skirt, open from the waist down to show a petticoat (now called an underskirt) beneath. The style was said to have been copied from Polish national dress, hence the name.

'very "tweetly" dressed'. They set off for the wedding in a fly with two aunts (one in 'a cream colour bonnet covered with lace and pearls' which 'looked very well indeed'; the other in 'a very ugly dress, a light brown silk gown trimmed with dark brown silk, a white hairy stuff, with silk stripes, polonaise with no sleeves—which suited her very badly indeed—and a peacock grosgrain and white lace bonnet'). At eleven they took their places in the church and the half-hour wait for the bride which followed gave the sharp-eyed Miss Troubridge time to take in what everybody else was wearing:

Lady Booba [*Lady Elizabeth St. Aubyn*], sister to the bride, had on a dark blue satin trimmed with light blue velvet. Lady Bute, who is lovely, quite tiny, with the most exquisite little figure, had a grena [*dark red*] silk dress, trimmed with salmon colour silk. Aunt Kitty, who looked very nice indeed, had a maroon satin dress, quite plain, with a very long train and a pouffe bonnet to match and a good deal of white lace about her neck. Freda Creswell had, as usual, a grey silk gown trimmed with pink. Little Eva North was there and looked very pretty in rose colour and white. The bridesmaids wore pale blue silk trimmed with gauze flounces of the same colour, and silk bows edged with dark grena velvet, long grena velvets round their necks and blue silk stockings and boots with rosettes. The five big ones had blue and grena bonnets, while the three little St. Aubyn girls had white straw hats, high and large-brimmed, lined with blue silk, caught up at one side with blue silk and blue and grena feathers. The five elder ones had silver bracelets with Lady Audrey's initials on them, and the three little ones had lockets the same.

Lady Audrey wore a white satin gown, trimmed with Brussels lace, and a Brussels lace veil fastened with diamond stars, a diamond necklace and earrings, orange blossom in her hair, and a very large bouquet. She trembled dreadfully as she came up the aisle on Lord Bute's arm (who gave her away), followed by her eight bridesmaids. I did pity her so, she did look so *agitée*. Everybody, of course, was staring at her. *Save* me from ever having a grand wedding. If ever I am married I should like to have nobody there but the clergyman and the bridegroom, and that reminds me of Mr. Howard, whom I have not spoken of yet. He looks rather old and stern, very like a surgeon, and not nearly good enough for her.

The ceremony was very impressive, it made one feel somehow what a very solemn thing marriage is. Soon after the service we walked up to the house and went into the Saloon, but there was such a crush there that we could not stay. . . . The breakfast, which was in the large Hall, was very good indeed.

Lord Bute proposed the health of the bride and bridegroom and Mr. Howard returned thanks, but they neither of them made speeches. For going away Lady A. had on a dark blue velvet gown with a very long train, but as she came to the door her maid threw over her shoulders a splendid Indian shawl, red embroidered all over with gold, which was a wedding present from Lord Bute and had, so L. told me, cost £400, but it made her look rather old and prevented us seeing her gown. They drove off in a regular shower of flowers and old satin slippers (one of which went straight into the bridegroom's hat as he was taking it off to bow). Everybody then said goodbye and drove off, and so ended the much longed for wedding day.

A newspaper account of a wedding which took place a few days before that of Lady Audrey Townshend shows the matrimonial pattern to have been very much the same amongst the wealthy middle class as with the aristocracy, and it also gives a delightful picture of a whole village entering into the festivities. The bride on this occasion was one of the nine Potter girls, a sister of Beatrice (later Mrs. Sidney Webb) of Fabian Society and London School of Economics fame. Beatrice, with four more of the sisters, was a bridesmaid, and a pretty formidable retinue they must have made: Malcolm Muggeridge (who married a niece of the bride) has described them as 'massive, dark, restless looking women, who, one feels, might easily have savaged the photographer as he emerged from under the protection of his black cloth'. The bridegroom was Daniel Meinertzhagen, of Viking and German descent; and the courtship was worthy of a romantic Victorian novel. Meinertzhagen a guest at the Potter home, Standish House, in Gloucestershire, had a bad fall while out hunting and was carried back to the house like a better-tempered version of *The Man Who Came to Dinner*; during an extended stay, his broken bones and convalescent spirits were tended by Miss Georgina Potter. Less than a year later, they married. And the *Gloucester Journal* of 13 September 1873, reported on the occasion at length:

> . . . The event caused no little stir among the inhabitants of the straggling village, who did their best to make it of a festive character. A small triumphal arch was constructed at the entrance to the drive leading to the house with the words 'Long life, health and happiness' and 'God bless you' on either side and there were small erections along the route to the church. At the entrance to the church was a pretty arch with the words 'health and happiness' on one side and 'Dieu vous garde' on the other, and a Union Jack blowing in the breeze from the old fashioned tower. The ceremony was fixed to take place at 11.00 o'clock and the bridal party began to arrive shortly before that hour, the organist (Mr. T. E. Boucher) gave a selection from 'The Creation' (Graceful Consort) as they were assembling. Just before the bride entered, the choir, mainly composed of several ladies living in the vicinity, began the well known hymn 'The Voice that breathed o'er Eden' singing it to the tune 'Magdalena'. The bride was adorned in a white corded silk dress, trimmed with white satin and tulle, and wore a wreath of orange blossoms and clematis. She was attended by the following bridesmaids: Miss Potter, Miss Meinertzhagen, Miss Blanche Potter, Miss Theresa Potter, Miss Margaret Potter, Miss Beatrice Meinertzhagen, Miss Beatrice Potter, Miss Rosalind Heyworth Potter and Miss Lina Heyworth. Their dresses were of pink or green silk, trimmed with Valenciennes lace and ribbons and muslin flounces and they wore tulle veils and wreaths of pink and white roses. When the bridal pair had entered and taken their places, and the villagers had crowded in behind them, filling the edifice, the scene inside the chancel was exceedingly pretty. The altar decorated with evergreens and jasmine entwined around the altar rails formed an excellent background to the richly coloured dress of the bridal party and the soft sunbeams stealing in at the plain glass windows gave a pleasing effect to the whole scene. The front of the choir was also decorated with choice flowers and the whole the work of the Misses Potter and the Misses Sheringham assisted by some of the parishioners. Tallis service in G was used and the psalm sung was the 128th. Mendelssohn's 'Wedding March' poured forth from the organ at the conclusion of the ceremony, the church bells rang out a merry peal, and as the bride and bridgroom left the church some of the village school children strewed flowers in their path. A sumptuous *dejeuner* was provided at Standish House.
>
> . . . The happy pair left shortly after 2.00 amid a shower of slippers, to catch

the 2.50 Express from Stroud to Paddington, en route for Switzerland. The wedding guests indulged in a dance in the evening and at nightfall there was a display of fireworks. The school children were feasted in the afternoon and the villagers were not forgotten.

The wedding tour (which was spent in Paris and the Black Forest, not Switzerland as reported) was fraught with what we now think of (no doubt unfairly) as typically Victorian difficulties. A son of the union, Richard Meinertzhagen, wrote many years later (in his *Diary of a Black Sheep*) that the honeymoon 'was not altogether a happy one, for my mother in her puritan chastity could not respond to father's exuberance. In Paris my father insisted on buying for my mother most unsuitable hats.'

Sometimes, instead of the squire feasting his tenants, the tenants laid on celebrations for the squire—as happened in February 1868 when Earl Beauchamp married Lady Mary Stanhope. Subscriptions were raised by the people of Malvern, the nearest town to Lord Beauchamp's seat, Madresfield Court, and bustling committees prepared a day and night of festivities. The marriage ceremony took place in London—at that sacred haven of society, St. George's, Hanover Square—but the church bells of Malvern peeled out all morning just the same; flags flew all over the town, and everyone was out and about, parading the streets in their best clothes and holiday spirits. Around one o'clock news that the marriage ceremony was complete reached the town by telegraph, whereupon the 'field guns of the Worcestershire Yeomany Cavalry, with a detachment of the artillery under the command of Captain Weaver, fired a salute from the knoll called St. Ann's Delight, and the bells of the Priory church were joyfully rung'. In the evening, Lord Beauchamp and his bride arrived on the scene themselves and were greeted by another ear-splitting salute and more bells. At seven o'clock a torchlight procession climbed up the hill called the Worcestershire Beacon to set light to the great bonfire half-way up:

> Three hundred torches of a peculiar construction had been provided, and the effect of this procession as it flashed among the ravines and on the syenite ribs of the hill, whether seen from below or above, was very picturesque and effective. On arriving at the bonfire rock, they made a halt; and then a little 'scene' was enacted, composed for the occasion by Mr. E. Lees, in which the marshall of the procession, with a personification of 'Modern Malvern' and 'The Genius of the Hills,' figured to the great satisfaction of the thousands of spectators, who joined in the choruses of 'Welcome to Earl Beauchamp and his lovely bride' with the utmost enthusiasm. This little masque being played out, a display of marine signal-lights and rockets, with mortars and the roar of artillery, announced that the bonfire was lighted. It burned so vividly as to be seen conspicuously far over the vale below, and it continued burning splendidly all through the night.

The *Illustrated London News*, which reported all this, gave special mention to 'Mr. W. Archer, of the Railway Hotel', who constructed this magnificent pyre from: '1300 faggots, twenty-four cords of ash, four truckloads of old railway-sleepers, one hundred tar barrels, six barrels of pitch, 1500 hop-poles, thirty-six gallons of petroline, 120 cartloads of gorse, six waggon-loads of larch-croppings, and two tons of coal.' At nine o'clock there was a display of 'rockets, shells, and coloured flares . . . in the presence of an immense number of spectators. In addition to this, several fire-balloons were sent up, and the electric and oxy-hydrogen lights were exhibited at intervals from the abbey tower and the top of the library with at times an almost magical effect among the old trees and buildings, raising the most singular moving shadows, finely contrasting with the changing coloured lights.' The boys of Malvern College also built a bonfire, in the school grounds, in honour of the marriage, Lord Beauchamp being the 'liberal patron, and president of the council of that rising and popular college. Many hearty cheers were given by the boys for the noble Earl and his bride.'

Schoolchildren less privileged than those at Malvern College were regularly feasted on these occasions—as at the Meinertzhagen-Potter wedding—though often they had to sing for their supper first. These were the days of charity schools and the lady of the great house was usually actively engaged in the running of them; when a child of the great house married, the charity children were lined up in matching uniforms, either along the aisle inside the church, or the path outside it, and were often given the task of strewing flowers before the bride. In October 1847, the Duchess of Leinster's school turned out in force for the marriage of her son, the Marquis of Kildare to Lady Caroline Leveson-Gower. In this case, according once more to the *Illustrated London News*: 'The centre aisle was supplied by between fifty and sixty little girls educated in the Duchess' own school, all of whom wore white dresses and straw hats trimmed with a wreath of green leaves, each bearing a small basket filled with choicest flowers. All the boys wore white favours.' In 1863, at the wedding of the Prince of Wales (later Edward VII), the children of the Queen's schools were lined up outside St. George's Chapel, Windsor, the girls dressed in scarlet cloaks and the boys in grey.

At the beginning of the century the wedding group in church was still mostly very small, with a wider circle of relatives and friends being asked to the breakfast. But, by the 1850s, a large congregation had become the fashionable aim, and 'the church was crammed' was a most gratifying thing to be able to say. In November 1851, the marriage of the Duke of Richmond's daughter, Lady Augusta Lennox, to Prince Edward of Saxe-Weimar, was particularly successful in this respect. Lord Malmesbury recorded (in his *Memoirs of an Ex-Minister*), that it 'went off very well, to the great edification of an immense congregation. The church was so full that several ladies got into the pulpit'. With such a mass of spectators, charity children lining the aisles, and the bride sweeping in late with ten or twelve bridesmaids, it is not surprising that wedding music was now introduced as the final flourish: it was invaluable for signalling the important moments, bridging awkward gaps, and pulling the whole spectacle, in general, into one neat and dramatic package. What is surprising is that the chosen music should have come, in most cases, from the repertoire of the profane rather than the sacred. Mendelssohn's *Wedding March*, which was the first piece to become inextricably linked with the marriage ceremony, was composed as part of his incidental music to Shakespeare's *A Midsummer Night's Dream* (and it was composed in 1826, when Mendelssohn was only 17); twenty years later, Wagner wrote his wedding march (strictly speaking his *Bridal Chorus*) for the secular *Lohengrin* and his bride, Elsa of Brabant. Even in Catholic France, at the magnificent Notre Dame wedding of Napoleon III, it was music from the stage rather than the church which accompanied the Empress Eugénie on her way to the altar: the march from Meyerbeer's *Le Prophète*, an opera which had been premiered in Paris four years earlier.

Mendelssohn's *Wedding March* is thought to have first been played at a wedding in 1847, the year Novello's originally published the music—as a piano duet. Samuel Reay, an enterprising young organist (who was later to become famous both as a performer and composer) immediately adapted it for his own instrument—and one pair of hands—and played it at a wedding in the parish church of Tiverton, Devon. In 1858 it accompanied Queen Victoria's eldest daughter, the Princess Royal, as she walked out of St. James's Chapel on the arm of Prince Frederick William of Prussia, and it has been fashionable ever since; though it was not chosen when the Princess Royal's brother, Albert Edward, Prince of Wales (the future Edward VII) married the beautiful Princess Alexandra of Denmark five years later. According to Queen Victoria's own account of that occasion (set down in detail in her Journal on the night of the wedding), Handel's *Processional March* was played for the entrance of the bride and Beethoven's *Hallelujah Chorus* (from his oratorio, *The Mount of Olives*) for her exit. In between, *Albert's Chorale* was sung, a work composed by the Prince Consort, who had died only fifteen months before the wedding. The whole congregation turned their beady, intrusive eyes on the newly-widowed Queen at this point, and rushed to record how she had taken it as soon as they got home: 'When a chorale composed by Prince Albert began, she gave a look upwards, which spoke volumes', wrote Lord Granville. The Queen herself noted, with sad simplicity, it 'affected me much'.

Until the 1880s, Handel's *Occasional Overture* was the music which immediately meant the arrival of the bride to most people, and this also was played at several royal weddings. Princess Beatrice, the last of Queen Victoria's children to marry, was accompanied to the altar by it in 1885; but, four years later, at the next important royal marriage (that of Princess Louise of Wales), the *Illustrated London News* reported: 'As the well known music of Wagner's March from "*Lohengrin*" came from the organ the bride entered on the arm of the Prince of Wales.' Both in America —where, three years earlier, it had been played at the wedding of President Grover Cleveland (with Sousa conducting)—and in Britain, the *Bridal Chorus* had arrived to stay. Though in America, perversely, Wagner's *Here Comes the Bride!* was played for the *departure* of the bride at some weddings (as it was at President Cleveland's), while Mendelssohn heralded her arrival.

There was great scope for marches at royal weddings since there were so many processions. The clergy usually arrived first—the Archbishop of Canterbury at the head of a dozen or so deans and chaplains. (At the wedding of Queen Victoria's third son, the Duke of Connaught, this priestly assemblage took their places to 'the minuet to the overture to Samson', by Handel.) The royal guests and their suites were next up the aisle; then the Queen with her household; followed by the bridegroom with his supporters; and finally the bride. Handel's march from *Hercules* and his *Processional March* were often played; while Mendelssohn's march from *Athalie* usually accompanied the bridegroom, sometimes the Queen, and at the wedding of the Prince of Wales it was played for the royal guests. The royal organist at Windsor, Sir George Elvey, composed a special march, called *Albert Edward*, for the Prince of Wales himself, and this was also played (by Sir George) for the entrance of the Prince of Wales's brother, the Duke of Connaught, on his wedding day. When the Queen's youngest son, Leopold, Duke of Albany, married in 1882, Her Majesty very grandly commissioned Charles Gounod to write a special march for his German bride.

Handel's *Hallelujah Chorus* from the *Messiah* was sung on at least one occasion, and Beethoven's, from *The Mount of Olives*, on several.

At humbler weddings, 'the service was fully choral' was now a nice thing to be able to include in the wedding notices. ('The service was fully choral, and the church, which was crowded to excess, was tastefully decorated with palms and flowers', read a *Lady's Pictorial* wedding report in July 1893, greatly to the comfort of the bride's mother, no doubt.)

For the celebrations which followed, military bands were favoured both by royalty and those subjects who could afford such magnificence. Jeaffreson wrote of 'the military band retained by wealthy hosts to play dance-music and operatic selections at a bridal-ball or garden-party'. He also showed that, at the other end of the musical scale, the marrow-bone-and-cleaver bands of butchers were still in operation:

> . . . even yet it seldom happens that a London butcher brings his bride home without receiving a rattling expression of the kindly feelings cherished for him and her by his blue-sleeved brethren. Occasionally, also, it still happens in 'the city' and old-fashioned quarters of the capital that the neighbouring butchers turn out in force at night, or at daybreak, and raise a bony riot before the house, to which some especially affable customer or patron of an influential meat-salesman has brought his bride a few hours before. I could name an eminent London physician to whom the harmony of the bones was thus accorded some years since by a strong regiment of Newgate Market butchers on his return from his wedding-trip to his residence in Finsbury Square.

During most of the 19th century, twelve noon continued to be the deadline for weddings performed in church without a special licence, and this was, no doubt, the main reason for the great popularity of wedding breakfasts, or, more genteelly, *déjeûners*. An early start to the great day also allowed bride and groom to set out on their fashionable wedding-trip at a reasonable hour. Some marriages, like that of Sarah Burney, took place at eight o'clock in the morning, and then the wedding breakfast really was a breakfast, though a superior one. But even when the ceremony was squeezed in at the other end of the canonical time-table, the meal which followed—by rights a luncheon—was still called a breakfast, and so it continued to be until a few years ago, when 'wedding reception' became a general cover-all for everything from full-blown dinner to *canapés* and curled sandwiches. Very early on the pattern became much the same as the one we follow still, with all its pleasures and all its agonies. Disraeli told his sister on 15 July 1841: 'Yesterday Lord Villiers was married to Peel's daughter; the church crammed, and at the breakfast Prince George proposed the health of the bride and bridegroom. Peel acknowledged the toast, and spoke shortly, but so pathetically that Lord Jersey burst into violent tears. During his sketch of the character of a *good* man, Wilton was seen gradually to grow redder and redder, till at length the personal allusions overcame him, and he also audibly wept.' For every bride today who dreads the same upsurge of parental pathos, who *knows* that the speech which was going to be so jolly is bound to end in a flood of tears, there may perhaps be some small consolation in the knowledge that even the great Sir Robert Peel couldn't help himself, either.

The centre-piece of the feast was now a towering cake, such as we know today, and towards the end of the century, newspaper reports of marriages often ended with the name of the maker: 'The wedding cake was supplied by Messrs. W. and G. Buzard, of Oxford Street, W.' added a touch of class to the account, while 'The wedding cake was supplied by Messrs. Bolland and Sons, of Chester', indicated that absolutely no expense whatsoever had been spared. At royal weddings it was, and still is, the custom for great baking concerns to present a cake to the bride, and in 1871, when Queen Victoria's fourth daughter, Princess Louise, married the Marquis of Lorne, Messrs. Bolland and Sons sent a magnificent example of their wares to Windsor Castle. According to the *Illustrated London News*, it was made 'in three tiers, placed on a gold stand weighing about 2 cwt., and measuring at the base of the lower cake 2 ft. in diameter, and in height nearly 5 ft. The gold plateau had the Royal arms at four equal distances, with Cupids and flowers. The lower tier was ornamented with blue panels, baskets of flowers, fruit, and love-birds between a scroll leaf, and medallions containing likenesses of the Marquis of Lorne and Princess Louise, with their respective coronets above. The second tier was festooned with the rose, shamrock, and thistle. The third tier was entirely of network, with cornucopias and shields, on which were the monograms of the bride and bridegroom. The whole was surmounted by a handsome vase of flowers, with silk banners edged with silver fringe, containing the armorial bearings of the Princess and of the Marquis. Each tier of the cake was bordered with trellis-work studded with pearls.' However, the 'principal cake on the table, at the wedding breakfast', was that made by Her Majesty's chief confectioner at Windsor Castle. This 'perfect triumph of the confectioner's art', was 5 ft. 4 in. high, and had a diameter of 2 ft. 6 in. 'The base was decorated with white satin, bearing coats of arms, and initials "L.L." entwined in blue, wreaths of orange-blossom, and small vases containing the same flowers. Within an alcove above the base was a fountain, with doves drinking, and around this miniature temple were four statues, representing Agriculture, Fine Arts, Commerce, and Science. The upper part was crowned by a figure of a vestal virgin. All the figures and ornaments were of sugar.' Besides these two giants, there were also 'presentation cakes for the Royal Family', and '300 lb. of wedding cake for distribution' (all made by Gunters of Berkeley Square).

Grand weddings in America were also occasionally graced by more than one cake, though here it was brought about by the great American tradition of 'his' and 'hers'. In October 1874, when the guests filed into the Chicago dining-room of Mr. Henry Hamilton Honoré, following the marriage of his daughter to young Colonel Frederick Grant (eldest son of President Ulysses S. Grant), they found at one end of the 14-foot table a 'Bride's Cake, decorated with natural flowers', and at the other end a 'Groom's Cake decorated with natural flowers'—and, as the lilac-coloured menus also informed them, these were supplemented by stewed terrapin, escalloped oysters, sweetbread, turkey and oyster patties, chicken and lobster salads, fillet of snipes 'in Paper cases', boned quail and boned prairie chicken, both 'in jelly form', plus a multitude of other cakes, ices, meringues, wine jellies, fresh fruit, and fruit salad; and, to see it all smoothly digested, tea, coffee, and that king of champagnes, Krug.

The marriage ceremony had been performed in the 'back parlour', which, like the front parlour, the dining-room and most of the rest of the house, was banked, draped, and twined with flowers and greenery; Mendelssohn's *Wedding March* was played— for the bride's entrance—and later there were selections from Strauss (including his waltz, the *Myrtle Bouquet*) and medleys from the opera. The bride wore a white satin gown from Paris (with a hundred boned stays in the bodice), an over-dress of Brussels lace, a tulle veil reaching almost to the floor, and a bunch of orange blossoms over her left ear. The band of the Grand Western Light Guard provided a concert for the spectators outside the house, and the bridegroom, a serving officer in the United States army, delighted everyone by arriving in an open wagon drawn by four army mules. The ceremony took place at three o'clock in the afternoon, and at nine that night Colonel Grant and his bride left, by train, for St. Louis on the first leg of their honeymoon (part of which was spent in a nostalgic visit to the bridegroom's old academy, West Point). It was, as the newspapers were happy to report 'one of the most brilliant weddings ever witnessed in the West'.*

The custom of threading cake through the ring, for the 'dreaming emolument', as Parson Abdy called it, was still popular, though with one small change: the Victorians, more superstitious than their 18th century forebears, were not so willing to tempt fate by removing their wedding rings once they had been put in place at the altar. The cutting and threading was now done the day before the ceremony. According to the immortal Mr. Minn's *Manual for Ladies*: 'To the bridesmaids, the day before the wedding, is assigned the duty of cutting small strips of cake and passing them through the wedding ring—woe betide them should they lose it! The pieces, about the size of a small little finger—are then wrapped up in ornamental papers of the latest novelty in design and colour . . . and fastened with some pretty device. These mystic condiments are distributed at the wedding breakfast to the young unmarried guests if any desire to possess the charming morsel.'

In America, in 1820, Louisa Quincy Adams, wife of the then Secretary of State, complained after the wedding of President Monroe's daughter: 'I didn't get a bit of cake and Mary had none to dream on.' Eight years later, when John Quincy Adams was President and 'Mary' (Mrs. Adams' niece) had grown old enough—and beautiful enough—to stir all three Adams boys into a fine romantic uproar, Mrs. Adams was again concerned with wedding cake. On 26 February 1828 she wrote to her youngest son (who had been first engaged to and then discarded by the troublesome Mary) to tell him that his ex-*fiancée* had finally married his older brother and nothing but more misery could be foreseen. It was the day after the White House wedding, and she explained: '. . . I am not much in a humour to write. I shall therefore only announce to you the fact that the wedding is over, that Madame is cool easy and indifferent as ever and that John looks already as if he had all the cares in the world upon his shoulders. . . . I send you a piece of cake as it is the fashion. Judge Cranch declined taking any as he said old people had "nothing but dreams" on such occasions.'

By 1884, however, the fashion for sending cake had changed. In that year, Mrs. Sherwood reported: 'Wedding cake is no longer sent about. It is neatly packed in boxes, each guest takes one if she likes as she leaves the house.'

In Britain people continued to find all kinds of curious things to do with wedding cake quite apart from eating it, or dreaming on it. Oatcakes were still broken over the bride's head in Scotland, and in some parts of England elaborately iced creations

---

* Two years later, Colonel Grant, one of General Custer's officers, narrowly missed being massacred by the Sioux in the General's 'last stand' on the Little Big Horn, Montana: he was away on compassionate leave, awaiting the arrival of his first child.

received the same rough treatment. According to Jeaffreson: 'So tenacious are men of superstitious practices and pleasant social ways, that a monstrous, costly wedding-cake, fresh from Chester—*the* English capital for wedding confectionery—is even yet knocked and wrenched into fragments, in a north country yeoman's parlour, over the head of a blushing lass.' Yorkshire wedding guests had a different way of dealing with it: 'when an East-Riding bride is on the point of crossing her father's threshold after returning from church, a plate containing a few spare pieces of cake is thrown from an upper window of the house, for the purpose of learning whether she will be a happy or wretched wife. If the plate on reaching the ground breaks, she will be happy; but if it is unbroken, she will not escape injury. It is needless to say that the near kinsman of the bride, who sends the platter from the window, takes good care that the omen is satisfactory. In some parts of Lancashire and Cumberland it is customary to put a ring amongst the ingredients of the cake, and to invite the guests in turn to cut a slice. The person who holds the knife when it comes upon the hidden ring, is deemed to be sure of happiness for at least twelve months.'

At most wedding feasts, the presents were put on show for the guests to admire—and the display became progressively more splendid as the century wore on. In 1826, shortly before her marriage to Thomas Carlyle, Jane Welsh described the giving of them as 'the most unreasonable species of *taxation* that could be devised'. She was thanking a childhood friend, Eliza Stodart, for her offering of a pair of earrings, and went on to quote her Uncle Adam Ramsay's 'exposition' of the theme, inspired by an earlier marriage: 'There canna be a mair needless, daftlike thing, than to gie presents to a woman at the very height of mortal happiness. It is *she* rather should gie to puir single folk, that ha' na Major Waddely to set them up.' Though many may have agreed with Miss Welsh's Uncle Ramsay, it would have been a reckless fellow who acted on the thought, for, as Jeaffreson wrote nearly fifty years later: 'Of late years, instead of decreasing in number and value, these customary offerings have surpassed, in variety and richness, the presents given to brides in Georgian England. In the gentle and fairly prosperous middle classes they sometimes comprise such costly tributes as a grand piano, a harp, a carriage, a silver or silver-gilt tea equipage, a service of choice porcelain. The bride, who receives these handsome gifts from her more affluent well-wishers, and, it may be, considerable sums of money from rich uncles, aunts, or god-parents, is also the recipient of scores of those tasteful, and comparatively inexpensive, articles that dealers in jewelry and fanciful contrivances are wont to press upon their customers as things suitable for bridal offerings.'

The most remarkable thing about these presents, to Jeaffreson's mind, was that: 'they are given to the gentle bride by her social inferiors, as well as by her equals and superiors—by the servants of her father's household, his tradesmen, and his tenants. On no other occasion but her marriage would the well-to-do and self-respecting paterfamilias consent that his daughter should become the recipient of material favours that may, in the least offensive sense of the term, be called benefactions. Given to her at any other time, the gifts, which, on the eve of her wedding occasion him lively satisfaction, in being tokens of his child's and his own popularity, would be repudiated indignantly as so many insults.'

By the end of the century relatives, and even friends, often simplified the deal by giving cheques—a custom which, said Miss Betham Edwards, deeply shocked the

Plate Nine

French. It was true, she wrote, that 'grandparents, uncles, and cousins may present a [*French*] bride with an elegant purse containing money or notes', and that 'a considerable sum of money enclosed in an envelope' had become an acceptable substitute for the bridegroom's traditional *corbeille*—the 'rich velvets and silks, furs, old lace, family and modern jewels, a fan, and a missal, all packed in an elegant basket or straw box lined with satin' which had for centuries been the French bridegroom's customary offering to his bride—but, 'a wedding gift in the form of a cheque shocks French susceptibilities'. On the other hand, the British shuddered at the exhibition of the 'entire trousseau . . . the spreading before everybody's eyes of slips and stockings . . .' which went on at wedding feasts in France. Jewellery was the most usual present for a British bridegroom to give his bride, and of all the jewels, a pearl necklace was, for those who could afford it, the most popular gift of all. Among the not-so-wealthy, something on more practical lines was often chosen, like the ivory fitted work-box which Charles Dickens gave to his bride and which, perhaps with a young author's justifiable pride in his own best-selling name, he had inscribed: 'From Chas. Dickens to Kate, April 2nd. 1836'. In America, Mrs. Sherwood ruled: 'The bridegroom is allowed to make what presents he pleases to the bride and to send something in the nature of a fan, a locket, a ring or a bouquet to the bridesmaids; he has also to buy the wedding ring and of course he sends a bouquet to the bride.'

There was no legal or canonical bar to marriage at any time of the year during the 19th century, though most Christians voluntarily considered Lent as too solemn a season for wedding festivities. It was now that the tag 'Marry in Lent, and you'll live to repent' superseded 'Marry in May, and you'll rue the day', which had been the warning when the church forbade weddings during the greater part of that month. The Romans had also thought May an inappropriate time to marry since they then had feasts to appease the spirits of the dead. One of Ovid's lines on this, '*Mense malas maio nubere vulgus ait*'—'Wantons marry in the month of May'—was pinned to the gates of Holyrood Palace on 15 May 1567, the day Mary Queen of Scots made her fateful marriage with Bothwell. But there was no such vulgar incident when Queen Victoria's daughter, Princess Louise, married the Marquis of Lorne during the Lent of 1871. Sunday, however, was now sacrosanct indeed, and a wedding on this once most popular wedding day of all would have met with a universal frown of disapproval. 'Victorian Englishmen', said Jeaffreson, 'very generally concur in holding a particular day of each week, i.e., a seventh of the entire year, as too sacred for bridal mirth. A fashionable wedding, celebrated on the Lord's Day in London, or any part of England, would now-a-days be denounced by religious people of all Christian parties as an outrageous exhibition of impiety.' Even Queen Victoria, who thought the gloom of a British Sunday vastly overdone, didn't go against that one.

The one church ruling which did prove irksome was the ban on marriages after mid-day. Now that the actual ceremony was carried out in such splendour before a full church and followed by a considerable feast, often for several hundred people, this time-limit was thought to concentrate the main festivities in the wrong half of the day and to leave a nasty gap before the grand finale of dinner or ball could begin. There were other discomforts, too, as Jeaffreson pointed out: 'The Victorian gentlewoman, who seldom rises from her bed before half-past eight, or breakfasts earlier than half-past nine, must be up long before her usual rising-hour, if she would make an elaborate toilet, take a leisurely first breakfast, see half-a-score of friends, and drive to church in time for marriage before twelve o'clock.' When the main breakfast had 'terminated with hilarity, occasioned by drink, which every feaster has done his best to shirk, several hours must be spent in a dismal affectation of jollity till the time for the evening dance arrives. If the weather is fine, and the bridal-house in the country, the men of the tedious *fete* may go away for a cigar and a walk, whilst the bridesmaids are sleeping off the fatigue of the morning, and refreshing themselves for the ball.'

But if it were wet, the only answer was the billiard room, and, as Jeaffreson had to admit, even in Victorian England, not every house had a billiard room. Then, in this jaundiced view of such jolly occasions, there was the problem of eating a large dinner after coping with a bridal breakfast: 'The man must combine the distinguishing characteristics of an alderman and a boa-constrictor, who can dine happily after the violent delights and cloying pleasures of a wedding-luncheon.' Jeaffreson (and one can't help feeling he wrote all this after a particularly heavy wedding) hoped that the church's hours for celebrating marriage would be extended 'so that a bride may be married at church late in the afternoon, and a pleasant bridal dinner be substituted for the inopportune wedding-breakfast'.

In 1885, his wish nearly came true. The government brought in a three-hour extension. Speedier journeys on the new-fangled railroads still allowed brides and grooms to reach their honeymoon destinations (the fashion magazines greeted the new hours with much talk of brides now getting married in their going-away clothes), while the friends they left behind them could drift almost painlessly on from wedding tea to gala dinner.

Earlier in the century, the Marriage Act of 1836 had made life easier in other directions: this was the bill which introduced civil marriages, and set up the machinery for civil registrars and registry offices. It also made wedding ceremonies in Catholic churches and the meeting houses of Protestant dissenters legal, so long as a civil registrar was present at the time. Before this bill Catholics and dissenters still had to go through two wedding ceremonies—the Catholic, or dissenting, one to satisfy their religion, and the Anglican one to please the State. The complications which this could cause are described, in many crazy variations, in *The Recollections of a Northumbrian Lady, 1815–1866*, the memoirs of Barbara Charlton, daughter of one old northern Catholic family (the Tasburghs, of Yorkshire), who married into another (the Charltons of Hesleyside, Northumberland). Writing her recollections in her late seventies, this doughty, and snobbish, old lady looked back on the Catholics of her youth as a golden race. At the time of her first London season (1834) they were, she wrote, 'much handsomer and more distinguished than they are now; they have sadly dwindled down and uglified since then. . . . The depression of the old Catholic type seems to have come on very rapidly; occasioned, it may be presumed, by an influx of converts and colonists'. But when these ravishing young girls and dashing young men decided to marry it was often not only true love which refused to run smooth. The first wedding in the Tasburgh family had been a model of how such things should be done; but it was not to be repeated. The bride was Barbara Charlton's elder sister Fanny, and she was quietly married by the Tasburgh family chaplain, the Abbé le Roux, in the chapel of the Tasburgh home, Burghwallis Hall; and then, with two bridesmaids, the family and guests, went to the local Anglican parish church for 'a pretty country wedding'. (In these cases, the Catholic ceremony was usually by far the quieter of the two; often being performed before breakfast and before the family had dressed in their wedding finery.)

Three years later, Mary, eldest of the three Tasburgh girls, fell in love with a non-Catholic (Charles Fairfax of Gilling Castle) and where for her sister everything had gone right, for her everything went chaotically wrong. First of all her father turned nasty, and then the priesthood played up. Life became so uncomfortable at home that she went to live with the previously married Fanny and the wedding was planned to take place from her house. On the morning of her marriage:

> Unfortunately, Mr. Simkiss, the priest, positively refused to marry a couple of different religion, although no canon law deterred him from doing so, his argument being that the Church of England ceremony was all that would be necessary. No other priest was available, so a hasty change of plan was contrived at the last minute. The Protestant ceremony, enjoined by law, was advanced to an early hour, and the bridal couple, after breakfast, posted with four horses to Burghwallis, a distance of forty miles, on a day of snow and bitter cold so that the roads were quite impassable in places, in order to be married according to the rites of Holy Church by our old French priest, Abbé le Roux, who was then in his eightieth year.
>
> The wedding couple did not reach the old priest's house till ten at night, and then they had to go for some distance on foot along a snowy path leading to his cottage. Of course, no one was up, but after loud knocking for some time the Abbé's maidservant appeared en deshabille and listened to their story with dismay. With difficulty, she roused her master, but it was still more difficult to get him to understand the intricacies of the situation, as he was not only deaf, but had a very imperfect knowledge of English. A fire was lit for the shivering twain and, after a long wait, the Abbé entered in a dirty old snuff-coloured dressing-gown and slippers, surmounted by a white night-cap sticking up a foot and a half above his head. The poor old man looked quite bewildered, not even then realizing what was expected of him. But when Mary explained the dilemma in beautiful Parisian French, he grasped the knotty point and sent at once for his Book and Holy Water. Alas! there was no *aspergés* with which to give a nuptial blessing. So the maidservant took a lantern, went out into the garden, and cut a spray of old man, a plant that grew in every cottage garden then, and that was used; somewhat of a reproach, it may be, on Charles Fairfax, who was considerably older than his pretty bride.
>
> When the marriage ceremony was over the Abbé retreated to his bed, and the bridal couple drove on to Burghwallis, where they were welcomed at nigh midnight. . . .

Barbara Tasburgh's own marriage was even more dramatic. Although she had chosen an eminently suitable Catholic partner, her disagreeable father this time found fault with the marriage settlement and finally drove his youngest daughter to elope to Gretna Green. After months of family arguments and manoeuvrings, parental edicts never to see the young man again, clandestine letters, and helpful aunts coming across with promises of legacies, Barbara Tasburgh and William Charlton decided to escape across the border in June 1839:

> We had turned over in our heads every feasible plan for getting married privately, naturally wishing to go through the Catholic ceremony first. The

137

Catholic chapel in Doncaster would have served our purpose, but unfortunately it was not licensed for marriages. At last, finding every scheme of the sort impracticable owing to the strict surveillance under which I was kept at home, William offered me, as our only possible means of union, 'a trip over the Border'.

On 19 June, having kissed her mother goodnight, Barbara retired to her own room, locked herself in and changed her light-coloured summer frock 'for one of a dark *cachemire*'. At half-past eleven, she lit up her room, opened wide the window, and prepared to await her *fiancé*:

> At a quarter to midnight, on Wednesday the 19th June, William was under my window, having posted from Doncaster and left the chaise at the end of the lane so that the noise of wheels should not disturb the house. I threw my soft bundle of belongings out of the window, and then by means of torn-up sheets fastened to a heavy, old-fashioned sofa, I swung out and, wonderful to say, got down without a scratch. We ran for our lives to where the chaise was standing, the object of getting posters from Doncaster instead of from Robin Hood's Well (only a mile from Burghwallis) being to leave no clew behind for pursuit in the morning.
>
> We posted through the night, and all next day, until we reached the Blacksmith's house at Gretna Green at 6 p.m. on the evening of June 20th, when we became man and wife. The wily old blacksmith, recognizing the name of Charlton and well-knowing that William was heir to two Cumberland estates as well as that of Hesleyside in Northumberland, charged us £20 for his services, which for us runaways was a heavy charge enough, and drained our ready cash. Luckily, I had with me my jewels, very handsome and chiefly presents from my sister Fanny, and the next day I pawned them in Carlisle. The jeweller shrewdly guessed that the pledges would be likely very soon to be redeemed, and, without haggling over the price, gave us for them a very liberal sum. It was only later that we heard my brother George had set out after us on horseback, and had given up the chase at Barnside Bar. . . . As fast as wheels and steam could convey us, we transplanted ourselves to London.

There, two more weddings followed: one in a Protestant church, to make quite sure the marriage was legal—the bride dressed in a borrowed 'pink muslin dress (far too big for me)'—and a second, not by any means so easy, by the rites of the Catholic church:

> We had the greatest difficulty in getting a priest to marry us in London; not on account of our escapade, but for the reason, if you please, that our great-grandmothers, Theresa and Isabel Swinburne, were sisters, and also, perhaps, a little on account of the Protestant ceremony having preceded the Catholic one. Mrs. Charlton and Mrs. Riddell threw themselves with zest into the good cause and at last, between them, unearthed a Jesuit, Mr. Lythgoe, the one solitary Jesuit then in London, who consented to perform the Catholic ceremony privately in his room.

The only stones which Barbara Tasburgh and William Charlton appear to have left unturned in their pursuit of matrimony, were the ones newly introduced specifically to ease the lot of non-Anglicans. No mention is made of the possibility of a civil wedding at a registry office, or of a Catholic ceremony with a civil registrar present; but these possibilities were less than three years old at the time, and the one, the civil wedding, doubtless seemed unattractive to the religious, while the other, the civil witness at a Catholic ceremony, would have been more difficult to arrange for runaway lovers.

For more conventional brides and bridegrooms the honeymoon was now firmly established, and though borrowing the home of a friend or relative, or going to one of the bridegroom's own estates, for the first few days or weeks, was still popular, a Continental tour was now the fashionable thing to do. Lord Clarendon's daughter, Alice, who married Lord Skelmersdale on 16 August 1860, took a typically leisurely and wide-sweeping excursion immediately following her wedding. On 20 September, the Earl wrote to the Duchess of Manchester from Wiesbaden, to say that 'the Skelmies' had just joined up with him there ('and two such happy faces as those wd: enliven anyone'); they were to stay a few days and then go off again on their own 'via Lucern and St. Gothard to Venice'. Paris was another favourite spot—when the rebellion wasn't raging: Charles Lamb's adopted daughter, Emma Isola, and her bookseller husband Edward Moxon, made directly for this traditional city of romance, after their wedding on 30 July 1833; on 9 September they were still there—'Moxon, who is flaunting it about *à la Parisienne*, with his new bride, our Emma, much to his satisfaction, and not a little to our dulness', Lamb wrote to H. F. Cary, on that date— and they did not return to cheer up the Lamb household until the end of the month. In the 1890s Norway came into favour, and a 'Norwegian Yachting Cruise' could be embarked on for '12 Guineas, including a sumptuous table'. The vessel was the 'Midnight Sun (Captain Nivison R.N.R.), 3020 tons, 2860 horse-power, sailing fortnightly'. In 1893, the Great Eastern Railway boasted the 'Cheapest Continental Holiday—Brussels and back: 29s.', while 97 shillings bought honeymooners a return ticket to Switzerland.

Of the English resorts, Brighton (made popular by the Prince Regent at the beginning of the century) was much in vogue. Thackeray in *Vanity Fair* arranged for 'Miss Emilia's honeymoon' to be spent there; she and Captain George driving down from London, in 1815, in their carriage with the four horses thought to be most suitable for such journeys. They had 'engaged apartments at the Ship Inn', where they 'enjoyed themselves . . . in great comfort and quietude', until presently they were joined by the bride's brother, Jos, the Regency beau. The Isle of Wight was also popular, though not quite so smart. Here, according to Jeaffreson, 'to afford suitable accommodation for spouses desirious of passing the first days of their matrimony in retirement and charming scenery, speculators built in the choicest spots of the lovely island those attractive honeymoon hotels, such as the Sandrock and Shanklin inns,— ivy-and-myrtle-covered tenements, partitioned into little pigeon-hole sitting-rooms and bedrooms,—in which proud boys and happy girls still [*1872*] delight to bill and coo in blissful unconcern of everything but love'.

Jeaffreson set down the pattern of 19th century honeymoons like this: 'In the first two decades of the present century the honeymoon trip of a married couple, who, though of gentle quality, were too busy or thrifty to think of spending much time or money on a romantic excursion, seldom exceeded ten days or a fortnight. The London merchant or lawyer took his London bride to Bath or Tunbridge Wells or Brighton for seven or eight days, and on returning to town she entered her new home in Finsbury Circus or Guildford Street, feeling herself to have seen much of her native land. The country clergyman or provincial doctor took his spouse for as short a time to London, to see the parks and theatres, St. Paul's and the Tower. . . . But in these later years the increasing facilities for travel have caused the majority of our spouses to regard the trip to the nearest of our Channel islands as too tame and unadventurous for the happy pair, who have time and money for a run to the Pyrenees, Switzerland, or the Italian lakes.' Sir William Des Voeux, a distinguished British colonial administrator with aristocratic connections, described (in *My Colonial Service*) a very upper-class mixture of foreign and British travel. Following his wedding in July 1875 he said: 'After a wedding tour of three weeks we returned for a few days to Footscray Place, Mr. Pender's residence in Kent, and then went for a round of visits in Scotland. . . . Returning to Footscray Place and spending the final fortnight there.' In late September (after a two-month honeymoon—though Des Voeux never mentioned the still fractionally low-class word) he sailed with his new bride to become Administrator and Colonial Secretary of St. Lucia in the West Indies.

Queen Victoria, never as stuffy as she has been made out to be, embraced the word honeymoon very early on and used it in a letter to her uncle, King Leopold of the Belgians, two years after her own wedding. Writing of the intended marriage of Prince Ernest of Saxe-Coburg-Gotha, brother of the Prince Consort, she said: 'Ernest's marriage is a *great, great delight* to us; thank God, I say, as I so ardently wished it, and Alexandrina is said to be really *so* perfect. I have begged Ernest beforehand to pass his honeymoon with us, and I beg you to urge him to do it; for he witnessed our first happiness, and we must therefore witness his.' Journals like the *Illustrated London News* evolved their own code on such delicate matters, and it was often extremely subtle: by 1870 the word honeymoon was generally used for all except royal brides and grooms; but Princess Louise, who married a non-royal, the Marquis of Lorne, in 1871, was reported to have 'returned from her honeymoon', while the Mediterranean cruise of her brother, the Duke of Connaught, and his Prussian Princess, in 1879, was described as a 'wedding tour'.

Whatever the social status of the 'newly-married pair', the traditional send off as they left for their honeymoon or wedding tour was a shower of old shoes—or satin slippers, as they were usually described. Flowers were also sometimes thrown, and by the 1870s another missile had appeared—rice. (How odd it is that the prim Victorian era should have brought forth all these fertility symbols.) By 1884 the custom had become so firmly established on both sides of the Atlantic, that Mrs. Sherwood could rule: 'As the happy pair drive off a shower of satin slippers and rice follow them. If a slipper alights on top of the carriage, luck is assured to them for ever.' This last good omen was not always left to providence alone; at the wedding of Alice Lee Roosevelt in 1906, 'a slipper was placed on top of the automobile for good luck'. Slippers were thrown at all royal weddings in England, and at the marriage of Princess Louise a broom was added to the barrage—an ancient Highland custom, it was said. At the marriage of the future King George V and Queen Mary, in 1893, the bridegroom's father and uncle, the Prince of Wales and the Duke of Connaught, and the bride's uncle, the Duke of Cambridge, stood inside the railings of Buckingham Palace looking like a group of naughty schoolboys, ready to throw rice at the bridal couple as they drove by *en route* for Paddington Station and Sandringham.

Although public emphasis was now all on the romantic aspect of matrimony, private belief in the solid marriage settlement and the 'suitable' match continued to run deep. Not everyone shared Lord Clarendon's broad-minded view that 'provided the poverty was not extreme' a girl should marry the man most likely to make her happy; many a stern Victorian father still showed quite reasonable suitors to the door—and many a daughter still, undutifully, ran off to Gretna Green. In May 1835, all London was 'en émoi', according to Lord Malmesbury, over the elopement of Sir Colquhoun Grant's daughter with Brinsley Sheridan, grandson of the playwright. Sneakily, they had waited until Sir Colquhoun was in Poole, canvassing his constituency, and then made a dash for Scotland. Ten years later, Malmesbury recorded: 'Nothing is talked of in London to-day but the elopement of Lady Adela Villiers with Captain Ibbotson. Poor Lady Jersey is much distressed.' However this wasn't exactly a new scandal in the Jersey family, for in 1804, Lady Adela's father had run off with her mother, the Earl of Westmoreland's eldest daughter, heiress to Child's banking fortune.

The conspiracy to turn all Gretna Green couplers into blacksmiths was still going strong. Barbara Charlton said she was 'taken to the house of the blacksmith' in 1839; and at the most celebrated abduction trial of the century, the flamboyant statesman and barrister, Henry Brougham, using one of the oldest legal tricks in the book, persisted in calling the man who had performed the marriage 'Mr. Blacksmith', even though he established early in his cross-examination that the fellow, hardly the build for a man of the forge, anyway, had previously been a pedlar. This trial was held at Lancaster Assizes in March 1827 and the chief of the accused was Edward Gibbon Wakefield, a widower with several children, who had neatly plucked a 15-year-old heiress, Ellen Turner, from her Liverpool boarding school (by saying that her father was ill and wanted her), and then persuaded her to marry him at Gretna Green. William Hone printed much of the evidence in his *Table Book* which was published the same year as the trial. The coupler in the case was David Laing who was dressed in spanking-new, vaguely clerical dress for the occasion and conducted his own case 'with a ludicrous expression of gravity upon his features'. The practice of the abductor in such enterprises was to get the girl to pay the 'parson'—and often to order the horses for the last stage from Carlisle—to prove her willingness in the affair; Laing testified that having 'married them after the Scotch form, that is, by my putting on the ring on the lady's finger. . . . I think I told the lady that I generally had a present from 'em, as it may be, of such a thing as money to buy a pair of gloves, and she gave me, with her own hand, a twenty-shilling Bank of England note to buy them.' Asked if the couple had both talked freely to him, Laing answered:

'O, yes; he asked me what sort of wine they had in Linton's house [*the inn where they were married*], and I said they had three kinds, with the best of Shumpine (Champagne). He asked me which I would take, and I said *Shumpine*, and so and so; while they went into another room to dine, I finished the wine.'

It was now Mr. Brougham's turn to cross-examine:

'What did you get for this job besides the *Shumpine?*' he asked. 'Did you get money as well as *Shumpine?*'

'Yes, sure I did, and so and so.'

'Well, how much?'

'Thirty or forty pounds or thereabouts, as may be.'

'Or fifty pounds, as it may be, Mr. Blacksmith?'

'Maybe, for I cannot say to a few pounds. I am dull of hearing. . . .'

'How long are you practising this delightful art?'

'Upwards of forty-eight years I am doing these marriages.'

'How old are you?'

'I am now beyond seventy-five.'

'What do you do to get your livelihood?'

'I do these.'

'Pretty doing it is; but how did you get your livelihood, say, before these last precious forty-eight years of your life?'

'I was a gentleman.'

'What do you call a gentleman?'

'Being sometimes poor, sometimes rich.'

'Come now, say what was your occupation before you took to this trade?'

'I followed many occupations.'

'Were you not an ostler?'

'No, I were not.'

'What else were you then?'

'Why, I was a merchant once.'

'That is a travelling vagrant pedlar, as I understand your term?'

'Yes, may be.'

'Were you ever any thing else in the way of calling?'

'Never.'

Laing was proud to testify that he had 'been in the courts of Edinburgh and Dublin', and that his marriages had always 'been held legal'; which proved to be the case with the Wakefield–Turner marriage. The bridegroom was jailed for abduction, but it took a special Act of Parliament to dissolve the union.

The days of *Shumpine* and £50 fees were soon to come to an end in Gretna Green. In July 1856, a law was passed making all marriages invalid in Scotland unless one of the parties had resided there for 21 days prior to the wedding. There was no longer anything to be gained by a trip over the border.

The forbidden match which had the whole of high society in a ferment of gossip and a flurry of note-sending (all the latest details), was that of Lady Susan Clinton, daughter of the Duke of Newcastle, and Lord Adolphus Vane-Tempest, son of Lord Londonderry, which took place in London, four years after the demise of Gretna Green. Queen Victoria herself was deeply concerned with this one, since Lady Susan had been a bridesmaid at the Princess Royal's marriage two years earlier. 'Only think,' Her Majesty wrote to her eldest daughter in April 1860, 'Lady Susan P. Clinton has gone and married Lord Adolphus Vane, who drinks and has twice been shut up for delirium tremens. . . . Lord Adolphus is a good creature and not the one who did all those dreadful things,* but between drink and his natural tendency to madness there is a sad prospect for poor Susan.' In May, the Queen followed up with a delightfully naughty postscript: '. . . There is a dreadful bon-mot about Lady Susan Vane (Clinton) that there is a bet which of the two will be confined first!!'

Most brides considered the drama of the new style church weddings as romantic

---

* The one who *did* do all the dreadful things was Lord Ernest Vane-Tempest, and perhaps the worst of them was his attack on the actresses' dressing-rooms in a Windsor theatre. When the Manager objected, Lord Ernest threw him down a flight of stairs.

as any elopement and these were now the aim of all classes. To be married in white was a dream within the grasp of almost all. The price of clothes (thanks, no doubt, to the industrial revolution) had become a great deal more reasonable, and almost every girl who wished to wear white on her wedding day could now afford to. In 1874, Peter Robinson advertised 'Wedding dresses. 18s. 9d. to 200s.' (though they, like most other dress firms, were far more interested in providing mourning, in all degrees of grimness, and must have devoted at least 75 per cent of their advertising budget to this dismal end). In 1871, the material for even a sumptuous crinoline of rich, white 'Moire Antique' could be bought for as little as '£3. 17s. the Dress of 11 yds.' and 'Brussels kid gloves', ideal for a wedding, cost 1s. 11½d. So, dressed in as close a copy of an aristocratic wedding gown as she could manage, the less fortunate bride planned celebrations of as genteel a nature as she could command. After the church ceremony, a wedding dinner at the bride's own home was the thing to aim for, and Dickens described just such an event in his story of *The Mistaken Milliner. A Tale of Ambition* (from *Sketches by Boz*). In this case, as was often so in previous centuries, it was the bridegroom, an 'ornamental painter and decorator's journeyman', who provided the feast:

> It was a charming party; Somers'-town the locality, and a front parlour the apartment. The ornamental painter and decorator's journeyman had taken a house—no lodgings nor vulgarity of that kind, but a house—four beautiful rooms, and a delightful little washhouse at the end of the passage, which was the most convenient thing in the world for the bridesmaids could sit in the front parlour and receive the company, and then run into the little washhouse and see how the pudding and boiled pork were getting on in the copper, and then pop back into the parlour again, as snug and comfortable as possible. . . .
> Then the dinner. There was baked leg of mutton at the top [*of the table*], boiled leg of mutton at the bottom, pair of fowls and leg of pork in the middle; porter-pots at the corners; pepper, mustard, and vinegar in the centre; vegetables on the floor; and plum-pudding and apple-pie and tartlets without number, to say nothing of cheese, and celery, and watercresses, and all that sort of thing.

Deep in the country genteel fashions held less sway and many of the most ancient customs continued to thrive, with entire neighbourhoods still turning out to honour the bride and groom and take part in nuptial sports. Canon John Atkinson, vicar of Danby in the North Riding of Yorkshire until his death in 1900, gave an excellent account of weddings in his part of the world in his book *Forty Years in a Moorland Parish* (1891). Riding for the kail had died out just before his incumbency, but racing on foot for the bride's colours continued to flourish. The most typical Dales wedding he had witnessed, he said, took place in about 1850, on Martinmas Day:

> But I should not have spoken of the event in the singular number; for there were, in point of fact, four weddings, all to be solemnised. After the ceremony was over, great was the scramble among the small boys for the coppers which it was and is customary for the newly married man or his best man to scatter the moment the chancel door is left. And then an adjournment to the field adjoining the churchyard was made, and there was a series of races, all on foot to be run for the ribbons which were the gifts of the several brides; and as some of them gave

more than one, the races were multiplied accordingly. . . . More than once, too, I have known when the bride in some way incurred the suspicion of niggardness, through not complying with the recognised usage of supplying one ribbon at least, to be run for, the 'stithy was fired upon her' i.e. a charge of powder was rammed into the hole in the anvil (much after a shot in a mine) and fired in derision: well pronounced, if the loudness of the report counted for anything, as the wedding party passed on the way home from the church. The direct converse of this was the firing of guns as the party passed the residences of friends and well-wishers. The race still lingers on, and only a week or two since the bride gave 'Two ribbons to be run for'; and a few years ago one young chap, fleet of foot, and with as much inclination for 'larking' (playing) as for sticking to work— some folks said more—was quoted as the fortunate winner of almost enough to start an itinerant haberdasher in trade.

An editor's footnote in Strutt's *Sports and Pastimes of the People of England* (1903 edition), which carried this quote from Canon Atkinson's book, added some startling spice to the story: an old parishioner of Danby swore that he had seen 'a stark naked race of young men over the moors from Danby-in-Cleveland Churchyard at the conclusion of a wedding at which Canon Atkinson officiated in the year 1851'. Needless to say, added the editor, the sport did not begin till after the rector had left: 'I had some interesting correspondence with the Canon on this subject, and was able to convince him by the evidence of several that this occasional stripping for a race after a wedding was only abandoned soon after he entered on his incumbency.'

There doesn't appear to have been much nakedness at Highland weddings of this period, but the firing of guns was very much a part of the ritual. According to a splendidly detailed account written by John Hay Allan, Esq., for Hone's *Table Book* (1827), the approach of a Highland bridegroom was announced 'at a distance by a continual and running discharge of fire-arms from his party. These signals are answered by the friends of the bride, and when at length they meet, a general but irregular feu-de-joie announces the arrival.' When the bridegroom lived a day's march away from the bride's home, and his party did not arrive till nightfall, the scene was even more spectacular, 'the plaintive pealing of the pipes approaching upon the stillness of the night, the fire-arms flashing upon the darkness, and their reports redoubled by the solitary echoes of the mountains, and when at length the train draws near, the mingled tread of hasty feet, and full clamour of the pipes, the mixed and confused visionry of the white figures of the girls, and the dark shadows of the men, with here and there the waving of a plaid and the glinting of a dirk'. The number and quality of the guests each side could attract to the wedding was a matter of pride—everyone from the laird to the lowliest villager was pressured to attend, and to attend in the greatest magnificence he could muster. 'Girls, who the yester even were seen bare-headed and bare-footed, lightly dressed in a blue flannel petticoat and dark linen jacket, are now busked in white frocks, riband sashes, cotton stockings on their feet, and artificial flowers on their heads. The "merchant's" and the miller's daughters frequently exhibit the last fashion from Edinburgh, and are beautified and garnished with escalloped trimmings, tabbed sleeves, tucks, lace, gathers, and French frills! As it has been discovered that tartan is nothing esteemed in London, little or none is to be seen, except in the red plaid or broached tunic of some old wife, whose days of gayety are past, but who still loves that with which she was gay in her youth.' Even the men mostly wore 'lowland fashion', though those who appeared in the 'noble dress of their ancestors' were always treated as 'an honour and ornament to the day'. Bride and bridegroom each entertained their own fine supporters to mid-day feasts at their own houses (often the partitions were taken down to make room for the gathering), and the tressels sagged under the weight of 'barley broth, or cock-a-leeky, boiled fowls, roasted ducks, joints of meat, sheep's heads, oat and barley cakes, butter, and cheeses; and in summer, frothed buttermilk, and slam. In the glens where goats are kept, haunches of these animals and roasted kids are also added to the feast.' And all the while (and for two hours before) the 'uisga' (or whisky) bottle circulated: 'each empties a bumper as it passes'. As soon as the bridegroom's feast was done, his party set out for the bride's home with the pipers before it and fire-arms at the ready. At the end of the journey, more whisky and more food greeted the travellers; then the two parties combined—no matter what time of day or night it had become—to march upon the church. The bride linked arms with an appointed bridesmaid and bridesman, a white scarf festooned from the one to the other across her body; and, bringing up the very rear of what must have been an awesome procession, there were always two young girls, with another white scarf festooned between them. The bagpipes skirled out *Fye, lets a' to the Bridal*, and the party moved off. The chapel ceremony was short and very simple, but often held impressively by candlelight. Afterwards, the celebrations continued at a nearby inn or the house of a relative, as it was considered unlucky for a bride's own house to be the first she entered after her wedding. The bridesmaid and bridesman broke an oat cake over her head as she crossed the threshold; then reels and strathspeys—and the regular passing of the whisky bottle—filled the gap till supper, to which each male guest escorted the lady of his choice and paid for her meal as well as his own.

The bride and groom were allowed to retire for a few hours, but most of the guests kept the dancing going till dawn, when a breakfast of tea, 'multitudes of eggs, cold meat, a profusion of oat cakes, barley "scones," and sometimes *wheat bread*' was provided for the stayers. The bride then prepared to leave for her husband's home, accompanied by her family and neighbours to the border of her father's land, or that of the 'tacksman' he lived under. There, at the burn-side (for the boundaries were usually formed by streams), they danced a parting reel; the bride kissed all her friends, and then marched away into the distance with her new kinsfolk and neighbours. 'When, however, the circumstances of the bridegroom will permit,' wrote Mr. Allan, 'all those who were present at the house of the bride, are generally invited to accompany her on her way, and a renewal of the preceding festivities takes place at the dwelling of the bridegroom.' Thus turning the whole thing into a nightmare marathon. The account ends with the logistics of a wedding at which two 14-year-old bridesmaids, by the time they reached the bridegroom's house, had walked thirty-one miles in two days, and danced all the intervening night.

A little earlier in the century, Benjamin Malkin returned from a *Tour of South Wales* convinced that anyone who met a wedding on the road there would be 'inclined to suppose that he had fallen in with a company of lunatics escaped from their confinement. It is the custom of the whole party who are invited, both men and women, to ride full speed to the church-porch; and the person who arrives there first has some privilege or distinction at the marriage-feast. To this important object all inferior considerations give way, whether the safety of his Majesty's subjects, who are not going to be married, or their own, be incessantly endangered by boisterous, unskilful, and contentious jockeyship.'

How spiritless these hot-blooded northerners and Celts must have thought the southern English with their pretty little country church weddings, the bride neatly turned out in white or pale grey with artificial orange blossom round her bonnet, and the bridegroom in a countryman's smock, embroidered for him by the bride herself in the traditional pattern of the district. Even penny weddings had disappeared, though, according to W. T. Marchant (in a charming little book full of bridal gossip, called *Betrothals and Bridals, with a chat about wedding cakes & wedding customs*, 1879): 'In some of the rural parts of this country it is usual to fix a floral rope across the street on the day of a wedding; all who pass through on that day have to pay toll.' In many corners of the country, even the simplest wedding was too costly for some villagers, as Richard Meinertzhagen discovered when his family went to live at Mottisfont Abbey in the Test Valley in the 1880s. In his book *Diary of a Black Sheep*, he tells how his mother (the former Miss Georgina Potter) was asked to tidy up the long-established habit of 'living in sin' in that corner of England:

> When we first went to Mottisfont many of the villagers were living together as man and wife without having been through the ceremony of marriage. This practice was deemed perfectly honourable, but it shocked the new rector, Mr. Slocock, who consulted my mother on the subject. My mother was a practical woman, always facing facts and, of course, saw the comic side of it. She rather enjoyed the honest and practical manner in which a village can manage its own affairs without the help of the Church, but Slocock being an orthodox priest was outraged at promiscuous living in sin (hateful expression) in his parish. The people of Mottisfont were not immoral and this marriage without ceremony was partly due to Church neglect and partly due to poverty. It was the fate of old couples who, as young people, had been unable to afford the marriage fee of half a crown. Under Mr. Slocock's persuasion, my mother offered to pay the fee and many old couples nearing the stage of a golden wedding became respectably married.

Wife selling, that other instance of the populace calmly taking the laws of land and church into their own hands, was still going on, too. Thomas Hardy, in 1886, set the story of *The Mayor of Casterbridge* round the selling of a wife at a fair and the retribution which followed; and, according to Robert Chambers, a good deal of surprise and resentment was felt in Yorkshire in 1837 when a man was sentenced to a month's imprisonment at the West Riding Sessions for selling, or attempting to sell, his wife, 'the right to do this being believed in more extensively than we are apt to imagine'. In 1815 a man auctioned his wife in Pontefract, offering her at a minimum bidding of one shilling, and finally knocking her down for eleven. In 1820, a man named Brouchet led his wife into the cattle-market at Canterbury, and when the auctioneer refused to handle her, took a cattle stall for the price of 6d. and sold her from it for five shillings. A Birmingham woman, sold for the handsome sum of £15 in 1834, had the satisfaction of outliving both husbands, marrying for a third time, and inheriting from her first husband's estate, despite strong competition from his relations. The *Annual Register* for 1832 gave a fascinating account of a Carlisle wife-sale which took place in April of that year (quoted in Chamber's *Book of Days*). Having been miserably married for three years, Joseph Thomson, a farmer, took his wife to Carlisle, where he had the bellman announce around the town that he was about to sell her. At noon he stood her on a chair with a halter of rope or straw around her neck and let fly with enough invective to put off, one would have thought, the most willing buyer:

> Gentlemen, I have to offer to your notice my wife, Mary Anne Thomson, otherwise Williams, whom I mean to sell to the highest and fairest bidder. Gentlemen, it is her wish as well as mine to part for ever. She has been to me only a born serpent. I took her for my comfort, and the good of my home; but she became my tormentor, a domestic curse, a night invasion, and a daily devil. Gentlemen, I speak truth from my heart when I say—may God deliver us from troublesome wives and frolicsome women! Avoid them as you would a mad dog, a roaring lion, a loaded pistol, cholera morbus, Mount Etna, or any other pestilential thing in nature. Now I have told you her faults and failings, I will introduce the bright and sunny side of her, and explain her qualifications and goodness. She can read novels and milk cows; she can laugh and weep with the same ease that you could take a glass of ale when thirsty. . . . She can make butter and scold the maid; she can sing Moore's melodies, and plait her frills and caps; she cannot make rum, gin, or whisky, but she is a good judge of the quality from long experience in tasting them. I therefore offer her with all her perfections and imperfections, for the sum of fifty shillings.

The anti-sell worked: 'after waiting about an hour, Thomas knocked down the lot to one Henry Mears, for twenty shillings and a Newfoundland dog; they then parted in perfect good temper—Mears and the woman going one way, Thomson and the dog another.'

Unfortunately, added Chambers, 'the occasional instances of wife-sale, while remarked by ourselves with little beyond a passing smile, have made a deep impression on our continental neighbours, who seriously believe that it is a habit of all classes of our people, and constantly cite it as an evidence of our low civilization.'

In America, the chief problem lay in finding wives rather than getting rid of them: as in most pioneering societies, the men still outnumbered the women by an uncomfortable margin. Being in such short supply, what girls there were tended to marry young, and according to Mrs. Frances Trollope, who visited America in the late 1820s, lived pretty wretched lives from that time on. Mrs. Trollope was the mother of author, Anthony Trollope (though in her life-time, that would have been phrased the other way round—'a son of Mrs. Trollope the writer', as Disraeli once wrote to his sister). In 1827, she and her barrister husband went to America in an effort to repair their shaky finances; an unsuccessful attempt, as it turned out, but the book she wrote on her experiences in the 'Union'—*Domestic Manners of the Americans* (1832)—did eventually put a few pounds into the kitty. She saw America and its people as: 'A vast continent, by far the greater part of which is still in the state in which nature left it, and a busy, bustling, industrious population, hacking and hewing their way through it.' After that, she pretty well ran out of nice things to say. Most of the men, it turned out, were even more attached to 'ardent spirits' at 'lamentably cheap' prices and untaxed tobacco, than they were to hacking and hewing and it was the wives and daughters who were the true 'slaves of the soil'. After living in the small village of Mohawk, near Cincinnati, for some months, Mrs. Trollope wrote: 'One has but to look at the wife of an American cottager, and ask her her age, to be convinced that the life she leads is one of hardship, privation, and labour. It is rare to see a woman in this station who has reached the age of thirty, without losing every trace of youth and beauty. You continually see women with infants on their knee, that you feel sure are their grand-children, till some convincing proof of the contrary is displayed. Even the young girls, though often with lovely features, look pale, thin, and haggard. I do not remember to have seen in any single instance among the poor, a specimen of the plump, rosy, laughing physiognomy so common among our cottage girls.'

Their life was brightened by 'no periodical merry-making, no village *fête*', and was changed only 'for the still sadder burden of a teeming wife. . . . "We shall get along," is the answer in full for all that can be said in way of advice to a boy and girl who take it into their heads to go before a magistrate and "get married". And they do get along, till sickness overtakes them, by means perhaps of borrowing a kettle from one and a tea-pot from another; but intemperance, idleness, or sickness will, in one week, plunge those who are even getting along well into utter destitution; and where this happens, they are completely without resource.'

The creed of equality ruled out the notion of domestic service and girls were usually only lured into it by the desire to buy themselves some fine new clothes. Their wardrobes complete, they left. When Mrs. Trollope asked her first young 'help' (the word servant was taboo) how much she should pay her a year, the girl replied, with a laugh: '"Oh Gimini! . . . you be a downright Englisher, sure enough. I should like to see a young lady engage by the year in America! I hope I shall get a husband before many months, or I expect I shall be an outright old maid, for I be most seventeen already; besides, mayhap I may want to go to school. You must just give me a dollar and a half a week, and mother's slave Phillis, must come over once a week I expect, from t'other side the water to help me clean."'

This young lady left after two months because Mrs. Trollope refused to lend her the money to buy a silk dress for a ball—saying as she went: 'Then 'tis not worth my while to stay any longer.' If she did find herself a husband before the dread onset of old-maidenhood at seventeen, she doubtless went to 'help' someone else for a while to pay for a silk dress for her wedding, but the ceremony and celebrations on that occasion were, on Mrs. Trollope's evidence, not likely to have been very exciting: 'as the thinly-scattered population of most villages can give no parties, and pay no priests, they contrive to marry, christen, and bury, without them', said our commentator. She had thought that one of the 'glorious institutions' of the Union, which everyone talked about but no one could define, was probably the institution of marriage which the Americans had 'made purely a civil and not a religious rite, to be performed by a justice of peace, instead of a clergyman', but the people she asked said no, that wasn't what they meant at all. And, of course, they had not made marriage a purely civil rite; weddings did take place in churches and others were performed by clergymen in private homes—though the latter perhaps was a prerogative of the wealthy, and Mrs. Trollope approved of their way of life no more than she did that of the poor.

American women were still dressing outrageously for their pioneering life: 'the expense of the ladies' dress greatly exceeds in proportion to their general style of living, that of the ladies of Europe,' she said, and, with the exception of Philadelphia, the results were far 'from being in good taste'. Even in heavy winter snow, they walked around 'with their poor little toes pinched into a miniature slipper, incapable of excluding as much moisture as might bedew a primrose' (though she was quick to admit that 'almost universally' Americans had 'extremely pretty feet'), and seemed 'extremely shocked at the sight of comfortable walking shoes and cotton stockings'. One young lady of Mrs. Trollope's acquaintance had her 'pretty little ear' frost-bitten by wearing an unsuitably frivolous bonnet, and muffs were never carried. They had other strange ways of adding to their charms, too: 'They powder themselves immoderately, face, neck, and arms, with pulverised starch; the effect is indescribably disagreeable by day-light, and not very favourable at any time. They are also most unhappily partial to false hair, which they wear in surprising quantities; this is the more to be lamented, as they generally have very fine hair of their own.'

A few years later, the American poet, Ella Wheeler Wilcox, included false curls in a bridal outfit when she wrote:

> Up in the cosy chamber
> Where, on the snowy bed,
> The dress, the pearls, and the new false curls
> For tomorrow's use were spread.

Mrs. Trollope put this partiality down to laziness and a dearth of 'accomplished ladies' maids'. Like most earlier travellers in the New World, she noticed that the main fashion display went on in the churches and chapels: 'I am tempted to believe that a stranger from the continent of Europe would be inclined, on first reconnoitering the city [*Cincinnati*], to suppose that the places of worship were the theatres and cafés of the place. No evening in the week but brings throngs of the young and beautiful to the chapels and meeting-houses, all dressed with care, and sometimes with great pre-tension; it is there that all display is made, and all fashionable distinction sought. . . . Were it not for the churches, indeed, I think there might be a general bonfire of best bonnets, for I never could discover any other use for them . . . were it not for public worship, and private tea-drinkings, all the ladies in Cincinnati would be in danger of becoming perfect recluses. . . . I never saw, or read, of any country where religion had so strong a hold upon the women, or a slighter hold upon the men.' American men she thought disgusting boors, always talking commerce and the dollar, eternally chewing tobacco and spitting it out. The negroes were far more gentlemanly, and she had often been amused by 'observing the very superior air of gallantry assumed by the men, when in attendance on their *belles*, to that of the whites in similar circumstances. On one occasion we met in Broadway [*New York*] a young negress in the extreme of fashion, and accompanied by a black *beau*, whose toilet was equally studied; an eye-glass, guard-chain, nothing was omitted; he walked beside his sable goddess un-covered, with an air of the most tender devotion. At the window of a handsome house which they were passing, stood a very pretty white girl, with two gentlemen beside her; but alas! both of them had their hats on, and one was smoking!'

However, she did feel that in New York there was society to be met with which 'would be deemed delightful anywhere'. Social occasions in the rest of America continually surprised and depressed her: 'Mixed dinner parties of ladies and gentle-men are very rare,' she wrote, 'and unless several foreigners are present, but little conversation passes at table. It certainly does not, in my opinion, add to the well ordering of a dinner table, to set the gentlemen at one end of it, and the ladies at the other; but it is very rarely that you find it otherwise.' And at gala functions, more often than not, the gentlemen sat down to supper in one room, while the ladies wandered forlornly round in another, balancing their meal in their hands as best they could—an 'arrangement. . . . owing neither to economy nor want of a room large enough to accommodate the whole party, but purely because the gentlemen liked it better'. The men sometimes played cards by themselves at evening parties; if a lady played too, it could not be for money; 'no ecarté, no chess; very little music, and that little lamentably bad . . . to eat inconceivable quantities of cake, ice, and pickled oysters—and to show half their revenue in silks and satins, seem to be the chief object they [*the ladies*] have in these parties'.

Even at this early date, visitors were being astonished by the exuberant combination of foodstuffs in America: 'I have seen eggs and oysters eaten together', proclaimed Mrs. Trollope; 'the sempiternal ham with apple-sauce; beefsteak with stewed peaches; and salt fish with onions. . . . They are "extravagantly fond," to use their own phrase, of puddings, pies, and all kinds of "sweets," particularly the ladies.' Already, Johnny cake was on the menu.

The most 'agreeable meetings', she had been assured by all young people, were those to which no married women were admitted: 'of the truth of this statement I have not the least doubt. These exclusive meetings occur frequently, and often last to a late hour; on these occasions, I believe, they generally dance.'

Mrs. Trollope's sour view of the country understandably met with howls of rage and contradiction in America, but her belief that the young had a gayer time socially than the old, or even the middle-aged, appears to be confirmed by Mrs. Vanderbilt's description of wedding parties in Flatbush. Writing in 1880 of the present and the past, she said that the older guests usually left a wedding party at a fairly early hour, while the young ones 'continued the festivity until after midnight, as they are wont to do even at the present day'.

At the beginning of the century there were still no honeymoons in America, and the wedding celebrations of the wealthy went on for a week or longer. Miss Eliza Southgate Browne, of New York, wrote in 1804: 'Miss Pell was married last week to Robert MacComb; they are making a prodigious dash. I went to pay the bride's visit on Friday; they had an elegant ball and supper in the evening, as it was the last day of seeing company; 7 bride's maids and 7 bride-men, most superb dresses; the bride's pearls cost 1,500 dollars; they spend the winter in Charleston.' Mrs. Earle, who quoted Miss Browne at the turn of the current century, said the 'seeing company' took the place 'of our present wedding-tour'. Everyone who knew the bride or bridegroom, or their parents, called on the bride. 'Sometimes she received one day, and her husband had men callers the next day,' which sounds like the kind of segregation Mrs. Trollope complained of. 'At other times ladies and gentlemen visited her in one parlor, then went to another room and drank to and with the groom, who, as one chronicler said, generally got "reasonably pleasant".'

Towards the end of the 1800s, Mrs. Sherwood announced that the 'wedding of today in England has "Set the Fashion" for America'; everything had become very elaborate and showy—'Even the cushion on which a wealthy bride in New York was lately expected to kneel was so elaborately embroidered with pearls that she visibly hesitated to press it with her knee at the altar.' She regretted that the English wedding breakfast had not become more popular in the States, but was inclined to be complacent about the way Americans handled the question of wedding favours. Not for her the

Plate Ten

English habit of giving knots of 'white ribbon and artificial flowers' to everyone; in America, she was happy to report, such ornaments were 'used for the horse's ears and the servants' coats. . . . Here the groom wears a boutonniere of natural flowers'. A similarly limited distribution of favours sometimes took place in Britain, too, but a more bountiful largesse was certainly not sneered at. Mr. Minn's invaluable guide to correct etiquette told him that: 'The box of wedding favours intended for the servants and coachmen are distributed when the ceremony is over outside the church and those intended for the guests are flying about in the busy hands of the bridesmaids, who, each with the pins already provided for each favour, fastens the white knot on the coat of one of the bridegroomsmen while he essays to pin a similar one on her shoulder. Every guest is provided with a favour.'

At royal weddings most of the guests and the cheering spectators, both men and women, provided their own favours (like those at Queen Victoria's marriage, some of which were 'of huge dimensions' with branches rather than sprigs of orange blossom). The bridegroom usually wore a white rosette on his dark frock-coat when he left for his honeymoon, and for the ceremony itself, both he and his chief supporters wore large flat bows of white satin ribbon over each shoulder, attached to the epaulettes of their uniforms. The horses in royal wedding processions did not wear favours, but they were themselves, of a suitably festive colour—'I drove in a sort of state coach with many windows & 4 of the Creams', wrote Queen Victoria after the wedding of her grandson, the Duke of York. (The 'sort of state coach with many windows' was one of the first royal glass coaches.) The other principal performers and guests at this wedding rode in open landaus—also drawn by four cream horses apiece—and this was the type of carriage most often used at other upper-class but non-royal weddings. William Francis Freelove (in *An Assemblage of 19th Century Horses & Carriages*) said that on such important occasions they were often driven by a postilion sitting ceremonially in the saddle of the lead horse, rather than from the coachman's box; and that the whips were decorated with white bows, while the horses 'were bedecked with white ear coverings and white tassels'. ('Could this', suggests a friend who delights in the absurd, 'be the origin of the expression "cloth ears"?')

By the 1870s grand American weddings, held in the bride's home, were also very spectacular occasions indeed, and magnificent were the arrangements made for them. A low platform was usually constructed at one end of the drawing-room, for the bride, bridegroom and priest to stand upon. Swathes of flowers and greenery turned the area into a sylvan bower, with a vast bridal bell, made of fresh white blooms, hanging in the centre above the principals' heads. Garlands of flowers and greenery festooned the house, often criss-crossing the rooms like Christmas decorations; the chandeliers dripped with foliage; floral monograms of the bride's and bridegroom's initials decorated the walls; potted palms concealed the fireplace, and horseshoes made of flowers filled in the gaps. In May 1874, all these preparations were made at the White House for the President's daughter, Nellie Grant, the pet of the nation, who was about to marry an Englishman and sail off across the Atlantic, much to the disgust of her parents and the country as a whole. The bridegroom was Algernon Sartoris, nephew of the actress Fanny Kemble; a young man with fine moustaches, melodious singing voice, and a tendency to drink. Theirs had been a ship-board romance, and President Ulysses S. Grant had made them wait eighteen months for the wedding, since Nellie was only 17 and Sartoris 21 when he first asked for her hand. Grant hoped his much-loved daughter would change her mind—and not many years later, Nellie wished she had, too. However, at eleven o'clock on the morning of 21 May 1874 the bride at least was happy, as a forty-piece Marine band struck up a wedding march in the East Room of the White House and the bridegroom appeared on an aisle marked out with white satin ribbons—carrying a pink and white bouquet of his own, with, in its centre, a small silver banner saying 'Love'. The 'most brilliant White House wedding of the century' was under way, and there were 200 guests to see it. Eight bridesmaids, dressed all in white, four carrying pink bouquets and four carrying blue, preceded the bride, who wore a white satin gown, made in New York and said to have cost $5,000. Fashions now tended towards the bustle rather than the out and out crinoline, and frills and trimmings were elaborate. Lace, orange blossom and even miniature oranges, banded Nellie's dress; a white tulle veil hung down behind her to the floor, and on her head was a wreath of orange blossom, small white flowers and green leaves. She carried a bouquet of white flowers and a pearl and lace fan. $75,000-worth of presents were on show, and the bride was even honoured by the poets (well, by a poet) in the ancient manner: Walt Whitman wrote an epithalamium for her—*A Kiss to the Bride*.

If ever a wedding breakfast was misnamed, it was the one that graced this marriage —though set beside the twenty-nine-course dinners President Grant liked to give, it appeared a mere snack. The seven courses (starting with soft crabs on toast, and passing lightly through such dishes as croquettes of chicken with green peas, wood-cocks and snipe, before reaching the strawberries and cream, small fancy cakes, punch *à la Romaine*, coffee and chocolate) were served in the State Dining Room, at a table burdened with pyramids of nougat and candy, 'Corbeils glaces a la Jardiniere', 'Epigraphe la fleur, de Nelly Grant', and, at the centre, a giant 'Bride cake' from which streamers stretched to either end of the table and disappeared into bowls of flowers bristling with flags wishing 'Success to the President', 'Success to the Army', 'Success to the Supreme Court' and 'Hail Columbia'. Each guest had a piece of wedding cake, already boxed and tied with white silk, and a menu printed on white satin beside his place. The bells of the Metropolitan Methodist Church (whose minister had performed the marriage) rang out with Mendelssohn's *Wedding March*, *The Wedding Pearl*, *God Save the Queen*, *Hail Columbia*, *Then You'll Remember Me*, *Auld Lang Syne*, the *Grand March* from *Tannhauser*, and *Home Sweet Home*, as Mr. Sartoris and his bride drove to the Baltimore and Potomac depot to take train for New York. Their special Pullman palace car (made for the Vienna Exposition) was decorated with more flowers and foliage, and a generous assortment of British and American flags. Next day the sad President and his wife joined them at the Fifth Avenue Hotel, and later waved them off from the dockside as they sailed for England.

Twelve years later, Grover Cleveland, the only President ever to be married at the White House, arranged a quieter wedding for himself. His was very much a 'daddy-long-legs' love affair, the bride being his 21-year-old ward, Frances Folsom, whose guardian he had been since the death of her father (and Cleveland's law partner) ten years earlier. It had been planned to hold the wedding at the home of the bride's grandfather, at Folsomdale, near Buffalo, but old Colonel Folsom died while his grand-daughter was away on a pre-marriage tour of Europe with her mother, and the President had to cope with organising something else by the time she got back.

Marriage by Fascination

Everything to do with the new arrangements received his personal attention, from the writing of the invitations to the music and the flowers. The very few Cabinet members, relatives and friends who were invited received simple hand-written notes dated only five days before the wedding:

> My dear Mr. ——
> I am to be married on Wednesday evening at seven o'clock at the White House to Miss Folsom. It will be a very quiet affair and I will be extremely gratified at your attendance on the occasion.
> > Yours sincerely,
> > Grover Cleveland.

By Presidential edict, floral bells and horseshoes were forbidden, but some thwarted artist managed to add the date, 2 June 1886, in yellow pansies (the figures nearly a foot high) to the permitted monograms. When it came to music, the President was able to turn to John Philip Sousa, director of the Marine Band, for assistance. Looking back on his life later, (*Marching Along*, 1928), Sousa recalled suggesting a piece from one of his own operas, *Désirée*, as part of the incidental music for the evening —a quartette called *The Student of Love*. Studying the proposed programme, the 49-year-old, portly, bachelor bridegroom said with executive decision: 'I think I'd play that number just as "A Quartette," leaving out "The Student of Love".'

The marriage was a popular one, as the crowds showed when the President reviewed the Memorial Day parades in New York the Sunday before the wedding. They cheered him rapturously, especially when one of the military bands lost its collective head and played a few bars of *He's Going to Marry Yum Yum*. The bride was smuggled back into the country at the end of her Atlantic voyage, and a few days later, at 5.30 a.m., arrived in Washington on the morning of her wedding day—with the *trousseau* she had chosen in Paris. In the 1820s Mrs. Trollope had said that anything French was the vogue in New York and that Broadway might have been taken for a French street; whilst anything English was 'decidedly *mauvais ton*; English materials, English fashions, English accent, English manner, are all terms of reproach; and to say that an unfortunate looks like an English woman, is the cruelest satire which can be uttered'. She supposed that family quarrels were the most difficult to patch up and that even 'fifteen years of peace' had not been enough 'to calm the angry feelings of brother Jonathan towards the land of his fathers'. By the time Miss Folsom married there had been another half-century and more of peace, but loyalty to French fashions had not wavered. It was to Paris Miss Folsom went for her wedding gown, and very handsomely Paris served her: there, corded ivory satin had been splendidly draped and tucked over an underskirt of silk muslin, fashioned into a bustle and long court train behind, and trimmed with orange blossom in a restrained and elegant manner. Her 5 ft.-long tulle veil reached to the hem of her dress in front, and the end of the train behind, and was held in place by a simple tiara of orange flowers. There were no bridesmaids, and the President himself, wearing a black dress suit, led the bride into the Blue Room of the White House; there, beneath the central gas-lit chandelier they were married by the Reverend Byron Sunderland of the First Presbyterian Church, and, on this unlikely occasion, the word 'obey' was purposely omitted from the bride's vows. Sousa conducted Mendelssohn's *Wedding March* for their entrance and Wagner's *Bridal Chorus* for their exit. Church bells pealed out all over Washington, whistles blew, and the cannons in the Navy yard were fired in salute. Outside, the crowds, who had been allowed to wander over the White House lawns to the portico of the main entrance, cheered.

Supper was served in the small family dining-room, which like the other reception rooms had been turned into a bower of flowers (one of the fireplaces in the Oval Room was full of glowing begonias, with Centaureas scattered on the hearth beneath like ashes); the centre-piece of the supper table was a three-masted floral schooner—the 'Hymen'—with a flag for each mast: the stars and stripes on the main mast and C-F in gold on the others. Each guest had gifts of sweetmeats in satin bags and a satin-covered box of wedding cake, with a hand-painted spray of flowers on the lid, and a card signed personally by both bride and groom (a box and card—rare trophies from this select gathering—can still be seen at the Smithsonian Institution).

Rice and slippers were thrown after the carriage as the President and his bride set out for Deer Park, Maryland, late that night, for what should have been a secluded honeymoon in a superior resort. But the journalists were there before them, ready to spy on the honeymooners for the whole week and file reports on every fleeting glimpse ('Mrs. Cleveland Fishes'), just like the odious royalty-watchers and Jackie Kennedy Onassis hounders of today.

And so, from the first families of the new world, to those of the old. In Britain, royal weddings during the 19th century went public, and gathered a wealth of new glories as they went along. The most important marriage of the early years was that of the heir presumptive, Princess Charlotte of Wales, daughter of the Prince Regent (later George IV). Loathing her mother (Caroline of Brunswick), the Regent was not over-fond of the daughter, and tried to marry her off to the Prince of Orange, an unprepossessing young man, whose main virtue, in the Regent's eyes, was that he would desire his wife to live in Holland. The 17-year-old Princess, who had somehow managed to grow up with a great deal of character (and most of it good), refused to agree to the match unless the stipulation that she should not be forced to live abroad against her will was written into the marriage settlement: 'My reasons', she wrote to her uncle, the Duke of York, 'arise no less from personal feeling, than from a sense of personal duty.' After this show of spirit, the Princess became a virtual prisoner until the spring of 1816, when another suitor appeared, a minor German prince, Leopold of Saxe-Coburg, who 'had many good qualities as well as good looks'. He was acceptable, if nothing more, to all parties, and so on the evening of 2 May 1816, the Princess was married at Carlton House, her father's London residence, wearing a wreath of roses and a silver gown which managed to look both magnificent and pretty (and which can still be seen at the London Museum). A few days later, a drawing-room was held in her honour at Buckingham House, as Buckingham Palace was called before the Regent commissioned Nash to turn it into a palace fit for a king. Princess Charlotte's short marriage was almost magically happy (Sir Thomas Lawrence, engaged in painting her portrait, described in moving detail the almost arcadian life at Claremont, Surrey where the couple lived); but nineteen months later it came suddenly to an end: the Princess died on 5 November 1817, a few hours after giving birth to a still-born son.

The double death of the heir presumptive and her child left the royal family in an embarrassing situation. Although George III and Queen Charlotte had seven middle-aged sons (and six daughters) living, these royal princes could not now produce a single legitimate heir between the lot of them. The Duke of York, a model of decorum compared with his brothers, had married the Princess Frederica of Prussia in 1791, but there were no children of the union; Augustus, Duke of Sussex, had married twice—once in Rome and once in St. George's, Hanover Square—and had a 23-year-old son, but as the lady concerned (she was the same at both ceremonies) was not of royal blood and as the Duke had failed to ask the King's prior permission, the marriages had long since been declared illegal (under the provisions of the 1772 Royal Marriages Act); the son (and his younger sister) were therefore deemed illegitimate. Ernest Augustus, the 46-year-old Duke of Cumberland, George III's fifth son, had been married only one year, and was not to produce a legitimate child until 1819. The three remaining brothers were nominally bachelors, and as such were pressured into speedy marriages with German princesses of promising fecundity. Queen Charlotte did the match-making, and managed to get all three off her hands by the summer of 1818. The 44-year-old Duke of Cambridge, the seventh son, was first to go: he married Princess Augusta of Hesse-Cassel, at Cassel on 7 May (and again in London on 1 June); the Duke of Kent, 51, the fourth son, was dispatched to Coburg three weeks later, where he married a 32-year-old widow, Victoria Mary Louisa, daughter of the Duke of Saxe-Saalfeld-Coburg, at a Lutheran ceremony. The most senior of this mature trio, the 52-year-old William, Duke of Clarence, was matched with the sweet-natured, 25-year-old Princess Adelaide of Saxe-Meiningen.

The Hanoverians had always been boorish bridegrooms, waiting in their palaces for their brides to come to them, but the Duke of Clarence excelled them all. He was out of town when his bride and her mother arrived, and they were greeted by no more august a personage than the proprietor of the hotel in Albermarle Street at which they were to stay. A messenger was sent to inform the Duke, who duly drove up Piccadilly in a coach and four an hour or so later. The marriage took place very quietly at Kew (a favourite retreat of Queen Charlotte's) on 18 July 1818, and they were joined by the Duke and Duchess of Kent, who took the opportunity of going through the Church of England ceremony with them. After a family dinner and tea at a cottage in the grounds of Kew Palace, the Duke of Clarence drove his bride and her mother to his bachelor apartments in the Stable Yard of St. James's Palace. Next day, the Duchess of Saxe-Meiningen returned to Germany, and the new Duchess of Clarence was left to cope alone, not only with an unwilling bridegroom, twenty-seven years her senior, but also with the ten children of his liaison with the actress Mrs. Jordan, who had died two years earlier. (This whole pride of princes was notoriously short of cash, and as Mrs. Jordan had continued to work during her relationship with the Duke of Clarence, the wags had all asked whether the Duke was keeping Mrs. Jordan, or Mrs. Jordan was keeping the Duke?) Princess Adelaide had been chosen by Queen Charlotte on her 'reputation for amiability' and she must have had this in marvellous measure: she charmed her husband; charmed his children ('the saving angel of the family', they called her); charmed the country when the Duke became William IV, the sailor king; and, after the bitter loss of two baby daughters of her own, wrote charming letters to the daughter of the Duke and Duchess of Kent, who had shared her wedding day. And that daughter was to become Queen Victoria.

With the marriage of this young Queen in 1840 the pattern of royal weddings began to change. The first alteration was fortuitous rather than planned: she chose to be married in the Chapel Royal of St. James's Palace, scene of most royal weddings of the previous century, but as she did not live at St. James's like her predecessors (Victoria was the first monarch to make the newly refurbished and titled Buckingham Palace her official home) she had a short journey to make on her wedding day, a journey which could be watched and shared in by her subjects, and which turned the occasion into a public event. Another novelty had been the emphasis placed on the desires of the bride when it came to choosing a husband. The match-making was still there, but it had become more subtle—there was to be no more parental bullying to take a life-partner sight-unseen. Prince Albert was brought to the notice of the future Queen a year before her accession, when she was just 17, and Albert (three months her junior) had not quite reached that elevated estate. He, his elder brother Ernest, and their father the Duke of Coburg, took an English holiday in the spring of 1836, staying part of the time with the Princess and her mother, the Duchess of Kent, at Kensington Palace. When they left, Victoria wrote in her Journal: 'I cried very very bitterly after my dear beloved cousins had left. Dearly as I love Ferdinand, and also good Augustus, I love Ernest and Albert more than them, oh yes, *much* more. . . .' (Albert wrote in his diary: 'She is very amiable and extraordinarily self-possessed!') Before the parting, the Princess and the Duke acknowledged that a marriage might take place. Albert was not told, but a gruelling course of education was mapped out (largely by King Leopold of the Belgians) to fit him for the role. King Leopold, Victoria's uncle (her mother's brother), played constant Svengali to the match, and he was in a particularly good position to know what was needed in a consort for a queen of England, for he was the same Leopold, the minor German prince, who had been married for so tragically short a time to Princess Charlotte. Since those days, Leopold had advanced in the world, turning down an offer of the throne of Greece in 1831, and accepting that of Belgium a year later.

Prince Albert was still deep in his studies when King William IV of Britain died in June 1837, and Victoria became Queen; he did not appear in England again until the autumn of 1839, and by that time the 20-year-old sovereign was greatly enjoying her new role—and her new freedom. The girl who only two years earlier had still been sleeping in her mother's bedroom and was forbidden to walk downstairs without someone to hold her hand, was now the crowned head of the United Kingdom of Great Britain and Ireland. Romance and Albert had a lot to compete with. Shortly before Prince Albert and his brother arrived for this second visit, the Queen described in her Journal a conversation she had had that day with her Prime Minister, Lord Melbourne: 'Talked of my cousins Ernest and Albert coming over—of my having no great wish to see Albert, as the whole subject was an odious one which I hated to decide about; there was no engagement between us, I said, but the young man was aware there was a possibility of such a union.'

One look at Albert, and all such sniffy superiority vanished: 'At $\frac{1}{2}$ past 7 I went to the top of the staircase and received my 2 dear cousins, Ernest and Albert—whom I found grown and changed and embellished. . . . It was with some emotion I beheld Albert—who is *beautiful.*' That was 10 October. On the 12th, the Queen: 'Talked of Spain with Lord M. . . . Talked of my cousins . . . the length of their stay being left to me; and I said seeing them had a good deal changed my opinion as to marrying, and that I must decide soon, which was a difficult thing. . . .' On Monday the 14th: 'Talked of my cousins having gone out shooting. After a little pause I said to Lord M.

I had made up my mind (about marrying dearest Albert)—"You have?" he said. . . .
"I'm very glad of it; I think it is a good thing, and you'll be much more comfortable;
for a woman cannot stand alone for long, in whatever situation she is.". . . Then I
asked if I hadn't better tell Albert of my decision soon, in which Lord M. agreed.
"How?" I asked, for in general such things are done the other way round. Which
made Lord M. laugh. . . .'

Next day: 'Saw my dear Cousins come home quite safe from the hunt. . . . At about
$\frac{1}{2}$ p. 12 I sent for Albert. . . . After a few minutes I said to him that I thought he must
be aware *why* I wished him to come—and that it would make me *too* happy if he
would consent to what I wished (to marry me). We embraced each other, and he was
so kind and *so* affectionate. There was no hesitation on his part. He is perfect in every
way. . . .'

'It was a nervous thing to do,' she said later, 'but Prince Albert could not possibly
have proposed to the Queen of England. He would never have presumed to take such a
liberty.' At the time, she wrote in her Journal: '"I have got well through this with
Albert," I said to Lord M.'

Greater ordeals lay ahead. Not only did the young Queen have to do the proposing
and consult with her Prime Minister on the progress of her romance, but it was also
her job to inform the Privy Council ('I wore a beautiful bracelet with the prince's
picture and it seemed to give me courage. . . . I felt my hand shake but I did not make
a mistake') and, later, Parliament. (Lord Melbourne and his Monarch looked up the
records of how George III had coped with such a situation, since he was another
youthful sovereign who had married shortly after accession, and followed this
precedent.) On 16 January 1840 Queen Victoria opened a new session of Parliament,
announcing her proposed marriage at the beginning of her speech from the throne.
The following day she was able to write to Albert: 'Everything went off exceedingly
well yesterday. There was an immense multitude of people, and perhaps never,
certainly not for a long time, have I been received so well; and what is remarkable *I
was not nervous*, and read the speech really well.'

Her ministers, however, were not handling things so deftly. They failed to make
clear that the Prince was a Protestant even though rumours were flying about, on the
one hand that he was a Roman Catholic, and, on the other, that he was 'a radical and
an infidel'; they tried to railroad the House into granting him the sum of £50,000 a
year (even after admitting the cost of his household would not be more than £7,000
and despite 'great commercial distress' in the country); and they attempted to slip
the tricky question of 'precedence' into the naturalisation bill, which caused an
ungracious delay in inviting the Prince to become a British subject. The English
constitution makes no provision for male consorts; each case is worked out afresh as it
arises, and usually provokes a surprising amount of bad feeling before it is settled.
Queen Victoria wished to make Albert her 'King-Consort', saying that she did not
want him to be in the same position as that 'stupid and insignificant husband of Queen
Anne'. As in the case of a Queen Consort, he would then have been of undisputed rank,
next only to herself. But the Opposition said, 'What? Have precedence over the
Prince of Wales, the heir to the throne, when there is one? And what if the Queen
died young? Would he then take precedence over *everyone*?' In the end the Liberals
had to drop the over-heated issue in order to get the naturalisation part of the bill
through in time for the wedding. It was not until seventeen years later that the Prince-

And the Bride Wore . . .

Consort, who had long since been given that title by public acclaim, had it conferred on him by Royal Letters Patent, and in the meantime there were many uncomfortable moments, especially abroad, when any protocol-crazed little Archduke could claim precedence over the husband of the Queen of England, 'merely', as Queen Victoria wrote, 'because the English law did not know of him'. His rank, to anyone who wanted to be nasty about it, remained that of a younger son of the ducal house of Saxe-Coburg and Gotha.

Queen Victoria and Prince Albert did so much to stabilise the British crown and rub up an image heavily tarnished by the sons of George III that it is easy to forget to what a low ebb royalty had sunk when she first came to the throne. At the time of her wedding, the newspapers and magazines were delighted to hint that the young Queen was fully as badly-behaved as her relations, and gave generous space to 'the rumours abroad' that the elderly charmer, Lord Melbourne, 'will, of course, be retiring after the marriage'. Even her bridal wardrobe came under attack in a letter from 'a dress-maker' to *The Times* four days before the ceremony:

> The papers constantly announce that the dresses of Her Majesty's Court are composed wholly of British manufacture. . . . This assertion is wholly un-founded. Her Majesty's dress makers and milliners are foreigners and no other find favour at Court. . . . I am told that five of Her Majesty's vans were loaded at the Customs House. . . . I believe it is also understood that Her Majesty's dress is to be Brussels Lace instead of Honiton Lace though Honiton Lace has been purchased as a blind.

The Court Newsman was later to stress that the wedding dress was of white Spital-fields satin 'with a very deep trimming of Honiton lace, a design similar to that of the veil. The body and sleeves were richly trimmed with the same material to correspond. The train was of white satin and was also lined with white satin trimmed with orange blossom. . . . exclusively of British Fabrication.' Details of the guests' *ensembles* also included 'exclusively of British fabrication', in brackets, where appropriate.

Although Victoria's wedding clothes were costly, they were far simpler than those of her predecessors; silver brocade, encrusted with jewels, was out, and she was the first British monarch to be married without a heavy velvet and ermine royal mantle. Having described her bridal *toilette* (rich by our standards, certainly), *The Times* reported: 'Her attendants were arrayed with similar simplicity.' The lace she wore *was* made at Honiton (or, to be absolutely precise, at the village of Beer nearby); it cost £1,000 and was worked by 'two hundred poor lace workers' who 'could not sufficiently express their gratitude.' During the Queen's lifetime, most of this truly exquisite lace was taken off the dress (to be worn on many other occasions) and replaced with something a little less expensive. The gown itself, with the original lace Bertha and sleeve flounces, plus the substitute lace, can still be seen at the London Museum— which is quartered in Kensington Palace, the birthplace of Victoria, and the home of her youth. It is a lovely, tiny dress (the Queen was only 4 ft. 11 ins. tall), with a low neck and very pretty sleeves, gathered into two puffs, above the elbow. The bodice is deeply pointed at the waist, the skirt pleated and full—though not monstrously so; crinolines had not yet become the fashion. The veil was only one-and-a-half yards square. She also wore diamond earrings and necklace, and the insignia of the Order of the Garter. The Dowager Lady Lyttelton, one of the Ladies in Waiting, wrote a few days after the ceremony: 'The Queen's look and manner were very pleasing; her eyes much swollen with tears, but great happiness in her countenance; and her look of confidence and comfort at the Prince, when they walked away as man and wife, was very pleasing to see. I understand she is in extremely high spirits since. Such a new thing for her to *dare* to be *unguarded* in conversing with anybody; and with her frank and fearless nature the restraints she has hitherto been under, from one reason or another, with everybody, must have been most painful.'

Lord Malmesbury recorded that the Queen's uncle, the Duke of Sussex (of the clandestine marriages) had given her away—'and the "John Bull" says that he is always ready to give away what does not belong to him. There were only two Tories present at the ceremony, the Duke of Wellington and Lord Liverpool. The Queen was very much cheered by the mob on her way to and from the chapel.' (The Queen had earlier vowed that she would not invite 'a single Tory' to the wedding, as punishment for the way they had argued over Prince Albert's allowance and precedence. She had obviously been persuaded to make two exalted exceptions.)

The bridegroom had also been very much cheered by the mob on his journey to London. Earlier, there had been grumbles that he was too young and that Britain had had enough of German princes, anyway; but when he landed at Dover, four days before the wedding, his handsome looks and youthful dignity won over the country as they had won over the Queen, and he was cheered all the way to London. He arrived at Buckingham Palace on 8 February, taking the oaths which made him a British subject the same day—'He looked superbly handsome', wrote the bride. The following day she made him a Knight of the Garter, and he wore the collar of the order on his wedding day, over the uniform of a Field Marshal of the British Army. Round the left knee of his skin-tight white breeches was the garter itself, and on each epaulette was a large bridal bow of white satin ribbon. (The Duke of Sussex, an imposing figure of a man, much girt about with collars and decorations, also appears, from Sir George Hayter's official painting of the marriage ceremony, to have sported wedding favours—in this case, a white rosette on each shoulder.) The Dowager Queen Adelaide wore a white gown with a train of violet velvet, lined with white satin, and on her head feathers and a diamond tiara. The bride's mother, the Duchess of Kent, also wore feathers and diamonds and a veil, but less illustrious guests were instructed by the Court Circular, on the morning of the wedding, that 'the exclusion of feathers is particularly desirable as they would interfere with the view of the passing scene'. White wedding favours were, specifically, permitted to everyone, and the day after the marriage *The Times* reported: 'Every lady exhibited a white favour, some of which were admirable specimens of refined taste. They were of all sizes, many of white satin riband, tied up into bows and mixed with layers of rich silver lace. Others merely of riband intermixed with sprigs of orange flower blossoms . . . here and there were seen bouquets of huge dimensions of riband and massive silver bullion having in their centre what might almost be termed a branch of orange blossoms. Large as they were, however, they were not more so than the apparent devotion of their owners.'

After a family wedding breakfast at Buckingham Palace, the royal bride and groom prepared to leave for a brief honeymoon at Windsor Castle, Prince Albert changing into 'a plain dark travelling dress and H.M. in a white satin pelisse trimmed with swansdown, with a white satin bonnet and feather' (*The Times*). 'Dearest Albert

159

came up and fetched me downstairs,' the Queen wrote in her Journal, 'when we took leave of Mamma and drove off near 4; I and Albert alone. . . .' But not for long: Mamma and the Duke of Coburg visited them two days later, and on the 14 February, the 20-year-old Queen and her 20-year-old Consort returned to London. On the 19th Her Majesty held a *levée*, and the Prince stood at her left hand.

The day after her wedding, the Queen wrote to Baron Stockmar: 'There cannot exist a dearer, purer, nobler being in the world than the Prince'; they were sentiments which were not to fade.

Queen Victoria, like her great-great-granddaughter, Queen Elizabeth II, was all for marriage, when it was her own she was thinking of; but, like Queen Elizabeth I, felt much abused when any of her household decided to take the plunge. In May 1842, she had obviously been grumbling to Lord Melbourne about the engagement of one of her Maids of Honour, Susan Cavendish, to Lord Emlyn, for the good Lord M. gave her an unmistakeable wigging in his letter of 15 May: '. . . . Your Majesty having generally chosen handsome and attractive girls for the Maids of Honour, which is very right, must expect to lose them in this way. Lord Melbourne is very glad of the marriage. Lord Emlyn always seemed to him a very pleasing young man, and well calculated to make a woman happy.' In her widowhood she was even more put out by such marriages and was very angry when her resident physician, Sir James Reid, became engaged to Susan Baring, a Maid of Honour for little more than a year. Lady Lytton (in her *Court Diary*) recorded that the doctor finally 'won round' his august patient 'by promising never to do it again'.

The marriages of her own children, however, were quite a different matter and Queen Victoria worked hard and long to find suitable partners for them; even the 'Baby' of the family, Princess Beatrice (who was only four when the Prince Consort died and was firmly clamped to her mother's side ever after), was allowed to wed, though under somewhat stringent conditions and not until the age of 28. The nine royal children (five girls and four boys) all married in pretty much the same sequence in which they had been born, and it was the eldest of them all, 'Vicky', the Princess Royal, who was the first to go. In January 1858, two months after her 17th birthday, she married Prince Frederick William of Prussia, at the same place—the Chapel Royal of St. James's Palace—and in a ceremony much the same in every respect as that of her mother. She and her husband also spent a brief honeymoon at Windsor, where they were visited by their parents as Queen Victoria and the Prince Consort had been. But on this occasion everything was a little more grand. That marvellous new invention, the railway, brought royalty from all over Europe to witness the event: Disraeli thought the final gathering included 'as many princes as the Congress of Vienna', while Charles Greville, the diarist, recorded that all went off with 'amazing *éclat*'. *The Times* was struck by the 'exquisite taste' of the floral arrangements and commented on the masses of flowers, leaves and berries which were used. Of the bride's arrival at St. James's it reported: 'The gorgeous veil she wears depending from her headdress is thrown off and, hanging in massive folds behind, leaves the expression of her face completely visible as she walks slowly, her head slightly stooped in bashfulness and her eyes cast down upon the ground.' Her dress was 'so thoroughly in good taste' it was 'difficult to remark anything, save that it is exquisitely becoming, beautiful, and white . . . manufactured by Miss Janet Fife and composed of a rich robe of white moire antique, with three flounces of Honiton lace.' In the end, they also managed to remark that the 'train of unusual length of more than three yards is of white moire antique trimmed with two rows of Honiton lace surmounted by wreaths similar to those on the flounces of the dress with bouquets at short intervals'. It was more floral and fussy than her mother's had been, trellised with garlands and wreaths of roses, shamrocks and thistles. On her head she wore a wreath of orange blossom and myrtle.

The bridesmaids—eight maiden daughters of dukes, marquises and earls, a selection which was to be followed at most future royal weddings—wore frothy dresses designed by the bride herself. All had six deep tulle flounces, looped up with bouquets of roses and white heather—the latter said (by the *Illustrated London News*) to have been 'modelled from a sprig of heather which the Princess gathered during her last walk in the mountains near her Highland home'. The bridegroom 'wore the dark blue uniform of Prussian Service, and over his breast the orange ribbon of the order of the Black Eagle'. Lord Malmesbury, a man with a dry sense of humour, noticed that the *Morning Post* had Lord Palmerston (the Prime Minister) carrying the sword of State 'with an easy grace and dignity', while *The Times* thought 'with a ponderous solemnity'.

There had been some rumours in Germany that the wedding might take place there, but Queen Victoria instructed her Foreign Secretary, Lord Clarendon, to tell the British Minister at Berlin not to '*entertain* the *possibility* of such a question. . . . The Queen *never* would consent to it . . . the assumption of its being *too much* for a Prince Royal of Prussia to *come* over to marry *the Princess Royal of Great Britain* IN England is too *absurd*, to say the least. . . . Whatever may be the usual practice of Prussian Princes it is not *every* day that one marries the eldest daughter of the Queen of England. The question therefore must be considered as settled and closed. . . .' And so it was.

The whole of Britain was given a holiday and despite the cold, raw weather, crowds lined the route from Buckingham Palace to St. James's, and were waiting again to watch the departure of the bride and groom for Windsor in the afternoon—and the arrival of the guests for the ball in the evening. There were complaints in the papers about the cost of the wedding in relation to the 'numbers of poor people with no bread' and a suggestion in the letter columns of *The Times* (23 January) that 'the poor in their workhouse should have a meat dinner (instead of soup) and a pint of porter each for their dinner on Monday next in order that they might have cause to rejoice in the auspicious event of the day'. But, on the whole, the country was in good humour, celebrating everywhere to the sound of pealing bells and crackling bonfires.

This was the only wedding of their children at which both Queen Victoria and her consort were present. In December 1861, Prince Albert died at the age of 42, and the next royal wedding which took place the following year, was a sad affair indeed. The bride was Princess Alice, the second daughter and third child of the Queen. The bridegroom was Prince Louis of Hesse. And they were married, six months after the Prince Consort's death, in the dining-room of Osborne House, on the Isle of Wight. The Queen gave her daughter a Prayer Book 'like one dear Mama gave me on *our* happy wedding morning' and wore deep mourning, with 'my "sad cap," as baby calls it'. Her Majesty surveyed the dining-room before the guests arrived and found it 'very prettily decorated, the altar being placed under our large family picture. All the furniture had been removed, and plants and flowers placed everywhere. . . .' The bride wore white lace, the bridegroom a black tail-coat, and the dress worn by the guests (said the *Illustrated London News*) 'was mourning dress; the gentlemen in black evening coats, white waistcoats, grey trousers, and black neck cloths, and the ladies in grey or violet dresses, and grey or white gloves.' The Queen entered with her four sons, sat in an armchair throughout, and had (she wrote in her Journal) 'a great struggle all through, but remained calm'.

The romance had blossomed in happier days. In a letter to her Uncle Leopold (King of the Belgians) in December 1860, a year before Prince Albert's death, Queen Victoria wrote with pleasure of their daughter's engagement (giving, at the same time, a splendid picture of the kind of setting which was then thought ideal for a proposal):

> Dearest Uncle,—I hasten to announce to you that yesterday our dear young couple were engaged, and that we *are all* very happy. Louis was spoken to yesterday on our return from Aldershot by Albert,—who told him he would have an opportunity of speaking to Alice—and this opportunity he took last night after dinner when he was standing alone with her at the fire, and every one else was occupied talking. They whispered it to me, and then, after we left the drawing-room, we sent for good Louis—and the young people met and confirmed in a very touching manner *what* they had merely been able to whisper to one another before. He was very much overcome. He is a dear, good, amiable high-principled young man—who I am sure will make our dearest Alice *very* happy, and she will, I am sure, be a most devoted and loving wife to him. She is *very, very* happy, and it is a pleasure to see their young, happy faces beaming with love for one another.

About her eldest son, Albert Edward, Prince of Wales, the Queen could never write with such contentment. 'Bertie' she could not love. Whatever he did was wrong, and even his looks aggravated her: 'Handsome I cannot think him, with that painfully small and narrow head, those immense features and total want of chin', she wrote to her eldest daughter in November 1858. Everyone appears to have agreed that Bertie had better be 'settled' early, with a girl who appealed to him and who had enough character to cope with him, or there would be trouble. As soon as the Princess Royal was married and living in Berlin, the Queen set her scouting all the unmarried princesses of Europe for possible talent, demanding photographs and reports of likely candidates. When the Prince was only 18, *The Times* (5 July 1858) reported that there were seven princesses under consideration, with Princess Alexandra of Denmark fifth on the list. That low rating, if correct, was solely due to politics: Germany and Denmark were baring their teeth at each other and Britain did not want to appear to be taking sides. Other candidates were sought, but Princess Alexandra was so obviously superior to the rest ('She is the most fascinating creature in the world', wrote the Princess Royal), that, in the summer of 1861, a 'casual' meeting was arranged between the Prince of Wales and the Princess of Denmark, in Germany where they were both on holiday. By remarkable coincidence, they both toured the Cathedral at Speier at the same hour on the same day. Next morning, they chanced to meet again at Heidelberg. Reactions were watched with gimlet-eyes, and reports fired back to Britain. When the Prince of Wales himself returned, his father wrote to Baron Stockmar: 'he has come back greatly pleased with his interview with the princess at Speier.'

But, with the death of the Prince Consort a few months later, the impetus was lost. The proposed marriage of his eldest son was shelved and was only taken down and dusted off again when the news reached Britain of other suitors for the hand of the peerless princess. In the late summer of 1862, after eight months of widowhood, Queen Victoria rallied herself and did 'alone . . .what, under other, former happy circumstances, had devolved on us both together'. At her Uncle Leopold's palace at Laeken she met Princess Alexandra for the first time ('such a beautiful refined profile, and quiet ladylike manner, which made a most favourable impression'), with her parents, Prince and Princess Christian, and arranged the engagement. 'I said that I trusted their dear daughter would feel, should she accept our son, that she was doing so with her whole heart and will. They assured me that Bertie *might hope* she would do so, and that they trusted *he* also felt a real inclination, adding that they hoped God would give their dear child strength to do what she ought, and that she might be able to pour some comfort into my poor heart.'

The Princess was delighted to do 'what she ought'; indeed, according to Lord Clarendon, she told one of her new sisters-in-law on her wedding day: 'you perhaps think that I like marrying your Brother for his position but if he was a cowboy I shd: love him just the same & wd: marry no one else.' (Sentiments which must have puzzled the young man's mother.) The second day at Laeken, Queen Victoria gave Alexandra 'a little piece of white heather, which Bertie gave me at Balmoral, and told her I hoped it would bring her luck.' Six days later, the Prince of Wales wrote somewhat truculently to his mother, who had, by then, moved on to Reinhardtsbrunn: 'Now I will take a walk with Princess Alexandra in the garden and in three-quarters of an hour I will take her into the grotto, and there I will propose and I hope it will be to everybody's satisfaction.' The announcement of the engagement stressed that it was 'based on mutual affection and the personal merits of the young princess', and was 'in no way connected with political considerations'.

The marriage celebrations in March 1863 were very grand indeed. The royal yacht, the *Victoria and Albert,* was sent for the bride and her family (the brides of British princes were no longer packed off alone to meet their destiny, though this still happened on the Continent). Three days before the wedding on the morning of 7 March, the Thames estuary was almost solid with small craft, as the yacht, dressed over all, and escorted by battleships, docked at Queenborough near Gravesend. The Lords of the Admiralty were there to greet her—and so was the bridegroom. A great cheer went up as he stepped aboard and kissed his bride on deck, in full view of the waiting crowds. Sixty girls in Danish colours scattered spring flowers in Princess Alexandra's path as she came ashore. A bouquet was handed to her, and the Mayor, Corporation and Town Clerk presented a welcoming address; the Princess replied in English 'as pure as if she had been born and bred in England'. The chairman and directors of the Chatham and Dover Railway were in personal charge of the special train which took the royal party to London; cheering crowds packed every station and flags sprouted even from the haystacks along the line. At the Bricklayer's Arms, Southwark, the party transferred to open carriages for a triumphant drive through London to Windsor. 'Welcome Rose of Denmark', 'Welcome to your new home' read the arches over the streets; London Bridge was flanked by gigantic effigies of every king of Denmark including the reigning sovereign; and, despite the rain, huge crowds—every man, woman and child of them with a wedding favour—thronged the route. 'The first Danish conquest came with fire and sword,' rhapsodised the newspapers, 'but this one comes with the mightier power of love.' Alfred, Lord Tennyson saluted the bride:

Sea-king's daughter as happy as fair,
Blissful bride of a blissful heir,
Bride of the heir of the kings of the Sea.

The wedding took place in St. George's Chapel, Windsor—the first royal marriage to be solemnised there since that of the Black Prince in 1361. Over 900 guests were invited; foreign royalty once more crowded in from all over Europe; all the diplomatic corps, and all the Knights of the Garter (in their robes) were there. The day, 10 March, was a national holiday and the route from Castle to Chapel was crowded with sightseers; bare-foot urchins sold wedding programmes at a penny a time; Eton boys in shiny top-hats and bum-freezers looked on superciliously. At noon the processions began to form up. First of all the clergy: the Archbishop of Canterbury was always the chief star on these occasions, assisted by many a Bishop and Dean. The royal guests who had no actual part to play in the ceremony were next to leave the Castle, with their various suites, in a long line of carriages; then the Queen, wearing her weeds, 'but a silk gown with crape, a long veil to my cap, and, for the first time since December '61, the ribbon, star, and badge of the Order of the Garter, the latter being one my beloved one had worn, also the Victoria and Albert Order, on which I have had dearest Albert's head put above mine, and a brooch containing a miniature of him set round with diamonds, which I have worn ever since '40.' With members of her household she entered the Royal Closet through a side door, and from there could see the whole Chapel: 'full of smartly dressed people, the Knights of the Garter in their robes, the waving banners, the beautiful window, altar, and reredos to my beloved one's memory, with the bells ringing outside, quite had the effect of a scene in a play.' The Queen, who was a spectator only on this emotion-charged occasion, watched her family arrive: the three younger daughters, all in mauve and white; her second daughter, Princess Alice of Hesse 'looking extremely well in a violet dress, covered with her wedding lace, and a violet train, from the shoulders trimmed with the miniver beloved Mama had worn at Vicky's wedding'; and then 'Vicky' herself, the Princess Royal, 'in a white satin dress trimmed with ermine. . . . (leading little William)'. Little William, then aged four, was to grow into Kaiser William II. It is nice to think that for the marriage of his British uncle, he was kitted out in full, if miniature, Highland dress.

Queen Victoria, who would have made an excellent reporter, recorded all this in her Journal on the night of the wedding. For the arrival of the bridegroom, she supplied an appropriately dramatic introduction: 'There was a pause, and then the trumpets sounded again, and our boy, supported by Ernest C [*Coburg, elder brother of the Prince Consort*] and Fritz [*the Crown Prince of Prussia, married to the Princess Royal*], all in Garter robes, entered; Bertie looking pale and nervous. He bowed to me, and during the long wait for his Bride kept constantly looking up at me, with an anxious, clinging look, which touched me much. At length she appeared, the band playing Handel's Processional March, with her eight Bridesmaids, looking very lovely. She was trembling and very pale.'

Lord Clarendon, father of one of the bridesmaids, also described the scene, for the beautiful Duchess of Manchester. As always with these events there were people everyone thought should have been invited who weren't, and people who were invited that everyone thought should not have been. The Disraelis were only asked at the last moment, and Lord Malmesbury, a former Foreign Secretary, was left permanently out in the cold. The Duchess of Manchester, who had been Mistress of the Robes to Queen Victoria, was another who could reasonably have expected an invitation which never came. Her friends, angry and amazed, dashed off high-spirited accounts of the day in compensation, as soon as they got home. (Thus making the Duchess's loss, our gain.) According to Lord Clarendon: 'The P: of Wales waited for The Pss: more than 10 minutes at the altar wh: was rather trying & people began to wonder if the Bride was coy & to hope she had not changed her mind. However she came at last with an enormous long train held up by the 8 b:maids who were a nice looking lot, tho none very pretty except Di Beauclerk. On either side of her were the D: of Cambridge & her Father.' The bride's eyes '& the tip of her nose were a tiny bit red & accounted for by her having cried all the morng: at leaving her mother, for ever, as she must feel'. The Prince of Wales, thought Lord Clarendon, 'in the robes of the Garter looked very like a gentleman & more *considerable* than he is wont to do'.

Lord ('Puss') Granville, another of the Duchess's devoted correspondents, thought the bride's 'dress (in my opinion, but Constance says I am wrong) was too much sunk in the Greenery—covered with too much orange flowers & green leaves'. The Queen wore a wedding favour, he said, and 'The Bridesmaids looked well in their uniform dresses, when their backs were turned. They were hideous when in full view, excepting Lady Di. Beauclerk who looked as if she had just stepped off the stage of the opera.' Lady Palmerston forgot her prayer book: 'Palma Vecchio [*Palmerston*] scrambled over the pews and after extraordinary acrobatic feats brought her three—which she thought at least two more than she required.' (Lord Palmerston was Prime Minister, and 79 years old.)

The *Illustrated London News* gave more detailed descriptions of the clothes:

> The dress of . . . the bride was a petticoat of white satin trimmed with chatelaines of orange-blossoms, myrtle, and bouffants of tulle, with Honiton lace, the train of silver moire antique, trimmed with bouffants of tulle, Honiton lace, and bouquets of orange-blossom and myrtle.
> Her Royal Highness wore a veil of Honiton lace, and a wreath of orange-blossom and myrtle.

The eight bridesmaids wore:

> . . . wreaths of . . . blush roses, shamrocks and white heather, with long veils of tulle falling from the back of the wreath. The dresses of white tulle over white glacé were trimmed to correspond.

While the Prince of Wales, the bridegroom:

> . . . wore his mantle of the Kt. of the Garter, with white ribands on each shoulder, over his uniform of General in the Army, which was so concealed by the ample folds of the blue and ermine that only a glint of the scarlet tunic and the extremity of his gold-striped overalls, boots and spurs were visible. [*The Prince was the last Royal bridegroom to add the splendour of his Garter robes to such an occasion.*]

And the Bride Wore . . .

A salute was fired at the end of the ceremony, the Queen kissed her hand to the bride; the choir sang Beethoven's *Hallelujah Chorus*, from *The Mount of Olives*, and the bridegroom led the Princess to a waiting carriage. The procession up the hill again to the Castle was wildly cheered, hats were tossed in the air and handkerchiefs waved. One journalist was so carried away by the magnificence of it all, he vowed that the shrubberies of Windsor sprouted nothing but orange blossom and myrtle flowers. The Queen, having taken a short cut home, was there to greet the newly-weds, rushing down the 'Grand Staircase (the first time since my misfortune) where all the Beefeaters were drawn up. My *only* thought was that of welcoming *our children*'. The register was signed in the White Drawing-room, and it 'took a very long time', so many royals having, in courtesy, to be asked to witness the event. A 'family luncheon of thirty-eight' followed (the Queen's favourite, the Maharaja Duleep Singh, was always counted as family at such times); but the Queen herself, widowed scarcely more than a year, and constantly aware that all the 'joy, pride, and happiness' which had accompanied the Princess Royal's wedding five years earlier, was being repeated '*without* the principal figure of all, the guardian angel of the family, being there', took her lunch with only five-year-old Princess Beatrice for company. For non-family like Lord Clarendon, 'A magnificent standing luncheon was provided . . . in St. Geo's Hall.' Lord Granville thought there was rather a scramble for it, and the Chancellor 'confided to Lady Shaftesbury that he thought the women (not the chickens) were skinny & boney'.

As the guests dived into the wedding breakfast, the beautiful bride and her considerable rise in fortune were the chief topics of discussion, for, as Clarendon wrote to the Duchess: 'Prince & Pss: Christian have not till quite lately had more than £800 a year pour tout potage & their children tho *very* well educated have been brought up in the simplest manner. What a change for The Alexandra! The P. of W. has expended £3000 in trousseau & £15,000 in jewels—some of the latter are I hear quite beautiful.'

Both royal luncheons finished, Queen Victoria rejoined the family: 'Bertie soon appeared, then darling Alix, looking lovely in a white silk dress, lace shawl, and white bonnet with orange flowers. She was much agitated and affected, and was embraced by all her family, who were in tears; then I once more embraced her and Bertie, with feelings I cannot describe, and gave them my warmest blessing.' The Queen then darted from window to window to watch them leave in an open carriage: 'They stopped for a moment under the window, Bertie standing up, and both looking up lovingly at me. Then we hastened to my room, where I saw them drive off, through the enthusiastic crowds.' They were away, in a shower of slippers, to Osborne for a week. (By 17 March they had returned to London, and on the 20th they held court at St. James's Palace.)

Most of the guests returned to London by special train, amidst (so Lord Malmesbury was told) scenes of considerable confusion: 'The Duchess of Westminster, who had on half a million's worth of diamonds, could only find place in a third-class carriage, and Lady Palmerston was equally unfortunate. Count Lavradio had his diamond star torn off and stolen by the roughs.' At Windsor, the sun had 'shone brilliantly all the time', but Lord Clarendon's servant in London met him with the news that there they had been 'obliged to light candles on acct: of the dense fog. . . . It now rains torrents & the illuminations tonight must be swamped.'

Nevertheless, on every high peak in the country a bonfire burned that night; church bells pealed out throughout the land; banquets were held for rich and poor; and many a city was lit up like fairyland.

The marriage of the Prince of Wales set the pattern for the weddings of four more of Queen Victoria's children. The Princesses Helena and Louise, and the Princes Arthur, Duke of Connaught, and Leopold, Duke of Albany, were all married in St. George's Chapel, with only slightly less pomp and fewer guests.

The Queen took a greater part in these later marriages, giving away her daughters, and walking in the processions of all. The carriages started to leave the Castle for the Chapel shortly after noon, the royal guests and their households first, the Queen next, then the bridegroom, and finally the bride, who started for the Chapel at 12.30. All were surrounded by their own suites and were led to their places by heralds in glittering tabards, the Lord Chamberlain, the Vice-Chamberlain, and the Master of Ceremonies. The chief of the royal guests were seated on either side of the *haut pas*, near the altar, and the principals stood in the area between. The ceremony (conducted always by the Archbishop of Canterbury) complete, a salute was fired outside, the bells were rung, the choir finished singing, the organ played Mendelssohn's *Wedding March*, and all the processions merged into one for the grand exit. The *Illustrated London News* gave this departure plan for the wedding of the Duke of Connaught:

Herald   Herald

Master of Ceremonies

Gentlemen in attendance of H.R.H. the Bride

Members of the German Embassy

H.E. the German Ambassador

Household of H.R.H. the Bridegroom

The Lord Chamberlain   The Vice-Chamberlain

THE BRIDE AND BRIDEGROOM

Supporters of their Royal Highnesses

THE QUEEN

With Princess Beatrice and Prince Albert Victor*

The Royal Family and Royal Guests

After the signing of the register, which always took place at the Castle, not the Chapel, the royal family and royal guests sat down to *déjeûner* in the dining-room. There were no speeches, just two toasts: to the Queen, and to the bride and bridegroom. A mounted military escort accompanied 'the happy pair' to the station and around 4 p.m. at both ends of their train journey bouquets were presented and short speeches of farewell/welcome and congratulation made. Towns and villages through which they drove were festooned with flags and garlanded with flowers. At night there was usually a ball or dinner at Windsor Castle for the royal guests left behind.

Royal honeymoons remained quiet and brief, except for that of the Duke of Connaught: he took his Prussian bride on a two-and-a-half month Mediterranean cruise,

---

* Prince Albert Victor—eldest son of the Prince of Wales, later given the title Duke of Clarence and Avondale. Died, 14 January 1892, aged 28.

taking in Gibraltar, Algiers, Sicily, Malta, Greece, and many another romantic spot, travelling from place to place in a royal yacht called the *Osborne*.

Even when a royal wedding did not take place in Britain, there were celebrations throughout the land: Queen Victoria's second son, Alfred, Duke of Edinburgh, married the Grand Duchess Marie Alexandrovna, only daughter of the Tsar Alexander II ('a just, benevolent, and truly liberal Sovereign') in January 1874, and travelled to St. Petersburg to do so, but the festivities in Britain were almost as great as those for his elder brother, the Prince of Wales, had been. The city of Edinburgh, understandably, put on a special show: the castle and old town being magnificently illuminated and: 'At an early hour in the evening a bonfire, consisting of fifteen tons of railway sleepers soaked in tar, was lit on the summit of Arthur's Seat, and told the district for fifty miles around that Edinburgh was rejoicing.' Bride-cake, as it was called in the newspapers, was distributed in the streets from great wicker baskets.

The Lord Mayor of Liverpool, 'with his characteristic munificence, chose to celebrate this joyful occasion in the good old English fashion, by giving a dinner for the poor.' On the night of the marriage and the one following, he entertained 1300 poor old men and women (2600 people in all) to dinner in St. George's Hall. Roast beef, plum-pudding, beer, tea, fruit and cakes were served, and both evenings were 'filled up with speeches, glees, performances by Mr. Best on the grand organ, and instrumental performances by the local police band.'

At Windsor the bells of St. George's Chapel and the parish church rang all day, flags flew all over the town and the Royal Standard was raised at the Castle. Royal salutes were fired in the Long Walk, at Fort Belvedere and at Virginia Water and, on relieving the Castle guard in the morning, the band of the Grenadier Guards played *Haste to the Wedding* followed by 'the Russian national air'. Every ship of war in all the ports of the country was dressed from stem to stern and, at one o'clock fired a royal salute and hoisted the English and Russian colours together. At night another salute was fired, and blue lights burned.

Piesse and Lubin, 'Royal Perfumiers', produced 'with consummate skill' a new scent called *Duchess of Edinburgh* ('Sold in bottles, 2s. 6d. to 21s. each, in all parts of the globe'); while the composers got busy with musical offerings such as the *Princess Marie Galop* and the *St. Petersburg Quadrille*.

At Osborne, the Queen read over the marriage service, 'thinking much of the young couple' and 'felt it very trying to be absent!' Many of the royal family, including the Prince and Princess of Wales, were in Russia for the ceremony, but the Queen gathered together a few who had been left behind for a celebration dinner. 'At half past seven', she wrote in her Journal, 'the ships, the guardship *Zealous*, and the *Royal Alfred* (sister ship) which had come over on purpose from Portsmouth, and the *Alberta*, all moored in Osborne Bay, lighted up and displayed fireworks.' Her Majesty wore the Star and Ribbon of the Order of St. Catherine, in tribute to the Russian bride, and Princess Beatrice (now 17), wore her Victoria and Albert Order for the first time. After dinner the royal party 'went down to the servants' hall, which was very prettily decorated with wreaths and flags, where a servants' ball took place. We remained through ten dances, Beatrice dancing the first country dance with George [*Duke of Cambridge*]. . . . Did not get back to my room till half past one.'

When Queen Victoria's cousin, Princess Charlotte of Belgium, daughter of King

Marriage by Fascination

Leopold, married the ill-fated Archduke Maximilian in 1857, the Queen wrote to her uncle: 'We do all we can to *fêter* in our very *quiet* way this dear day. We are all out of mourning; the younger children are to have a half-holiday, Alice [14] is to *dine* for the first time in the evening with us; we shall drink the *Archduke and Archduchess's* healths; and I have ordered *wine* for our servants, and grog for our sailors to do the same. . . .' Wine and grog were no doubt also provided for healths to the Duke and Duchess of Edinburgh.

In St. Petersburg the festivities for the Duke of Edinburgh had been even more impressive. All the church bells in the city had been ringing for days and a heavy programme of dinners, balls and operas, both in St. Petersburg and Moscow, went on for a month. There were two wedding ceremonies: the first in the chapel of the Winter Palace, where the Duke of Edinburgh and the Grand Duchess were married according to the rites of the Greek Church, carrying candles and being crowned. When that was done, at about 1.30 p.m., the principals and their guests progressed to the other side of the Palace, where, in the Alexander Hall, an Anglican altar had been prepared and the Dean of Westminster was waiting to take them through the marriage service of the Church of England. The Grand Duchess was dressed in the kind of splendour which Queen Victoria's white satin and lace had made unfashionable in Britain thirty-four years earlier. The 'august bride' at St. Petersburg wore 'a silver embroidered robe and an Imperial mantle of crimson velvet lined with ermine; a diamond crown and diamond collar, and rich lace veil, adorned with orange flowers'. Her train was 'supported by four chamberlains and borne by the Equerry of the Court of her Imperial Highness'.

Royalty were always very nice about wearing little symbols of the land they were visiting, and when the new Duchess of Edinburgh arrived in Britain six weeks later, Queen Victoria was able to record: 'Marie . . . wore a light blue dress with a long train and a white tulle bonnet with white roses and white heather, which I had purposely sent to Antwerp in the yacht.' The entry into London on this occasion was as spectacular and as warmly cheered as that of Princess Alexandra. This time it snowed instead of raining, but the royal party—including the Queen—still turned out in open carriages, and the crowds were there to cheer them.

These great alliances which were to spread a network of cousinship throughout the courts of Europe, are now looked on as one of Queen Victoria's greatest achievements; but the Queen herself became heartily sick of the whole business. When her fourth daughter, Princess Louise, refused to contemplate a Prussian prince (proposed by her sister, the Princess Royal) and became 'most *decided* in her wish to *settle* in her *own* country', her mother was delighted. The Prince of Wales was not so happy, and used an argument which must have won the day many a time before—that his father wouldn't have liked it. On this occasion, however, Her Majesty was not to be swayed. Times had changed, she told her son, in a letter written on 29 November 1869:

> There is nothing about which I am more anxious than that you and I should hold together about so important a subject as this concerning Louise's future. . . .
> Times have much changed; great foreign alliances are looked on as causes of trouble and anxiety, and are of no good. What could be more painful than the position in which our family were placed during the wars with Denmark, and

169

between Prussia and Austria? Every family feeling was rent asunder, and we were powerless. The Prussian marriage, supposing even Louise wished it and liked the Prince (whereas she has not even seen him since she was a child), would be one which would cause nothing but trouble and annoyances and unhappiness, and which *I never* would *consent* to. Nothing is more unpopular here or more uncomfortable for *me* and everyone, than the long residence of our married daughters from abroad in my house, with the quantities of foreigners they bring with them, the foreign view they entertain on all subjects; and in beloved Papa's lifetime this was totally different, and besides Prussia had not swallowed everything up. You may not be aware, as I am, with what *dislike* the marriages of Princesses of the Royal family with small German Princes (German beggars as they most insultingly were called) were looked [on], and how in former days many of our Statesmen like Mr. Fox, Lord Melbourne and Lord Holland abused these marriages, and said how wrong it was that alliances with noblemen of high rank and fortune, which had always existed formerly and which are perfectly legal, were no longer allowed by the Sovereign. Now that the Royal family is so large (you have already five, and *what* will these be when your brothers marry?) in these days, when you ask Parliament to give money to all the Princesses to be *spent abroad*, when they could perfectly marry here and the children succeed just as much as if they were the children of a Prince or Princess, we could not maintain this exclusive principle. As to position I see no difficulty whatever; Louise remains what she is, and her husband keeps his rank (like the Mensdorffs and Victor), only being treated in the family as a relation when we are together.

I wish you would talk to the Dean and Lord Granville about it, you would see how well every side has been weighed, and how strong the reasons are for such an alliance. It will strengthen the *hold* of the Royal family, besides infusing new and healthy blood into it, whereas all the Princes abroad are related to one another; and while I could continue these foreign alliances with several members of the family, I feel sure that *new* blood will strengthen the Throne *morally* as well as physically.

The Queen was right about the sneers at German beggar-princes. In 1816, when Princess Charlotte married Prince Leopold of Saxe-Coburg, even the bride was said to have laughed as he repeated the words 'with all my worldly goods I thee endow' (*The Court of England under George IV*).

Princess Louise's eventual engagement to the Marquis of Lorne, heir to the Duke of Argyll, in October 1870, was exceptionally well received by the country. (Queen Victoria's children followed the revived fashion for betrothals. These were always publicly announced, and the wedding generally followed six months later.) Parliament still made a fuss about the marriage settlement but finally agreed to an annuity of £6000 and a dowry of £30,000. The people were less grudging. Presents poured in from all over the country (royal brides received many of them personally, from a steady stream of gift-bearing deputations) while the *Illustrated London News* embraced 'the innovation upon courtly custom', claiming 'there is no affectation in saying that the nation would have regretted—let us, rather, put it in the nation's own homely phrase, "would have been very sorry if Princess Louise had been going away". . . . Dismissing, as unworthy of serious argument, the political considerations which have been imported into the question, we would say that the Queen's true womanly courage in regard to this marriage is proof that the high spirit of her race is unsubdued. Where a desirable union, one party to which held princely rank, was offered, the Queen naturally and properly mated her child in her own degree; but the Queen of England would not consign her child to celibacy or to undesirable wedlock because a Royal match did not present itself. The Sovereign recognises a higher and holier rule than that of the Courts.'

Royal weddings always inspired the composers of popular dance music—and the publishers of souvenir albums ('handsomely bound in boards' with 'beautiful' portraits of the bride and groom, 'lavishly embossed in gold'), but this bride also inspired 'The Princess Louise Crinoline—does away with the unsightly results of the ordinary hoops'. In it a lady might now 'ascend a steep stair, lean against a table, throw herself in an arm-chair, pass to her stall at the opera, or occupy a fourth seat in a carriage without inconvenience to herself or others'. The price: 8s. 6d. ('with Pannier' 10s. 6d.) from Mrs. Addley Bourne, 37 Piccadilly. In the more regular line of tributes, were a *Grand Bridal March*, 'composed in honour of the Princess Louise', by W. Smallwood. (Beautifully illustrated. Price 3s.); *The Bride of Lorne* Polka-Mazurka, by J. T. Trekell ('a melodious and most graceful specimen of an elegant form of choregraphic music. Price 3s.'); and 'The Bridal Morn—Wedding Fantasia for Piano, by W. F. Taylor. Introducing "Haste to the Wedding", "God Save the Queen," "The Campbells are coming," "The Wedding March," &c., with illustrated title, Inverary Castle. Sold for 2s.'

With the wedding of Princess Beatrice, Queen Victoria's youngest child and the last to marry, the royal bridal pattern broke down. The Queen was now 66, and the bride 28—rather older than her sisters and sisters-in-law had been on their wedding days. Also, at the time of the Princess's engagement, the royal family was still in mourning for Queen Victoria's youngest son, Prince Leopold, Duke of Albany, who had died in March 1884. A quiet wedding on the Isle of Wight was thought to be most suitable in all the circumstances, and no doubt 'Baby', as Princess Beatrice was called, was astonished and thankful to be marrying at all.

It must have been a very pretty occasion: the date was 23 July 1885, and the sun shone as, ideally, it always should shine at the height of an English summer. This was the first royal wedding to be held in a parish church, and the small 'edifice' at Whippingham, close to Osborne House, which had been chosen for the honour, was suitably banked with flowers and had a wide striped awning from church porch to decorated lych gate ('adorned with evergreens, ferns roses and a magnificent garland of lilies') to take overflow guests as well as the bridal procession. Breaking all the rules, Princess Beatrice had ten bridesmaids instead of the usual eight; they were all the daughters of her sisters and brothers and all rather younger than previously ('some of them quite small children', said the *Illustrated London News* in surprise). There were also two pages, another royal innovation. The Queen, assisted by the Prince of Wales, gave her daughter away, wearing jewels among which 'the Koh-i-Noor was conspicuous'. The bridegroom, Prince Henry of Battenberg, eighteen months younger than his bride, looked extraordinarily dashing in white uniform, many orders, thigh-high boots and a handsome moustache. (The Princess of Wales is said to have taken one look at all these trappings of a Prussian guardsman, and dubbed him 'Beatrice's Lohengrin'.) Queen Victoria, always susceptible to male beauty, was delighted to have him around, as long as it truly meant gaining a son and not losing a daughter. After the 'sumptuous wedding breakfast', served in the marquees which dotted the lawns at Osborne, and a two day honeymoon six miles from her mother's side, it was firmly established that the Princess and her husband should live with Her Majesty.

The chief bridesmaid at Princess Beatrice's wedding was the eldest daughter of the Prince of Wales, Princess Louise, and four years later it was her turn to marry. At the age of 22, she became engaged to the 40-year-old Duke of Fife, and once again Queen Victoria was delighted to think of a British princess making her home in Britain.

The wedding was to take place exactly one month later, and the bride asked for it to be held in the chapel of Buckingham Palace. This had not been used since the days of Prince Albert, nor had the State rooms leading to it. A speedy renovation job was put in hand. 'When the decorations are finished, the floor will be carpeted, and on the marriage day the interior will be adorned with palms, foliage, plants, and the choicest flowers from the conservatories of the Royal gardens at Frogmore', announced the *Illustrated London News* a week before the ceremony.

At noon on Saturday, 27 July, the bridal party drove from Marlborough House, London home of the Prince of Wales, through great crowds to Buckingham Palace, where 'as the well known music of Wagner's March from 'Lohengrin' came from the organ the bride entered [*the chapel*] on the arm of the Prince of Wales. . . . His Royal Highness in the uniform of a Field Marshal.' Women's fashions were now extremely becoming—nothing outrageous, but all splendidly curvaceous. The bride's gown was of white lace, with a low V-neck in front and a small stand-up collar behind. It was 'well-built', in the fashion phrase of the time, but simple. Too simple, thought Queen Victoria, who complained to the Princess Royal in Germany: 'Little Louise was vy pale. . . . She was not near so pretty a Bride as my dear Children, & she was too plainly dressed—& had her veil over her face wh. *no Pcess* ever had & wh. I think unbecoming & not right. . . .' The six 'Brides-Maids', however, she thought 'looked vy pretty'. They broke away from the white tradition by wearing what the newspapers described as 'dresses in a lovely shade of blush pink faille with demi-trains draped with crêpe de Chine, over which were arranged broad moiré sashes'. They all carried bouquets of pink roses and had more pink roses in their hair. (Two of them were the bride's sisters, and another was a distant cousin, Princess May of Teck.) The bridegroom wore the uniform of the Banffshire Volunteer Artillery, and his best man, Mr. Horace Farquhar, was in 'a scarlet uniform'. Although the bride was the eldest daughter of the heir to the throne, the ceremony was scaled down to that of a private occasion—gone were the two supporters each for bride and groom, and gone the elaborate processions. The Archbishop of Canterbury, however, was in charge, as usual.

Princess Alexandra, the mother of the bride, who almost invariably wore white at other people's weddings (at that of her sister-in-law, Princess Beatrice, four years earlier, she had been 'looking radiant in a costume of white satin trimmed with moss roses'), chose lavender figured silk for her daughter's marriage. Queen Victoria was, as always, in black. The ruling for lesser guests was: 'Levée dress to be worn by gentlemen. Evening dress (demi-toilette) by ladies.'

When Princess Louise's brother, Prince George, Duke of York, married after another interval of four years, the low key of this last wedding was set aside. After his father (the Prince of Wales), the Duke was next in line to the throne, and therefore warranted all the pomp and circumstance which could be mustered. St. George's

Chapel, Windsor, should once more have been the scene of this splendour, but there were sad reasons which made it unsuitable. The Duke of York's bride was Her Serene Highness Princess Victoria Mary Augusta Louise Olga Pauline Claudine Agnes— more affectionately known as Princess May of Teck (and later to be called, with equal affection, Queen Mary). Only eighteen months earlier, Princess May had been engaged to Prince Albert Victor, elder brother of the Duke of York, and he, one month after the announcement of the engagement and one month before the proposed marriage, had died of influenza and pneumonia, at the age of 28. His funeral had been held in St. George's Chapel; Princess May's orange-blossom wreath, prepared for the wedding, had been placed on his coffin; and May blossom—'*Her* flower *now* being woven for the wedding train!' as her mother wrote to Queen Victoria—had filled the dead prince's room. Overnight, Princess May had become a tragic heroine, and the nation had truly mourned: 'The newspapers full of touching accounts', wrote the Queen in her Journal. 'Special services almost everywhere. London a wonderful sight, every possible house, shop, and theatre voluntarily closed, and everyone in mourning.'

That had been in mid-January 1892. By July 1893, all had marvellously changed, and, as a cartoon in the *Lady's Pictorial* put it: 'Now is the Winter of our discontent made glorious summer by the sun of York.' The second son of the Prince of Wales had become number two in succession to the throne and number one in Princess May's affections. After an eight week engagement, they were married in the Chapel Royal of St. James's Palace, in a blazing summer so glorious it had London gasping. A few weeks earlier, Queen Victoria had written to her eldest daughter: 'The wedding of Georgie is to be in the first week of July, & alas! in the Chapel Royal. Windsor is lovely for a marriage in the summer—but I quite feel it cld not be *after* the sad funeral in St. George's. . . . The Chapel Royal is . . . small & *very* ugly.' It was also where both the Queen and the Princess Royal had been married, which brought back many memories as Her Majesty watched her grandson at the altar: 'I could not but remember that *I* had stood, where May did, fifty-three years ago, and dear Vicky thirty-five years ago, and that the dear ones, who stood where Georgie did, were gone from us! May those dear children's happiness last longer!'

Princess May, who had gone through all the rigours of choosing wedding clothes during her first engagement—'we get trousseau things sent to us on approval from all parts of England, Scotland & Ireland so that we are nearly driven mad & have not a moment's peace'—had to go through it all again during the second. The Royal Wedding Number of the *Lady's Pictorial* described, as only 'a portion of the trous- seau', forty outdoor suits, fifteen ball-gowns, five tea-gowns, and bonnets, shoes and gloves without number.

The royal wedding presents (3,500 'articles of value', estimated to be worth £300,000, ranging from a 'golden bread-basket' and 'an old French ormolu clock' to 'golf sets' and gongs) were put on show to the public at the newly opened Imperial Institute. After the presents came the royal relations, the heads of most of the states of Europe. The wedding was the most public there had ever been in Britain and the build-up of gala opera nights and dinners was gruelling, especially in the incredible heat. The day before the ceremony, the Prince of Wales gave a garden party in the grounds of Marlborough House. Queen Victoria, always the best reporter on such occasions, described in her Journal how she arrived there at 5.30 p.m., rather later than everyone else: 'drove with Beatrice and Irène (the others having gone on before) to Marlborough House, where a gigantic Garden-party took place, 5,000 people having been invited! All the steps crowded, so that I got out at a side door, where Bertie [*the Prince of Wales*] met me, and led me to the tea tent in the garden. Alix, Georgie, the girls, and all the family as also the Paris [*the Comte and Comtesse de Paris and their daughter*]. . . . Hélène (in great beauty), and four Indian Princes. The Salisburys, Mr. and Mrs. Gladstone, etc., were brought up to speak to me, some before and some after tea. The heat was quite awful.' And the Duchess of Edinburgh (formerly the Grand Duchess Marie Alexandrovna of Russia) did nothing to make it seem better. According to the *Lady's Pictorial*, she wore 'a rather hot looking gown in green and garnet coloured silk brocaded with velvet and a green bonnet trimmed with red roses'. (The temperature that day was over 80 degrees and humid.)

At night there was a 'great dinner' at Buckingham Palace, at which the 74-year-old Queen (after a brief rest in her own garden, 'which refreshed one a little') presided, sitting between 'the King of Denmark who led me in, and the Cesarewitch, who is charming. His great likeness to Georgie leads to no end of funny mistakes, the one being taken for the other! The Artillery Band played. The men of the Indian Escort were posted in the four rooms, but one nearly fainted from standing so long motionless.'

All the main characters in the wedding drama were staying at Buckingham Palace, and next morning, while the Queen was being dressed in her own wedding lace, 'over a light black stuff', and her wedding veil, 'surmounted by a small coronet', the bride was led in, in all her finery, to receive Her Majesty's blessing. She 'looked very sweet', wrote Queen Victoria. 'Her dress was very simple, of white satin with a silver design of roses, shamrocks, thistles and orange flowers, interwoven. On her head she had a small wreath of orange flowers, myrtle, and white heather surmounted by the diamond necklace I gave her, which can also be worn as a diadem, and her mother's wedding veil.' (The previous silk of woven May blossom had been discarded as too sad a reminder of the past. The *Bradford Wedding Journal*, doing a round-up of royal weddings in 1911, said it had been cut up on the bride's instructions and distributed to friends.)

Princess May's wedding gown can still be seen at the London Museum and it is certainly not what we would call 'simple' today. The brocade itself is very rich, incorporating heather and true-love knots in the design, as well as the symbols listed by Queen Victoria. The low-cut bodice is engineered rather than sewn, sleeveless apart from a small frill of lace over one of chiffon, and lavishly trimmed with orange flowers and leaves. The brocade overskirt is open down the front, showing plain white satin beneath, garlanded with three flounces of lace and decorated with more orange blossom and heather; behind, it forms a short train, trimmed with a wide ruche of white satin. The Honiton lace veil was very small and must have looked old-fashioned even when the Duchess of Teck wore it in 1866. Lady Geraldine Somerset, lady-in-waiting to Princess May's grandmother, and never a loyal supporter of the Tecks, thought it a wretched little thing. 'May . . . was not veiled *at all*!!' she wrote in her diary, 'her veil hung in a little tiny narrow strip but a couple of inches wide *quite* at the *back* of her head only like an elongated lappet!' (Lappets were the decorative frilled streamers—'unmeaning pendants', according to Horace Walpole—which dangled from ladies' caps and bonnets throughout the 18th and 19th centuries.) A modern touch, however, was the bride's huge 'shower bouquet', a shape which had only recently ousted the posy.

Outside Buckingham Palace, the whole of London was splendid with garlands and banners, 'Venetian masts' and triumphant arches. Spectators were now actively considered on such occasions, and for their benefit, the long route to the Chapel Royal—along Constitution Hill and Piccadilly—had been chosen for the procession. Garlands of greenery and flowers hung overhead all the way, and St. James's Street was, thought Lady Geraldine Somerset, 'like a bower from end to end. . . . garlands of green across and between the Venetian masts with bracelets of flowers suspended from them, *too* pretty'. All the houses in the street were so thickly hung with silk and velvet flags and banners that scarcely a brick could be seen, and at the Pall Mall end there were two Corinthian columns of imitation marble, crowned with 'floral trophies and tall tufts of waving Pampas grass'.

Twelve open scarlet and gold carriages, each drawn by four cream horses, formed the first procession of royal guests which set off from Buckingham Palace at 11.30. The bridegroom followed, supported by his father, the Prince of Wales, and his uncle, Prince Alfred, Duke of Edinburgh, all three in naval uniform with white satin bridal bows on their shoulders. Queen Victoria left next, in what she described as 'the new State glass coach with four creams, amidst a flourish of trumpets'. In the new coach with her was the bride's mother, the Duchess of Teck. (The Duchess had been born Princess Mary Adelaide of Cambridge, and her father, the Duke of Cambridge, was one of the three sons of George III sent so unceremoniously to the altar when Princess Charlotte died.) She was fat and jolly, a first cousin to Queen Victoria, and immensely popular. The glass coach took the short route down the Mall to the Chapel, the same journey the Queen had taken fifty-three years earlier, when she was herself a bride, and when royal weddings were still thought of as private rather than public occasions.

Princess May was last to leave the Palace. Supported by her father, the Duke of Teck, and her brother, Prince Adolphus, she rode in the last carriage of all. Her ten bridesmaids, all of them the bridegroom's sisters or cousins ('of whom there are a great number', as the Queen rightly said), joined her at the chapel, wearing white satin with 'a little pink & red rose on the shoulder & some small bows of the same on the shoes'. Princess Alexandra, mother of the Duke of York, was back in white again: 'a very lovely white dress trimmed with chiffon and embroidered with silver and magnificent diamond ornaments. The Princess of Wales has seemed to look lovelier and lovelier on each occasion that her highness has appeared in public', thought the *Lady's Pictorial*. This journal also reported that the Queen of Denmark, mother of the Princess of Wales and grandmother of the bridegroom, was in white, 'and so was the Duchess of Fife whose dress, as usual, was simple but of an exquisite build'. The Marchioness of Ormonde, 'who was one of those bidden to the wedding, was dressed in white satin, with clever and delicate touches of pink. Lady Ormonde wore magnificent jewels.' And, 'The Marchioness of Londonderry was dressed . . . in pure white satin, and wore a high coronet of diamonds.' Many of the gentlemen, according to the *Illustrated London News*, wore 'Court dress or uniforms and the chains or badges of Knighthood; the ladies were in evening dress, without trains, and made a great display of jewels.'

Queen Victoria, taking the short route home again, was first to arrive back at the

Palace, where she nipped quickly out onto the balcony, alone, to much cheering from the crowds below. Then: 'Very soon the Bride and Bridegroom arrived, and I stepped out on the balcony with them, taking her by the hand, which produced another great outburst of cheering.' A royal bridal tradition was born.

After the signing of the register in the 'Bow room saloon', protocol was set aside as the Duke and Duchess of York led the royal guests to luncheon in the large dining-room, where they were seated at seven small tables. 'It was very prettily arranged', wrote Queen Victoria. 'I gave two toasts, the Bride and Bridegroom and the King and Queen of Denmark, the King giving out my health.'

Luncheon ended shortly after 4 p.m.; photographs were posed for; and then the Duke and Duchess changed into their going-away clothes. 'Dear May came in looking very pretty in her dress of white poplin edged with gold, and a pretty little toque with roses.' (A 'toque', the hat for which Queen Mary became famous, was already on the scene.) The Duke of York wore a black frock coat and top hat. Lady Geraldine Somerset described the departure: 'May kissed us all and went off—we saw her and the Duke of York get into the carriage receive the shower of slippers and drive *au pas* round the Quadrangle amid cheers and as they passed under the portico we rushed into the bedroom and from the balcony saw the Prince [*of Wales*], the Duke of Edinbro: and Duke [*of Cambridge*]! and all the Princes standing round the *grandes grilles* of the outer railing and as the Duke and Duchess of York drove into the Mall shower them with rice! Then they drove along the Mall with the magnificent Blues amid ringing cheers.'

Cheers followed them all the way as they drove through 'the principal streets of London' to Liverpool Street Station, where (announced a writer in *The Star*) 'great things' had been done. 'The grimy girders on the roof have been hung with flags and, startling as it may appear, the glass roof outside the main booking office has been scrubbed. Nothing but a stern sense of duty would have induced the Company to take so serious a step.'

A special train took 'the happy pair' to Sandringham, where the Prince of Wales had 'lent, and had arranged for them the Cottage'. As the bride's first *fiancé*, the Duke of Clarence, had died at Sandringham, Queen Victoria was not alone in thinking it an odd choice for the honeymoon. She regretted it, she told the Princess Royal, thinking it 'rather *unlucky* & sad'. But there was certainly nothing mournful about the welcome which greeted the young couple when their train pulled into Wolferton Station, near Sandringham, at eight o'clock that night. Velvet-pile carpets covered all the floors, flowering plants, ferns and palms were everywhere, and in the station yard, more Venetian masts bore 'lines of pennons'. The Chief Constable of Norfolk, a 'strong force' of whose men lined the route, was on the platform to welcome them, and an escort of the Royal Suffolk Hussars waited outside. As they left the station yard, their carriage passed under one triumphal arch of greenery and crimson cloth, bearing the royal insignia, and 'on the brow of the hill leading from the railway premises another arch of graceful proportions bore upon its face, in bronze and gold letters on a crimson ground, the word 'Welcome'. The flanks were entwined with ribbons bearing the mottoes 'God bless our Princess May,' 'God bless the happy pair,' 'Long live the Duke of York,' 'Health to the Royal pair,' and 'God bless our Sailor Prince.' It was surmounted by a Prince of Wales's coronet, behind which rose a flagstaff bearing the national standard, and at each end of the structure were displayed ducal coronets and flagstaffs flying the naval and blue ensign and the ensign of St. George.' Masts with 'medallions emblazoned with the initials G. and M., trophies of flags, and true-lovers' knots' also decorated their route and over a thousand 'Sandringham tenantry, work-people, and cottagers', who had been given a three o'clock wedding feast in a marquee on the estate, were there, with thousands of other spectators, to cheer them. 'York Cottage was reached at about half-past eight o'clock', said the *Illustrated London News* (who gave all the other information, too): 'An interesting surprise awaited the royal pair after reaching home. Suddenly, to their evident astonishment, the islands and the rocks in the ornamental waters were illuminated with fairy lamps, the rustic bridge and boat-house being outlined with the same, while the girths of about fifty trees were illuminated by fairy lamps and Japanese lanterns. On the highest part of the park there was a display of fireworks.'

Queen Victoria appears to have had no objection to the union of cousins—even first cousins—but did not believe in marrying more than one child into the same family. At the wedding of the Prince of Wales, several people had been taken with the good looks and nice manners of the bride's brother, Prince William of Denmark (who later became King George I of the Hellenes) and thought, like Lord Clarendon, that such 'a gentil looking lad . . . wd: do very well for one of our little Princesses but The Q: won't hear of it. She says one of a family is enough.'

On proxy weddings, Her Majesty's views were less definite. They had gone out of fashion in Britain at the end of the previous century, and the Queen wrote of them as though they were part of some strange but interesting foreign cult. In May 1858, with the marriage of the Princess Royal still fresh in her mind, she was moved almost to tears by the beautiful Princess Stephanie of Hohenzollern-Sigmaringen, who had been married by proxy at Berlin to King Pedro V of Portugal. On her way to her new country, Queen Stephanie stayed at Buckingham Palace, and Queen Victoria wrote to her own daughter of the proxy ceremony: 'How touching it must all have been. How I should have liked to have seen it—and yet how strange to be married without one's husband!' A week later, the day before Stephanie was to sail for Portugal, the Queen continued: 'Poor dear child, what an undertaking—do think to go alone to a husband she don't know—without a mother—or mother-in-law she knows!! Think of all this and all you know and feel must be gone through and no mother at hand! You may imagine what I feel for the dear sweet child!'

Such romantic sentiments bore no sway in the management of royal matrimonials in most Continental countries, and certainly not in those of France. Lord Malmesbury told of three typical alliances manipulated by the French, with not a drop of romance in one of them. Of the much talked of 'Spanish marriages' of 1846, he wrote:

News from Spain has been very interesting of late. The marriage of the Queen with the Duke of Cadis is settled, in spite of her abhorrence of him; and that of her sister with the Duc de Montpensier is announced to take place at the same time. This is a masterpiece of Louis Philippe's cunning, because it is known that the Queen would not have children, even if her own bad health made it possible. Her sister will then be heir to the throne. The English Government, especially Lord Palmerston, are much displeased, and Mr. Bulwer and M. de Bresson, their respective Ministers at Madrid, are on the coolest terms since the announcement has been made, it having taken Lord Palmerston completely by surprise.

And the Bride Wore . . .

In March 1860, Malmesbury quoted a philosophically brave Princess, trapped in another political match:

> The annexation of Savoy, together with the neutral States of Chablais and Faucingny, which is now a *fait accompli*, has shaken the confidence of the people in the Government. There is a *bon mot* of the Princess Clothilde on this subject which is worth recording. Alluding to the transfer of Savoy to France and her own unwelcome marriage, she said: '*Quand on a vendu l'enfant, on peut bien vendre le berceau.*'

At non-royal level, marriages arranged by friends were still accepted practice on both sides of the Channel. Miss Betham Edwards (in *Home Life in France*) tells of a summer picnic near Besançon, where a companion asked her: 'Do you see that young lady in pink, beside her wet nurse and baby? . . . Her marriage to Professor T——— was arranged by friends of mine. After the first introduction he declared that no, nothing on earth would induce him to marry a girl with such a nose; she has a very long nose, certainly. But on further knowledge he found her agreeable and accomplished, and now they are as happy as possible.'

Barbara Charlton (*Recollections of a Northumbrian Lady*) wrote of a match she arranged between two of her friends who had never met each other. After a series of letters from both sides to Mrs. Charlton, a meeting was organised: 'Major Darell came to Hesleyside by special invitation on the 17th and Isabella Eyre, by a curious coincidence, put in an appearance on the 18th. The stage was set; the proposal was duly made and, as duly, accepted. . . . Archbishop Manning married the happy pair. At the wedding reception an accident threw a transitory depression on the newly married couple. One of the young Eyres, perhaps too full of champagne, removed his sister's chair when she rose to cut the cake, in consequence of which she sat down heavily on the ground. It was a typical piece of Catholic horse-play.'

Catholic, Protestant, or anything else, this was the century for innocent superstitions; none of them taken too seriously and many of them still with us, just for fun:

A bride must not be completely dressed until the last moment of setting out for church—when a final stitch should be added to her dress for good luck;

A bride should not look in a mirror before she is dressed, nor after her toilet is completed;

> To change the name, and not the letter,
> Is to change for the worse, and not for the better.

Each day of the week was now given an omen:

> Monday for wealth,
> Tuesday for health,
> Wednesday the best day of all;
> Thursday for crosses,
> Friday for losses,
> Saturday no luck at all.

The superstition that bride and groom should not meet on their wedding day until they do so at the altar also began in Victorian times, though when Princess May of

Marriage by Fascination

Teck and the Duke of York caught sight of each other from opposite ends of one of the long, long corridors of Buckingham Palace on their marriage morning, they took it as a happy sign. They were a constrained couple, always writing to explain how much they loved each other and apologising that they could not actually *say* so; both were warmed by the brief encounter. The Duke, according to Queen Mary's official biographer (James Pope-Hennessy) 'swept her a low and courtly bow. This gesture she never forgot.'

Colours, always deeply significant, were now lined up like this:

> Married in white, you have chosen right,
> Married in green, ashamed to be seen,
> Married in grey, you will go far away,
> Married in red, you will wish yourself dead,
> Married in blue, love ever true,
> Married in yellow, you're ashamed of your fellow,
> Married in black, you will wish yourself back,
> Married in pink, of you he'll aye think.

Blue retained its ancient connections with constancy, which no doubt accounts for its inclusion in the most famous—and most regarded—rhyme of all:

> Something old, something new,
> Something borrowed, and something blue;
> And a silver sixpence in your shoe

but this "traditional" good-luck jingle was not to become really popular until the 20th century.

Chapter Eight

Some things old, some things new
The Twentieth Century

June means weddings in everyone's lexicon,
Weddings in Swedish, weddings in Mexican.
Breezes play Mendelssohn, treeses play Youmans,
Birds wed birds, and humans wed humans.
All year long the gentlemen woo,
But the ladies dream of a June 'I do.'
Ladies grow loony, and gentlemen loonier;
This year's June is next year's Junior.
Ogden Nash: *Here Usually Comes The Bride*

ND so to the present century—and a wedding world apparently run mad. During the last ten or fifteen years, there have been brides in hot pants, brides in Arab caftans, brides in tatty ancient finery culled from the nearest jumble sale; unmarried 'brides' presenting their new-born children to the world and proclaiming they feel just as much married as anyone who ever walked to the altar.

But these are the exceptions which hit the headlines. The dull black print of the majority of wedding notices, and the pages of wedding photographs in local and provincial papers, put the balance straight: for most people, things haven't changed. Not two world wars, nor Women's Lib, nor all the social turmoil of the last half-century have made more than a tiny crack in the upper crust of the great white wedding tradition.

Brides themselves may long for a quiet and private affair—as Dorothy Osborne did in the 17th century, and young Laura Troubridge in the 19th—but when it comes to the crunch they are mostly overwhelmed by family pressure and find themselves involved in a celebration much the same as any random sample taken from the last hundred years.

Winefride Jackson, writing in the *Sunday Telegraph* in April 1972, told of a recent 'grand white wedding' which she had attended, a wedding which 'almost never happened' because the bride and bridegroom wanted a quiet registry office ceremony while the bride's parents were determined to have 'a traditional happening in their local cathedral'. The parents won 'due to us all, including the groom's parents (who wouldn't have to pay for the reception) nagging the bride and groom not to be selfish, that the occasion was as much the bride's mother's day of pride as the bride's day of joy'. It's a well-known battle. What won the day in this particular case—conscience or 'an excess of gin taken during stress'—was never clear, but whatever the cause the result was the same: the bride in long white dress and long white veil; a great gathering of friends and relations, a slap-up party, and champagne flowing like lemonade.

In the same article, Miss Jackson told of another kind of good old-fashioned wedding still going strong—a Scottish celebration, on the Isle of Lewis, which remained in full decibel swing at midnight. 'The reception was at the hotel where I stayed. I swear that not even waiting at an international airport with jets screaming back and forth created so much noise. Sleep was impossible. At midnight I went downstairs and there leaning against the lower banister was a disconsolate bride, still in her long white dress and veil, waiting patiently for a groom reluctant to break up the party.'

The laws covering church marriages in England still require that banns should be called on three successive Sundays (and a licence—present cost £5—purchased), and that the ceremony should take place within the district in which one of the parties lives, or at the church at which they usually worship, between the hours of 8 a.m. and 6 p.m. on any day of the year, with open doors and in the presence of two witnesses. Both bride and groom have, at some point of the ceremony, to vow that they take each other as man or wife, and solemnly declare they know of no lawful impediment to the match. (The reason for the open doors is to ensure that anyone who does know of a lawful impediment can get into the church to say so.)

Special licences, granted only by the Archbishop of Canterbury, are still available, though they are hard to come by. (They are no longer particularly expensive, however; while other marriage costs have slowly risen, this one has remained the same: £25.) These, as formerly, permit the marriage to take place anywhere, at any time, but the 'special circumstances' which demand such accommodation have to meet with his Grace's approval.

In Scotland weddings can be held anywhere at any time by law—no licence, special or otherwise, being necessary. And, although three readings of the banns are legally specified, 'by immemorial practice proclamation on one Sunday' only is accepted. The posting of a notice of the intended marriage for seven days in a prominent place at a registrar's office, is also allowed in lieu of banns (though a clergyman can refuse to perform a marriage which has not been declared in church). One of the parties still has to have lived (or to have had a parent living) in the district for fifteen days before the ceremony, but, even with this limitation, getting married in Scotland is just quicker and simpler enough to tempt runaway lovers over the border. For a brief time during the 1950s, eloping became almost as fashionable as in the 18th century, and one young man of slender means and large ambition kept himself in style for several years by heading north with a series of romantic heiresses, getting caught before the knot was tied, and allowing himself to be 'persuaded' by angry—and rich—fathers to relinquish all claim to the young ladies. In September 1972, the *Daily Mail* told the story of a couple of English school-children who married in Dumfries while their parents thought they were on holiday in Wales. The 16-year-old bride decided not to go back to school afterwards to take her A-levels. She thought she would get a job and keep her 17-year-old husband at technical college. Children are maturing earlier, say the experts.

And the Bride Wore . . .

Easter and June are still thought of as the high peaks of the year for 'traditional' weddings, though in the middle years of the century the main wedding rush came at the end of March: it was discovered that no matter how late a man married in the tax year, he could claim a full year's tax benefit for having a wife. The popularity of this mean-spirited manoeuvre killed it. The men at the Inland Revenue changed the rules.

The Anglican wedding service, little changed since the reign of Elizabeth I, is happily followed by most Protestant brides, though it can be adapted to suit individual tastes. Some girls, even in the rosy glow of their wedding day, now find the word 'obey' too subservient, and ask to have it left out, feeling terribly modern and liberated as they do so. They may well be liberated, but they are not particularly modern: the word was having a tough time even at the beginning of the century. Constance Gore-Booth, the stunning Irish beauty (who was to be jailed by the English for her part in the 1916 Irish troubles) did not promise to obey the Polish Count Casimir Dunin-Markievicz when she married him in September 1900, though, in every other way, the wedding at St. Mary's Church, Marylebone, London, was splendidly conventional. According to her biographer, Anne Marreco: 'A large trousseau was bought. She chose a wedding dress of white satin with a bodice of lace and chiffon and a full court train of silver brocade. Her jewels for the great day were gifts from her mother: a pearl necklace, a diamond pendant, and a diamond crescent. . . . She was supported by four bridesmaids—her two sisters dressed in violet satin, and her friends, Miss Rachel Mansfield and Miss Mildred Grenfell, in green trimmed with lace in compliment to Ireland. The bridegroom wore a nobleman's court uniform consisting of a black tunic trimmed with gold braid, and white trousers.'

An occasion on which the word 'obey' might understandably have been omitted was the wedding of Princess Elizabeth, heiress-presumptive to the British throne, when she married Lieutenant Philip Mountbatten R.N. in November 1947. But she did in fact promise to 'love, cherish and obey' her husband; and so did her sister, Princess Margaret, thirteen years later, though many of the newspapers then noted that 'it is a word often omitted from their promises by modern brides'. The Duchess of Gloucester brought particular praise from male journalists covering her wedding in 1935. Being married in an Episcopalian ceremony, which does not usually demand obedience of the bride, she could have escaped without censure, but particularly asked for the word to be included.

In March 1972, a less exalted bride dispensed with a different piece of the wedding service—the ceremony of being given away. According to the *Daily Mail* (in a story headlined 'Now It's Equal Rites for the Bride'—9 March 1972), the idea came from her father, Mr. Tom Cullingworth, of Sale, Cheshire, who thought the practice 'inappropriate today', when women are 'no longer the chattels of their father or husband'. The 22-year-old bride, Marilyn, said: 'This is not a great Woman's Lib thing. The ceremony will be perfectly normal and my father will make a speech as father of the bride at the reception. The idea not to give me away was his, but I am in entire agreement. It seems superfluous in this day and age.'

The minister of Nuthall Methodist Church, the Reverend D. Matthew Wilkes, who was to perform the ceremony, thought the idea 'logical'. The new Methodist marriage service, introduced in 1971, made the question 'Who gives this woman to be married to this man?' optional, so he would simply be leaving it out.

Even in New Zealand, which for so long seemed to be two islands of sanity in an

Plate Eleven

otherwise dotty world, the marriage pattern is occasionally exploded by free-thinking youth. In June 1972, the Deputy Prime Minister, Mr. Robert Muldoon, was photographed with a brave smile and his daughter and new son-in-law—the bridal pair both wearing long hair, matching embroidered kaftans and what looked very like Dr. Scholl's best remedial sandals. The New Zealand *Listener* (8 November 1971) told of even more way-out occasions, like the wedding of two Wellington students who returned from a visit to India with 'very definite ideas about the ceremony they wanted'. In the living-room of their 'small cottage flat', with ten to fourteen guests seated on cushions around them, bride and groom read 'appropriate extracts' from two books—one by Sri Nadhava Ashish and a piece from Katha Upanishad. Then a friend played a little Bach on his guitar, while the bridegroom went 'to a sort of altar set up against the wall where he symbolically offered up the elements air, earth, fire and water to Khrishna'. At the end of the half-hour ceremony, in which the Victoria University chaplain also performed, all the guests joined in a haphazard jam-session on any instrument which came to hand. More guests were invited to a curry feast afterwards.

The symbolic offerings to Khrishna, 'A reminder to the couple of "something bigger than themselves"', are also a reminder of the symbolic offerings of fire and water at Roman weddings.

Another event echoed the bride-ales and penny weddings of the 16th and 17th centuries: 'Bernice and Mel King had a traditional church wedding and were thoroughly satisfied with it. Together they planned the whole celebration, made their own cake, chose the hymns to be sung . . . tied the ribbons to deck the pews. . . . Most of their 120 guests were church people. Women of the church banded together to provide the wedding breakfast, which was a lunch in the church hall.'

In May 1971, shortly before the wedding of U.S. President's daughter, Patricia Nixon, the London *Daily Mail*'s New York correspondent reported:

> When Tricia weds Ed and becomes Mrs. Cox in the White House rose garden next month, it will be as proper a nuptial as was ever laid on. But outside the influence of Presidential protocol and formality, the conventional wedding is taking a bashing.
>
> This spring, marriage American-style is being held down in the meadows, up on the mountains, bare-footed on beaches, at midnight or in the rosy light of dawn.
>
> Even that temple of tradition, New York's St. Patrick's Cathedral, conceding to changing tastes, had dispensed with Lohengrin and substituted guitar music, and now offers a choice of twenty-one variations in the wording and style of the marriage vows and service.
>
> The Rev. Joseph Bishop, of a New York Presbyterian church, says one in four of the marriages he performs these days have been altered, if not completely rewritten, to personal specifications of the bride and groom.
>
> With an unsentimental recognition that one in every four American marriages ends in divorce, 'Till Death us do Part' often becomes 'For all the years that are to be.'

The *Mail*-man didn't mention the wedding palaces springing up around the land, with special stage effects on hire, geared to make the whole show look more like a night at the opera than the sacred rite of matrimony, but he might have done:

And the Bride Wore . . .

America has always been one delirious leap ahead with the unconventional. In December 1944, when many an English bridegroom still felt conspicuous in a registry office, Elliott Roosevelt, second son of President Franklin D. Roosevelt, married his third wife (film star Faye Emerson) in a glass-enclosed observation platform on the edge of the Grand Canyon, with nothing but snow and swirling mists below them. The maid-of-honour was the bridegroom's ten-year-old daughter by a previous marriage. The bride thought it was 'probably the most beautiful wedding there ever was'. Since then couples have been married in swimming pools in the States and on horseback in England. Dogs have appeared as bridal attendants—and in America, at any rate, the dogs have been dyed to match the bride's ensemble. James Lascelles, an heir to the British throne (albeit only 20th in line of succession) married in April 1973, wearing a Tibetan wool jerkin over cream leather jeans, with two necklaces of beads and flowing shoulder-length hair; and had the Global Village Trucking Company Progressive Rock Group to accompany the informal reception afterwards.

But these are the oddities, the way-out events which catch the publicity just because they are so different. For every one of them a dozen women's page writers say, with astonishment, 'still the traditional white wedding persists'. In June 1972, *Sunday Express* columnist Veronica Papworth said the same thing, though not with satisfaction. The money could be better spent, she thought. Instead of 'the tents and togs, cars and catering, flowers and frill-me-downs—not to mention buckets-full of booze' she suggested her own style of wedding reception: held in a Buckinghamshire field in hot sunshine, with the two witnesses and a bottle of champagne. She didn't expect to change anything though and included pictures and details of the latest range of long, white, organdie wedding dresses priced from £25 to £31·50, as her contribution to cutting down the cost of the customary grand affair.

Throughout the century the tradition has been under attack: in the Twenties, Bright Young Things thought it 'old hat'; in the Thirties, the politically conscious refused to contaminate their ideals with such bourgeois display; during the Fifties and Sixties, Modern Youth wanted to 'do their own thing'. But the white wedding refused to die and during the Forties, in wartime, when it could not have been more difficult to arrange, it became the most desired aim of all—a comforting and defiant return to normality.

In the early 1930s, *The Bride's Book, or Young Housewife's Compendium*, 'Compiled and Written by two ladies of England', described what a bride should wear, and, with few exceptions, the advice holds good for most weddings at any time during the century:

> If you have a large number of conventionally minded friends whom you desire to please rather than flout, you will not depart much further from the traditional white or ivory bridal gown than present custom readily permits—silver, pale gold, or the very lightest of blue, pink, or lilac shades.
>
> The orange blossoms, the lace or tulle veil, the long train sweeping from the shoulders—all these, extravagant though they be, and ephemeral in their usefulness,—must be chosen so as to fulfil the demands of tradition. In the dress itself fashion will be followed, but at a distance. Nowadays, young ladies frequently turn their bridal robes into evening dresses when the honeymoon is ended; but unless your wardrobe is a very meagre one, we recommend the old

sentimental custom of preserving this gown, the only one of its kind you will ever possess, in its pristine glory as a treasure for your descendants.

With regard to the honeymoon, the 'two ladies of England' said resolutely that they were not going to 'look upon the black side' of this 'institution which may truthfully be said to be a success much oftener than it is a failure. We will content ourselves by stating the simple fact that some honeymoons *are* failures.'

Trousseaux, on the other hand, they were prepared to study from all angles. The quantity of 'lace-trimmed garments, of diaphanous linens, of exquisite tea-gowns, of wraps and bonnets and shoes and gloves and smart dresses' required to make a young wife feel respectably equipped 'a generation or two ago' would, they believed, 'startle the modern journalist and judges who comment on women's extravagance in dress as if it were a new thing. The rule was simply this—A Dozen of Everything. . . . Such reckless expenditure is unknown today except in the ever-diminishing class which is ostentatious as well as rich.'

Under the heading *Lingerie*, they instructed:

> Unless you are very rich or very busy it will be a serious extravagance for you to buy in a shop any lingerie that you can possibly produce with your own hands. The price of good made-up underwear is out of all proportion to the cost of the material. And the sewing of small silk garments is by no means arduous: they can be packed so easily into a case containing your scissors, needles, and other requisites, and taken about with you on informal visits, or picked up at any time in your own home to work on while you are talking. Fifteen pounds' worth of silk, lace and embroidery thread will provide you with as many night-dresses, bed-jackets, chemises, and knickers as would cost you about fifty pounds bought ready-made in materials of the same quality.

Any bride-to-be who carted partially-sewn knickers to informal gatherings today, might perhaps raise an eyebrow or two, but what the two lady authoresses had to say about pyjamas still seems valid: 'If men have one aversion that is fully and invariably justifiable, it is for the sight of a woman clad in pyjamas. (We are referring here to bedroom, not beach pyjamas.) Some women are misguided enough to wear pyjamas even on a honeymoon; it would be a bitterness to us to think that you were one of these.'

The standard etiquette book rule that 'the bride's father pays for the *trousseau*', now produces a hollow laugh from many a working girl; but no one doubts that it really is his job to provide the party, even if he goes bald and bankrupt in the process. In 1973, a secretary marrying an electrician estimated that her father would be £500 the poorer after the festivity: 100 guests had been invited and food and champagne would come to about £3 a head; there was £23·50 for the photographer; £20 for the church (£4 fee for the service, then the organist and choir); £30 for the hall for the reception; £15 for the mobile discotheque which would provide the music; £5·61 for the printed invitations; and a whole lot more on things like 'serviettes and matches'. Her 'plain' dress was to cost about £35 and she was paying for her bridesmaid's, too—another £15. The bridegroom would be taking charge of the florist's bill: £8 for a bouquet for his bride and £3 for one for her bridesmaid; and the car hire: £8·50 each for two Austin Princess limousines for an hour. (And his friends kept telling him that at 26 he was 'too young to die'.)

There would also be the ring to buy and a gift for the bridesmaid from the bridegroom (lockets and bracelets are still popular) and for the bride (pearl necklaces have recently begun to wane). At the wedding reception there would be a speech to make—at a cost only to his nerves—but he might get out of that since speeches at weddings are going out of fashion and a simple toast to bride and bridegroom coming in. Even when there are no set speeches, the best man is still usually called on to read out the telegrams from friends who could not be there (and wits who are there but can never resist an opportunity to be publicly funny). Until recently, someone could generally be relied upon to send the hoary telegraphed hope that the only troubles to inflict the happy pair would be 'little ones', but that really must be too well known now to produce even a groan. At the 1906 wedding of U.S. Congressman Nicholas Longworth and Alice Lee Roosevelt (dashing daughter of President Theodore Roosevelt) an old friend cabled the bride: 'I always knew Old Nick would get you', which is as good a piece of wedding humour as any.

The cake is still the centrepiece of the feast, and small pieces are mailed in little white boxes (with silver lettering and silver wedding bells and horseshoes on the top) to friends and relatives who could not attend. I've heard of people wishing on wedding cake, but not dreaming on it any more. Three tiers or more remain in vogue for grand weddings, the top tier (in theory if not in practice) to be kept for the first christening —except in the case of President's daughter, Luci Baines Johnson: her cake in 1966 had six tiers of 'summer fruit cake', decoratively iced, with sugar-icing arches and sugar-icing lilies-of-the-valley between each tier, and on the top, decorated with real lilies-of-the-valley, a small 'bride's cake' (chocolate flavour beneath the white frosting) which she took off with her on honeymoon to the Bahamas. While rich fruit mixtures topped with a layer of marzipan are traditional for all celebrations in Britain, the less solid sponge is more popular in America, and when the next President's daughter (Patricia Nixon) married, in 1971, the White House chef provided a more typically American lemon sponge mixture beneath all the icing. A scaled-down version of the exotic recipe (ten egg whites for a 12-inch cake) was released to the nation, so that in every home throughout the land, the very same brand of ambrosia could be savoured by every last American man, woman and child, on the great day. It was a happy thought, but something went wrong with the culinary calculations: eruptions of lemon lava gummed up cookers from coast to coast. There were tales of it hitting ceilings and flowing over floors; it was like soup on the outside, glue on the inside. A red-faced White House chef thought again, and produced amendments.

At the beginning of the century, a lucky wedding ring was still sometimes baked into the cake. 'Bride Cuts the Cake; Sister Gets Ring; All Dance the Tango' announced a *Washington Post* headline when President Woodrow Wilson's second daughter, Jessie, deserted the 'Gilded Portals of the White House to Rule Humble Home as Mrs. Francis Bowes Sayre'.

In Britain, at the 1934 wedding of Princess Marina of Greece and Prince George, Duke of Kent (son of King George V and Queen Mary): 'Concealed in the large wedge cut from the lower tier at the wedding breakfast were seven charms of solid gold, representing respectively a wedding ring, thimble, bachelor's button, horseshoe, dove, donkey, and threepenny bit.' Even compared with other royal wedding cakes, this one was spectacular. Made by Mr. Borella, of McVitie and Price—and said to be the thirty-third he had produced for royalty—it was 9 ft. tall, weighed 800 lbs., was decorated in 'semi-Greek' style and contained 'ingredients from Empire sources, with the addition of Greek currants sent to the bride by maidens of Greece'.

At less illustrious matches, the cake often bears handsome witness to the deeds of bride or groom. When cricketer Colin Cowdrey married in 1956, cricket bats, stumps and balls, 'all made of pure sugar' surrounded his three-tier cake, and the horseshoe on the top was worked with 'the same cricket motif'. (The chief pastry cook at the Lewisham store owned by the bride's father made the cake, which weighed 60 lbs., and contained 60 eggs, 4 lbs. of butter, 12 lbs. of marzipan, and 15 lbs. of dried fruit from that cricket-crazy country Australia.) In the same year, bandleader Ray Ellington's wedding cake was decorated with a miniature set of bongo drums and a packet of cornflakes made of sugar-icing—bride and bridegroom had met at Barnes television studios when he was recording a session with his quartette and she was doing a breakfast cereal advertisement; and in 1961, a certain author, who had shortly before declared to the press that he was married to his typewriter and intended to stay that way, found a white sugar typewriter on the top of his wedding cake when he decided to marry a woman after all.

Miniature figures of white-gowned bride, and morning-suited groom, top many a cake on both sides of the Atlantic, but, to use the jargon of the 20th century, they are (like silver-printed invitation cards) non-U. Top cakes continue to be topped by small vases of fresh flowers.

The record for the greatest number of cakes ever prepared for any one wedding goes to the present Queen: twelve 'official cakes' were presented to her. When she married, in 1947, Britain was still weary and underfed after the Second World War; austerity was the word the country had to live with; and what food there was, was rationed. But the royal wedding was seen as a bright turning point, a hopeful pointer to better times ahead, and the people made it *their* wedding with heartening enthusiasm. Twelve baking firms prepared twelve gleaming tributes to the young Princess and 'the sailor bridegroom'. Huntley and Palmer's four-tier offering, with 'gracious permission of Her Royal Highness', was first put on show at a London store, to aid the Royal Naval Benevolent Fund. Peek, Frean's six-tier 'masterpiece of the confectioner's art' was staunchly British and naval: made from 'ingredients from all Commonwealth countries'; it was crowned with a magnificent sugar-icing St. George on his rearing charger, and had panels showing the Princess's arms, Glamis Castle, St. George's Chapel, Windsor, H.M.S. *Vanguard*, and the Royal Naval College, Dartmouth, with many an anchor and coiled rope in between. But, once again, it was McVitie and Price's offering which was chosen by the bride to be cut at the wedding reception, and, once again, the *Illustrated London News* had all the details:

> The cake, 9 ft. high and weighing 500 lb., was made with four tiers, supported by silver pillars, and decorated with the armorial bearings of Princess Elizabeth and Lieutenant Philip Mountbatten, R.N.; plaques modelled in sugar depicting Buckingham Palace, Windsor Castle and Balmoral; figures illustrating the sporting activities and interests of the bride and bridegroom; the crests of the

And the Bride Wore . . .

Royal Navy and Grenadier Guards; the badges of the A.T.S., the Girl Guides and the Sea Rangers; and shields bearing monograms of the bridal couple.

Filigree sugar arches and canopies, with 'musical Cupids' beneath them, decorated the whole. On top was a solid silver vase of fresh roses, and more fresh roses were arranged around the base. Before the cake was presented to the Palace, a section was cut from the bottom tier, looped around with satin ribbon, replaced, the cracks iced over, and the ribbon tied in a bow outside to mark the spot. On the wedding day, using the ribbon as a guide, bride and groom had an easy task: two light strokes through the icing only, with the bridegroom's sword, and the whole wedge could be pulled clear by the bow.

Much was made of the fact that like 'any ordinary bride of a Naval officer, the Princess cut her cake with her husband's sword'. The sword itself was, however, rather more exalted than most, having originally belonged to the bridegroom's grand-father, Prince Louis of Battenberg, the first Marquis of Milford Haven and a former Admiral of the Fleet.

Both the bride's dress and this noble cake arrived at Buckingham Palace the day before the wedding. The gown had only a short journey—from Norman Hartnell's salon—which it made in a 4-foot long box, inside a green Board of Trade van; but the cake was given more spectacular treatment, travelling from Harlesden, North London, in a 'pantechnicon', escorted by a 'courtesy cop' on a motor-cycle, and fol-lowed by another van in case of accidents to the first.

The bride's home is still considered to be the most suitable place for a wedding recep-tion, with hired caterers, extra staff, and a marquee on the lawn if necessary. Hotels are also popular in the middle ranks of society, and superior London clubs, which not so long ago barred their doors to the most modest female invasion, are now happy (financially, if in no other way) to open their reception rooms to wedding parties on Saturday afternoons and provide elegant food in extremely elegant surroundings. At the other end of the middle class range come tennis clubs, which also hire out their facilities for the weddings of their members (and offer an appropriate setting for jokes about love matches).

Whatever the time of day, and whatever the kind of food provided, champagne is still the expected accompaniment. Searcy's, the great London caterers (whose name on the fluted pastry cases is a guarantee both of contented guests and a generous host), say its popularity never wavers: 'But most people have a bottle or so of whisky tucked away for those older men who can't take a fizzy drink.'

At the wedding of Franklin D. Roosevelt's youngest son in June 1938 a different kind of problem guest had to be catered for: 500 bottles of champagne (United Kingdom *cuvée*) and 12 gallons of temperance punch were provided for the 616 guests at the smart Nahant (Mass.) Tennis Club reception.

At the beginning of the century, according to one bride, quoted in *Brides* magazine, claret was the festive drink at working-class weddings. Describing her own 1912 marriage, she recalled: 'The reception was at home. We folded back the doors, and the trestles were groaning with roast meats and puddings. There were mountains of jellies and trifles. We drank claret then, never champagne.' On the way home from church, the wedding party was held up in the crowd, the bride in her long white dress and veil, carrying a great trailing bouquet; the bridegroom in best suit, starched white collar and carrying white gloves: 'all the people on top of one of the new open buses cheered'. Her 'going away suit was specially tailored in navy blue serge' and with it she wore a 'plum colour Breton hat with crossed wings of feathers at the back. This was a tribute to the new Royal Flying Corps. We left in a motor car and I was very anxious in case friends tied cans and boots to the back. I thought we were lucky but some of them distracted us by waving Kruger's ticklers in our faces so we didn't see them tying things on. Kruger's ticklers were big curled ostrich feathers, nick-named during the Boer War, and popular then.'

Although marriages up till 6 p.m. have been legal since 1934, evening weddings have only recently come into favour, and even now, their popularity is limited mainly to London and other large cities. (The previous restriction to daylight hours only was a measure against skulduggery, and the extension was due more to the wide-spread use of electric light than to social pressure.) A late wedding allows guests to join in straight from work (and takes the load off Saturdays); but it can also mean that they arrive looking businesslike rather than festive, and keep checking the time of the last train home.

In the 1950s, when most of my friends were getting married, between 2.30 and 3.30 on a Saturday afternoon was the most popular time. After the half-hour service in a church decorated (but, as a rule, not particularly lavishly) with white flowers, an odd mixture of sandwiches, cocktail savouries, cakes and champagne was served at the bride's home or a nearby hotel. There were always lots of aunts with moist eyes saying they had always known the dear girl would 'make a lovely bride', and lots of strange faces 'from the other side'; the bride was regularly kissed in best wedding tradition, and the bridegroom, who had often had a bet with a friend as to who would 'get caught' first, ruefully paid up. Bride and bridegroom left after an hour-and-a-half or two hours, and the party swiftly lost impetus. The parents of either the bride or groom had often organised a quiet dinner party for their own contemporaries for later in the evening, but arrangements for the young were more chancy. It was always the hope, and aim, to drift on from the wedding reception to dinner and dancing at some other establishment, the men still dressed (against all the rules of etiquette) in their black morning coats and pin-striped trousers, with carnations in their buttonholes. If this failed, there was nothing more desolate than to be young, full of champagne and on your way home at 6 p.m.

Occasionally, there were morning weddings followed by a luncheon served at small round tables in a marquee on the lawn, everyone sitting on spindly gold chairs (supplied by the caterers) which looked particularly elegant in the out-door setting. Full-blown wedding breakfasts, with long, white-draped tables arranged like a city banquet, went out of favour with the Second World War.

Most fun of all were long-distance events. These involved staying at least one night in the bridal house, or an annexe provided by nearby relatives or friends. Then, there was usually a party the night before the wedding (often given by a married sister of the bride) and the occasion took on the atmosphere of the three- and four-day festivities of old—and the saying that one wedding leads to another was given plenty of romantic opportunity to come true.*

* 'One Wedding, the Proverb says, begets another'—John Gay, *Wife of Bath*, 1713.

And the Bride Wore . . .

There haven't been too many instances of whole villages and towns putting out the flags and triumphal arches for weddings this century, but it does still happen. Romsey in Hants. was very much *en fête* in January 1960 when Earl Mountbatten of Burma's daughter, Lady Pamela Mountbatten, married Mr. David Hicks. The main streets were lined with banners and bunting, and if it had not been for a persistent snow-storm, there would have been a bridal procession on foot from Romsey Abbey where the ceremony took place. There were two receptions afterwards: one for the 'Royal party and the principal guests' at Broadlands, the bride's home, and another at a hall in the town for 'tenants and staff'. The bride and some of the royal guests divided their time between the two, and an 11-year-old Prince Charles charmed the tenants and staff by taking over from his bridesmaid sister, Princess Anne, and straightening the bride's train as she entered the hall. (Lady Pamela had 'had the unusual and delightful idea of wearing white mink on her wedding dress'.) Nearly forty years earlier Lady Pamela's parents had had a spectacular marriage themselves, with the then Prince of Wales (later King Edward VIII) as best man and sailors instead of horses to pull the bridal carriage from church to reception.

For humbler weddings, the church hall has been the most popular setting for the feast throughout the century, usually with caterers providing the food. Higher up, Assembly Rooms sometimes make a grand setting for a grand affair—like the marriage of the Earl of Dalkieth in January 1953. This was the first major social event of Coronation Year, and the new Queen, Elizabeth II, was present—the first time, it was said, that a British sovereign had attended a wedding in Scotland since 'the Union of the two crowns'. The ceremony took place in St. Giles' Cathedral, Edinburgh, with music composed especially for the occasion by the cathedral organist and choir-master, and Isobel Baillie to sing Mozart's *Laudate Dominum*. Afterwards, the guests left, between pipers of the City Police pipe band (wearing kilts and bearskins), for 'a reception in the Assembly Rooms, George Street, where, in addition to the Royal guests, some 1600 people were entertained'.

The very first year of this century saw one of the most spectacular non-royal weddings there can ever have been. The bride was Clara Butt (later to be made Dame Clara Butt), a 27-year-old from Bristol with a contralto singing voice of alarming depth. She received the kind of dizzy acclaim reserved for pop-stars today—and even they don't warrant a half-holiday for all the factories, shops and offices in their home towns when they marry.

The bridegroom was another singer: 30-year-old baritone, Robert Kennerley Rumford, a favourite of Queen Victoria. He wooed Miss Butt with songs, and pen-cilled little notes in the margins of her music—sometimes such embarrassing little notes that, having opened the score in a public place, such as Paddington Station, she snapped it fast shut again (even though Mr. Rumford's language of love was German). He proposed to her while they were singing a duet called *The Keys of Heaven*, and they left the concert platform engaged to be married.

In the words of her biographer, Winifred Ponder: 'Clara Butt was paid the supreme honour of the offer of St. Paul's Cathedral for her wedding—an honour almost unprecedented for a commoner; but she refused it, in order to be married in Bristol, among her own people and friends of her girlhood. The Dean of Bristol then came forward with the offer of Bristol Cathedral (in which only one wedding had previously taken place within a century) for the ceremony. An offer she accepted and the day was fixed for Tuesday June 26th 1900.'

There were special trains to and from London; the Cathedral was 'crammed with Duchesses, prima donnas, and what not', church bells pealed throughout the city, and the crowd which had started to gather before 7 a.m. for the 1.30 ceremony, grew so dense the police had to clear a way for the trams to get through. Hundreds of presents rolled in, including one from Queen Victoria. (Bristol's gift was a brooch with the initials CB—standing conveniently both for Clara Butt and the City of Bristol—shot through with a ruby arrow.) Sir Arthur Sullivan composed an anthem (*O God thou art worthy to be praised*) and Madame Albani sang it. Dame Nellie Melba, Clara Novello Davies (mother of Ivor Novello), Forbes Robertson, and many another famous singer, sat in the choir stalls and added even greater lustre to the Cathedral choir.

There were six bridesmaids, three of them sisters of the bride, and two pages. The wedding dress, of heavy crêpe de Chine trimmed with a deep silk fringe, was made by Madame Wyatt of Clifford Street, who had made the bride's most popular concert gown—her famous 'grape dress'. (When booked for a return concert, Clara Butt was often asked to wear the gown she had worn the time before, and in Australia, both she and her 'grape dress' were engaged over and over again.) Twenty-five years later, the white fringed crêpe de Chine was remodelled for the now Dame Clara's silver wedding concert. As her biographer said: 'It is an interesting example of how mere redrapery can bring a long-out-dated gown back into fashion. In this case the skirt portion was simply taken out of the waist and draped from the shoulder.' In charge of the redraping was 'Lucille' (otherwise known as Lady Duff Gordon).

In America the tradition that a bride should wear her wedding dress again for the 25th anniversary lives on. One anguished look at what a quarter of a century has done to the waistline usually vetoes the idea, but an American friend tells me she has seen it done—'though mostly by gals without daughters!' Alice Lee Roosevelt Longworth (daughter of President Theodore Roosevelt) was one bride who had no trouble following the tradition, though she chose to wear a favourite *trousseau* gown (yellow satin with brilliants at the waist and down the front) rather than the wedding dress itself for her silver wedding in 1931, and she had her hair upswept in the same Edwardian style she had worn for the marriage ceremony in February 1906—a ceremony which was said to have been the most lavish in the history of the White House, and the most publicised.

Alice Lee Roosevelt had been a racey young lady—she smoked cigarettes; it was said that she even drank cocktails; and she had definitely been seen wearing riding breeches out at Rock Creek Park. All that, and beauty too, made her a journalist's dream. The press converged on Washington from all over the world to cover her wedding, and the following day the *Washington Post* devoted its entire front page to the event. She was one of the handful of presidential daughters who have been awarded the mostly affectionate title of 'Princess', and, as is fitting in royal circles, she received some noble gifts: King Edward VII of Great Britain sent a gold and blue enamelled snuff box with his miniature on it; the Kaiser sent a bracelet with his miniature on it; King Victor Emmanuel of Italy sent an enormous mosaic table, without his miniature on it; and the Dowager Empress of China gave a generous mixed bag of eight rolls of gold brocade worked with the Chinese sign of longevity, white jade, a pair of earrings, two finger rings, and two fur coats—one of white fox, the other ermine. The French government presented a Gobelin tapestry, and the Republic of Cuba (where the honeymoon was to be spent) sent a $20,000-pearl necklace—sixty-two matched pearls with a diamond clasp—as much in gratitude to the President for his help in Cuba's war with Spain as in tribute to his daughter.

Six-hundred-and-eighty guests (including Nellie Grant Sartoris—the White House bride of 1874) were present for the ceremony; seventy-two policemen were on duty outside, and the Marine band, brilliant in scarlet and gold, played wedding music in the hall. There were no bridesmaids and no small page boys at this wedding: just Alice and firm masculine support. A few minutes before noon, a military *aide* led the Episcopal Bishop of Washington, between lines of satin ribbon, to the altar set, against the east windows of the East Room, in a bower of palms, smilax and Easter lilies. They were followed by the bridegroom, the 36-year-old Congressman from Ohio, Nicholas Longworth, and his best man. On the stroke of twelve, with the band playing the march from Wagner's *Tannhauser*, eight ushers escorted the bride and her father up the green-carpeted aisle to join them.

The wedding dress had been made in New York—like the rest of the *trousseau*— and was magnificent: cream satin, with an 18-foot long train of silver brocade. The neckline and wide, ruffled, elbow-length sleeves were trimmed with lace from the wedding gown of the bride's mother (who had died twenty-two years earlier—two days after the bride was born). A wreath of orange blossom and a tulle veil (kept very much to the back of the head) completed the outfit. As she stepped up to the altar, Alice Roosevelt handed her large and trailing orchid bouquet to her father, and left the straightening of her train to her cousin, Franklin Delano Roosevelt (who, having married only the year before, understood such things).

In regal style, 'Princess' Alice entertained her own intimate friends to a wedding breakfast in the family dining-room, while less honoured guests were feasted in the State Dining-room. Never one to quit a party that had some life left in it, this bride left *after* her guests. At 4.30 p.m., the Congressman and his lady, dressed in beige, drove to a mansion on the outskirts of Washington (the grounds of which are now the McLean Gardens on Wisconsin Avenue), which had been lent to them for the first few days of the honeymoon. Later, they sailed for Cuba.

Alice Roosevelt's gown of cream and silver could well have started a fashion trend, for five years later, on the other side of the Atlantic, the *Bradford Wedding Journal* (August 1911) high-lighted the popularity of these two colours in a round-up of news from the recent wedding season:

Out of Date
   Bridal white seems to be almost extinct, so rarely does one now see the old style of dead white wedding gown and the usual bouquet of pure white flowers.

Easily Held
   Miss Margaret Glyn carried a prayer book instead of the usual bouquet but of course she is the daughter of a bishop.

Silver the Rage
   During the London season just closed, silver, in the form of brocade, wreaths etc. has been much employed in bridal costumes which have largely been designed in the mediaeval style, generally in white brocade. Black, which superstition

would not at one time allow to be seen at a wedding, has been frequently used in hats. Indeed it is quite evident that the bride of today does not possess that fear of superstition which her grandmother had.

Silver, having made a come-back for bridal trimming, remained popular for another fifty years. Many royal wedding dresses, like that of the Queen Mother, have been embroidered with silver, while Princess Marina wore a sheath of brocade more silver than white; and, in 1922, Princess Mary (only daughter of King George V) and all her bridesmaids shimmered with a silvery light:

> The scheme of Princess Mary's wedding cortège was white and silver. Not only was the bride's dress woven of silver and sewn with pearls and diamonds, but her eight bridesmaids wore gowns of glistening silver. Their headdresses were wreaths of silver leaves with diamante centres, over veils of white tulle. (*Illustrated London News.*)

Silver lamé was another favourite of the Twenties, and white lace embroidered with silver thread was popular in the 1950s.

The urge to bring black into the wedding picture was determined but short-lived. In 1901 when the daughter of the Secretary for War, Mr. St. John Broderick, married Lord Tweedmouth's son, the Hon. Dudley Marjoribanks, at St. George's, Hanover Square, *The Tatler* reported that the bridesmaids wore white with black picture hats and carried bouquets of violets; and a week or so later the writer of 'My Lady's Mirror', in the same magazine, described a fashionable bridesmaid's ensemble as made by 'Mesdames Hancock & James, Grafton Street':

> The bridesmaid's gown was of white mousseline de soie over pale green glacé silk, trimmed with transparent ecru insertion, the tucked bolero, which opened over the soft full front of the mousseline being edged with insertion and lace. Sleeves distinguished by wide volants over little tucked manchettes and a green silk belt supplied the all important finishing touch. As might have been expected, just now, a huge granny muff with a bunch of real lilies-of-the-valley and a wide frill on one side of pale green silk with ruches of silk and black lace, replaced the conventional bouquet and the hat was a charming confection of silk and lace with a triple brim adorned with lace ruches and a black ostrich feather falling over the hair.

Another 'fashion writer' (quoted in C. W. Cunnington's *English Women's Clothing in the Present Century*) said that the spring season of 1901 had 'been productive of several innovations in wedding ceremonies. It has redeemed black, once and for all, from its reproach in its function as a wedding garment, Lady——, that recent bride, setting a seal on this by gowning her bridesmaids in picturesque black frocks.'

Three years later, at the society wedding of the 1904 winter season, at least one of the one thousand guests wore black. This was the marriage of Lady Marjorie Greville, daughter of the exquisite Daisy, Countess of Warwick (friend of King Edward VII—and others), which took place at Warwick Castle in January 1904. On January 30, the 'Ladies' Page' of the *Illustrated London News* described what everyone wore, except, curiously, the bride. The beautiful Countess, heavily pregnant in suspicious circumstances, was in velvet—'a long wide coat of creamy tint' trimmed with 'an abundance of lovely lace and worn with a sable stole and a hat of pale-brown gathered chiffon trimmed with shaded ostrich feathers, it was an enhancement of her dress of striped satin gauze, with yoke of point d'Alençon embroidered with silver'. The bridegroom's mother, the Countess of Feversham, 'choose a rather bright shade of green relieved by a lace vest, and a green hat with pink velvet and violets for trimming'. Theresa, Countess of Shrewsbury, 'had a handsome grey velvet gown with a cape of the same; and Lady Maitland was in black velvet.' The bridesmaids (there were fourteen of them) had 'rich red velvet "early Victorian" scarves, and rosettes of the same material on their wide hats of white beaver' as a 'happy addition to the soft pure white of their satin and chiffon dresses'. The few guests who did not wear velvet 'patronised soft, supple face-cloths'.

The daughter of another friend of King Edward VII, Sonia Keppel (whose mother Mrs. George Keppel brought joy and stability to the later years of the amorous monarch's life) was also given a grand society wedding. In 1918, at the age of 18, Sonia had fallen in love with Roland Cubitt, fourth son of Lord Ashcombe. (The three older Cubitt boys all died in action during the First World War and so Roland, against all the odds and his own expectations, was by then his father's heir.) There was some strong Ashcombe opposition to the match; then, as Sonia Keppel was to tell in her autobiography:

> Sometime during the spring of 1920 Rolie's parents decided that we had crossed the borderline from adolescence into maturity and, after nearly two years of waiting and hoping, we became officially engaged, with our wedding planned to take place in the autumn.
> We had been 'unofficially' engaged for so long that the formal announcement only seemed a question of sticking on fresh labels. But now we were allowed to dine alone together and to motor down alone to stay with friends, which seemed to me as emancipated as it was delightful.
> Rolie gave me a half-hoop ring of a ruby and two diamonds, and a little diamond Coldstream star to pin into my hat. I gave him some 'engagement' cuff-links; we gave each other photographs; and the future seemed but a vista of exchanging presents to confirm our love.

The *trousseau*, ordered by 'Mamma', was formidable:

> . . . three dozen night-gowns, petticoats, bodices, chemises, knickers, stockings, handkerchiefs, gloves. A dozen pairs of evening and day shoes; six pairs of stays. I had a pink satin peignoir, trimmed with ostrich feathers, for summer; and a quilted blue velvet dressing-gown, with a real Valenciennes lace collar, for winter. (At last Nannie was satisfied.) As, now, I was to be married in November, I had two evening dresses suited to winter: a black velvet square-necked ball dress, and a pink velvet ball dress trimmed with silver lace. (My wedding gown, of silver lamé, was to act as my presentation gown the following summer.) I had two tea-gowns, one trimmed with Chinese embroidery, and the other of billowing chiffon; three day dresses and three afternoon dresses; and three tweed suits and a travelling coat, with matching hats and jerseys and shirts. My going-away dress was of pale blue marocaine, with a skirt cut into petals, topped by a black velvet coat with a grey fox collar, and a grey cap trimmed with ospreys.
> The presents began to arrive and, foremost among them, an heirloom from

Mamma in the shape of Nannie, bequeathed to me as a lady's maid. (I felt dreadfully disloyal, but a trifle dubious, as Rolie's and my combined ages fell short of Nannie's by nearly thirty years.) Next in importance from Mamma came a diamond tiara; and an emerald and diamond pendant; and an enchanting eighteenth century diamond brooch in the shape of a sheaf of wheat. And Papa gave me a piano and a Georgian writing-table; and Violet and Denys gave me two crystal and diamond hat-pins; and Rolie's parents gave me a turquoise and diamond pendant; and Rolie himself gave me a bigger ring and a bigger Coldstream badge. Uncle Arnold and Aunt Gertie gave me a Georgian sideboard; and Uncle Archie and Aunt Ida gave me some nineteenth century gilt candlesticks. Mamma's friends coughed up nobly: Maggie [*Mrs. Ronald Greville— Sonia's godmother*], with an emerald ring; the Grand Duke Michael [*her godfather*] and Countess Torby with a Fabergé snuff-box; Stavey and Lady Ilchester, with a huge aquamarine and diamond brooch; Sir Ernest Cassel, with a fat cheque. (When this arrived, to my disappointment, Mamma said that cheques were vulgar, so it had to be transformed into a long stole and muff of Canadian sables, which I did not particularly want.) Marshalled by Marjorie Jessel eighty of my girl friends gave me a breakfast, dinner and tea service of Spode china; nearly all my boy friends gave me individual presents; and my dentist appositely gave me a tiger's tooth, attached to a bell. Rolfe [*the family butler*] and all the house servants gave me a silver salver, and almost best of all I loved Nannie's two toast-racks with each strut spelling a letter of 'Rolie' and 'Sonia', in silver plate. And Rolie too had an impressive array, from his family; from his friends; from his father's tenants. Every purse within reach seemed to have been opened for us, to line our future home in the nicest way.

A year earlier, when Sonia's elder sister married, the music had been one of the greatest features of the wedding, with Dame Nellie Melba singing Gounod's *Ave Maria* as the register was signed, and 'an organist of great talent' playing Purcell's *Trumpet Voluntary* for the entrance of the bride and Wagner's *Bridal Chorus* for her exit. Music has also been a particularly impressive—and imaginative—feature of royal weddings this century, and, in most cases, it is the bride who has been given the credit. When the present Queen married in 1947, much was made in the press of the many personal consultations she had had over the pieces to be played and sung, and how many of them were her own personal choice. The inclusion of the 'Scottish metrical version of the 23rd Psalm', 'delighted Scotland', and produced much speculation: by some it was seen as 'a tribute to the impression made upon her at services in that country when she heard the version sung to the Scots tune of "Crimond"'; others decided she had made the choice 'because she learned the Psalm as a baby from her Scottish mother'.

Before the arrival of the bride, Dr. Osborne H. Peasgood, sub-organist of Westminster Abbey, played a sonata by Elgar, Widor's *Cantabile*, Bach's exquisite *Jesu, Joy of Man's Desiring*, and selections from Handel's *Water Music*. The Princess walked up the aisle, on the arm of her father, King George VI, to Parry's *Bridal March and Finale*, and was the last British princess to walk down the aisle again to the sound of Mendelssohn.

Rebecca West, reporting the occasion from the organ loft of the Abbey, was particularly moved by the fanfares, which had been composed for the ceremony by Sir Arnold Bax, Master of the King's Musick. After writing much about post-war austerity, evident even within the Abbey, she said: 'at last the fanfare of trumpets was heard which greeted the bride as she arrived. . . . It was like a shower of shooting stars in a winter sky expressed in sound . . . and it added to the wedding a luxury greater than all the money the most fortunate country could have bought for a child of the head of its State.'

Thirteen years later, 'magnificent fanfares' were also composed for Princess Margaret—this time by Sir Arthur Bliss, who had succeeded Bax as Master of the Queen's Musick—and, as at her sister's wedding, they were played by the trumpeters of the Royal Military School of Music. Princess Margaret made the not-too-usual choice of walking to the altar while the choir sang a hymn—*Christ is made the sure foundation*. During the service the 23rd Psalm was sung once more, but this time, by special desire of the bride, to Schubert's setting. While the register was being signed in the small chapel of St. Edward the Confessor, two more anthems—by William Byrd and Gustav Holst—were sung. Another of the splendid trumpet fanfares sounded as bride and bridegroom returned to the Sacrarium, and as that died away, Purcell's gay *Trumpet Tune and Airs* took over for the procession down the aisle.

In 1923, when the mother of these two royal brides married, *The Times* said of the music: 'The dominant note will be one of cheerfulness, and that which is obscure or complicated on the one hand, or weakly sentimental on the other, will be avoided.' The result was a pleasant mixture of the old and fairly new: pieces by Purcell, the minuet from Handel's overture to *Berenice*, Saint-Saëns' *Benediction nuptiale* were all played before the ceremony, and, as her younger daughter was to do, the bride chose to enter to the sound of the choir rather than the organ. As Lady Elizabeth Bowes-Lyon, the present Queen Mother walked up the aisle to the hymn *Lead us, Heavenly Father, lead us*; as the Duchess of York, she made the return journey to Mendelssohn's *Wedding March*, and 'proceeded to the West door of the Abbey' to *Marcia Eroica*, which had 'just appeared from the pen of Sir C. V. Stanford'.

The Times made no claim that it had just appeared from the pen of the 70-year-old composer for this purpose, and, most probably, it had not. Curiously little music has been commissioned for royal weddings, and apart from the fanfares only one other piece appears to have been written specifically for a royal bride this century: an anthem, *Beloved, let us love one another*, which was first sung at the marriage of Princess Mary (only daughter of King George V) in 1922, and was again featured the following year, at the wedding of her brother, the Duke of York.

A royal bride thought to be particularly well qualified to supervise her own wedding music, was Miss Katherine Worsley, who married the Duke of Kent in June 1961. The Queen Mother, the Queen and Princess Margaret had all been described as 'accomplished pianists' at the time of their marriages. Miss Worsley was said to be 'an accomplished musician'. The wedding took place in York Minster and the music was a match for the magnificent surroundings. The bride walked to the altar to Parry's *Laudate Dominum*, and in one of those nice gestures at which royalty—even royalty by marriage—are so good, the first anthem sung was *I sat down under His shadow*, by Sir Edward Bairstow, a former organist of the Minster. Gustav Holst's setting of Psalm 148 and his *Alleluia* were also sung, and the *Toccata* from Widor's Fifth Symphony was played for the final procession of the bride and bridegroom. (The same *Toccata*, followed by William Walton's *Crown Imperial*, was also played at the marriage of the Duke of Kent's sister, Princess Alexandra, two years

Some things old, some things new

later.) A splendid musical flourish to the Duke of Kent's wedding was described by the *Illustrated London News*:

> When the newly-married pair came out together from the Minster, the rain which had fallen during the ceremony had ceased and the sun shone on the Duke and Duchess as they emerged through the arches of swords of the guard of honour from the Duke's own regiment, The Royal Scots Greys, and two pipers played the Scots folk tune, 'I hae a wife of my own'.

In America, Luci Baines Johnson was another bride who took particular interest in the music for her wedding—and again, the result was both impressive and original. This magnificent 'private family affair' took place in the spanking-new National Shrine of the Immaculate Conception, Washington: the largest Catholic Church in the United States (capacity 3,500 plus). It was the first wedding to be celebrated there, and Luci Baines Johnson was the first presidential daughter to be married anywhere but in a private house—the White House or otherwise. One more first, was the fact that she was the only daughter of a President ever to be married at a Catholic ceremony (having left the Episcopalian Church and been baptised into the Catholic faith when she was 18). For an hour before the noon wedding, the fifty-six-bell carillon, in the slender tower above the Shrine, heralded the event: Purcell's *Trumpet Tune and Airs*, Haydn's lovely *St. Anthony Chorale*, Massenet's *The Angelus*, pieces by Handel, Bach, Tallis and the first performance of Franco's *Pronunciamento for Carillon*, were played from a giant keyboard within the building. Shortly after twelve o'clock, with the 700 guests assembled, the organist, Robert F. Twynham, played his own *Paraphrase on a Trumpet Tune by Henry Purcell*, and the bridal procession began.

First of all the eleven 'groomsmen' (wearing morning suits, cravats and white roses in the buttonholes of their 'cutaway' coats) walked up the aisle, followed by the bridegroom, Patrick Nugent (in morning suit, cravat and a small sprig of lily-of-the-valley) with his father (standing in as proxy best man for the bridegroom's brother, away on active duty in Vietnam). Next came a line of nine bridesmaids, one matron-of-honour, and one maid-of-honour, Lynda Bird Johnson, sister of the bride—all walking in single-file and all wearing different shades of pink with long fine tulle veils tinted to match. (Nieman Marcus's emporium in Dallas, Texas, supplied the dresses, and Mr. Marcus himself suggested the choice.) Then came the 'ring bearer', 5-year-old Lyndon Hand (dressed in a smart white suit with long white socks), keeping up nobly with the others. Following him, at a more individual pace, was a single flower girl, of equally small size, in a long white dress and carrying a basket of flowers designed for decoration rather than strewing. Finally, on the arm of President Johnson, the bride appeared, wearing a slender gown of white Alençon lace, decorated with seed pearls, a three-yard train of matching lace flowing from her shoulders, and a starched, short and bouncy, tulle veil framing her dark hair. (The high neck of her dress was described as 'wedding band style', while the slightly lower, padded necklines of the bridesmaids' gowns were said to be 'wedding ring style'.)

With honest Texan belief in sheer size, two choirs were chosen to sing at this wedding in place of the usual soloist: 150 men and boys from Baltimore made memorable music within the great Shrine as they sang Bach's *Jesu, Joy of Man's Desiring*,

197

Cesar Franck's setting of the 150th Psalm, and, by special request of the bride, one Episcopalian hymn: Ralph Vaughan Williams' *King's Weston*.

Representative Hale Boggs of Louisiana, a Johnson family friend as well as a member of Congress, read from Chapter Five of the *Epistle of Paul the Apostle to the Ephesians*: 'Wives should be submissive to their husbands as though to the Lord; because the husband is head of the wife just as Christ is head of the Church . . .' and a budding army of Women's Liberationists (this was only 1966) tore at their bras in outrage.

The Pope, who had met both bride and bridegroom when he visited New York the previous autumn, sent his blessing, and his personal message, praying for 'abundant heavenly favour in their married life', was read out by Archbishop O'Boyle at the end of the nuptial Mass.

Bride and groom then led the procession back down the aisle, and rode in a 'bubble-top limousine' to the White House for the reception. As usual on these occasions, the Executive Mansion was a blaze of flowers (a team had stayed up all night arranging them both at the White House and the Shrine). A pink-lined canopy—its poles and ropes entwined with pink and white carnations—had been placed over the Jacqueline Kennedy Garden to protect guests from the hot August sun, and it was here that they gathered before filing along a corridor lined with white petunias and pink geraniums to the Blue Room and the reception line—which included Mrs. Alice Lee Roosevelt Longworth, the White House bride of 1906, still sparkling and elegant at 82.

There were buffets in the East Room and the State Dining-room, and Peter Duchin's orchestra to dance to. Later in the afternoon, Luci stood on the South Balcony in her shocking pink going-away outfit, and threw her bouquet to her elder sister, Lynda Bird, while her then Hollywood beau, George Hamilton, looked on. There was 'a secret getaway' to a secret 'honeymoon hideaway' which later turned out to be a luxurious beachside villa in the Bahamas, lent by millionairess Rebekah Harkness Kean.

The next presidential daughter to marry was Patricia Nixon: tiny, blonde and, once more, given the title 'Princess'. She chose a ten-minute Episcopalian ceremony in the rose garden of the White House in June 1971, at which music had little chance to shine. But earlier in the century, at the weddings of two of President Woodrow Wilson's daughters, and two of President Franklin D. Roosevelt's sons, all the brides walked up the aisle to Wagner's march from *Lohengrin*, and down again to Mendelssohn's *Wedding March*—the two pieces which still mean weddings to most of us.

In the search for something 'unusual', some good music has been chosen, some disastrous, but the prize for the most surprising must surely go to an English bride of the 1930s who walked down the aisle to the march from Berlioz' *The Damnation of Faust*. She was a music teacher, liked the piece and thought, appropriately, to hell with its associations. At a more recent wedding, I joined the rest of the congregation in singing the hymn which begins 'He who would true valour see, Let him come hither', and listened to my husband muttering: 'They might just as well have had *Fight the Good Fight*, and be done with it!'

As incidental music for the feast, the military band and light operatic selections have had a tough time in recent years. Pop groups and travelling discotheques have been hired for some of the noblest liaisons in Britain, while the majority of weddings are

Plate Twelve

musicless after the church service. However, I know of one 1973 summer marriage, in the enchanting little village of Ewelme in Oxfordshire, where the bride and groom and all the guests wandered back from the church on foot, leaving the drivers of the big, black, white-ribboned limousines disconsolately bereft of custom at the porch, to find a melodious old barrel organ grinding away on the lawn. The bride's father had originally suggested hiring the local brass band, but his wife and daughter had murmured about the hazards of hot weather—'they always play in their braces'. And the highlight of the nicest wedding I went to in 1972 was the appearance of a small, light-hearted group of madrigal singers, of which the bride had been a member. In younger days, it was always a great comfort to find a certain forlorn-looking trio (piano, accordian and double bass—with other instruments on the side) installed for the reception: they played at the dances we all went to, and their presence was taken as a sign that though time was passing and friends were falling by the wayside, some things quite obviously went on for ever.

The eternal wedding tune then was *The Girl that I Marry*, from Irving Berlin's *Annie Get Your Gun*, with Robert Wright and George Forrest's romantic songs from *Kismet* following hard behind: dancing dreamily to *Younger than Springtime* helped many more bridesmaids to wedding rings of their own than catching the bridal bouquet ever did, and 'Hold my hand, I'm a stranger in Paradise. . . .' from the same show, was almost as potent and just as certain to appear in the repertoire.

Irving Berlin's ideal bride wore a gardenia in her hair ('And I'll be there . . .') which was a break with tradition suited to the times, for after leading the field for more than a century, orange blossom began to lose ground in the 1950s, and royal brides changed their allegiance back to the more solid glory of jewels even earlier than that. The present Queen Mother was the last major royal bride to wear flowers rather than diamonds. For her wedding to the then Duke of York (son of King George V), in April 1923, she wore a typically hideous 1920s arrangement: a veil clamped down over her head to the eyebrows and firmly held there by a garotte—in this case, a narrow band of myrtle leaves with two white roses and sprigs of orange blossom above each ear. At the next marriage of a son of George V, the Duke of Kent's bride, the exquisitely elegant Princess Marina of Greece ('she has that polish which living in Paris gives to a woman') wore a diamond fringe tiara—straight bars of gems graduating like the rays of the sun. That was in 1934, and it set the fashion for all future royal brides—and many non-royal ones, too. The makers of bridal head-dresses were quick to bring out 'costume jewellery' crowns, coronets and tiaras for girls with no access to the real thing, and these are still worn, though the present cult of honesty in everything and a return to the simplicity of Nature has brought fresh flowers back into fashion to rival them. In 1971 and '72, large floppy hats (and no veil) were popular, and before that, the women's magazines backed peasant-style three cornered handkerchiefs, with non-peasant-style ruffles round the edges.

One 1973 bride who had no difficulty in deciding what she should wear was Miss Mari Prichard, daughter of Welsh poet and writer, Caradog Prichard: she chose one of her father's three Bardic crowns—the one he won for his poem called *The Wedding*.

It was in the 1960s according to a 'London wedding wear expert' (quoted in the *Daily Mail*, 15 October 1971) that orange blossom really began to disappear and brides 'moved on to one artificial rose stuck on top of six yards of tulle—what we call the "miner's lamp" in the business'. Early 1971 fashions, he said, had been influenced by the extraordinary success of two television series, based on the lives of Henry VIII and Queen Elizabeth I, but that was passing: 'We're just getting over the Tudor bit, thank God. I'm absolutely sick of dressing brides to look like Elizabeth R, or one of the beheaded wives of Henry VIII.'

Tapping another cult, two years later, Young's, 'Britain's biggest bridal hire firm', introduced a collection of 'horoscope dresses'. For Taurus brides (21 April–21 May) the result was a frilly milk-maid number—the nearest they thought their customers would like to get to a bull.

Both Young's and Moss Bros (who hire out clothes for the bride as well as the bridegroom) say girls who go to them are prepared to pay an average of £20— and hire rather than buy because they want to look 'romantic' on their wedding day. (For a £20 rental charge, a girl gets a gown which would sell at £100, say Moss Bros.) The most expensive dress Young's ever hung on their racks was 'the original copy of Princess Alexandra's wedding dress, which cost us £435'. Both firms say that business is booming. Young's, who started up in 1949, were pleased to report that the figures for the first few months of 1973 were up '30 per cent against last year's increase of 21 per cent' and that brides were demanding more 'elaborate and costly dresses. In fact dresses which normally retail for £60 or under, remain unhired.' Fifty per cent of their clients also hire the dresses for their bridesmaids. Their advertising is based on the idea that by hiring, a bride can 'get beautifully married for half the price'. 'There are two ways to be outstandingly elegant on your wedding day', they say. 'One is to be rich. The other is to be clever. . . . You might very well get rich later. But right now, be clever.'

Brides who feel currently rich enough to ignore this advice and decide to buy their wedding dresses are usually torn between choosing something which is so perfect for the event it will never look right for anything else, or compromising with a dress which will look good, though not marvellous, at the altar, yet can be turned into an evening gown afterwards. The compromise is rarely successful; there is nearly always something about the dress, and the girl inside it, which shrieks bride for ever more, no matter what the alterations or how many trips it has made to the dyers. In the 1950s when strapless evening dresses were in fashion, brides and bridesmaids often wore these boned and bare constructions under a chaste jacket or bolero of matching material. It was a good idea, but it never looked right. Strapless dresses had an unfortunate habit of drooping or sticking out at an odd angle, and when covered with the jacket could make the most upstanding young woman look like an over-endowed matron.

There is a superstition that an old veil is luckier than a new one, and that luckiest of all is a borrowed veil, especially if on loan from someone who has been happily married, or from a member of the bride's own family. But superstition is no match for fashion, and as crisp, fresh tulle has been in vogue for wedding veils during most of this century, crisp, fresh tulle is what most brides have worn. In the Twenties, it was clamped over the forehead and fell to the hem of the gown, or, when the skirt was short, sometimes formed a train. During World War II when dresses, of necessity, were often short, the veil was sometimes no more than shoulder-length and attached to a hat. In the Fifties, with the arrival of nylon, a more bouncy effect was achieved, and very full, waist-length veils became popular. Now there is a demand for 'two-tier' or 'three-layered' veils: the bottom tier or layer forming a train; the second adding body to the mid-section, and the third short and full to frame the face and to be worn over it for the arrival at church. (And just to prove there is no new fashion under the sun, it is exactly the same arrangement as that worn by Ethel duPont in Delaware in June 1937, when she married Franklin D. Roosevelt, Jr. Then, fastened to a tiny Juliet cap of orange blossoms, she had three layers of white tulle, one ten feet long, one six feet long, and the other three feet—all edged with silver thread. Like Patricia Nixon, the 1971 bride, she also wore elbow-length mittens to match her dress.)

Some brides, however, lucky enough to have a lace heirloom in the family, do choose to wear it on their wedding day. In 1904, Princess Alice of Albany, a grand-daughter of Queen Victoria, borrowed the much criticised veil—the 'elongated lappet'—which Princess May of Teck had worn in 1893, and her mother, the Duchess of Teck, in 1866. (The bridegroom at this wedding was Princess May's youngest brother, Prince Alexander, later Earl of Athlone.)

In 1923, Princess May—by then Queen Mary—lent another family veil to her daughter-in-law-to-be, the Lady Elizabeth Bowes-Lyon, when she married the future King George VI. This was a much larger affair, of old *point de Flandres*, which had aged to a soft ivory colour, and the silk crêpe moiré for the wedding dress was dyed to tone with it.

Since then most royal brides have worn veils designed and made to match their dresses, though Princess Alexandra combined old and new by having her newly-woven wedding veil trimmed with a wide border of Valenciennes lace which had belonged to her grandmother, the Russian-born Princess Nicholas of Greece.

In wartime, the borrowing of a veil often became not a matter of choice or super-stition, but one of necessity. As with many things in life, the great white wedding is usually longed for most when it is most difficult to achieve; and during the Second World War, when everything was against it—from clothing coupons and food ration-ing, to a ban on church bells (except in case of national invasion) and bridegrooms sent suddenly abroad on active service—the desire to have one marvellous day to remember became iron determination. (It was no coincidence that Sir Alan Herbert's *Bless the Bride* brought such rapturous applause in 1947, or that his lyric, 'This is my lovely day, It is the day I shall remember the day I'm dying', had half his audience in tears.) One wartime bride who had set her heart on her wedding being 'the real thing', and achieved it even in 1944, later described how it was managed for *Brides* magazine. She was a schoolteacher; her bridegroom was an Army officer; and they had known each other since they were 12. Just before the Battle of Alamein, in 1942, when he was sent out to the Middle East, romance blossomed. (His father wrote to him soon afterwards: 'Is there anything between you and Margaret?' and was told: 'Yes—5,000 miles.') They wrote to each other; they saw each other when he came home on leave; then:

> Suddenly at a week's notice, Douglas came back for a course with a week's leave at the end. I came in from the shelter and there was the letter saying 'How about getting married?' It was a fantastic rush. I wanted the 'real thing' in every respect and raked in all the coupons possible. It was so nice that people didn't need to be asked for them. They offered. I bought my dress and head-

dress one Saturday morning scuttling up and down Oxford Street in a taxi—something I'd never have done normally. My dress was obviously pre-war; white figured satin that cost about £20 at Debenhams. The headdress was imitation orange blossom which was just about unobtainable so it cost £6. 4s. 10d., which horrified my mother, but time was so short. I had enough coupons for this but no more, so my bridesmaid wore a blue net dress that I'd worn at a friend's wedding in 1938. I'd saved a pair of treasured silk stockings. Any stockings were terribly scarce. I remember going bare-legged on our honeymoon which was in December. My veil and shoes were borrowed, and I didn't have the coupons for a new going away outfit, so I made do with a brown coat and a blue dress I'd had before. But almost everything for the wedding itself was new, right down to the satin pants. My own nightmare was that the house would be bombed and I'd lose the lot.

The wedding was gorgeous. We had a full peal of bells, which Churchill allowed because there was no fear of invasion anymore. And the reception, thanks to the black market, was as lush as any in peacetime. Somehow we got hold of a turkey and drink, and the cake was made and given by the parents of one of my pupils. Then we had a four-day honeymoon in Hove. The weather was lovely but the beach was lined with barbed wire. After that we didn't see each other again for eleven months and we had our real honeymoon in April 1946 when Douglas was demobbed.

A more unlikely bride to long for the 'real thing in every respect' was French singer, Edith Piaf—the 'Little Sparrow'—tiny, frail, a child of the streets (born, the daughter of a Paris street acrobat and a street singer, on a policeman's cloak under a Paris street lamp in 1915); acclaimed around the world, hooked on drugs, and, on the evidence of her half-sister, sad and wounded if a man—any man—did not want to sleep with her. At the age of 37, Edith Piaf married for the first time. 'She kept repeating dizzily, "This is my first marriage, so I really must love him".' She wanted it all to be like the song *Mariage*, which Henri Contet had written for her some years before. 'A wedding is a church and pealing bells, it's a love feast', she told her sister. But there were problems:

What worried her most was the wedding dress. She wanted to have one. 'But it would be ridiculous if I got married in white. That would be going a bit far. I can't wear a veil either, can I? You know, that was something I always wanted. I never celebrated my First Communion with the dress and the crown and all the rest of the stuff. First communicants look like little brides. I used to be so jealous of them.'

She was transformed, happy. Physically she looked ill, but she was less tense. What I didn't know was that she had found the solution—she had stopped rationing the drugs. She wanted to be well for the wedding; afterwards . . . *on verra*.

She had also solved the problem of what to wear:

I've been thinking about it. The virgin's colours are blue and white. There's nothing purer than Our Lady; I'll get married in sky blue. I'll have a little violet tulle hat instead of the veil. It'll look white in the photos.

And so, on 29 July 1952, in the Town Hall of the sixteenth arrondissement of Paris, Edith Giovanna Gassion (stage-name Edith Piaf) married René Victor

Eugène Ducos (stage-name Jacques Pills—one half of the duet act, Pills and Tabet), aged 46. But it wasn't what she had longed for. 'It didn't mean anything. They galloped through it. It wasn't a real wedding at all', she said. 'But I'm going to make up for it. We're going to go through it again in New York, in style, in a church.'

Two months later they left for America where both were to appear in cabaret—Piaf at the Versailles in New York, and Jacques Pills at La Vie en Rose—and on 20 September they were married again in the church of St. Vincent de Paul. Her French agent Louis Barrier gave the bride away, and Marlene Dietrich, having helped her to dress in her suite at the Waldorf Astoria, acted as a witness at the ceremony. Piaf wore sky blue from top to toe; the church bells rang, the organ played, and the bridegroom wore a white carnation in his dark blue suit. The priest blessed the rings, and outside, friends and fans gave their blessing with a shower of rice.

Two receptions were arranged: a luncheon at New York's most *chic* and expensive restaurant, Le Pavillon, and a cocktail party given by the Versailles, where, a few hours later, Piaf was back at work. Several blocks away, Jacques Pills also sang that night—a new song which he had written for his new wife, *Formidable*.

Twenty years on, wanting bridal white so much, Edith Piaf might well have gone right ahead and worn it, for, as Winefride Jackson wrote in the *Sunday Telegraph* (2 April 1972): 'no one seriously considers the implications of a white dress and veil for the bride. It is now a fashion and not a symbol.' A theory backed up by a wedding photograph in the *Sunday Express* five months later, showing the bride, in full-length white dress and frilly white mob-cap, hugging her new husband, a 29-year-old 'service engineer', and her former husband, an ex-painter and decorator turned boutique owner, and the three-year-old daughter of the previous marriage. Husband No. 1 had acted as best man to Husband No. 2. 'He's been just great about the whole thing', said the bride. 'We were very happy he was here', said the service engineer.

But in April 1973, when Miss Bernadette Devlin (leader of street fighters in the cause of Catholic Ireland, an 'honourable member' of the British House of Parliament, and the well-publicised mother of a baby born out of wedlock) married a man who, it was equally well-publicised, was not the father of the child, the newspaper columnists asked: 'Was virginal white brocade REALLY a good idea?'

For bridesmaids this century white has not been popular—for purely aesthetic reasons. Except at royal weddings (when it has been the majority choice) or for small child attendants, a colourful contrast is more usual. In Britain all the bridesmaids are generally dressed in the same style and shade, but American brides are more enterprising. At Patricia Nixon's wedding there were four attendants all dressed in 'opalescent layered gowns of mint green and lilac with fluttery necklines and hems', but while three of them wore 'lilac underskirted with misty green', the matron-of-honour (Julie Eisenhower, the bride's sister), wore 'a similar dress of pale green organdie with an underlayer of lilac'. All had halo hats and carried small posies. The idea of having each dress in a different shade of the same colour, which was so effective at Luci Baines Johnson's wedding, was also followed at a much earlier White House marriage: Jessie Wilson, daughter of President Woodrow Wilson, in 1913, had four bridesmaids plus her elder sister as maid-of-honour, and once again all wore pink—palest rose for the maid-of-honour, deep rose for the bride's younger sister, and something in between for the other three attendants. To modern taste the dresses themselves were hideous, with silver lamé underskirts, 'Elizabethan ruffs of silver lace' and draped pink charmeuse everywhere else. They showed four inches of ankle, which was thought to be rather daring. The headdresses were equally unbecoming: 'small rose velvet caps, trimmed with silver lace wired to stand up in the Russian fashion'. The result looked like a mad, fluted crown, higher one side than the other and was worn, inevitably, at eyebrow level. Nine years later, in England, the seven bridesmaids at the marriage of the Hon. Edwina Ashley and Lord Louis Mountbatten (later Earl Mountbatten of Burma) also wore wired silver lace, but this time made up into 'Dutch bonnets'. (It was the bride at this wedding who went Russian, wearing a triangular jewelled headdress, clamped, once more, low down on the forehead.)

At the very beginning of the century wide-brimmed hats were most popular for bridesmaids and these (usually made of lace or light-weight straw) became fashionable again in the Thirties. Garlands or sprays of imitation flowers—often incorporating corn or wheatears—have been almost continuously in favour, but recently, there has been a trend towards no headdress at all. The long, straight hairstyles which have been the general fashion for the last five years or so, are often presented just as they are, or with a very small circlet of flowers or narrow ribbon, worn either in the hair or round the forehead. The result has been eerily Mediaeval: a band of virgin(?) maidens with their hair hanging, and a bride who could just as truly be said to have 'married in her hair' as any girl in the 14th or 15th centuries.

In the 1950s I worked on a weekly newspaper in Kent and one of my many, many tasks was to write the wedding notices. Like most local papers, we sent out printed questionnaires to all brides in the area, and they filled in the details from which the reports were written. Without having to feed the answers into a computer, or even take a random survey, it was quite obvious then what was the most popular headgear for bridal attendants. Far more often than not, the question 'What did the bridesmaids wear?' received the same crisp reply: 'Dutch caps and a gold locket, present of the groom.' And that was all. (The bride often took her own white dress and veil so much for granted that all she claimed to have worn herself was: 'A pearl necklace, present of the groom.')

Pageboys always appear to be most in evidence at either end of the social scale. At royal and society weddings they usually wear kilts, sporrans and shirts with frills at the throat and cuffs. White satin court dress, very popular during the first half of the century is on the wane. Instead, miniature guardsmen often march up the aisle now—in uniforms hired for the day. (In 1973 it cost £5·50 to kit out a junior guardsman; 'an alternative fur busby' instead of a 'toy soldier hat' brought the total up to £6·75. Also on offer: 'Boy's morning suit'—scaled down model of black tail coat, striped trousers, grey waistcoat, and carnation in the buttonhole—£3·95.)

Who pays for the outfits worn by the attendants is still open to doubt. A generous father of the bride usually does the decent thing and takes care of the lot. Otherwise, accepting the honour of accompanying a friend to the altar can mean forking out for a dress designed to make the bride's younger sister look like an angel, but which does nothing at all for anyone else.

Married bridal attendants are not too common in England, where there is still a tacit assumption that after marriage a girl puts such public frolics behind her. When one is chosen, she is usually a recently married sister of the bride, or a lifelong 'best friend', whose support, at the last great trial before a husband takes over, is considered indispensable. In either case, her relationship to the bride, as much as her married status, fits her for the title of matron-of-honour and she is automatically platoon commander. When there is no married attendant, the head girl is called, simply, the 'chief bridesmaid' in Britain; but, in America, she is given the more romantic name of 'maid-of-honour' and the whole question of rank is more complicated.

Often a bride has both a maid-of-honour and a matron-of-honour—and the maid can be senior to the matron (especially if she is the sister of the bride). Of Luci Baines Johnson's thirteen attendants, one was a 5-year-old male ring-bearer, one a 5-year-old flower girl; two of the nine 'bridesmaids' were married (the husband of one of them was a 'groomsman', while the husband of another, the bridegroom's brother, would have been best man if he had not been fighting in Vietnam). Then there was a matron-of-honour, known to the bride for only three years; and the head girl, Lynda Bird Johnson, sister of the bride and maid-of-honour.

Children of previous marriages often appear, and even divorcees get listed as nominal bridesmaids. Cecil Beaton, present at the epic Hollywood wedding of Bessie Love in 1930, described the entrance of the bridal procession with relish in his *Diaries 1922–1939*:

> Excited screams could be heard from the crowd outside, heralding the arrival of the bride. The organist was having the time of his life, pulling out all stops. The air vibrated with thunderous fanfare.
>
> One by one, at intervals of six yards, the bridesmaids moved up the aisle with jerky, funereal pace. And what bridesmaids! Divorcees and mothers alternated with famous stars, all wearing large hats and flower-trimmed crinolines. Rather naively, I still believed that most bridesmaids were virgins. But perhaps they realised they couldn't find enough; so the retinue had been culled from the bride's friends, both married women and divorcees. Norma Shearer crept towards the altar, looking chiselled from alabaster. Her unseeing eyes stared out of a flawlessly complexioned face. Bebe Daniels, once a Mack Sennett bathing beauty and now a big star, walked behind Blanche Sweet, the maid of honour.
>
> Here comes the rock-pippet bride! Bessie Love entered on the arm of her very proud over-dressed father. She wore a shroud of white tulle and looked like a terrified bird. Bessie radiated love.

Beaton himself was wearing his evening tails, for the first time since arriving in Hollywood, and had a gardenia in his buttonhole. While the guests arrived, a woman 'in surplice and cap sang semi-religious love songs'. After the 'short and sweet' ceremony, performed by 'an affected minister', bride and bridegroom marched together down the aisle, between gilded baskets of pink gladioli tied with pink tulle, and disappeared into the hysterical crowd of fans and autograph-hunters outside. At the reception, at the Ambassador Hotel, Lilyan Tashman, 'with an escort of eight or nine vaguely *louche* young men, looked ever so ladylike in a chinchilla cape. Her scrambled-egg curls were done in a Greek fashion.' Mae Murray, 'with painted pout and daffodil-yellow hair, was a miracle of agelessness in spite of being a grandmother. She looked a fat dimpled cherub in a Kate Greenaway dress of silver lace. She chirped away to her sweating, long-haired husband, Prince Mdivani.' Hedda Hopper was there;

And the Bride Wore . . .

Cecil B. DeMille and family; William Powell, Ronald Colman, Laura LaPlante, Anita Loos, who escorted Beaton, and many, many more.

Mr. Beaton doesn't say what the bridegroom wore and until recently it has been the least interesting aspect of the whole commotion (we didn't even have a slot for it in the wedding forms I used to send out); but in Britain, at any rate, it is the one thing which can cause more pre-marital uproar than almost anything else. In England, much of Europe, America, and what used to be called the colonies, brides of all social rank wear white or reject it according to their own personal taste; but until a few years ago, the bridegroom's clothes had deeper significance: they were taken as a measure of the class he was born into, had succeeded to, or was aiming at, and to some extent that remains true. If a man who is still only aiming decides to wear a morning suit, he can walk a stormy path to the altar, with every other male involved in the affair challenging aggressively: 'Just let anyone try to dress *me* up in a monkey suit, that's all!' At the top of the scale, the situation used to be exactly reversed: for the first half of the century, a bridegroom who did not wear a morning suit (or a uniform) met with icy politeness, condescending civility, or searching questions as to his antecedents.

But now, as one lively 83-year-old recently told me: 'Weddings have changed! Not among the lower-middle class and middle class but among certain groups of the so-called aristocracy. When Lord Bath's son was married some two years ago, all the important males were in fancy dress—every colour of trouser and waistcoat, very lavishly embroidered, and hair hanging to the shoulders! In such cases, the bride takes almost second place!'

This trend towards male glory has filtered down to some middle-class weddings, too, where the latest 'formal' fashion for the bridegroom is a dark green velvet lounge suit (though 'lounge' is a very inadequate description) worn with a wide and colourful tie. To off-set the turbulence at the top, Moss Bros. (branches everywhere, including two in Paris) say 'there is a tendency for morning coat suits to be worn slightly down the social ladder these days'—which has kept business steady. But they are obviously keeping a wary eye on the situation, and are 'encouraging' the search for 'variations from formal morning wear'. (In 1973, they launched a competition for fashion students, to produce a modern alternative.) In the meantime their catalogue, under a line of identical penguins, says:

> *Morning Wear is not a uniform.* Although it is the custom for Bridesmaids to be dressed alike, it is incorrect for the men at a wedding to be dressed identically. For example, they should not all wear grey morning suits.
> The morning coat can be black or grey, the waistcoat black, grey, or almost any other colour, and the trousers striped, dark or light, or shepherd's plaid.
> Morning dress is capable of almost as much variation as a lounge suit, and each man should express his individual personality.

In a mass swing towards expressing their individual personality, many men now choose the all grey morning suit (matching coat, trousers and waistcoat—usually in 'bird's eye' cloth), and find that instead of being the one glorious exception at the wedding, the fellows who kept to the more traditional black coats and striped trousers are the ones that catch the eye.

Some things old, some things new

At 'fashionable London or country weddings', many, if not most of the male guests still wear morning dress (even when the bridegroom does not), 'but lower down the social scale only the bridegroom, best man, ushers, and the two fathers dress up and most of the remainder of the male guests wear lounge suits. There is a tendency, of course, that if a man is invited as a guest to a wedding and he has a morning suit in his wardrobe he will wear it.' (And there must be many such men in England, since this one firm has been *selling* 'between 2,000 and 3,000 morning suits for very many years', as well as hiring out 'many thousands' more.)

In Wales, it has been discovered that 'many wedding attenders prefer black short jackets rather than morning coats', while in Scotland it is difficult to get men to wear top hats. (Could this be thrift? After all it is an extra 80p for the usual grey one, and £1·25 for black. And even if you do get 'Braces and Studs supplied at no extra charge', a pound's a pound for a' that.) The Isle of Thanet—'Canterbury, Margate, etc.'—has a bad sartorial record with Moss Bros. 'Far too many men get married in lounge suits there', they say.

In America formal morning wear looks much the same as in England, but an American description of it strikes oddly on the English ear. The *New York Times* News Service put it like this after Patricia Nixon's 1971 marriage: 'All the men in the wedding party, including Nixon, wore grey, swallow-tail cutaways with striped trousers, Ascots, stiff wing collars and gloves.' Ascots (grey silk cravats) and wing collars have made an occasional reappearance in Britain recently, just as, occasionally, an American bridegroom wears a tie (and is then said to have dressed 'in the English style'). The social pressure to wear a 'swallow-tail cutaway' can obviously be great: the late President Lyndon Johnson wore one for his daughter Luci's wedding, though he refused to do so for his inauguration as President three years earlier.

In Australia, for grand evening weddings, the bridegroom wears evening tails, as did the demon interviewer of British television, Robin Day, when, at the age of 41, he swapped his spotted bow tie for a white one and married a ravishing 24-year-old Australian barrister, at St. Mary's Anglican Cathedral, Perth, in 1965. (She wore an elegant white turban with a veil attached to the back. He said the whole deal had been 'more nerve-racking than any TV show'.)

Except for the caftan and Mongolian-shepherd's-jerkin fringe, a lounge suit is the only alternative to morning dress in Britain; but in America dinner jackets are often worn, and in the summer the wedding pages of many a newspaper look suitably tropical, with all the bridegrooms pictured wearing white tuxedos.

For the first few years of the century, frock coats were worn for daytime weddings on both sides of the Atlantic, and many older guests continued to wear them into the Twenties. There is a splendid, laughing wedding photograph of King George V and two of his sons, taken at the marriage of the King's niece, Princess Maud of Fife, in 1923: the King wearing a rather old-fashioned, but magnificent, frock coat (satin-faced collar and velvet ribbon trimming), while the 28-year-old Duke of York, and his brother, 21-year-old Prince George (later Duke of Kent) wear equally gorgeous silk-bound morning coats, pearl-grey ties and spats.

The King and Prince George both sported white carnations in their buttonholes at this wedding, and for most of the 20th century this flower has been the modern version of the wedding favour. Only a limited distribution, to the main wedding party, is now expected; though many other guests supply their own. As with the clothes which provide the buttonhole, how a man wears his carnation is yet another indication of class. Top men take them neat; lesser men add a backing of asparagus fern and a twist of silver foil round the stems for containment and preservation purposes. In the unfortunate circumstance of a suit not having a workable buttonhole in the lapel, the *boutonnière* is pinned in place—with a gleaming expanse of silver on show.

Two carnations, one below the other, and a little asparagus fern, is the feminine version, but once again, not for top ladies. They might wear an orchid perhaps, or a rose, but not two white carnations.

The custom of giving flower and ribbon favours to all the guests died suddenly at the end of the 19th century, and was only briefly revived at the beginning of the 20th. The *Illustrated London News* (16 January 1904), described one instance of the revival in an account of Viscount Fincastle's wedding, but first of all it set the scene with details of the multi-coloured costumes worn by the bride's attendants:

> The bridesmaids' dresses were extremely pretty: they were of white gauze over white silk, made with deep collars and edged with brown fur, and having wide folded sashes with long ends of turquoise-blue satin, against which the shower bouquets of pink roses showed up well; then their hats were of pale-green crumpled felt, trimmed with plumes shaded from blue to green, and with folds of blue chiffon. These six attendant maidens had committed to them the pretty task of distributing 'favours' to the guests in the church while the register was being signed—a white rosebud mingled with sprays of white heather and lilies-of-the-valley, tied with a tiny piece of ribbon. This is a pretty old custom, and one that Fashion is smiling upon again; it fills up the tedious quarter of an hour while the couple and their nearest friends are in the Vestry, and gives the whole bridal party a feeling of community in the celebration.

The rose was not only the 'Queen of Flowers' and symbolic of love, and thus 'very suitable at a wedding', but according to this writer, signified different aspects of love at different stages in its development:

> The half-opened bud is a symbol of the beginning of affection: the maiden who accepts it with a smile is understood to be expressing her willingness to be courted. The full-blown rose speaks of the perfumed sweetness and the un-equalled beauty of a happy passion.

Myrtle, on the other hand, was 'emblematical of the evergreen nature that ought to distinguish wedded love: and white heather is the established symbol of "good luck".'

Now, even white carnations for men are going through troubled times. At many society weddings less than half the principal men wear flowers of any kind, and at the last grand royal wedding—that of Princess Alexandra of Kent in 1963—red carnations, not white, were worn. One 1973 bridegroom who struck an even greater blow for originality was John Grimond, journalist son of the former leader of the British Liberal Party, Mr. Jo Grimond. For his May wedding to the daughter of actress Celia Johnson, he wore a velvet suit with a large daisy in the buttonhole.

Able Seamen in the British Navy have a charming custom all their own: 'when they marry in Square Rig, instead of tying their bag with blue tapes, they tie it with white satin ribbon'. Which, in non-nautical terms, means when they marry in bell-bottoms and jerkin, they tie the scarf which goes under the sailor collar with festive white ribbons, and end up with a satin bow and streamers on their bosoms. On the day of the wedding a wreath with fluttering white ribbons is hoisted at the main mast-head of the ship in which they serve. Officers, who also marry in their uniforms, are not allowed bridal ribbons (or carnations), but they have the privilege of a guard of honour of fellow officers, who present a crossed swords archway for bride and bride-groom to walk through as they leave the church porch.

In America, the marital tradition of 'his' and 'hers' is kept alive by the bride-groom wearing a buttonhole of the same flowers used for the bride's bouquet—and it looks very attractive indeed. President Franklin D. Roosevelt's youngest son, John, wore a fairly large arrangement of one white orchid backed by lilies-of-the-valley for his wedding in 1938; and the bride, Boston socialite Anne Lindsay Clark, carried a large, round bouquet of the same flowers. She also wore 'real imported orange blossoms' in her hair, while the bridegroom was in 'English' morning dress—soft collar and tie and slightly lighter striped trousers than are usual in America. (He also wore grey spats, and carried gloves and a black top hat, instead of the grey more favoured in Britain.)

At Luci Baines Johnson's 1966 wedding, the bridegroom wore a small spray of lilies-of-the-valley, to match his bride's small posy.

Bridal bouquets have steadily diminished in size during this century. The 'shower' arrangement, which came into fashion during the 1890s, had a good run, but in the late 1920s it was replaced by a double-ended style, which was cradled like a baby in the crook of the arm, rather than carried. The bridesmaids at this time often had 'a sheaf' of flowers—sometimes delphiniums, since delphinium blue was a popular colour for bridesmaids' dresses. In the Forties and Fifties, large, round jobs were much favoured —or, as a more demure alternative, a white Prayer Book with floral bookmark and trailing satin ribbon. During the Sixties the posy made a come-back, large to begin with, then gradually dwindling until it reached the neat dimensions of most arrange-ments today. The choice of flowers has also changed: stephanotis, for many years virtually indispensable, has gone into retreat, while lilies-of-the-valley are sprouting everywhere. The most recent development of all is the coloured bouquet. These haven't appeared at society marriages yet, but a random sampling of the wedding pages of the Kent newspaper, the *Bromley Times*, for April 1973, produced descrip-tions like this:

The bride, who was given away by her father, wore a full-length lace-trimmed dress of lawn. Her short two-tier veil was secured by a single white rose, and she carried yellow freesias and white pipped hyacinths decorated with turquoise ribbon.

The bride . . . carried a bouquet of pink, red and white roses.

The bride . . . wore a white dress trimmed with blue, and carried a bouquet of white roses, blue carnations and lilies-of-the-valley.

Given away by her uncle . . . the bride wore a traditional white embossed organza gown trimmed with velvet, a matching cap and a ᵇhree-layer veil also trimmed with velvet. She carried a basket of mixed spriʳ   ᵃrs.

The bride, who was given away by her father, worʳ   ᵈle dress of white crepe Courtelle with flower motif trimmings anᵈ   ᵖil was

flowey

secured by a Juliet cap, and she carried a shower of freesias, hyacinth bells and cheerfulness.

. . . she carried a Victorian posy of mauve and white spring flowers.

'Cheerfulness' and 'pipped hyacinths' (or 'hyacinth pips' as they are also called) are new to the wedding scene since I dealt with such things in the Fifties. And 'mixed spring flowers' were then reserved for the bridesmaids.

The throwing of the bride's bouquet—the girl to catch it will be the next to marry—is talked about a great deal in Britain, but is performed more often in America. At Jessie Woodrow Wilson's 1913 wedding, superstition was cruelly tested: the lucky wedding ring in the cake was found by the bride's elder sister, Margaret, while the tossed bouquet went to her younger sister, Eleanor. The bouquet proved to have the stronger magic, and sister Eleanor became another White House bride within six months.

In Britain, 'Brides who throw their wedding bouquets are traditional; those who preserve them, sentimental', said the *Daily Telegraph* in April 1972; and went on to suggest a means of throwing the bouquet and saving it, too: 'You need only keep back a representative bloom or two . . . to have an everlasting memento. From these Mrs. Philippa Atkinson, in Sussex, can fashion a dried and pressed picture arrangement either on a suitable fabric background or a piece of the wedding dress or veil. Glazed and framed in narrow white, inside size 8 in × 7 in, it costs £6·50, including the container she provides for you to post the flowers and foliage to her.'

Floral decorations in the church and for the reception in Britain nowadays tend to be like many of the brides they are prepared for—nice, but dull. Even at royal weddings all the effort goes into two huge and beautiful arrangements flanking the altar—after that, inspiration dies. This is not the case in America. There, it is not only the lavishness which impresses (though it can hardly fail to do so), but also the brilliant attention to detail: even the cassocks on which the bride and principal guests kneel are given a bridal boost. At Alice Lee Roosevelt's 1906 wedding, 'the *prie-dieu* was upholstered in nuptial white fabric, tied with white satin ribbons and filled with the petals of Bride's roses and lilies'. At Luci Baines Johnson's wedding, 'miniature markers' of ivy, roses, babies breath, arum lilies and white delphiniums, decorated the 'kneelers' set in the chancel of the National Shrine of the Immaculate Conception for the chief wedding party, while larger versions of the same thing decorated the end of every fourth pew. The Shrine was turned into a young forest, with small locust and ficus trees, laced with lilies-of-the-valley, white roses and babies breath, and even the 'ropes' cordoning off the pews not in use for the ceremony were made of green smilax.

For Ethel duPont's 1937 marriage (which took place in the tiny church at Christiana Hundred, Delaware, founded by Colonel Henry duPont in 1859), 2,000 sprays of jasmine were shipped across the continent from California, to scent the chapel and, with peonies and lilies, decorate the end of every other pew.

I have never heard of this delightful custom being followed in Britain, but a friend, in March 1973, seeing 'the wedding awning up' outside Vere Street Church, just off London's Oxford Street, strolled inside and found the end of every pew decorated with a rosette and streamers of white satin ribbon, which she thought 'looked charming'.

Some things old, some things new

A recent Hollywood wedding, which revived all the excesses of the good old days of the film capital, was said to have taken place amidst £25,000-worth of blooms: two-hundred dozen white lilacs and ninety-two dozen white tulips, flown in from Paris, fraternized with 'thousands of Californian varieties'. The bridegroom was 55-year-old singer, Dean Martin, father of seven, who had 'already been to his own wedding twice before'; the bride, 25-year-old Cathy Mae Hawn, had only made one previous excursion. Not to be outdone by the jungle of flowers around her, Miss Hawn wore a complete hair-do of lilies-of-the-valley, carried an outsize bouquet of the same flowers, and had the champagne glasses festooned with white satin ribbons and sprays of more lily-of-the-valley.

Doves were released at intervals; pews were borrowed from Warner Brothers and 20th Century Fox; Frank Sinatra was best man, and thought it 'a lovely but simple wedding'. 'Truly an old-fashioned Hollywood marriage', said the man in charge of the flower show—which was probably nearer the mark.

And so, from the not quite ridiculous, to the nearly sublime—royal weddings. These have altered considerably over the last seventy years and the most noticeable change of all—the fact that Westminster Abbey is now the 'traditional' place for them— came about, once again, by chance. Just as Queen Victoria's short wedding journey from the new royal residence (Buckingham Palace) to the old one (St. James's Palace) snow-balled into the public cavalcade we now expect on these occasions, so the 'unsafe condition' of St. George's Chapel, Windsor, in 1919, led to all the Abbey splendour of the present century.

In 1904, when Edward VII had been King for three years, and his niece, Princess Alice of Albany (now the Countess of Athlone) was about to marry, he decided that the weddings of the numerous descendants of Queen Victoria should be carried out as quietly as possible. As the *Illustrated London News* explained:

> The King has ordered that, as far as possible, the marriage of these junior members of the royal family shall be regarded as a domestic and not a public affair, as this event will set a precedent in some respects for others of a similar kind that may be expected in time to come. It has been decided to invite to the ceremony only personal friends and personages of State importance who are always asked to such events, and there will be no alterations in the chapel [*St. George's, Windsor*] to allow more than its usual complement of seats being provided.

This ruling was followed and Princess Alice's wedding was reasonably restrained. The guest list was pared down and she had only five bridesmaids, who wore blue, rather than the white of major royal marriages. The Princess of Wales (formerly Princess May of Teck), whose brother was the bridegroom, thought it 'a most cheerful wedding', with 'no crying' and the mother of the bride, the widowed Duchess of Albany, 'behaved like a brick'.

The pattern worked well until the end of the First World War, and the marriage of Princess Alice's cousin, Princess Patricia of Connaught, another grandchild of Queen Victoria. When her wedding was planned, for February 1919, St. George's Chapel was found to be 'structually unsound', and the Dean of Windsor launched an appeal to pay for repairs. The obvious alternative was the Chapel Royal, St. James's, which had been used for the marriages of Queen Victoria, the Princess Royal, and Princess May of Teck (who, after another name change, was now Queen Mary). But this was, as Queen Victoria had said, 'small & *very* ugly', and Princess Patricia was one of those lesser members of the royal family whose popularity was out of all proportion to their position; she was called 'our adored Princess Pat', and received rapturous applause wherever she went: a chapel holding only 200 guests was no place for her wedding— or for the first major royal event since the beginning of the war. And so Westminster Abbey was thought of; it had been the scene of many society weddings in the previous century, and with a minimum capacity of 2,500 was certainly the right size.

The newspapers were delighted. It would be, they calculated, the first royal wedding in the Abbey for over 500 years, since King Richard II married Anne of Bohemia in 1382. This piece of research was polished up afresh for the next two royal weddings: when Princess Mary, only daughter of George V and Queen Mary, married three years later, she was the 'first child of a sovereign' to have been married in the Abbey for more than 500 years, and the following year her brother, the future King George VI, was 'the first royal prince' to have been married in the Abbey for more than 500 years.

The newspapers and the nation had something else to ponder with these three marriages—both royal brides and the royal bridegroom had chosen non-royal spouses. And Princess Patricia, on marrying Commander Alexander Robert Maule Ramsay, D.S.O., R.N., third son of the Earl of Dalhousie, chose to relinquish her royal title, too.

Looking back on Princess Patricia's wedding (at the time of Princess Mary's), *The Times* recalled:

> The wedding of the adored 'Princess Pat' to Commander (now Captain) Ramsay in Westminster Abbey is still fresh in the public mind. An Armistice time wedding: a khaki and blue, a naval and military wedding. The beauty of the bride in her Venetian-looking white gown with silver embroidery and lace; the little pages, the eight bridesmaids in their dresses of 'love-in-the-mist' blue and picture hats, the white flowers and gold plate—there was something very gracious about it all within the soaring wistful beauty of the Abbey and the King and Queen were there and the Prince of Wales, and many others of the Royal Family. The Duke of Connaught gave his daughter away and she, who had come to the altar Princess Patricia of Connaught left it Lady Patricia Ramsay.
>
> Thus among many other ways does the Royal Family of Great Britain build itself firmly into the hearts and interests of Great Britain and of Britons overseas.

At the time, the paper had thought: 'her renunciation of her royal style and title, to become Lady Patricia Ramsay, was felt to be a sign of the new spirit of national union which the war and its perils, in which the bridegroom played such a gallant part, have created among the people'.

The war and its perils, had also made Britain relentlessly anti-German, and toppled many a European throne. The source of acceptable royal partners for British princes and princesses was drying up; an all-royal match was now to become the exception rather than the rule. Although Queen Victoria had encouraged the idea of members of the royal family marrying into the British aristocracy, only one of her nine children did so: Princess Louise, her fourth daughter, who married the Marquis of Lorne, son and heir of the Duke of Argyll. Of King Edward VII's children, two made royal marriages, one married into the aristocracy, and two died unmarried. With the children of King George V, however, the balance altered radically: only one of the five made a royal marriage (the Duke of Kent to Princess Marina of Greece); three married into the aristocracy; and the heir to the throne chose to give up his crown for a twice-divorced American.

There were more shocks to come in the next generation—though not of the same high voltage. At the beginning of the 1960s, the country was still getting used to the idea of a distant connection of the throne (Lady Pamela Mountbatten) marrying an interior decorator, when the Queen's sister announced she was to wed a photographer. As a Reuter's correspondent pointed out, it was the first time for 457 years that the daughter of a British king had married a plain 'Mr.' 'The last to do so was Princess Cecilie, daughter of Edward IV, who married an obscure "mister" named Thomas Kymbe, in a ceremony that passed almost unnoticed in its day.'

What was to be done about the plain 'Mr.'? And would—almost unthinkable—the Princess become a plain 'Mrs.'? The *Illustrated London News* called on the editor of *Burke's Peerage* to sort out this 'knotty problem' for which there was 'no precise precedent'. He had to admit he couldn't, but in doing so mentioned that the photographer, Mr. Antony Armstrong-Jones, came from the landed gentry, 'the untitled aristocracy as Sir Bernard Burke liked to call them'. It had a comforting ring to it. Mr. Armstrong-Jones was also found to have been educated at Eton, which was equally reassuring; and later to have coxed the Cambridge boat against Oxford, which was the right sort of thing to have done. His parents were, unfortunately, divorced, but his mother had married the Earl of Rosse and his half-brother was called Lord Oxmantown, which made that part of it all right. The chief trouble remained: Mr. Armstrong-Jones was too well-known in Fleet Street as a working photographer, and familiarity breeds—familiarity. While one half of the press was busy building him up; the other half was determined to keep him right down there at Street level like the friends he had left behind him.

In the end, the Princess stayed a princess and carried on with her public duties, while, the year following the marriage, the 'Mr.' was made an Earl (the Earl of Snowdon) and became a better photographer than ever.

And now, thirteen years later, Princess Margaret's niece, the only daughter of the Monarch, is to marry another 'member of the people', 'The commoner of her choice', the son of 'a company director' (after which some newspapers, in the interests of the whole truth, added, 'of the Walls sausage firm'). After months of excited speculation, stern and sometimes salty denials, countless fuzzy photographs of the 'just good friends' exercising their horses, the announcement was made on 29 May 1973 from Balmoral, where a loving family gathering had been staged: Princess Anne's elder brother flew in from his Royal Navy duties in the Caribbean; her two younger brothers were on half-term holiday from school; the bridegroom-to-be was on leave from his regiment, the Queen's Dragoon Guards, stationed in Germany. Next day all travelled in the royal train to London, where the Princess showed off her sapphire and diamond ring to the press; Lieutenant Mark Phillips told how 'petrified' he had been, asking her father for her hand (the Duke of Edinburgh had the final domestic

say, while the Queen took care of State approval); and Her Majesty gave a celebration lunch for the handsome Lieutenant's parents.

The press, this time, gave their unanimous blessing. It was a 'fairy-tale love
story'; 'A most suitable choice'; 'They have many interests in common'; 'the
Princess and her fiancé met through their common interest in horses'; and, from the
Daily Mirror, 'horses all over Britain must be neighing with delight'. Love had
conquered all 'at a canter', and the Princess had galloped 'blushing down the straight',
'rushing the last fence', just when everyone thought the romance had cooled. Within
hours of the announcement fashion editors had decided what the Princess should wear
on her wedding day and one paper even pasted a picture of Her Royal Highness's
face over that of a model in a modern wedding dress to show how right they were.
The general feeling was one of relief. As with Albert Edward, Prince of Wales—
Queen Victoria's problem heir 'Bertie'—more than a hundred years before, an early
marriage to a strong-minded partner was thought to be the wisest course. The *Daily
Mirror*'s caption 'Anne meets her match' was meant to be read two ways.

The *Daily Express* felt obliged to point out that 'Mark's great-great-grandfather
was a Lancashire coal miner, while Anne's was Edward VII', but all agreed with the
Daily Mirror that he was 'upper-crust enough'. (The editor of *Debrett* later spoilt
this big-heartedness by discovering that Lieutenant Phillips was descended from
Edward I, king from 1272 to 1307, and that the couple were in fact 'thirteenth
cousins, twice removed'. But then someone discovered that Mrs. Simpson was a
descendant of William the Conqueror.) The general feeling was that Princess Anne's
was a 'love match', there had been no 'royal match-making'. The mettlesome 22-
year-old daughter of the Queen and her 24-year-old Lieutenant were in love, the
Welsh Guards played *Congratulations* at the changing of the guard, and the country
loved the lovers.

'A love match.' It is what the newspapers have said of almost every royal engage-
ment this century; and it is what the royal family themselves have felt, too. In
November 1921 the 39-year-old Henry, Viscount Lascelles, eldest son of the Earl of
Harewood, proposed to the 24-year-old Princess Mary (later to be made Princess
Royal) at Sandringham, and Queen Mary, mother of the bride-to-be, wrote in her
diary: '—At 6.30 Mary came to my room to announce to me her engagement to
Lord Lascelles! We then told G. & then gave Harry L. our blessing—We had to keep
it quiet owing to G. having to pass an order in council to give his consent. Of course
everybody guessed what had happened & we were very cheerful & almost uproarious
at dinner—We are delighted.'

Between then and the wedding in February 1922, there was many an 'hilarious'
family tea-party, and great excitement, even among the Princess's brothers. '. . . as
far as I can make out the 28th is going to be a day of national rejoicing in every conceivable & unconceivable manner. . . . In fact it is now no longer Mary's wedding
but (this from the papers) it is the "Abbey Wedding" or the "Royal Wedding" or the
"National Wedding" or even the "People's Wedding" (I have heard it called)
"of our beloved Princess",' wrote the Duke of York to the Prince of Wales who was
away touring India.

A few days after the ceremony, the Queen took up the story for her eldest son:

. . . a beautiful pageant from start to finish, a fine service in the Abbey, Mary doing her part to perfection (a very great ordeal before so many people) & everyone happy & pleased. . . . Grannie [*Queen Alexandra*] was wonderful & looked very nice in violet velvet wearing the Garter & many fine jewels. Enormous crowds everywhere & a great reception when we stepped on to the Balcony.—We gave a large family luncheon (both families) in the state dining room and Mary & Harry L. drove off at 3.45—Papa & all of us throwing rice & little paper horse shoes & rose leaves after them. Papa & I felt miserable at parting, poor Papa broke down, but I mercifully managed to keep up as I so much feared Mary wld break down. However she was very brave & smiled away as they drove off in triumph to the station.

The bridegroom had worn the full dress uniform of the Grenadier Guards with the Order of the Garter conferred on him two days earlier by the King. Neither he nor Princess Pat's husband wore festive white satin bows attached to their epaulettes and this charming bridal fashion was never to reappear. Being non-royal, Lord Lascelles and Commander Ramsay were restricted to one supporter each, a 'best man', in accordance with the custom which emerged at the end of the previous century. Only the sons of the King were allowed two, in all cases their brothers.

The bridesmaids were the traditional eight; all maiden daughters of dukes, marquises and earls, with the exception of one Princess (Princess Maud of Fife, who, with her cousin, the present bride, Princess Mary, had also been attendant on Princess Patricia of Connaught.) Although the mixture was much the same as in Victorian times, the emphasis was now on relationship and friendship, rather than rank, and this was to become stronger with the years. (The ghost of grand old Sarah, Duchess of Marlborough must have walked in scorn through the corridors of Marlborough House. In 1734, when George II built his 'orange box' alongside her property, she had objected to the daughters of peers being asked to walk in the procession of the Princess Royal; now daughters of the monarch were carrying the trains of their cousins.)

At the turn of the century, when Princess Alice of Albany married, the *Illustrated London News* said that her 'wedding dress was cut, as those of royal brides always are, quite low at the neck'. It was a fashion which had gone out of favour for ordinary brides in the 1870s, and now both Princess Patricia and Princess Mary conformed to more general custom with demure necklines and long sleeves. Both wore silver and white. Queen Mary, who had worn 'aluminium grey silken crêpe' at Princess Patricia's wedding, chose for her daughter's 'a beautiful gold lamé into which a bold design of cream velvet brocade had been woven, creating a rich old-gold effect'. The *Illustrated London News* made a point of confirming that 'All the main dresses were British made and British designed.'

Less than a year after Princess Mary's wedding, her brother, the Duke of York, became engaged to one of her bridesmaids, Lady Elizabeth Bowes-Lyon, ninth child of the 14th Earl of Strathmore. Again, it was a 'love match', the Duke had been wooing her for more than a year and the King had told him: 'You'll be a lucky fellow if she accepts you.' They had first met in 1905, at a children's party, when she is said, prophetically, to have given him the crystallized cherries off her sugar cake. They did not meet again until 1920, at a small private dance given by Lord Farquhar, when the Duke was 24 and Lady Elizabeth 20. This time she was not so encouraging. Lady Elizabeth Bowes-Lyon was enjoying being launched into society, a 'coming out' which had been delayed by the war. She was quickly voted the best dancer in any London ballroom, and the prettiest and most charming girl anywhere, and, in the words of John Wheeler-Bennett (King George VI's official biographer) 'entertained a very natural reluctance to abandon the unfettered liberty of a great noble family for the restricted freedom of membership of the Royal circle, where every action was public property, every step must be watched, every word guarded'.

But, on 16 January 1923, the Duke was able to write to his parents: 'I know I am very lucky to have won her over at last.' King George V and Queen Mary were once more delighted. '. . . he looks beaming', wrote the King in his diary. The newspapers busied themselves with statistics again and discovered that both the Duke and his *fiancée* were descended from Robert the Bruce of Scotland.

Royal engagements now lasted a set three months, and the wedding was arranged for 26 April. Once more there were eight bridesmaids, two of them small nieces of the bride, two of them nieces of Queen Mary, one a fellow bridesmaid from Princess Mary's wedding. Though all were well-connected, only five were the daughters of peers. (Princess Maud of Fife didn't push her luck by appearing for a third time and it paid off: she was married in the autumn.) The year before, Princess Mary's attendants had worn veils but *The Times* announced that Lady Elizabeth's would not do so, 'as it is understood that the Duke of York does not care for them'. Instead they had the same kind of headdress as the bride (who did wear a veil, and a monstrously unbecoming one): 'A narrow fillet of myrtle green leaves with a white rose shaded pink on either side and sprigs of heather.' The result was unfortunately like earphones.

The day began grey and showery, but as the King recorded later: 'It stopped raining at about 9.30 & the sun actually came out as the Bride entered the Abbey.' On her way up the aisle on her father's arm, Lady Elizabeth paused to place her bouquet on the tomb of the Unknown Warrior. It was, as a writer was to say on the 50th anniversary of her wedding day, 'the first of countless thousands of gestures she has made in the half-century since demonstrating her unique ability to touch the human heart'. And wherever she has gone, through fifty years of service to her country, the sun has always seemed to shine.

The brand-new British Broadcasting Company (forerunner of the British Broadcasting Corporation) asked permission to relay the ceremony over the latest miracle invention, the wireless. The go-ahead Dean of Westminster Abbey was in favour, but the Chapter said No, and it was not until eleven years later that the first royal wedding was listened to by families throughout the land. Thirteen years after that, the marriage of Princess Elizabeth, daughter of the Duke of York and Lady Elizabeth Bowes-Lyon, received even more miraculous attention: '200,000,000 future subjects heard the tremulous "I will" as radio and television services relayed the majestic Abbey ceremony'. After another thirteen-year leap, Princess Margaret's wedding was not just televised, it was 'Eurovised', and in 1963 pictures of the marriage of Princess Alexandra of Kent were 'bounced by satellite' all around the world.

In the 1930s there were three royal weddings in quick succession: one a traditional Abbey spectacular; one a more subdued affair in Buckingham Palace Chapel; the third, notorious.

The first of the trio was that of King George V and Queen Mary's youngest son,

Some things old, some things new

Prince George, made Duke of Kent shortly before his wedding day. And it was splendidly romantic. The girl that he married was the only royal bride from over the sea of the century: the elegant and beautiful Princess Marina. She was the daughter of Prince Nicholas of Greece (uncle of the exiled King George II) and the Grand Duchess Hélène of Russia. And her great-grandfather was King Christian IX of Denmark, father of Britain's Queen Alexandra, consort of King Edward VII. The Duke, having left the navy because of ill-health, was at this time the 'first royal Civil Servant, attached to the Home Office as a factory inspector'. (A job he took very seriously, said a friend in the pre-marriage burst of publicity: 'He insisted, for instance, that no notification of his visits to factories should be made beforehand.')

Prince George and Princess Marina became engaged in the August of 1934 while staying with her sister and brother-in-law, Prince and Princess Paul of Yugoslavia, at their rustic summer home amidst the woods and above a lake in the mountains of Slovenia: 'The most romantic setting one could possibly have', said the bride-to-be. They were serenaded by peasants and presented with wild flowers—a garland for the head of the Princess, bouquets for both. They had known each other for five years.

Back in London, the 31-year-old Prince George made immediately for Cartier's to buy the ring: 'A large square-cut Kashmiri sapphire, flanked by two baton diamonds, set in platinum.' (Most royal engagement rings this century have had a sapphire, 'symbol of enduring love', and diamonds. Only the shape and metal have differed.) The 27-year-old Princess returned to Paris, where she had lived with her parents for twelve years, and began ordering her *trousseau*. In mid-September she boarded a cross-Channel steamer to make her first visit to England as 'Prince George's Bride-elect'. At Folkestone there was no official ceremony, 'but the crowd gathered to greet her witnessed a charming incident. Standing on the quay as the boat came alongside was a little grey-haired old lady carrying flowers, and Princess Marina, recognising her former nurse, ran to kiss her directly she landed. Cheers followed the Princess as she moved towards the boat train. As she entered the special carriage, the ropes gave way before the pressure of spectators, and they thronged the door with cries of 'Good luck, Princess!" and "Welcome to England!"'

Prince George, in morning coat and striped trousers, was on Victoria Station to greet his *fiancée* and his future in-laws, and that night escorted them to Scotland by royal train to stay with the King and Queen. At 7 a.m. next morning the Duke and Duchess of York, with their small daughter Princess Elizabeth, and the King's Guard of Honour of the 1st Battalion of the Argyll and Sutherland Highlanders, were at Ballater to welcome them, and when Prince George stepped from the train he was found to have cast off his formal morning dress for kilts and sporran. At Balmoral, His Majesty the King stood on the steps of the castle in Prince of Wales check jacket, Prince of Wales check plus-fours, and Prince of Wales check socks. The ladies of the party could not compete.

In mid-October tragedy cast an ominous cloud over the great royal romance— King Alexander I of Yugoslavia was assassinated by a Croat nationalist at Marseilles on his way to Paris for a political conference. Prince Paul (Princess Marina's brother-in-law and provider of the romantic engagement setting) became Chief Regent for the 11-year-old successor to the Yugoslavian throne, and Prince George and Princess Marina, who all along had had to share the news pages with pictures of Hitler stirring

217

the German nation to frenzy, were now over-shadowed by photographs of blood and bullets and relatives in deepest weeds.

But nothing was allowed to dim the second triumphant arrival of Princess Marina into Britain on 21 November, eight days before the wedding. This time she sailed into Dover, and there was a formal ceremony of greeting, with the Mayor 'expressing the town's welcome' and the Lady Mayoress presenting a bouquet of roses. The King and Queen, the Prince of Wales, the Duke and Duchess of York, Princess Mary and the now Earl of Harewood, were at Victoria Station in family force to meet the boat-train, and all returned to Buckingham Palace, through cheering crowds, in a motor-car cavalcade.

In the intervening week before the marriage the British press kept up a fevered commentary. There was talk of the Greek Orthodox wedding to be held in the Chapel Royal sometime after the Abbey ceremony, to conform with the bride's religion, but everyone was disposed to be interested rather than outraged by this side-step from pure Anglicanism. The bride was discovered to be 'a portrait-painter of decided talent. . . . Exquisitely beautiful, healthy in mind and body . . . not only witty and beautiful . . . but a cultured lady'. There were pictures of her as a shock-haired baby playing with bricks—'The builder'—and with dolls, 'The little mother'. The Prince was shown 'in cambric frock days'—complete with petticoats and sash; in 'Eton-collar days'; playing piano with the ship's jazz band as a 'Lieutenant R.N.' in the *Téméraire*; and with many a 'doggy friend'. ('In his canine friendships, it would seem, the Duke favours the larger breeds.')

Princess Marina's 'trained artist's eye' was put to wondrous use in the preparation of the *trousseau*, much of which was to be 'in her own Marina green'—a colour half Britain now wanted to wear. Captain Molyneux, an Irishman of Huguenot descent, was the *couturier* involved and he could not have been more enthusiastic: 'she has taken a more constructive and imaginative interest in her clothes than almost anyone I have ever worked for'. He incorporated many of her own designs into the 'three morning ensembles, five afternoon dresses, six evening gowns and two coats' and the result included a black velvet evening dress with 'a most intriguing belt and gloves of natural pigskin' and another black dress, a slinky number of cloqué satin, 'the skirt slit to reveal a stripe of silver lamé. The sash is of lamé lined with petunia crêpe.'

On 9 November, the *Daily Mail* had more hot news 'From our fashion editress':

> I was given further details of her wedding gown and the dress to be worn by the bridesmaids at the wedding. The magnificent court train fitted to the shoulders by a clever elastic 'harness' passing beneath the gown, is absolutely without ornament, the white and silver brocade of its material demanding this. It is lined with silver lamé to match the turn-back cuffs, and widens to nine feet at the end. The unbelted gown itself has a very tight skirt developing into a train three to four yards long. The neckline is draped. The bridesmaids' dresses of white crêpe, patterned with silver thread have draped necklines as well, the sleeves being only a little less wide than those of the bridal gown. The skirts billowing out just below the hip-line and the sashes are of silver lamé, tied at the left in front.

All the processions for this wedding set out from Buckingham Palace, since that was where the bride and her parents were staying. The route was no longer turned into a bower of greenery, with triumphal arches and buildings draped in silk (as had been done for the wedding of King George V and Queen Mary in 1893), but London looked festive enough with flags and streamers, and in Bond Street there was a 'great joy bell' made of flowers with garlands trailing from it. The railways ran special cheap fares to town for the day, and 'Vast crowds welcomed Princess Marina as she drove from Buckingham Palace to Westminster Abbey, accompanied by her father, Prince Nicholas of Greece', said the *Illustrated London News.*

Royal weddings now took place an hour earlier than in the previous century, the bride arriving at the Abbey at 11.30 a.m.

The Princess was driven from Buckingham Palace, in a closed State landau, drawn by two Royal Greys, with a coachman on the box. Eleven years earlier, Lady Elizabeth Bowes-Lyon, who had also journeyed to the Abbey in a closed landau (starting from her father's house in Bruton Street), returned to the Palace, with the Duke of York, in the same carriage, but open. That, however, had been an April wedding, and Prince George, Duke of Kent and his bride were to return through the bright November streets in a Glass Coach, protected from the weather, but clearly visible to the crowd.

During his 'moving address' to the Duke and Duchess of Kent, the Archbishop of Canterbury made a discreet reference to the uniquely large number of guests at their wedding: 'Never in history . . . has a marriage been attended by so vast a company of witnesses. For, by a new and marvellous invention of science, countless multitudes . . . are joining in this service. The whole nation—nay, the whole Empire—are the wedding guests. . . . We all wish you happiness.'

Microphones in the Abbey had come to stay.

The next royal wedding, the quiet one, was that of the Duke of Kent's elder brother, Prince Henry, Duke of Gloucester, aged 35, and Lady Alice Montagu-Douglas-Scott, aged 34, daughter of the Duke of Buccleuch. The wedding was planned for Westminster Abbey in the November. It was the same pattern as the previous year. But on 19 October the bride's father died and there was a hurried scaling down with a move to Buckingham Palace Chapel, where Princess Louise of Wales had married the Duke of Fife in 1889.

Norman Hartnell was in charge of the *trousseau* this time and made it a gold lamé and pearl satin wedding in contrast to the Duchess of Kent's silver and white. Except for the bride's sister, 28-year-old Lady Angela Scott, the attendants were younger than usual, four of them wearing short skirts trimmed with swansdown, and ankle socks. Princess Elizabeth, now aged nine, who had been a trainbearer to Princess Marina, was chosen again, and for the first time her sister, the five-year-old Princess Margaret Rose had a public part to play. She was the youngest bridesmaid and, inevitably, stole most of the limelight. The bridegroom 'the tallest member of the Royal Family', who looked and was 'every inch a soldier', wore the magnificent full dress uniform of the 16th/5th Lancers, the regiment in which he was serving as a Brevet-Major. His tunic was superbly frogged and braided and his calf-high boots betasselled and mirror-bright. The bride's bouquet, presented by the Worshipful Company of Gardeners, was 'carried in the crook of her arm so as to accentuate the slim lines of her gown'.

And the Bride Wore . . .

There was a striped awning spanning the pavement outside the Buccleuch house in Grosvenor Place and a carpet for the bride to walk on, when she left for the Palace in a Glass Coach—five minutes early. 'Instead of starting at 11.20, as originally arranged the bride's coach left at 11.15; so that it was due at the Palace at 11.23 instead of at 11.28, for the ceremony at 11.30,' noted the newspapers. A five-minute change in royal plans was bound to cause comment and even Queen Mary mentioned the circumstance in her brief diary round-up:

> A lovely day for the wedding of Harry & Alice in the Chapel here. We went down to the Bow Room at 11. Met various members of our family, & saw the bridesmaids who looked charming—Lilibet & Margaret looked too sweet. Alice arrived before 11.30 looking lovely in her wedding dress. We had a beautiful service & the Archbishop of Canterbury gave such a nice address. . . . We had luncheon in the supper room, about 120 guests, all our family & many of the Scott family—They left after 3. . . . May God bless the dear Couple.

There were two monster wedding presents, on show with all the rest at St. James's Palace: two table lighters in the shape of grenades with imitation flames shooting from them and two very carefully-written cards, one saying 'Lilibet and MARGARET', the other 'George and Gerald' (sons of Princess Mary, Countess of Harewood). A tribute, no doubt, to Uncle Harry looking every inch a soldier.

At the time of the Duke of York's marriage in 1923, *The Times* said: 'There is but one wedding to which the people look forward with still deeper interest—the wedding which will give a wife to the Heir to the Throne and, in the course of nature, a future Queen to England and the British peoples.' That wedding was not to take place until 1937, and when it did it was not what *The Times*, or anyone else, had had in mind. Edward Albert Christian George Andrew Patrick David, Prince of Wales (known to his family as David and later to the world as the Duke of Windsor), eldest son of King George V and Queen Mary, had given up his crown and his country the previous December for 'the woman I love'. That woman was the *chic*, notorious Mrs. Wallis Warfield Simpson, a Baltimore socialite, twice divorced. In the autumn of 1936 Cecil Beaton wrote in his diary (*Diaries 1922–1939*): 'The sound of her name implies secrecy, royalty, and being in-the-know. As a topic she has become a mania, so much so that her name is banned in many houses to allow breathing space for other topics.'

In June the following year Beaton was at the Chateau de Candé, near Tours in France, a privileged photographer, taking pictures of the self-exiled, uncrowned king and his bride, in her hard, blue wedding dress and little blue straw hat, the day before the marriage. Outside the gates there were 'swarms of journalists and their vans and motorcycles'; inside, the flowers were being arranged and telegrams were being dealt with; the 'obscure Darlington vicar', who had come forward 'at the eleventh hour' to perform a religious ceremony, arrived from England; the music room was being gutted of its piano and other furniture for the wedding next day. Thirty-two chairs were placed in rows and a hunt started for a suitable table to use as an altar. The one with the drinks on it was passed up for the chest in the hall:

> . . . a heavily carved, vastly ornate affair of no particular period, with a row of fat caryatids holding up bogus Renaissance carving.

Some things old, some things new

Wallis, rather harassed but not too harassed to laugh, wondered about an altar cloth. Pointing to the caryatids, she drawled, 'We must have something to cover up that row of extra women!'

It was a love match to end all love matches, but it left in its wake a whole nation jilted and bereaved.

On the abdication of King Edward VIII, the next eldest of his brothers, the Duke of York, became King—King George VI; and King George VI's eldest daughter, Princess Elizabeth, became heiress-presumptive to the throne at the age of ten. Her marriage was to be the next of vital importance to the British monarchy, and she chose impeccably. As *The Times* explained:

> By happy accident, the Princess has bestowed her hand in such a way that two apparently divergent opinions about the qualifications of a consort are simultaneously satisfied—the opinions of those on the one hand who would wish him to be a British subject and of those on the other who consider Royal blood essential.

They had known each other since she was 13 and he was 18, a Cadet-Captain at Dartmouth Naval College, and the engagement had only been delayed until after her 21st birthday because her parents could not believe that she had really fallen in love with the first young man she had ever met. So, it was a love match *and* a noble alliance.

Until four months before the engagement, Lieutenant Philip Mountbatten had been known as Prince Philip of Greece. His father was a younger son of the Greek Royal family (a branch of the more ancient Danish royal line) and his mother (a descendant of Queen Victoria's third child, Princess Alice) was a daughter of the first Marquis of Milford Haven and sister to Earl Mountbatten of Burma. The *Illustrated London News*, delving into his ancestry, found they could start off his family tree with Harold Bluetooth, King of Denmark. (Sweyn Forkbeard, King Canute's sister, and Harold, last of the Saxon kings of England, all appeared later.)

Prince Philip's home had been in England since he was 8 years old, and in March 1947 he became a British subject, relinquishing all his titles, and choosing to call himself Mountbatten (the anglicised version of his mother's name of Battenberg). He was not to remain a humble Lieutenant for long. Shortly before the marriage, in the following November, King George VI honoured both the bride- and bridegroom-to-be with delicate attention to detail, as he explained to his mother, Queen Mary:

> I am giving the Garter to Lilibet next Tuesday, November 11th, so that she will be senior to Philip, to whom I am giving it on November 19th. I have arranged that he shall be created a Royal Highness & that the titles of his peerage will be
>
> Baron Greenwich, Earl of Merioneth
> Duke of Edinburgh
>
> These will be announced in the morning papers of November 20th, including the Garter.
>
> It is a great deal to give a man all at once, but I know Philip understands his new responsibilities on his marriage to Lilibet.

As with Queen Victoria's Albert, even so much proved to be not quite enough. Lieutenant Mountbatten had been given the title of Royal Highness, but not that of Prince, and though he soon became known as 'Prince Philip' once more, he had no right to the name. It was not until ten year's later, five years after Princess Elizabeth became Queen, that 'Prince' Philip was accorded 'the style and title of Prince of the United Kingdom in recognition of the services which he has rendered to the country and to the life of the Commonwealth'.

Most of the major royal weddings of this century have taken place either in the threat or the aftermath of war. The three early ones followed hard on the heels of the First World War; when the Dukes of Kent and Gloucester married in the 1930s Hitler and Mussolini were flexing their muscles and Abyssinia was being put to 'the sword of Rome'. Now, in November 1947 when Princess Elizabeth was to be married, the Second World War had technically been over for two years, but the scars were everywhere. Rationing was still in force, London was pock-marked with bomb sites, money was scarce. There was to be no extra seating in the Abbey, since 'the King has decided that in present circumstances, it was undesirable to divert labour for this purpose from housing and other essential work'; instead of the 10,000 places available for the coronation, ten years earlier, there would be only 2,500 for the wedding. The dress ruling, too, reflected the times: 'Morning dress, lounge suits or service dress will be worn by men guests at the wedding. It will be the first time lounge suits have been permitted at a Royal wedding. It is an austerity departure from the tradition of court dress or full dress uniform for such occasions. Women will wear morning dress with hats.'

Only £4,000 was voted by the new Labour Government for decorations; after that, they said, the cost would have to be met by the Privy Purse. Even the list of wedding presents had forlornly utilitarian patches: Princess Margaret's gift to her sister was 'a practical well-designed picnic basket containing cutlery and equipment for four people'. The town of Leamington Spa sent an electric washing machine. Mahatma Gandhi crocheted a piece of lace ('worked by the Indian leader himself'). Northern Ireland's present was a selection of household linen, boxed and ribbon-tied like a draper's display. One solitary pair of nylons, precious then as finest silver, was also put on show, with the more magnificent china, plate, jewels and furniture, at St. James's Palace. A little American girl, used to 'bundles for Britain', sent a live turkey 'bought with money she had saved herself'.

It was announced that no 'full State functions' would be held in honour of the marriage, though 'some of the State rooms of Buckingham Palace, unused since the outbreak of war, have been restored to their pre-war condition'. At the 'wedding breakfast', there would be fewer than 100 guests, including all the visiting royal relatives (whose descent could always be traced back to Queen Victoria and invariably was). It was a blue and khaki wedding all over again, with the King in uniform on railway platform after railway platform meeting the exalted, uniformed, guests who travelled from all over Europe; many of them were still politely called King and Queen in the British press, though their own countries no longer owned them. Prime Ministers also arrived from all over the Commonwealth, even from New Zealand and Australia, the still astonishing aeroplane making such long distances possible.

One marvellously cheerful note, after the years of blackout: Buckingham Palace was to be floodlit on the night of the wedding, for the first time since the beginning of the war.

The celebrated writer, Rebecca West, having watched the marriage ceremony from the Abbey organ loft, wrote: 'It might have been folly to have a Royal Wedding in winter, but it was wise enough. People are tired of sadness, they need a party; they are tired of hate, they need to think of love; they are tired of evil, they need to think of goodness. And they are persuaded that the Royal Family are good.'

She recalled a scene on the streets of London some days before, when a man selling wedding favours called out: 'Buy a red, white and blue ribbon for the pair that's going to live happily ever after. . . . It'll be forever after with this pair, decent people they are.'

The 'poor bits of bunting round the window boxes on government buildings and an advertisement facing the Abbey concerning national savings . . . were the only signs of distress' outside Westminster Abbey. But inside: 'Distinguished Englishmen and their womenfolk made one think of the Flanagan and Allen song "Nice People with Nice Manners, But Got no Money At All". Shabby top hats, shabby fur coats, fine and disciplined faces.'

There was nothing shabby, however, about the bride's dress, nor those of her attendants. In an orgy of peacetime extravagance, hundreds of girls had spent hundreds of hours weaving the delicate fabrics and stitching on the individual pearls. (And each girl who had worked on the Princess's gown had worked into it a strand of her own hair—for luck.) Until the Duke of Kent's marriage in 1934, royal wedding gowns were made by ladies—like 'Madame Handley Seymour, the Court Dressmaker of New Bond Street', who was responsible for the tubular dress worn by Princess Elizabeth's mother in 1923. Now, the male *couturier* was firmly entrenched and Norman Hartnell, royal dressmaker, was again asked to design the gowns for a royal wedding.* Three-million silk-worms were kept working overtime in Ayot St. Lawrence, Hertfordshire, to produce the silk to make the satin for the gown; while firms in Dunfermline, Nottingham, Barnoldswick, and even France, started weaving for the *trousseau*.

The *Illustrated London News* described the result:

> The dresses designed for her Royal Highness the Bride, Princess Elizabeth, are of great beauty, masterpieces of British design and workmanship. . . . Norman Hartnell took his inspiration for the diaphanous beauty of the brides-maids' ivory silk tulle dresses from Buckingham Palace pictures by Winter-halter, Tuxen and Sir George Hayter. He designed the Princess's wedding dress of ivory Duchesse satin on classic lines. The idea for the hand embroidery on the skirt and bodice and on the Court train of transparent ivory silk tulle fifteen feet long was taken from a Botticelli picture. The pattern features Roses of York, ears of corn, star flowers and orange blossom in pearl and crystal.

The dress had a 'sweetheart' neckline, and the 'voluminous Bridal veil of crisp white tulle' was held by a simple, but stunning, diamond tiara, lent by the Queen, her mother.

* Twenty-six years later this pattern was to change again, with Princess Anne choosing to have her wedding dress made by Mrs. Maureen Baker, 'design director' of the 'medium to high price range' off-the-peg dress firm 'Susan Small', the house responsible for most of the Princess's clothes for the previous four years.

The eight bridesmaids (aged from 11 to 24) were not quite the traditional mixture: at their head was the 17-year-old Princess Margaret, fresh from the triumph of carrying out her first public engagement alone the previous month (she had launched the new Union Castle liner, the *Edinburgh Castle*). The youngest was the bride's cousin, Princess Alexandra of Kent; then there were a duke's daughter, a marquis's daughter, two daughters and a granddaughter of earls, and the daughter of a baron. All but one were related to the bride, and the war-work of all those old enough to have done any was carefully chronicled. Their dresses were 'Victorian', the frothy skirts scattered with appliquéd blossoms and pearls in a design echoing that of the bride's train. The two page boys (also called train-bearers since they did all the work) were Prince William of Gloucester and Prince Michael of Kent, 5-year-old cousins of the bride. They were the first pages to appear at a royal Abbey wedding since Princess Patricia's in 1919, and one of them, Prince Michael, added an endearing touch of humour to the occasion by getting bored in mid-photo session and giving his 5-year-old tummy a thorough and satisfying scratch.

The 26-year-old bridegroom, who had 'hurried away from the Palace by a side door' the previous night to a bachelor party with 'nine old shipmates' was, according to Rebecca West, late, and 'like many a bridegroom before him, greenish white in complexion'. He wore his naval Lieutenant's uniform, with the star of the Most Noble Order of the Garter, received from the King the day before, and below it the Star of the Greek Order of the Redeemer.

His best man (or 'groomsman' in the more dignified journals) was his cousin, the 28-year-old Marquis of Milford Haven, another descendant of Queen Victoria.

On the grey Thursday morning of the wedding, the Princess and her father left Buckingham Palace in the Irish State Coach 'exactly at the appointed time, 11.16 a.m.' and, with a Sovereign's Escort of the Household Cavalry in full dress, drove through cheering crowds to the Abbey. There, at 11.28, the bride stepped down from the coach as a military band played the national anthem and entered the West door of the great vaulted building as the trumpeters played one of the magnificent fanfares written for her by the Master of the King's Musick. Led by choristers, her two small pages holding her train, and her eight bridesmaids following behind, she walked to the altar on the arm of the King. ('I was so proud of you & thrilled at having you so close to me on our long walk in Westminster Abbey, but when I handed your hand to the Archbishop I felt that I had lost something very precious', His Majesty wrote to his daughter a few days later.)

'The day was grey and dark and little light shone through the great rose window of the South Transept', said the *Illustrated London News*; 'red and gold were the dominant notes of this scene of high romance and time-honoured pageantry'.

Up in the organ loft, Wynford Vaughan-Thomas described what was happening for radio listeners and television viewers, while on tall buildings and Admiralty arches outside Richard Dimbleby, Audrey Russell, Lieutenant-Commander Peter Scott and Frank Gilliard awaited the return procession.

In keeping with tradition, the Archbishop of Canterbury conducted the service, which was, as he said in his address, 'in all essentials exactly the same as it would be for any cottager who might be married this afternoon in some small country church in a remote village in the dales'. The royal couple knelt on silk and betasselled cushions placed on the top step of the first of two shallow flights leading up to the high altar. They were flanked on either side (as royal brides had been in St. George's Chapel, Windsor) by rows of closest family and most illustrious guests. On this occasion there were fifty-two such privileged spectators—among them five kings (ruling or exiled), eight queens and two regents. It was said to be the greatest gathering of royalty of the century. The promises made, and the union blessed, the choir sang an anthem while the Princess and her husband, her mother and father, her grandmother, Queen Mary, the bridegroom's mother, Princess Alice of Greece, with the Archbishop of Canterbury, in his white and golden vestments, made their way to the chapel of Edward the Confessor where the register was signed. The bride and bridegroom were last to return, waiting for stillness once more before enacting what has come to be one of the most exquisite moments of modern royal weddings. Another fanfare filled the Abbey with a shower of sound as the Princess and the Duke walked from the chapel and stood again before the altar; then, with the full length of her train spread out behind her, the bride curtseyed in deep obeisance to Their Majesties, her parents, while her husband beside her bowed. A moment later, to the joyous sound of Mendelssohn's *Wedding March*, in a simple procession, led only by a court usher and followed by their eleven bridal attendants, the Princess Elizabeth and the Duke of Edinburgh walked out of the Abbey 'to be received into the hearts of the people'.

One-hundred-thousand people strained against the police barrier near the Palace to see the royal carriages arrive. 'Although in keeping with post-war austerity, the decorations and arrangements could not compare with previous occasions, the number of people who assembled in London for the Royal wedding to demonstrate their loyalty and affection was greater than that on previous State occasions.' Between bouts of community singing, there were chants of 'We want the bride!—We want the Princess!' which brought the royal party out onto the central balcony of the Palace three times before the Princess and the Duke of Edinburgh left in the early November dusk for Waterloo Station and the first part of their honeymoon. In an open landau, drawn by two white horses, with a magnificently liveried postilion in front, and two top-hatted footmen behind, bride and bridegroom travelled to the station in the manner Queen Victoria's children had made tradition. The Duke's uniform (minus decorations) and the Princess's 'love-in-the-mist' blue wool coat (cut in the 'Princess style') and her hard, high beret hat, were still covered with paper rose petals, thrown by the royal guests, when they stepped from the carriage, and a great cheer went up from the crowd as the Princess's favourite Corgi stepped out after them. The Royal train pulled out at 4.20 p.m. and arrived at Winchester at 5.44 (royal times are always wonderfully precise). The Mayor of Winchester (a lady, Mrs. D. Crompton) was there to greet the honeymooners, with Lord Templemore and other local dignitaries. The Princess was presented with a huge bouquet which she managed to hold on to, along with the Corgi's lead. A royal limousine took them the last part of the journey to Broadlands, near Romsey, Hampshire, once owned by Lord Palmerston, now the home of Earl Mountbatten of Burma, uncle of the bridegroom, and lent by him 'for the first part of the honeymoon'.

In London that night, 'austerity was thrown aside' as the nation celebrated. At the Savoy, the Berkeley and Claridge's a new cocktail appeared on the wine list— 'Wedding Bells'; a 'Gala dinner dance' at the Mayfair hotel was advertised: 'Dinner, cocktail or sherry, half a bottle of champagne, brandy or liqueur, coffee, dancing, £3 per person.' Quaglino's promised 'decorations inside and outside', a souvenir menu card and a 'surprise dish by the chef'. Journalists were scandalized to find many a London hotel had charged £100 for guests staying in town the whole wedding week.

Buckinghamshire magistrates sourly refused permission for the bar of a Town Hall to stay open an extra half hour for a wedding night dance, saying it was not a 'special occasion': only the usual licence extension to 12.30 would be granted. But there were not many mean spirits abroad. Throughout the land, dance floors glittered with more renovated finery than had been seen since the first hectic days of war; the sound of the big band, the quickstep and the old-fashioned waltz; the spot-prizes, the Paul Joneses; the paper hats and paper streamers, made it seem like a marvellous new beginning to good old-fashioned pleasures: a fairy-tale come true.

Next day Reuter's reported that 3,000 people queued outside Westminster Abbey to see the marriage register with the seven names of the main wedding party signed in the Abbey, and the many more added later at Buckingham Palace. 'Women from America, France, India and Africa stood side by side with British housewives, some with their shopping baskets.'

The following week, thousands more went to view the wedding presents at St. James's Palace, to which the wedding gown and one of the bridesmaids' dresses had been added.

Thirteen years later when Princess Margaret married the atmosphere could not have been more different. In place of post-war austerity, there was the booming Britain of the 1960s, of Prime Minister Harold Macmillan and the slogan 'You've never had it so good'. It was the new Elizabethan era, with another young Queen Elizabeth on the throne. The marriage was to be in May and the May of 1960 was particularly bright and warm.

The bride had always been newsworthy and slightly unpredictable: in the early days there had been the night-clubbing 'Margaret Set', then the romance with a divorced man, a former Palace equerry, now there was the photographer, Mr. Antony Armstrong-Jones—'a man whom few people before February 26 would have placed high on the list of candidates for her hand.' Speculation about what she would wear was intense, for both the bride and the bridegroom were known to 'love clothes and have an abiding interest in fashions. He, in fact, has held a show of highly original ski-ing garments.' Norman Hartnell, King of the Sequin and the Bugle Bead, was once again in charge.

Speculation on what Mr. Armstrong-Jones would wear was equally intense. He was the first royal bridegroom who could lay no claim to a uniform. The obvious solution was morning dress. But morning dress for a royal bridegroom? It seemed so strange.

The royal yacht *Britannia* was to be used for a Caribbean honeymoon—a break with tradition which caused many a raised eyebrow, and voice. Previous royal honeymoons had followed the same pattern as Princess Elizabeth's: the first week or so at a charming private house loaned by a relative or friend, with one session for press photographers and an appearance at church; then a move to Scotland or Ireland for several more weeks of seclusion. It was all very dignified, patriotic—and cheap. Now,

226

the royal yacht was being spruced up from stem to stern for a costly, if romantic, six-week voyage: 'Seventy painters were employed and will probably have used 144 gallons, including twenty-four gallons of royal blue on the hull, thirty gallons of white on the upper works, and six gallons of buff on the masts and funnel', reported the *Illustrated London News*, without further comment; 260 officers and men would sail with her.

Westminster Abbey was sand-blasted of centuries of grime without, painted and gilded within (though this, it was said, would have been done anyway).

Tall masts topped by golden coronets went up along the Mall, with nylon banners bearing the initials of bride and bridegroom, fluttering beneath. Outside Clarence House, where the Princess lived with her mother, Queen Elizabeth the Queen Mother, 30,000 pink roses were fashioned into a double arch spanning the Mall and rising sixty feet high.

The bridesmaids were chosen, and all were to be children, aged from 6 to 12, with 9-year-old Princess Anne heading them. (It would be her second time as bridesmaid, the first having been six months earlier at the wedding of her distant cousin, Lady Pamela Mountbatten.) Having only child attendants was another break with royal tradition, but this time it was favourably received. Both bride and bridegroom were 'petite'; small bridesmaids would be 'suitable'. A best man of more-or-less appropriate size was also chosen, but the press, digging deep into his past, discovered a hint of scandal which they presented to the world. The best man was then found to have jaundice and retired on medical grounds. A new best man was chosen: Dr. Roger Gilliatt, 'tall, dark and commanding', who was to tower over the small cortège like a gaunt guardian angel.

The Dean of Westminster held a press conference, and asked journalists to 'put over' the spiritual significance of the ceremony.

Disregarding both the day's reputation for bad luck, and Ovid's reference to the kind of lady who married in that particular month, Princess Margaret chose Friday, 6 May, for her wedding, and the sun shone its defiance of all superstition. (Next day, she was to be called 'The Sunshine Bride'.) Shirt-sleeved crowds, six to eight deep, all with small Union Jacks to wave, lined the route from the Mall to the Abbey. (And 1,215 of them were to faint and be scooped up by the St. John's Ambulance Brigade before the day was out.) First they watched the Queen, the Queen Mother, and 11-year-old Prince Charles, in Highland dress, ride past together in Queen Alexandra's State Coach, with a Sovereign's Escort of the Household Cavalry in attendance. Then, into the Mall, from Clarence House, and under the arch of roses, came the maroon State Glass Coach, lined with blue silk, with the bride and her brother-in-law, the Duke of Edinburgh, who was to give her away.

At the Abbey, the dress 'which had caused so much speculation before the wedding, aroused complete admiration. It was of extremely simple design and set off effectively the magnificent tiara which the Princess wore. It was made from white silk organza with a closely-fitted bodice with a high V-neckline. The skirt consisted of three layers of organza over hundreds of yards of tulle, cut into twelve panels that widened down from the waist to hem. Her shoes were made of white crêpe with a white satin facing running round the edges. Her bouquet was of orchids.'

Apart from the tiara there was not a gem or a piece of embroidery to be seen, and the result was breathtaking in its surprising simplicity. The veil of fine white tulle with a narrow binding of organdie, had been designed and made by Claude Saint-Cyr of Paris, and the tiara was nestling against the first royal hair-piece to be put on public view. (At this time the Princess wore the 'Chrysanthemum cut', which she had helped to make fashionable, yet here was a large, glossy 'bun' on the top of her head! It was thought to be very progressive indeed.)

'The bridesmaids' dresses were based, at Princess Margaret's request, on the first evening dress that Mr. Norman Hartnell designed for her—when she was seventeen. It was a favourite with her father. They are frilly dresses, with puff sleeves, decorated with panels of *broderie anglaise* with pale blue ribbon slotted through. Their bouquets are all of lilies-of-the-valley—the flower *par excellence* of early May.'

The wedding ceremony was particularly praised for the music and interesting for two changes from the normal pattern: the Beatitudes were read in place of the usual sermon, and 'the Archbishop included in the service an ancient ritual, the binding of the hands at the moment the ring is blessed by the officiating priest'. For the exchange of vows, 'to have and to hold', bride and bridegroom held hands.

Then, after the signing of the register, the bride 'curtsied gaily to her sister', walked in simple procession to the Abbey's West door, passed under the striped awning between a guard of honour formed by members of the regiments of which she was Colonel-in-Chief, and entered the same Glass Coach for the ride back to Buckingham Palace with her husband, through 'delirious crowds'.

There had been 2,000 people in the Abbey, but once again the reception was small: '120 guests were entertained to a family wedding breakfast in the lofty white and gold ball supper room of the Palace', reported Reuter's.

At 1.20 p.m. the wedding party appeared on the balcony to wave to the massed crowds surrounding the Palace. Later there was a grand family send-off, with over a hundred cheering royal guests lining the steps of the Grand Entrance, and then racing across the quadrangle, the ladies holding up their long skirts, to fling one last handful of paper rose petals as bride and bridegroom left by open car for Tower Pier and the royal yacht.

The Princess's 'going-away clothes, by Victor Stiebel, were of pale sunshine yellow. The coat was of pure silk shantung cut straight and loose with a small upstanding collar and three-quarter sleeves. Her dress was of a double layer of draped fine silk chiffon with small sleeves.'

The open car, unaccompanied by any other vehicle, drove through the City in brilliant sunshine to the Thames. The ship had been dressed over all since 8 a.m. that morning; now her decks were lined with her men and the band of the Royal Marines was playing calypso music. As she stepped aboard, the Princess's banner was hoisted at the main mast. At 5.30 p.m. the *Britannia* sailed; ships' sirens, hooters and church bells sounded in salute as she began to move slowly downstream from the Pool of London with the Princess and her husband standing on the bridge to acknowledge the cheers. The promenade at Gravesend was trimmed with bunting and crowded to over-flowing as they passed. At Southend, an estimated 10,000 were crammed onto the pier, and thirty boats went out to greet the bride.

For this slightly prodigal Princess, the country had truly killed a fatted calf.

Six weeks, and many photographs of a progressively bronzed bride and bridegroom later, the *Britannia* returned to Portsmouth, where the Royal Marine band was seen to be still on board, and heard to be still playing calypsos.

Some things old, some things new

A year and one month after Princess Margaret's wedding, came the marriage of the young Duke of Kent, son of Princess Marina and Prince George, Duke of Kent, who had died in a Second World War aircrash when his eldest son was six. Once again the newspaper statisticians had a field-day: this time it was the bride who was non-royal, 'the first untitled girl to marry a Royal Duke since Tudor times'. York Minster, which had been chosen for the ceremony had 'not been the scene of a royal wedding since King Edward III married Philippa of Hainault there in 1328'. (Nearly a hundred years before that, it had seen the marriage of the 10-year-old Alexander III of Scotland and his 11-year-old bride, Margaret, daughter of Henry III of England —the marriage at which the Archbishop of York had provided '60 pasture cattle' for the feast and the quarrelsome supporters of both sides had worn such splendid clothes.) The Kent family, like Princess Patricia of Connaught earlier in the century, have always been particularly popular in Britain, and the Duke of Kent was thought to have chosen well. His bride was not royal, but her family was wealthy and distinguished. Her father, Sir William Worsley, had been Lord Lieutenant of the North Riding of Yorkshire for ten years, and lived in the beautiful Hovingham Hall, twenty miles from York.

The Queen and the Duke of Edinburgh, Princess Margaret and Mr. Antony Armstrong-Jones, the 12-year-old Prince Charles, in dark suit and huge white carnation, and many other British and foreign royalties travelled north for the occasion and there was the biggest party afterwards of any British royal wedding this century: a large marquee was set up near the cricket pitch at the bride's home and more than 2,000 guests were invited to the feast.

There were other departures from the royal pattern at this wedding too. It was an afternoon ceremony, and the bride arrived at the Minster with her tulle veil over her face. She had eight bridesmaids, 'a galaxy of youthful beauties', but they were nearly all small nieces, cousins or god-daughters, with Princess Anne among them for the third time. Her three pages wore white satin jackets and knickerbockers, with black, silver-buckled shoes, instead of kilts. Cars, not carriages, were used throughout, the bride and bridegroom returning to Hovingham from the Minster in a very modern bubble-top limousine lent to them by the Queen. It was the only major royal wedding not to be celebrated by the Archbishop of Canterbury: the Most Reverend Dr. Michael Ramsay, Archbishop of York, did the deed, but, by chance, he was also Archbishop-designate of Canterbury at the time. And they were the first royal couple to fly off on their honeymoon—spending the first part of it at the 18th century mansion Birkhall, on the Balmoral estate, where the Queen and Prince Philip had spent the second part of their honeymoon fourteen years earlier.

Miss Katherine Worsley's wedding dress was particularly approved. It was made by John Cavanagh, who had once worked for Molyneux, designer of Princess Marina's *trousseau* in 1934, and it was again almost starkly simple: made of white silk gauze, with a design of silver thread woven into it so that it shimmered. The bodice and long sleeves were very closely fitting, while the skirt swept out from the tiny waist to form a fifteen-foot train behind. The bridesmaids were in simple white organdie.

Two years later when the Duke of Kent's sister, Princess Alexandra, married (in Westminster Abbey, once more), there was a greater gathering of British and European royalty than at any time since the wedding of the Queen, and the Queen herself laid on two delightful entertainments for them. Two days before the ceremony, there was the 'largest ball held at Windsor in the last hundred years': a magnificent occasion with the Castle floodlit and 2,000 guests, arriving in sleek cars, a-blaze with more diamonds than Aladdin found in his cave. Next morning these glittering creatures were given a probably greater treat: at a not-too-early hour, they were loaded into charabancs and taken on a tour of Windsor Great Park and forest, with a midday stop at the Hind's Head Hotel, Bray, for lunch. The Duke of Edinburgh did some of the commentary, especially when they rounded the polo ground, and the Queen got a thorn in her thumb, which the massive King Olaf of Norway delicately removed. It was a royal mystery coach tour, and quite obviously an enormous success.

Royal brides have things thrown at them on their wedding day just like anyone else, and it is largely due to them that the up-dating of the missiles has been so well chronicled. When Princess Mary married in 1922, her mother wrote of 'throwing rice & little paper horse shoes & rose leaves after them', and the newspapers published photographs of the bride and groom being 'pelted by lucky horseshoes and silver slippers by the King, the Duke of York, Prince Henry and Prince George'. The following year, when the Duke of York married Lady Elizabeth Bowes-Lyon, the *Illustrated London News* said: 'As they started from the Palace they were bombarded with confetti and rose-petals and both looked supremely happy. The Queen herself dropped a shower of confetti upon them from the balcony.' Rice was out, and rose petals were in to stay. At the wedding of the Duke of Kent in 1934, the throwing of paper rose petals was seen as 'another British feature' of an occasion which was 'practically all British in character', and there were photographs of patriotic 'disabled ex-Servicemen' making them.

Confetti (the word for the tiny sweetmeats hurled by the crowd at fiestas in Italy) suddenly appeared in the English vocabulary at the beginning of the century and referred to the kind of mixed bag of paper symbols—horseshoes, slippers and hearts—which Queen Mary described. Soon afterwards very small circles of multi-coloured tissue paper were introduced, under the same name. Being the cheapest form of artillery on the market they quickly became the most popular and when this type of confetti came in, very little more rice was thrown in Britain—and vergers muttered un-Christian oaths as they tried to sweep up the new invention from the church porch, with no help from the birds, who had soon taken care of the rice. Now their patience is tested even further, by the use of computer punchings, scooped up off office floors, absolutely free and therefore more popular than ever—except with the bride and bridegroom (being made of card they are hard and sharp) and the verger again (being hard and miniscule, they are impossible to sweep up and won't blow away or dissolve with rain). In Yorkshire, where thrift is considered a cardinal virtue, they have had to be banned from at least one parish: in 1972, the vicar of Birkenshaw in the West Ridings, said 'no more'.

The throwing of satin slippers did not continue long into the 20th century, but old boots, thrown at less genteel weddings in the 1800s, have remained, and tying them to the bumpers of honeymoon cars has become a popular wedding sport. Rolls of toilet paper are also employed in the same manner. To escape this undignified start to married life, many a honeymoon couple sets off from the wedding party in a borrowed car, leads determined followers around the neighbourhood in a Hollywood-style chase, doubles back, picks up the proper car when the coast is clear, and finally sets off, alone at last, for the wedding trip.

In the 19th century details of where the honeymoon was to be spent were often given at the end of the wedding notice; this century, except for royal honeymoons, the plans have been kept as top secret as the bride's dress. Most girls still think it is bad luck for the bridegroom to see the wedding gown before the wedding day, though I know of one bride who married in 1970 in the dress she was wearing the night she and her husband first met—it happened to be white lace and high-necked, but I'm not sure that had much to do with it; and now that young men are turning peacock again, I've heard of several of them helping their brides to choose the dress—and making sure it sets off what they want to wear.

Another superstition which remains more or less unchallenged is the belief that bride and bridegroom should not see each other on the wedding day until they meet at the altar. There are, of course, couples who rise from the same bed, put on the clothes they have chosen together, and stroll round to the church or registry office hand in hand, and there always have been—a joke of the 1920s involved a couple kneeling at the altar and displaying the same room number chalked on the soles of their shoes—but they are still not in the majority.

Meeting a chimney sweep on your wedding day is lucky (and nowadays not too likely), but you have to speak to him or touch him.

A pig running across the road in front of a bride is a sign of evil (says one book of superstitions), but happily it is a hazard not too many girls have to face up to.

Carrying the bride over the threshold of her new home is a tradition still going strong from Roman days. A Liverpuddlian who married in 1920 tells me it was then thought of as 'carrying the *virgin* bride over the threshold' and she well remembers having it done to her. Now the custom depends more on the law of the possible than the laws of morality. A bridegroom who sizes up the proposition and has any doubts about it, is wisest to leave things alone.

The wedding superstition with the greatest following of all in the 20th century is that a bride should wear:

> Something old, something new,
> Something borrowed, and something blue

and, possibly, 'a silver sixpence in her shoe'. This is usually described as 'ancient' and 'traditional', its origins 'lost in the mists of time', but John Cordy Jeaffreson, who wrote on every conceivable and inconceivable aspect of the wedding in 1872 did not mention it, nor did that other mine of marriage lore, Dr. Brand in his *Popular Antiquities*. (Neither of them mention tossing the bouquet, either—another wedding custom which is younger than it looks.) Most 20th century books of quotations and phrases and fables also ignore 'Something old, something new', but a sprightly friend in her mid-eighties tells me: 'My Mother was married in 1889, and she used it at her wedding. When I was married first in 1922, I heard it for the first time from her, as she pinned a "blue" bow on to the bottom of my youthful corselette just before I went to Church! The "old" was covered by my great-great-grand-mother's wedding veil, the "new" by other garments!'

In America I know of a 1914 bride who followed the custom, also minus the six-pence in the shoe; but by 1966, when Luci Baines Johnson married, the coin was firmly established as part of the magic and she had several sent to her from well-wishers across the States. The other charms she used to bring her luck were a 58-year-old lace handkerchief made by her great-grandmother, a rosary given to her sister by Pope John XXIII, and a gold locket tied with blue ribbon. She also had her name and the date of the wedding day embroidered in blue on the hem of her wedding gown, which could have served for the 'something blue', too.

This century has also seen two brand new customs—one from America and one from England. The first is the 'shower'—a party given by the bride's friends shortly before the wedding when each brings a small gift for the new home. It is something like the 'bidden weddings' of old, when the neighbours were all expected to contribute to the new bride's household; but, now, the party is arranged by the girl's friends, instead of her family, and is, as a rule, restricted to her own contemporaries and her own sex. Often it is specifically a 'Kitchen Shower' or a 'Bathroom Shower', or some other kind of shower, and all the presents are aimed at kitting out that one room. The gift-wrap manufacturers do a nice line in wrapping paper with such events in mind—usually dotted with a design of open umbrellas. This kind of party has been popular in America since very early in the century, but only drifted across the Atlantic in the 1950s.

The other custom, which began in the City of London in or around 1967, is a great deal more curious, and bears no resemblance to anything else at all. There, and now in many other British cities, when a girl leaves her office job to get married she is 'dressed' by her colleagues 'according to their abilities'. The clothes can range from crêpe paper dresses to woollen gloves and ribbon bows. There is always a headdress of some kind and when the bride-to-be leaves for home she is expected to travel all the way in her astonishing office *trousseau*.

In the 1970s the real *trousseaux* of the swinging young can be almost as surprising. A 1973 bride, marrying, to please her parents, at St. Margaret's, Westminster (which usurped top society favour from St. George's, Hanover Square, sometime mid-century), collected this list together for her honeymoon (in Greece) and after:

    12 pairs of tights
    1 bra
    2 packs of paper panties
    1 pair suede lace-up-to-the-knee boots with platform soles
    2 trouser suits
    1 pair blue jeans
    2 skinny-knit sweaters
    1 'absolutely super beach thing' (a wrap-around, long skirt; a top, with short
        sleeves, tying under the bosom and leaving the midriff bare; plus a tiny
        bikini—all in filmy printed lawn. 'It cost £40—but it will do for *every-
        thing*!')
    1 mini-skirt
    1 ankle-length 'granny dress' for day wear
    1 slightly longer and barer dress for evening wear.

No nightdresses? '*No one* wears anything to sleep in any more!' No *negligée* or dressing-gown? 'Heavens! I wear an old shirt when I have to. I'll borrow one of Chris's.' Hardly any underclothes? 'Well, I have bought one bra. But I don't expect I'll wear it.'

232

Some things old, some things new

The bridegroom on the other hand was packing for the honeymoon: 1 lace shirt, 2 lace-trimmed shirts, a genuine hand-embroidered Japanese kimono, and six pairs of stretch bikini brief underpants, ranging in colour from sky-blue with flowers to fire-engine red.

And so the tradition continues. Each generation sifts the ingredients and comes up with a slightly different version of the well-known wedding cake. As the years go by, some things new are added, some things old return, and some people ignore, as some people always have ignored, the whole glittering confection. But, like the visions in a kaleidoscope, the pieces are all there, waiting only to be shaken to produce a pattern to suit every changeless 'happy couple'.

'Why do not you marry, Hugo?' said Bertram.
'I respect the institution,' said Hugo, 'which is admitting something in these days; and I have always thought that every woman should marry, and no man.'

The Rt. Hon. Benjamin Disraeli, *Lothair*, 1870.

Bibliography

(In the following list 'edited by' is abbreviated to 'ed.' The dates given in brackets are those of the editions used.)

ANGLO-SAXON POETRY, translated by Professor R. K. Gordon (1934)

ARMSTRONG'S NORFOLK DIARY, ed. Herbert B. J. Armstrong (1963)

BEATON, Cecil, *Diaries 1922–1939* (1961)

BERTEAUT, Simone, *Piaf*, translated by Ghislaine Boulanger (1970)

BETHAM EDWARDS, Matilda, *Home Life in France* (1905)

BOEHM, Max Ulrich von, *Modes and Manners* (1932–35)

BRAND'S POPULAR ANTIQUITIES, revised by Sir Henry Ellis (1908)

BRONTË, Charlotte, *Jane Eyre*

BRONTË, Charlotte, *Villette*

BRUCE, Philip Alexander, *The Social Life of Virginia* (1907)

BULLINGER, Heinrich, *The Christen State of Matrimonye*, translated by Myles Coverdale (1541)

BURNEY, Fanny, *Diary of*, ed. Lewis Gibbs (1966)

CARLYLE, Jane Welsh, *Letters and Memorials of* (1883)

CARLYLE, Jane Welsh, *Early Letters of*, ed. David G. Ritchie (1889)

CHAMBERS, Robert, *The Book of Days* (1886)

CHARLTON, Barbara, *The Recollections of a Northumbrian Lady 1815–1866*, ed. L. E. O. Charlton (1949)

CHAUCER, Geoffrey, *Canterbury Tales*, ed. A. C. Cawley (1958)

CHICKEN, Edward, *The Collier's Wedding* (1764)

COKE, Lady Mary, *Letters and Journals of, 1756–1799*, ed. the Hon. J. A. Home (1889–96)

COLLINS, Arthur, *Letters and Memorials of State: The Sydney Letters* (1746)

COOKE, E. Thornton, *Her Majesty, the Romance of the Queens of England* (1928)

CUNNINGTON, C. W. and P., their five *Handbooks of English Costume*

CUNNINGTON, C. W. and P., and BEARD C., *Dictionary of English Costume 900–1900*

CUNNINGTON, C. W., *English Women's Clothing in the Present Century* (1952)

DAVISON, Francis, *A Poetical Rhapsodie* (1611)

DELANY, Mrs., *Autobiography and Correspondence of Mary Granville* (Mrs. Delany), ed. Lady Llanover (1861–62)

DELONEY, Thomas, *The Pleasant History of John Winchcomb, in His younger years called Jacke of Newberrie, the famous clothier of England* (1633)

DICKENS, Charles, *Letters of*, Vol. 1, 1820–38, ed. Madeline House and Graham Storey (1965)

DICKENS, Charles, *Sketches by Boz*

DICTIONARY OF NATIONAL BIOGRAPHY (British and American)

DISRAELI, Benjamin, *Lothair* (1870)

DISRAELI, Benjamin, *Lord Beaconsfield's Correspondence with his Sister 1832–1852* (1886)

DREW, John H., *Kenilworth—An Historical Miscellany* (1969)

EARLE, Mrs. Alice Morse, *Colonial Days in Old New York* (1896)

EARLE, Mrs. Alice Morse, *Costume of Colonial Times* (1894)

EARLE, Mrs. Alice Morse, *Home Life in Colonial Days* (1898)

Bibliography

EARLE, Mrs. Alice Morse, *Two Centuries of Costume in America* (1903)

EIGHTEENTH CENTURY PLAYS, ed. John Hampden (1958), especially *The Clandestine Marriage* by George Colman and David Garrick

EVELYN, John, *Diary of*, ed. E. S. de Beer (1959)

FANSHAWE, *The Memoirs of Ann Lady Fanshawe* (1907)

FRASER, Antonia, *Mary Queen of Scots* (1970)

GOLDSMITH, Oliver, *The Good Natur'd Man*

GOLDSMITH, Oliver, *The Vicar of Wakefield*

GUMMERE, Mrs. Amelia, *The Quaker, A Study in Costume* (1901)

HEBER, *Dear Miss Heber, an Eighteenth Century Correspondence* (with letters from Mary Curzon), ed. Francis Bamford (1936)

HEYWOOD, John, *Proverbes* (1546)

HONE'S TABLE BOOK, ed. William Hone (1827)

HOUBLON, Lady Alice A., *The Houblon Family* (1907)

JEAFFRESON, John Cordy, *Brides and Bridals* (1872)

JENSEN, Amy LaFollette, *The White House and Its Thirty-four Families* (1958)

KEPPEL, Sonia, *Edwardian Daughter* (1958)

KILVERT, Francis, *Diary of*, ed. William Plomer (1956)

LAKE, Dr. E. J., *Diary of* (1847)

LAMB, Charles, *Essays of Elia and Last Essays of Elia* (1921) (also *The London Magazine*, June 1825)

LAMB, Charles and Mary, *The Letters of*, ed. E. V. Lucas (1912)

LATIN LITERATURE IN TRANSLATION, ed. Kevin Guinagh and Alfred P. Dorjahn (1952)

LELAND, John, *J. Lelandi . . . Collectanea*, ed. T. Hearne (1770)

LONGWORTH, Alice Roosevelt, *Crowded Hours* (1933)

LYTTON, *Lady Lytton's Court Diary*, ed. Mary Lutyens (1961)

MALMESBURY, the Rt. Hon. the Earl of, *Memoirs of an Ex-Minister* (1884)

MARCHANT, W. T., *Betrothals and Bridals, with a chat about wedding cakes and wedding customs* (1879)

MARLBOROUGH, Sarah Duchess of, *Letters of a Grandmother 1732–1735*, ed. Gladys Scott Thomson (1934)

MARRECO, Anne, *The Rebel Countess* (a life of Constance Gore-Booth, Countess Markievicz) (1967)

MARTIN, Theodore, *Life of the Prince Consort* Vol. 1 (1875)

MEINERTZHAGEN, Richard, *Diary of a Black Sheep* (1964)

MISSON, Francis Maximilian, *Memoirs and Observations in his Travels Over England*, translated by John Ozell (1719)

MONTAGU, Lady Mary Wortley, *The Complete Letters of*, ed. Robert Halsband (1965)

MY DEAR DUCHESS, Social and Political Letters to the Duchess of Manchester (many by Lord Clarendon and Lord Granville), ed. A. L. Kennedy (1956)

NORTHUMBERLAND, Duchess of, *The Diaries of a Duchess 1716–1776*, ed. James Greig (1926)

OSBORNE, *Letters of Dorothy Osborne to William Temple*, ed. G. C. Moore Smith (1959)

OVID, *Fasti*, Book III, ed. Sir James George Frazer (1931)

OXINDEN AND PEYTON LETTERS *1642–1670*, ed. Dorothy Gardiner (1937)

PARIS, Matthew, *English History from the Year 1235–1273* (1847)

PASTON LETTERS, ed. John Warrington (1956)

PENNANT, Thomas, *Some Account of London* (1790)

PENNANT, Thomas, *A Tour of Scotland 1769* (1771)

PEPPERELL PAPERS, THE, Massachusetts Historical Society (1886)

Bibliography

PEPYS, Samuel, *Diary of*, ed. Henry B. Wheatley (1952)

PERCY, Thomas, Bishop of Dromore, *Reliques of Ancient English Poetry:* ed. Henry B. Wheatley (1889)

PLANCHÉ, James Robinson, *A Cyclopaedia of Costume* (1876–79)

PLANCHÉ, James Robinson, *History of British Costume* (1834)

POETRY, the Oxford University Press anthologies, and collected works of poets mentioned

PONDER, Winifred, *Dame Clara Butt, Her Life Story* (1928)

POPE-HENNESSY, James, *Queen Mary* (1959)

PORTER, E. R., *Historic Weddings of the White House* (1906)

POWER, Eileen, *Medieval People* (1939)

QUEEN VICTORIA, *The Letters of* (with extracts from her Journals).
    First Series, ed. Arthur Christopher Benson and Viscount Esher (1907)
    Second and Third Series, ed. George Earle Buckle (1930)

QUEEN VICTORIA, *Dearest Child* (letters of Queen Victoria to her eldest daughter), ed. Roger Fulford (1964)

RICHARDSON, Samuel, *Sir Charles Grandison*

RICHARDSON, Samuel, *Pamela*

RICHARDSON, Samuel, *Clarissa*

ROGER OF WENDOVER, *Flowers of History*, translated by J. A. Giles (1849)

ROWSE, A. L., *The Elizabethan Renaissance* (1971)

SANDYS, Sir John Edwin, *A Companion to Latin Studies*

SEWELL, Samuel, *The Diary of*, Massachusetts Historical Society (1899)

SHAKESPEARE, William, the Yale edition (1917–27)

SHERIDAN, Richard Brinsley, *The Rivals*

SHERWOOD, Mrs. Mary Wilson, *Manners and Social Usages* (1884)

SINCLAIR, Sir John, *Statistical Account of Scotland* (1791–99)

SMITH, Marie and DURBIN, Louise, *White House Brides* (1966)

SMITH, J. T., *Nollekens and His Times* (1929)

SOUSA, John Philip, *Marching Along* (1928)

SOUTHEY, Robert, *Commonplace Book 1849–1851*

STEPHENS, John, *Essayes and Characters* (1615)

STRUTT, Joseph, *Sports and Pastimes of the People of England* (1903)

THACKERAY, William Makepeace, *The Book of Snobs* (1887)

THACKERAY, William Makepeace, *Vanity Fair*

THE COURT OF ENGLAND UNDER GEORGE IV (with letters of Queen Caroline), anonymous (1896)

THE EXETER BOOK, Part II (Anglo-Saxon verse), ed. W. S. Mackie

THE MABINOGION, translated by Lady Charlotte Guest (1913); and G. Jones and T. Jones (1949)

THRALE, Mrs. Hester Lynch, *Thraliana*, ed. Katherine C. Balderston (1951)

TROLLOPE, Mrs. Frances, *Domestic Manners of the Americans* (1832)

TROUBRIDGE, Laura, *Life Amongst the Troubridges*, ed. Jaqueline Hope-Nicholson (1966)

VANDERBILT, Gertrude Lefferts, *Social History of Flatbush* (1881)

VAUGHAN, William, *The Golden Grove* (1608)

WALPOLE, Horace, *Letters of* (1840), and Yale edition, ed. W. S. Lewis

WHEELER-BENNETT, John W., *George VI, His Life and Reign* (1958)

WOODFORDE PAPERS AND DIARIES, ed. Dorothy Heighes Woodforde (1932)

NEWSPAPERS

The Times, of London

The Washington Post

Bibliography

The Daily Mail
Daily Telegraph
Sunday Telegraph
Daily Express
Sunday Express
Daily Mirror
Daily Post

PERIODICALS
Brides (1956–.)
The Gentleman's Magazine (1731–1914)
The Illustrated London News (1834–.)
The Ladies Cabinet (1834–43)
The Lady's Pictorial (1890s)
The New Monthly Belle Assemblée (1835–70)
The Tailor and Cutter (1868–.)
The Tatler
The Weekly Belle Assemblée (1833 and 1834)
The World of Fashion (1824–39)

Index

Index

Beatrice, Princess, daughter of Queen Victoria, 160, 166, 167, 168; marriage (1885), 171–2, 173

Beauchamp, Earl, 128–9

bedding of the bride, 35, 36–7, Chap. 5 *passim*, 74

Beethoven, Ludwig van, *Hallelujah Chorus* (*Mount of Olives*), 166

Belle Assemblée, La, (1827) 115; (1835) 116–117, 117; *New Monthly*, 238; *Weekly*, 238

Beowulf, 8

Berlin, Irving, *Annie Get Your Gun*, 199

Berlioz, Hector, *Damnation of Faust March*, 198

Berry, Mary, 81, 82

Berteaut, Simone, *Piaf* (1970), 235

Bertha, wife of King Ethelbert, 6

Bertie, Lady Charlotte, 81

best man, 108, 121 and *passim*

Betham Edwards, Matilda, *Home Life in France* (1905), 111, 134, 178, 235

betrothal, 6, 16–17, 29, 30; becomes 'engagement', 111, 112; royal, 91, 170

Betson, Thomas, 12

'blacksmith' of Gretna Green, 105, 106, 138, 141

blessing of the marriage-bed, 36

Bliss, Sir Arthur, 196

Boehm, Max Ulrich von, *Modes and Manners* (1932–5), 235

Boleyn, Anne, Queen, 31

bonfires, 128–9, 167

bonnets à la bonne mamman, 83

Book of Common Prayer, 31, 45

Bothwell, James Hepburn, Earl of, 24, 135

bouquet, use of the, 7, 175, 209–10, 231

Bradford Wedding Journal, 174, 192

Bradshaw, William, *A Marriage Feast*, sermon (1620), 39–40

Braithwaite, Richard, 59

Brand, Dr. John, *Popular Antiquities* (1777), 4, 7, 7–8, 15–16, 22, 55, 231, 235

breaking of cake, etc., 3, 32–3, 56, 94, 145

bridal, *see* penny-bridal

Bride Flown, The, 108

bride price, the, 6

bride-ale (later 'bridal'), 32–3, 60, 98–9, 183; *see also* penny-bridal

bride-bush, or bride-stake, 33

bride-cake, *see* wedding-cake

bridegroom's dress, 206–9

bride-men (groomsmen), 108

bride-wain (Cumberland), 99–100

Brides, magazine, 188–9, 201–2, 238

Bride's Book or Young Housewife's Compendium, 184–5

bride's father's duties, 185–6

bridesmaid ('bride-maid'), 81, 108, 122, 124; royal, 161, 186, 205

bridesmaids' dress, royal, 86, 123, 124, 125; hire, 200; not white, 203–4

Bridges, John, *History and Antiquities of Northamptonshire*, 16

Brighton, 139

Bristol Cathedral, 190–1

Britannia, royal yacht, 226, 228

British Broadcasting Company (later 'Corporation'), 216

Britons, Ancient, 3, 5

Brittany, 3

broadcasting, 216, 219

Broderick, St. John, 193

Bromley Times, 209–10

Brontë, Charlotte, *Jane Eyre*, 111, 114, 235; *Villette*, 235

brooch, as wedding wear, 11, 12, 13

Brooke, Christopher, *Epithalamium*, 22

brose, running for the, 61

Brougham, Henry, 140

Browne, Eliza Southgate, 150

Bruce, Philip Alexander, *The Social Life of Virginia* (1907), 235

Brueghel, Peter, 35

Buckingham Palace, 9 (or 'House'), 154, 156, 159, 174, 176, 188, 211, 218, 222, 224, 226, 228; chapel, 172, 219

Budd, Rachel, 80

Bullinger, Heinrich, *The Christen State of Matrimonie*, tr. M. Coverdale (1541), 30, 31–2, 39, 235

Bunter's Wedding, ballad, 69, 69n

Burghwallis Hall, 136, 137

Burke, Maud, later 'Emerald', 118

Burke's Peerage, 213

Burn, J. S., *History of Parish Registers*, 6

Burney, Fanny, *Diary of*, (1966), 82–3, 88, 89, 235

Burney, Rear-Admiral James, 120

Burney, Sarah, marriage (1825), 120–1, 131

Butler, Samuel, *Hudibras*, 22

Butt, Dame Clara, marriage (1900), 190–1, 237

Byrd, William, 80

calling-card used as a bride's card, 123

Cambridge, Adolphus Frederick, Duke of, marriage (1818), 155, 175

Cambridge, George, Duke of, 140, 165, 168, 175

Campion, Thomas, 42

Canadian Indians, customs, 4

Candé, Château de, 220–1

canopy (talith), 8

240

Index

Index

Index

Index

Index

Index

Index

Index

Index

servants, marriage of, 102–4

Sewell, Samuel, *The Diary of* (1899), 49, 237

sexes, segregation of, 118

Seymour, Madame Handley, 223

Shakespeare, William, *Hamlet*, 27; *A Mid-summer Night's Dream*, 29, 129; *Much Ado About Nothing*, 23–4, 37; *Romeo and Juliet*, 24; *Taming of the Shrew*, 25, 37; *The Tempest*, 34

Shearer, Norma, 205

Sheridan, Brinsley, 141

Sheridan, Richard Brinsley, *The Rivals* (1775), 65–6, 237

Sherwood, Mary Wilson, *Manners and Social Usages* (1884), 121, 122, 135, 150–1, 237

shoe (or slipper), customs, 7, 140, 166, 230

'shower', of presents, 232

silver, royal brides' colour, 42, 193

silver wedding, dress, 191

Simkiss, Mr., priest, 137

Simpson, Mrs. Wallis, *see* Windsor, Duchess of

Sinatra, Frank, 211

Sinclair, Sir John, *Statistical Account of Scotland*, (1791–9), 2, 237

Sion Chapel, 71, 72

Sheffington, Hon. Clotworthy, 66–7, 91

Skelmersdale, Lord and Lady (Alice), 113, 139

slipper, bride's, use of, 6

Smith, Sir George, 81, 83, 91

Smith, Rev. Henry, *A Preparative to Marriage*, sermon, 32

Smith, J. T., *Nollekens and His Times* (1929), 237

Smith, Marie and Durbin, Louise, *White House Brides* (1966), 237

Smithfield matches or 'bargains', 64

Smithsonian Institution, 'First Ladies'' Collection, 117, 154

Snowdon, Anthony Armstrong-Jones, Earl, 213, 226–8, 229

Somerset, Lady Geraldine, 174, 175, 176

Somerset, Robert Carr, Earl of, 41–2

Sousa, John Philip, *Marching Along* (1928), 130, 153, 237

Southey, Robert, *Commonplace Book, 1849–51*, 105–6, 237

Southwell, Sir Thomas and Lady, 4

'Spanish Marriages' (1846), 177

Sparhawk, Col. Nathaniel and Rev. John, 79

special licence (*specialis licentia*), 17, 38, 57, 64, 67, 73, 82, 110, 131, 181

Spencer, Lady Georgiana, 78

Spencer, John, sen., 75–6; jun., later Lord Spencer, 76–7, 78

Spenser, Edmund, *Epithalamion*, 21; *Prothalamion*, 21

spinster, origin and use of word, 6, 110

sports at weddings, 33, 100, 143–4

stamp duty, 59

Standish House, Gloucestershire, 127

Stanford, Sir Charles Villiers, 196

Stanhope, Lady Mary, 128–9

Stapleton, G. T., ed., *Plumpton Correspondence*, 10

Star, The, 176

Statistical Account of Scotland, 99, 106

Steele, Richard, 66, 67

Stephens, John, *Essayes and Characters* (1615), 237; *A Plaine Countrey Bride*, 23, 40, 120; *A Plaine Countrey Bridegroome*, 40–1, 100

Stiebel, Victor, 228

stocking, flinging the, 36, 39, 51, 74, 102

Stockmar, Baron, 160, 162

Stoddart, Sarah, 124

Stonor Letters, The, 12

Stowe, John, *Survey of London*, 26

Strawberry Hill, Twickenham, 87

strewing, or 'strawing', flowers, 26

Strutt, Joseph, *Sports and Pastimes of the People of England* (1903), 8, 144, 237

Suckling, Sir John, *Ballad upon a Wedding*, 62

Sullivan, Sir Arthur, 191

Sunday Express, 184, 203, 238

Sunday Telegraph, 180, 203, 238

Sunday weddings, 25, 28; end of, 46, 135

superstitions, 178–9, 231–2

Sussex, Augustus, Duke of, 155, 159

swathbonds, 22

Swift, Jonathan, Dean, 75, 86

Symonds, Deputy Governor and Mrs. Rebekah, 47–8, 49

Tailor and Cutter, The (1886, 1899), 121, 238

taleth (or talith), canopy, 8

Tasburgh family, 136–8

Tashman, Lilyan, 205

Tatler, The, (1710), 66; (1877), 112, 121; (1901), 193; 238

tax year, 182

Teck, Duchess of, Princess Mary Adelaide, 174, 201

television, 216

Temple, Sir William, 43, 45, 57, **236**

Tennyson, Alfred Lord, 164

Tertullian, 17

Thackeray, William Makepeace, *The Book of Snobs* (1887), 123, 237; *Vanity Fair*, 119, 139, 237

Theodoric, King, 8

Thomson, Gladys Scott, ed., *Letters of a Grandmother 1732–5*, 75, 84–5, 86, 215, 236

Thomson, Joseph, sells his wife, 147

Index

Index